Teach Yourself VISUALLY™ COMPLETE

WordPress®

by Janet Majure

Visual™
A Wiley Brand

Teach Yourself VISUALLY™ Complete WordPress®

Published by

John Wiley & Sons, Inc.
10475 Crosspoint Boulevard
Indianapolis, IN 46256

www.wiley.com

Published simultaneously in Canada

Wiley publishes in a variety of print and electronic formats and by print-on-demand. Some material included with standard print versions of this book may not be included in e-books or in print-on-demand. If this book refers to media such as a CD or DVD that is not included in the version you purchased, you may download this material at http://booksupport. wiley.com. For more information about Wiley products, visit www.wiley. com.

Library of Congress Control Number: 2013934757

ISBN: 978-1-118-58395-1

Manufactured in the United States of America

10 9 8 7 6 5 4 3 2 1

Trademark Acknowledgments

Contact Us

For general information on our other products and services please contact our Customer Care Department within the U.S. at 877-762-2974, outside the U.S. at 317-572-3993 or fax 317-572-4002.

For technical support please visit www.wiley.com/techsupport.

Sales | Contact Wiley at (877) 762-2974 or fax (317) 572-4002.

Credits

Acquisitions Editor
Aaron Black

Project Editor
Lynn Northrup

Technical Editor
Donna Baker

Copy Editor
Kim Heusel

Editorial Director
Robyn Siesky

Business Manager
Amy Knies

Senior Marketing Manager
Sandy Smith

Vice President and Executive Group Publisher
Richard Swadley

Vice President and Executive Publisher
Barry Pruett

Senior Project Coordinator
Kristie Rees

Graphics and Production Specialists
Ana Carrillo
Andrea Hornberger
Jennifer Mayberry

Quality Control Technician
Jessica Kramer

Proofreading
Evelyn Wellborn

Indexing
BIM Indexing & Proofreading Services

About the Author

Janet Majure is an author, writer, and editor with more than 30 years in the publishing industry. She writes or has written for WordPress blogs (individual blog Foodperson.com and group blog Ethicurean.com) as well as two business sites using WordPress (Janetmajure.com and Givemestrength.net). She also has written and edited books, newsletters, and articles for daily newspapers, and edited technical white papers.

Author's Acknowledgments

The author gratefully acknowledges the WordPress community, which has made this remarkable software available, as well as the ongoing support of family and friends. In particular, she thanks friend, neighbor, colleague, and agent Neil Salkind; Acquisitions Editor Aaron Black; Project Editor Lynn Northrup; Technical Editor Donna Baker; and previous Project Editor Sarah Hellert.

How to Use This Book

Who This Book Is For

This book is for the reader who has never used this particular technology or software application. It is also for readers who want to expand their knowledge.

The Conventions in This Book

① Steps

This book uses a step-by-step format to guide you easily through each task. **Numbered steps** are actions you must do; **bulleted steps** clarify a point, step, or optional feature; and **indented steps** give you the result.

② Notes

Notes give additional information — special conditions that may occur during an operation, a situation that you want to avoid, or a cross-reference to a related area of the book.

③ Icons and Buttons

Icons and buttons show you exactly what you need to click to perform a step.

④ Tips

Tips offer additional information, including warnings and shortcuts.

⑤ Bold

Bold type shows command names or options that you must click or text or numbers you must type.

⑥ Italics

Italic type introduces and defines a new term.

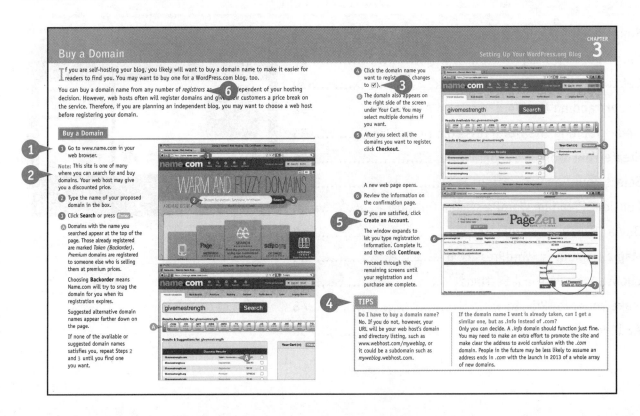

Table of Contents

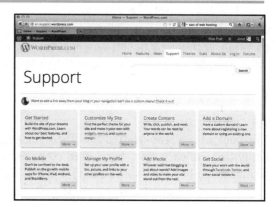

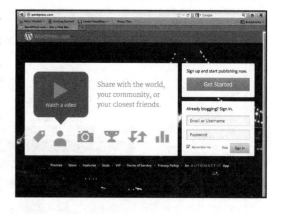

Table of Contents

Chapter 5 — Creating Visual and Audio Content

| Chapter 6 | Changing a Site's Look and Function |

Table of Contents

Table of Contents

Chapter 10	Maintaining Your WordPress Blog

Chapter 11   Expanding Your Posting Options

Chapter 12   Expanding Your Content Options

Table of Contents

Chapter 13 · Customizing Your Site's Look

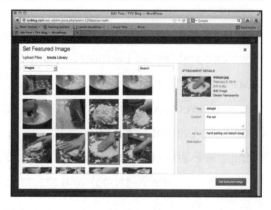

Author's Note

This book is intended to provide everything you need to know to start, run, and maintain a website using WordPress software. It should be noted, however, that no book can be truly complete where WordPress is concerned. That is because software developers are continually adjusting, modifying, and updating WordPress and its addons. Developers also are creating new addons and abandoning old ones, in the form of visual themes and plugins. Those options number in the thousands, and this book gives details on only a handful.

Also, because the software is open source — meaning, essentially, that anyone can use it and modify it — a *really* complete book on WordPress would tell you how to write code in the PHP language and how to write *cascading style sheets*, or CSS, to make your site look just the way you want it. Those subjects are beyond the scope of this book.

The great thing is, you do not need to know all there is to know about WordPress to run your WordPress site. My hope is that this book is complete enough to answer most of your questions, give you ideas, and steer you toward other resources when the answers are not here.

CHAPTER 1

Planning Your WordPress Site

WordPress is the platform of choice for new blogs, and increasingly it is the software chosen for websites of many different descriptions. WordPress lets you get your message out quickly and easily while giving you all the control you want.

Understanding WordPress and Blog Terms

Learning a few WordPress and blog terms before you dive in makes the process of learning the software and starting your website easier. Terms in this section arise again and again. These terms generally apply regardless of whether you host your own blog or use the WordPress.com hosting service. They are also pertinent even if you use WordPress to run a static website, meaning the information published on a site rarely changes. Terms that seem abstract now become clearer as you develop your site.

Blog versus Static Site

The term *blog*, which merges the words *web* and *log*, came about when software advances made it possible for nontechnical people to easily publish information to the World Wide Web. Although blogs typically publish posts in reverse chronological order and allow for reader interaction, WordPress also lets you create *static websites*, or sites that have fixed content and are not interactive.

Posts and Posting

Each entry in a blog is known as a *post*, and the usual presentation of posts is with the newest entry at the top of the screen. *Post* is also what you do. That is, you post a new post to your blog. Posts usually follow a standard visual style, although WordPress offers alternative post formats for specific kinds of posts, such as posts that highlight a quotation.

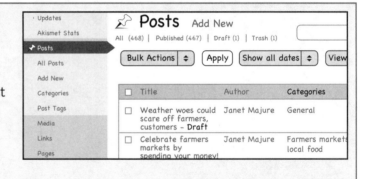

Pages

Think of a website as a collection of web pages, with each web page having its own content. With WordPress, the running blog page typically — but not always — is the home page, which usually displays the most recent posts. Themes provide page templates to display posts by category and to display an individual blog post with its own web address. You can have static pages, too. The most common static page on websites is an About page that explains the site to visitors.

Dashboard

The WordPress Dashboard is the online but behind-the-scenes control panel from which you create and modify your website. A *panel* is a display screen in the user interface. The Dashboard differs a little between the .com and .org versions of WordPress. "Get to Know WordPress Types," later in this chapter, describes those versions. The Dashboard main features are a left-hand navigation menu bar and a set of *panels* with information and links.

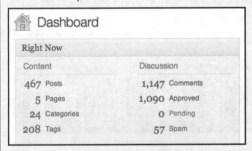

Permalinks

A *permalink* is the permanent link to a specific post or page. If you host your WordPress installation, WordPress gives you options on what your permalinks look like, which may make it easier for search engines to find your post.

SEO

SEO is an acronym for *search engine optimization*, and your interest in it depends on the purpose of your blog. SEO aims to improve your site's ranking in search results by search engines such as Google. A higher ranking leads more search engine users to find your site. SEO relies partly on making generous use of searched-for words.

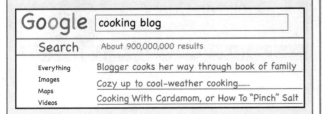

Themes and More

Other terms you need to know are *themes*, which refer to the sets of files that determine the overall design of your site; *widgets*, which give you options for presenting information; and *plugins*, which you can add to a self-hosted WordPress installation to add functionality. WordPress offers flexibility as to the content of your site's menus, your theme's options, and more.

Choose a Blog Topic

You can choose anything as your blog topic, but doing some research may help you identify the topic that you will love to write about and that readers will look for. In general, the more focused your topic, the greater your success in attracting readers. Even if you do not care about getting a large audience, you will spend less time trying to figure out what to write on your blog if you have consistent subject matter. You also may discover that you learn more about your topic the longer you blog. Consider different approaches before you decide.

Expertise

If you are an expert in some field, your knowledge could make an excellent blog topic. By writing about your area of experience you will have plenty of content and confidence, and you may be able to use your blog to attract business and advertising.

Hobby

Perhaps you have a hobby that you avidly pursue and continue to learn more about. This, too, is a good subject for a blog. Fellow hobbyists may look to you for ideas and advice, and they can offer ideas and advice in return.

Business

A blog is a great way to keep in touch with your customers and to attract more customers. It is like a newsletter, only easier. As with a hobby, you surely have plenty of content to offer readers, whether news about products, special offers, or holiday hours.

Scattershot

One option is not to choose a topic at all and simply write your blog as you might write a diary. This unfocused, or *scattershot,* approach is fine as long as you are content to attract a small audience. Only a few people, by virtue of their fascinating lives or captivating writing styles, can write a scattershot blog and attract a large number of readers.

Focused

The more focused your topic, the easier it will be for search engines to find it. A focused blog also has greater potential to generate advertising revenues later, if that is one of your goals.

Useful and Entertaining

Whatever topic you choose, you will get more readers if your blog is useful or entertaining — or both. As you narrow your list of possible topics, think about which ones give you the greatest opportunity to be helpful or engaging. Those may be your best bets.

Competition

If you are unconcerned about developing an audience or if you want your blog to focus on your personal life, you need not worry about competition. For other subjects, however, check out the competition before you settle on a blog topic.

Research the Competition

You can get clues as to what is being written about and what is popular at these websites:

- http://wordpress.com/tags: See the most popular recent *tags,* which are like keywords, on WordPress.com blogs.

- www.alexa.com: Search for websites on your topic, and Alexa lists them and their traffic ratings.

- www.technorati.com: Click **Top 100** or **Tags** to see the 100 most popular blogs among Technorati users and most popular tags.

- www.stumbleupon.com: Sign up with this service, select your topic of interest, and then *stumble,* which takes you to blog post after blog post on that subject.

- http://google.com/blogsearch: Search on a topic to find existing blogs and blog posts on the topic.

Plan Your Blog's Content

Your blog will be easier to create and maintain and easier for readers to follow if you plan your content before you start blogging. By planning ahead, you can give your blog a consistent approach that works for you, your content, and your readers. The word *content* refers to whatever you publish on your website. Aspects to consider include everything from writing style to visual presentation. WordPress gives you considerable flexibility to change, but you will be well served to consider these factors just as if you were publishing a book.

Words, Pictures, or Both?

Your choice of having content that is word heavy, picture heavy, or a balance of words and pictures affects not only the appearance of your blog, but also how you spend your time preparing your posts. Give thought now as to what medium best expresses the ideas you want to share.

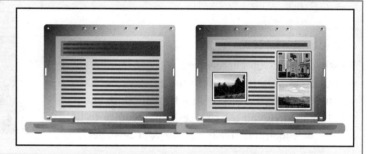

Consider Post Length

Although there is no ideal length, there may be an ideal length for you and your blog. Having a somewhat predictable length for your posts enables you to know how long it may take to write a post, and lets regular readers know how much time to allow for reading. You can break up long subjects into a series of posts.

Consider Post Frequency

Some bloggers post multiple times a day; others post once a week. Your blog's topic and your time constraints may dictate how often you can post, and that is fine. *More* is not necessarily better, but *predictable* is definitely better!

Make Your Blog Stand Out

After you study other blogs in your subject area, ask what will make your blog unique, aside from its being written by you? If your topic is broad — cars, perhaps — yours will stand out better and be easier to plan if you narrow the subject to, say, restoring Chevrolets from the 1950s, or reviewing late-model, two-seat sports cars.

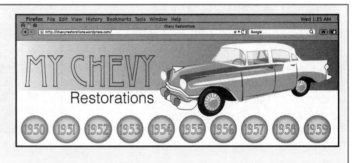

Make Your Blog Accurate

Even if you are an authority in your subject area, you need to check your facts and, where possible, link to your sources. Yes, you can find popular sites that use dubious information, but if you want credibility with most readers, you need to get your facts straight. Include fact-checking as part of your content plan.

Suit the Content to the Subject

If your blog is about sculpture or carpentry or any other highly visual subject, you need to have pictures. Podcasts are desirable on an interview blog. Make sure you have the equipment you need for the media you plan to use. If your blog is about grammar or creative writing, you can probably skip buying a top-flight digital camera.

Research Blog Titles

If you do not take care in naming your blog, you may find down the road that your choice does not serve you well. It may duplicate the name of an existing blog, or you may decide you want to get a domain name and find that a website with your blog's domain name already exists. You also want to avoid using a trademark as your blog title. Various strategies can help in your search for a memorable title that reflects your blog's content.

Blog Title versus Domain

Your *blog title* generally appears across the top of your blog's front page. A *domain name* is the part of a web address that includes *.com*, *.net*, *.info*, or one of the other domain name extensions. You can read about buying a domain name in Chapters 2 and 3.

Corresponding Names

It is helpful for the blog title and domain name to match, or at least to correspond, so that people can find you more easily. If you want to name your blog *In My Opinion*, it would be wise to see whether a domain such as *inmyopinion.net* or *imo.com* is available.

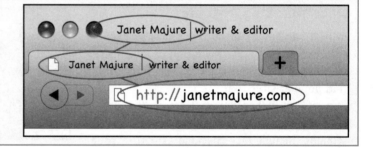

Consider the Long Term

If you are going to keep your blog private or are certain that you do not want to develop a significant audience, the blog title makes no difference. Most people start blogs, though, because they want to be heard. If you are one of those people, then consider the advice on these pages.

Brainstorm Names

Your blog topic is the place to start your search for blog titles. Write as many words and phrases as you can think of associated with your topic. If you have a personal blog, you may simply want to use your real name. But even your real name may not be as unique as you think, so write down many options. Narrow the options to a dozen or more and then see whether another blog uses those names.

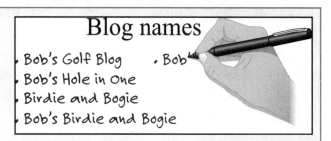

Blog names
• Bob's Golf Blog   • Bob'
• Bob's Hole in One
• Birdie and Bogie
• Bob's Birdie and Bogie

Try for a Unique Name

Increase your odds of having a unique blog title by:

- Typing your proposed title into the Google blog search engine at http://google.com/blogsearch to find blogs that use your title in full or in part.

- Typing your proposed title in your browser's address box followed by **wordpress.com**. For example, you could type **mythoughts.wordpress.com** to see if a WordPress.com blog by that name pops up.

- Typing the proposed title in the address box followed by **blogspot.com**, as in **mythoughts.blogspot.com**.

All the Good Names Are Taken!

So many sites are on the web these days that it may seem that all the good names are taken, but forge ahead. You can try alternate spellings, whimsical expressions, or combinations of your name and your interest. If you can make the title memorable and easy to spell, all the better. You also can try tools described in the following section, "Research Domain Names," to devise a good blog title.

Avoid Duplication

If someone else has a website with your preferred title, you can still use it, but it is a bad idea. Besides the potential for legal conflict if someone decides to trademark the title, the bigger issue is that readers may get your blog and the other site confused.

Research Domain Names

By researching domain names before you commit to a blog title, you can avoid the frustration of being unable to match your domain to your title. A few websites provide good brainstorming tools to help you. Most of these sites also link to pages where you can buy and register a domain, and they can advise you whether the name of your choice is available for purchase. However, you do not need to buy a domain name right away. Instead, you can use options described in Chapters 2 and 3.

Research Domain Names

1 In your web browser, go to www.dotomator.com.

2 In the Beginnings box, type a few words that describe your blog idea.

Note: This example uses *healthy food*.

3 Click the drop-down list ⬍.

4 Choose a category of endings.

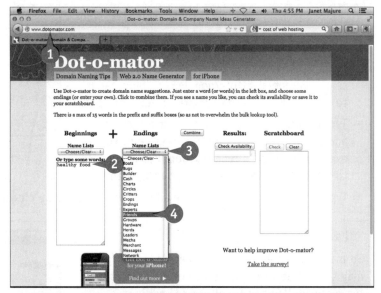

Ⓐ Endings related to the category appear.

Ⓑ Suggested domain names appear.

Ⓒ If a results list does not appear, click **Combine**.

5 Click a name that interests you.

Ⓓ The name appears under Scratchboard.

6 Repeat Steps 2 to 5 until you have several potential domain names.

7 Click **Check**.

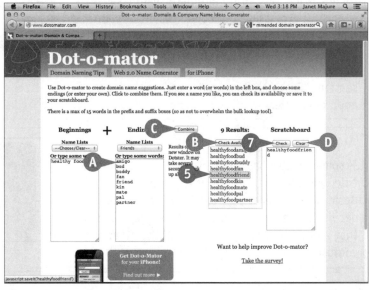

E A separate window operated by Dotster opens and displays availability of domains related to the names you chose.

8 Record the available names you like for future reference.

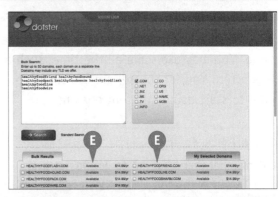

9 Type **www.panabee.com** in the address bar.

The Panabee home page opens.

10 Type two words related to your blog topic in the search box.

11 Click **Search**.

F Availability of a domain combining your words appears.

G A list of other suggestions and their availability appears.

12 Record the names you like for future reference.

TIPS

If I see a name I really like on these sites, should I go ahead and buy it?

You can, but in the long run you may be happier if you buy your domain registration through the web host you eventually choose. Doing so makes life simpler and potentially could save you money. Also, be assured that these sites do not have exclusive rights to sell the names they suggest to you.

Are there other sites that help with researching domain names?

The sites in this section are two of several such sites. Another good one is www.bustaname.com. Each of these sites has a slightly different approach to name generation, which is why it is handy to try more than one. Others include www.nameboy.com, www.namestation.com, and http://impossibility.org.

Think Ahead about Passwords

Making a password plan now will make life easier as you go about setting up your WordPress site, because chances are you are going to need multiple usernames and passwords before you are done. You may use some all the time, such as your site's logon information, but you may use others less often. You, of course, are too smart to use the same password for all situations, right? If not, plan to start using different ones now.

What Not To Do

Remember first what not to do: Do not use easily guessed words such as your spouse's or child's name, the word *password,* your license plate number, widely used combinations (such as qwerty or 123456), or any word in the dictionary spelled forward or backward. Also, do not put your password on a sticky note on your computer, and do not use the same word on multiple sites.

Choosing Passwords

Numerous strategies exist for choosing passwords. The basic approach is to choose a memorable phrase such as "My country tis of thee," use the first letters of the phrase's word — *Mctot* — and add numbers and special characters to get something like **Mctot!1*. The longer the password, the better. Have four or five passwords ready before you start your WordPress experience.

Saving Passwords

Experts agree that having your computer or browser remember your password for you is generally a bad idea because the bad guys are good at cracking those bits of software. The most secure plan is to *remember* your passwords, but that is not possible for many of us. Although there is some debate, the idea of writing them down and putting the list in a safe place is considered more secure than doing any of the items on the what-not-to-do list.

Get to Know WordPress Types

Whether you are setting up a WordPress blog or are using one set up by someone else, it is helpful to understand that WordPress comes in multiple flavors. They range from the relatively simple WordPress.com and basic WordPress.org installations to the enterprise-scale WordPress.com VIP and WordPress.org MultiSite options. After a quick look at each, you can get more detail on the focus of this book in the next two sections, "Look Closer at WordPress.org" and "Look Closer at WordPress.com." One nice feature is that you can choose one version and change to another later with few problems.

WordPress.com

WordPress.com is for individuals and organizations that like the WordPress ease of use and flexibility but do not want to concern themselves with details of hosting a website. If you skip some options, you can operate a WordPress.com site for no money.

WordPress.org

WordPress.org offers the greatest degree of flexibility and options for its users. It does, however, require a willingness to be involved at least on a low to moderate level with such website details as arranging for hosting and keeping software up to date.

WordPress.com VIP

The WordPress.com VIP service is aimed at large-scale websites, such as those of CNN and Dow Jones. It is expensive and not the service for beginners. This book does not cover operating a WordPress.com VIP site.

WordPress.org MultiSite

As the name implies, WordPress.org MultiSite is intended for running a network of websites. It uses the same software that you use for running a basic WordPress.org installation but is considerably more complex to operate. If you work for a large organization such as a public school system, your school may be running a WordPress.org MultiSite installation. This book does not cover installing and operating such an installation. If you are a user at such an organization, the information here for WordPress.com users generally applies to you.

Look Closer at WordPress.org

WordPress.org lets you take advantage of *open-source* software, meaning you — or anyone — can download it, use it, and change it, generally for free and with few restrictions. It has been around since 2003 as a program for self-hosted blogs, and this book uses versions 3.3.1-3.5. With WordPress.org you can customize all you want. Those customizations of everything from appearance to function usually are simple to create or install. WordPress.org websites also are known as *self-hosted sites*, because the trade-off is that you also have to take more responsibility for site management.

Hosting

With a WordPress.org installation, you need to find and engage a web host as well as a site name. If you plan a small site with low traffic, you may be able to operate it on your Internet service provider's site for no additional cost. More likely, you may seek out a host that caters to small site operators or one that provides automatic installation of WordPress.org software.

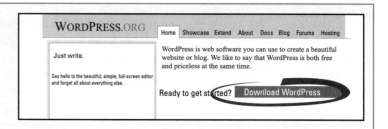

Appearance

Your WordPress.org site can look just about any way you want it to look. You can choose among some 1,600-plus themes that meet WordPress.org requirements — and many of them provide for further customizations. Most are free. Commercial sites that require a fee and often provide more support also are available.

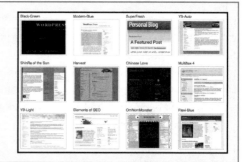

Plugins

Plugins are program-like extensions that work with WordPress to add functionality. You can have as many as you want on your self-hosted WordPress blog. Plugins, which are discussed in many places in this book, let you add innumerable functions, such as providing translation of your website, improving security, or linking to Facebook. Plugins let you make your site your own.

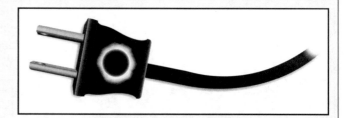

Advertising

With a self-hosted WordPress blog, you can publish zero to endless amounts of advertising. It is up to you. You can try the full range of Internet advertising media, from links that pay commissions when people purchase a product to pay-per-click ads, such as those provided by Google.

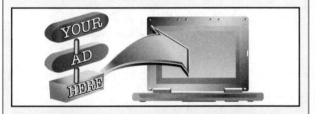

Business

You can use your self-hosted WordPress website to sell your own products or services without restriction, other than restrictions in law or in your web host's rules. Sell real estate, hand-made candies, computer advice, or whatever your business has to offer, and you will not have an issue with WordPress.org.

Di's Desserts
At Di's Desserts, we source the finest organic ingredients, then make each dessert with homemade care and pride. See our gallery of cakes for your next special occasion.

Cost

You pay nothing for your WordPress.org operating software. For a self-hosted site, you most likely will need to pay for a web hosting, which can run as low as $3.50 a month. Sometimes, your web host will provide one free domain registration when you sign up for hosting. If not, you may pay from a few dollars and up to buy a domain.

Support

In the spirit of WordPress's open-source development, support likewise is free and open source. That is to say, WordPress.org does not have staff to answer your questions. Many, if not most, answers can be found either in the WordPress.org support pages, called the *Codex*, or in the WordPress.org forums.

Look Closer at WordPress.com

With WordPress.com as your blog host, you can start blogging within minutes. The user interface is simple and similar to that of self-hosted WordPress.org blogs, but WordPress.com handles updates and maintenance and has staff to answer questions. WordPress.com developed as the hosting business of the people who started WordPress.org. The trade-off of giving WordPress.com the management duties, however, is that is has limitations that may or may not work for you. Also, although the hosting is free, you may choose options that do cost money.

Appearance

WordPress.com offers about 220 themes, and they are good ones. About 20 percent of them are *premium* themes, meaning you must pay for them. If you want to customize your theme by editing the *Cascading Style Sheets*, or *CSS*, you must pay an annual fee. With a self-hosted WordPress blog, you can choose among countless free themes or purchased themes, or create your own.

Widgets

Although WordPress.com, unlike self-hosted installations, does not let you add plugins, it has many more widgets than self-hosted blogs. A *widget* allows you to arrange sidebar information without writing code. The additional widgets at WordPress.com provide the same functions as similar plugins. The downside is that you have fewer options and that the widget panel can get a little cluttered.

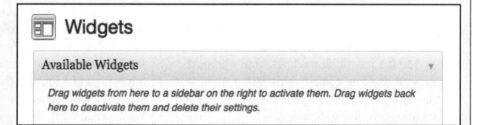

Ads

At WordPress.com, the blog host itself occasionally posts ads on your blog, unless you pay a no-ad fee. Also, WordPress.com does not allow most types of ads, including Google AdSense, and only allows *affiliate ads* — those that pay you a commission when someone buys by way

of a link on your site — under special circumstances. WordPress.com offers WordAds to allow some, but not all, bloggers to make money on their WordPress.com sites.

Cost

It costs nothing to publish your blog at WordPress.com. You may, however, decide to pay fees for a variety of options. Among them are options to eliminate their ads, buy a domain name, and edit the *Cascading Style Sheets,* or CSS, which set such styles as color and type face for your site's appearance. You also can pay to post videos — a cost absent from independent blogs — although you still can embed videos from sites such as YouTube.

Key Differences: Support

WordPress.com has a clearly written support section, redesigned in 2011, plus forums and a contact form for support. The support documentation for WordPress.org blogs is the Codex. Written by WordPress volunteers, its quality gets better all the time, but it is inconsistent. At WordPress.org, no support contact exists except for the forums, but they are excellent.

Sign Up at Gravatar.com

By signing up at Gravatar.com, you create a profile that promotes your online identity. Gravatar is a globally recognized *avatar*, which is an image that you associate with your e-mail address and that appears when you write a blog post or comment on someone else's blog. You can use a personal photo, your business or site logo, or some other image that you want associated with you or your brand. Although you are not required to have a Gravatar, it adds to the personal touch that makes WordPress popular.

Sign Up at Gravatar.com

1 In your browser, go to http://en.gravatar.com.

Note: You can type **http:// gravatar.com**, and the browser may take you to an address that presents the site in your language, such as http://es. gravatar.com, the Spanish-language version of the site.

2 Type your e-mail address.

3 Click **Get Your Gravatar.**

A confirmation screen appears.

Confirmation email sent!

We've sent an email to *tyvwp3@zoho.com*.

In the email you'll find a link that when clicked on will bring you back to the site so you can set your password and start using Gravatar.

If for some reason you do not receive the activation email, contact us and we'll do our best to get you back on track.

PLEASE check your junk/spam folder before contacting us, as it is very common to have email delivery problems because of automated filters.

④ In your e-mail inbox, open the message from Gravatar.

⑤ Click the activation link.

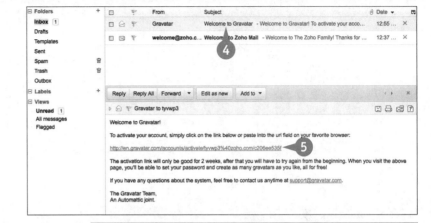

⑥ Type a username.

⑦ Type a password.

⑧ Retype the password.

⑨ Click the check box (☐ changes to ☑) to agree to the terms of service and privacy policy.

⑩ Click **Signup**.

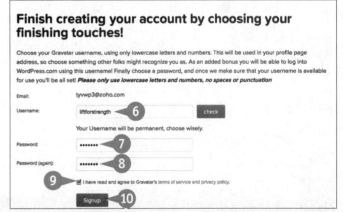

The Gravatar home page appears in your browser.

Ⓐ The presence of the My Account button shows you are signed in to the site.

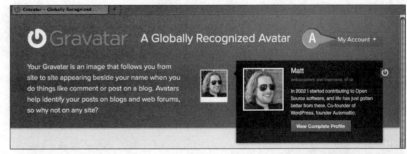

TIP

I am signed up, but how do I add an image with my membership?
You can add an image or images by clicking **My Account** and then selecting **Manage My Gravatars** from the pop-up menu. A new window appears with a link that says *Add one by clicking here!* When you click that link, Gravatar takes you step by step through the uploading process. Other items on the account menu let you add profile information for public view, such as favorite links or a brief bio about yourself.

CHAPTER 2

Setting Up Your WordPress.com Blog

Once you decide to run your blog on WordPress.com, setting it up is a snap. In this chapter, you sign up with WordPress.com, get familiar with its workings, choose among settings, and select a visual theme for your new blog's appearance.

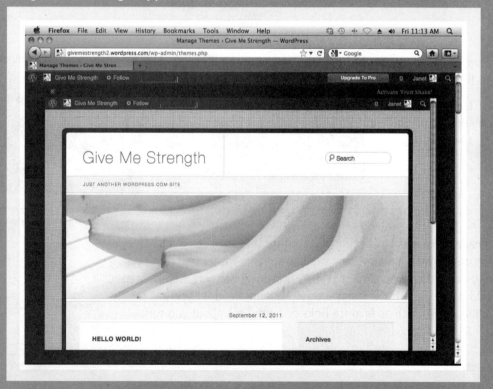

Sign Up with WordPress.com

With just a few simple steps, you can sign up with WordPress.com. When you do, you can start communicating, customizing, and getting in touch with the world as soon as you want.

Sign Up with WordPress.com

1 Navigate to http://wordpress.com in your web browser.

2 Click **Get Started**.

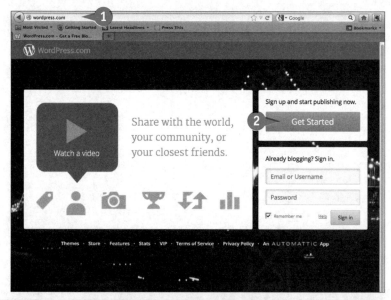

The signup screen appears.

3 Type your e-mail address.

WordPress.com inserts your e-mail name in the Username and Blog Address boxes. You can change those if you want, and WordPress.com will tell you if your selection is unavailable.

4 Type a password.

5 Click **No thanks, I'll use the free address**.

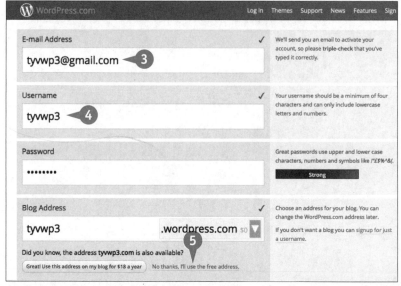

6 Scroll to the bottom of the page.

Ⓐ This link shows the site's terms of service.

7 Click **Create Blog**.

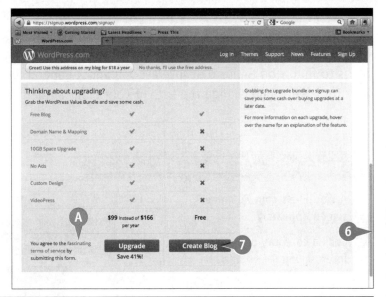

WordPress.com sends a confirmation link to your e-mail address.

8 Click **Activate Blog** in the e-mail you receive to confirm your account.

Note: WordPress sends you a second confirmation e-mail with links to helpful information for beginners.

TIPS

Can I just sign up without starting a blog?

Yes. You can add your own blog or site later. To sign up without starting a blog, click **Sign up for just a username** next to the Blog Address box, and follow the signup instructions. Signing up lets you comment on WordPress.com blogs or, if you are a WordPress.org user, gives you access to some services managed by the WordPress.com servers.

Now that I am a member, how do I sign in?

You can go to the home page at WordPress.com and sign in at the top of the page; you can type your blog's address plus **/wp-admin**, such as **example.wordpress.com/wp-admin**. After your blog is set up you may have a *Meta* section, which provides a link to log in from your blog's home page.

Sign Up with WordPress.com (continued)

Once you confirm you want a WordPress.com blog, you can get a jump-start on blogging and on full involvement with the WordPress.com community. You do it by making choices in the series of welcome screens that WordPress.com presents. By making selections there, you soon have a set of blogs to follow on topics that interest you and a general look, or *theme,* for your blog. You also can look for friends and change the title of your blog, all before you have published a single blog post.

Sign Up with WordPress.com (continued)

A WordPress.com welcome screen appears.

9 Click a category or two that interest you.

B The Follow button changes to Following after you click.

10 Click **Next Step**.

The Follow Your Friends screen appears.

11 Click **Next Step**.

Note: You can connect later with your friends, as described in Chapter 8.

The Set up your blog screen appears.

12 Type a blog title.

13 Type a tagline.

Note: You can leave the default tagline, delete it, or create your own.

C The Language drop-down list lets you choose among several languages.

14 Click **Next Step**.

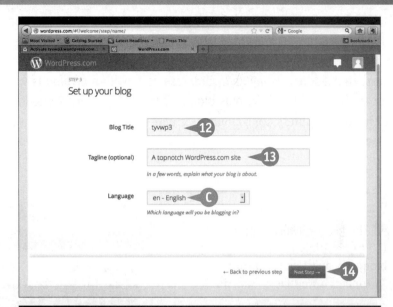

The theme screen appears.

15 Click a theme you like.

16 Click **Next Step**.

The customization screen appears.

17 Click **Next Step**.

The Create your first post screen appears.

18 Click **Finish**.

WordPress opens the first of four introductory screens.

TIP

What are the introductory screens?

They are a set of self-explanatory screens that give you a mini-tour of the WordPress.com administration pages. They give a brief introduction to all aspects of your WordPress.com installation. It is easy to be overwhelmed, so go ahead and view them, and then you can come to this book to review what you need later.

View Your New Blog

Now it is time to learn the parts and pieces that make up your new blog. That general understanding can help you to make decisions as to your blog's appearance and content and help you understand controls behind the scenes. See your new blog by typing your blog address. For most new WordPress.com users, that address is *myblog*.wordpress.com, where *myblog* is your blog name. There, you see your blog as the world sees it, plus blogging tools if you are logged in at WordPress.com. The About page, at *myblog*.wordpress.com/about, is created by default and shows many aspects of a WordPress page or post.

The Home Page

Ⓐ The header, which runs across the top of the screen, displays the blog title and tagline, in this case "A topnotch WordPress.com Site."

Ⓑ When you are signed in as a WordPress.com member, you see the black Admin Bar. It gives easy access to WordPress.com resources and tools.

Ⓒ Most themes include a sidebar, also known as a *widget area*, and you get to choose items that appear in them. Your first installation may include the Meta widget. *Meta* refers to *metadata*, or information about your blog and its contents. The Search and Archives widgets appear by default.

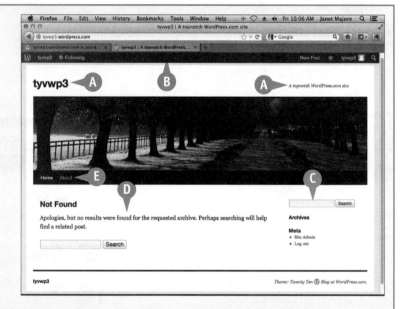

Ⓓ Once you create content, the blog posts appear in this area.

Ⓔ Your initial site lists two pages in the menu bar, About and Home, which WordPress creates by default.

The About Page

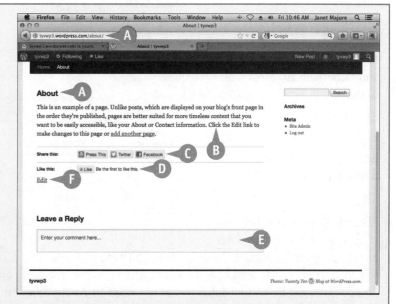

Ⓐ The title of the page, in this case *About*, corresponds with the page's web address, such as *myblog*.wordpress.com/about.

Ⓑ The default About page text explains the page's purpose and how to change it.

Ⓒ Sharing tools let readers tell their friends about your pages and posts. The Press This button, which is for sharing on WordPress.com, appears only to viewers who are logged in at WordPress.com.

Ⓓ The Like button lets readers endorse a page or post. If they are not logged in, they are asked to log in at WordPress.com or join.

Ⓔ The comment area lets readers respond to or comment on your page or post.

Ⓕ When you are logged in, your pages and posts include an Edit link. Clicking it puts you behind the scenes to edit the page or post you are viewing.

Get to Know Your Blog's Dashboard

Your blog's Dashboard is information central. The Dashboard's modules give you an overview of current and past activity on your blog, and you can add to your blog's content. WordPress includes introductory text and a video on the Dashboard when you are new. You can click **Hide this screen** to make it go away permanently. The address for your WordPress.com administrative panels is *myblog*.wordpress.com/wp-admin. If you are not logged in, typing that address prompts you to do so. If you are logged in, you can find several links to the Dashboard, depending on your location.

Dashboard Modules

Ⓐ Left Menu Bar

Contains navigation links for working on your WordPress blog. Most of the items expand when you click them to reveal more options.

Ⓑ Right Now

Provides the facts on how many posts, pages, and other content items your blog has.

Ⓒ Screen Options Tab

Expands module that lets you choose what content modules appear on your Dashboard. Other administration panels also have a Screen Options tab, and module choices vary according to what panel is active.

Ⓓ Help Tab

Expands module that provides links to WordPress.com support information and to information specific to the administration panel that is active.

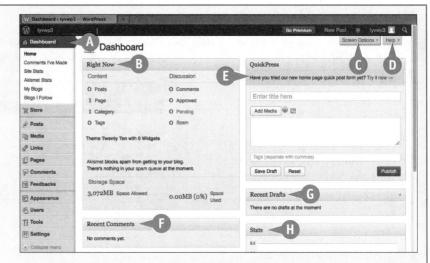

Ⓔ QuickPress

Lets you type and publish a blog post when you are in a hurry and do not need to do anything fancy.

Ⓕ Recent Comments

Reveals the names of recent commenters, the name of the post that they commented on, and the first line or two of the comment. You also can moderate comments from here.

Ⓖ Recent Drafts

Shows posts and pages you have written but not published.

Ⓗ Stats

Gives a snapshot of how many times people are viewing your WordPress.com blogs and what blog posts are getting the most interest.

Dashboard Modules (continued)

❶ Your Stuff

Lists your recent posts, edits, comments made, and comments received.

❿ What's Hot

Offers links to WordPress news and blogs.

❻ View All

Links to a page of detailed WordPpress.com statistics.

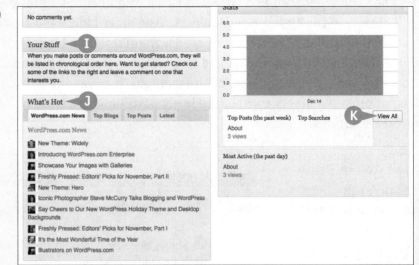

Screen Options

Ⓐ Show on Screen

Indicates with a checked box (☑) that the content item appears on your Dashboard.

Ⓑ Screen Layout

Shows with a selected radio button (⦿) how many columns WordPress uses to display your Dashboard information.

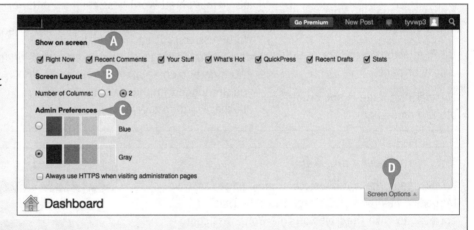

Ⓒ Admin Preferences

Shows with a selected radio button (⦿) the color scheme for your administration panels.

Ⓓ Screen Options Collapse Button

Collapses the Screen Options box when clicked.

Understanding the WordPress.com Admin Bar

When you are logged in at WordPress.com, the Admin Bar provides a wealth of tools. With just a click, you can start a new blog post, visit other blogs, and check out your site statistics. You also find links that let you log out, search WordPress.com blogs, and go to your Dashboard. In short, if you want to do something related to WordPress.com, you probably can get to the right location from the Admin Bar. Some Admin Bar menu offerings vary depending on where you are on your own blog or other WordPress.com blogs. Simply position your mouse pointer over the menu of interest to reveal its options.

The Admin Bar

A Opens the WordPress.com menu.

B Opens blog menu, specific to the blog being viewed.

C Toggles among Follow, Following, and Unfollow the blog being viewed.

D Toggles between Like or Unlike a post or page.

Note: This toggle is not visible on blogs' home page.

E Shows statistics graphic and links to blog statistics.

Note: Items **A**, **B**, **C**, and **D** are visible on all WordPress.com blogs when you are logged in at WordPress.com. Item **E** is visible only when viewing your own blog. A Reblog button appears when you are logged in and visiting another WordPress.com site.

F Opens New Post pane at the top of the screen.

G Shows recent activity on your blog or blogs.

H Opens your account menu.

I Opens WordPress.com search box.

The WordPress.com Menu

A Ⓦ opens the WordPress.com home page for logged-in members. That page has tabs that correspond with the items on this WordPress.com menu — New Post to open a new post panel, Reader for reading blogs you follow, Notifications that list activity on your blogs, Stats for site statistics, My Blog for blog information overview, and Freshly Pressed, which displays featured posts on WordPress.com sites. See the following section, "Understanding the WordPress.com Home Page," for more information.

B Opens your WordPress.com settings panel.

The Blog Menu

A Shows name of blog you are visiting.

B Takes you to your blog's Dashboard.

C Opens a menu to choose to add a new post, page, or favorite link or to upload new media.

D Opens administrative panel associated with item named — comments, menus, and widgets, all explained in later chapters.

E Provides a *shortlink* for current page or post, handy for Twitter or e-mail.

F Goes to a random post on the current site.

G Lists theme name.

H Opens a dialog box where you can report to WordPress.com that the post you are viewing — on your own or on some other blog — should be reviewed by WordPress.com staff as adult content, as spam, or for other reasons.

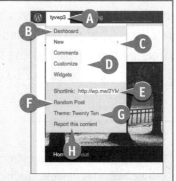

Note: Items **B**, **C**, and **D** are visible only when you are visiting your own site.

Your Account Menu

A Opens friend-finding page at WordPress.com.

B Opens My Blogs tab at WordPress.com home page.

C Opens main support page at WordPress.com.

D Signs you out of WordPress.com.

E Opens flyout menu for your blog. If you have more than one blog, each is listed here, and pointing to one opens the flyout menu for that blog.

F Provides links to each of the panels listed.

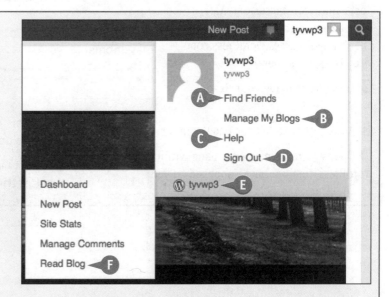

Note: The Read Blog option takes you to your blog's front page from other WordPress.com sites.

Understanding the WordPress.com Home Page

When you are logged in at WordPress.com, you have access to your WordPress.com activity at the WordPress.com home page. It has links that let you create a new post, read other WordPress.com blogs, review your site statistics, and get an overview of your blogs. In addition, the Settings panel, accessible through the home page, gives you one spot to update such account details as your password and the e-mail address where you get WordPress notices. WordPress.com offers multiple paths to the same destination. Go to the home page by typing **http://wordpress.com** into your web browser or by clicking the WordPress menu icon (Ⓦ).

Home Page Links

Ⓐ Opens pages corresponding to tab names. The default landing page is Reader, which shows posts in blogs you are following. The other pages let you see your site's statistics, see an overview of your blog or blogs, or take a look at "Freshly Pressed," blog posts that WordPress.com staff have selected to highlight. Chapter 9 discusses WordPress.com site statistics in detail.

Ⓑ Lets you manage your Reader page content.

Ⓒ Adds topics to Reader page content.

Ⓓ Opens a create new post page within the WordPress.com pages, as opposed to your administration panels.

Ⓔ Reveals list of recent activity related to your blog or blogs.

Ⓕ Opens menu leading to your administration panel, settings, help, and more.

My Blogs Page

A Links to your Posts, Pages, and Comment panels in your blog's administrative area.

B Link to your blog's Dashboard.

C Link to your blog's Themes panel.

Freshly Pressed

A Posts recommended by WordPress.com staff.

B Toggle to switch between list and grid views.

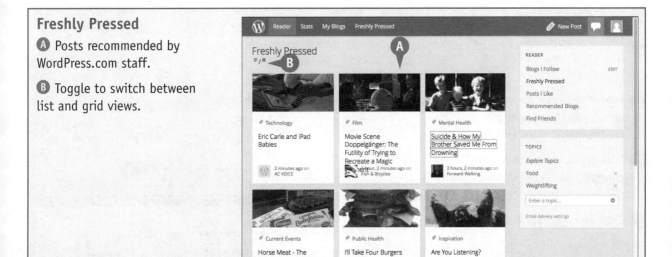

Create Your WordPress.com Profile

Your WordPress.com public profile allows you to tell the world who you are through words, pictures, and links. This information is public and displayed at Gravatar.com, so do not include any information you want to keep private. The image also appears along with your name whenever you leave comments on other WordPress.com blogs. You can complete your profile by clicking **Users** and then **My Profile** in the left menu bar of your blog's Dashboard. If you prefer, on the WordPress.com home page when you are logged in, you can click your avatar, then click **Settings** in the menu that appears, and then click **Public Profile**.

Create Your WordPress.com Profile

Note: This example is on the My Profile panel in your administration panels.

1. Type your first name.

2. Type your last name.

3. Type the name that you want to appear on your blog as your posts' author.

4. Type a sentence or paragraph about you that you think readers might want to know.

5. Click **Update Profile** to save changes, and scroll down to reveal more profile options.

6. Click **Change your Gravatar**.

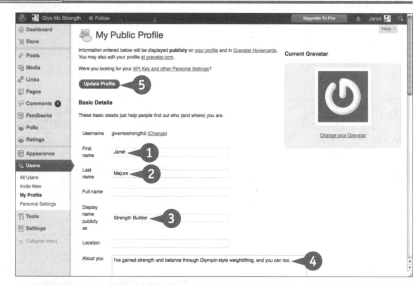

The Upload your Gravatar window opens.

7 Choose an option for uploading an image if you want, and follow the directions that appear.

8 Choose **Edit My Profile** from the Main Menu.

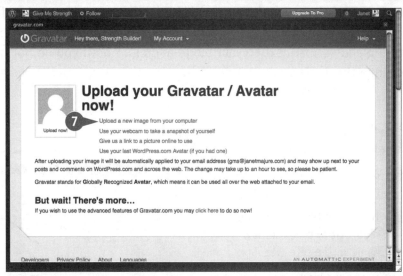

The My Public Profile page opens.

9 Type the web address in the URL box of any web page you like plus a name for the page in the Title box.

10 Click **Add Link**.

11 Click **Update Profile**.

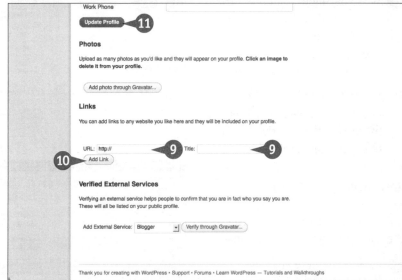

Where does my profile appear?
Several places, all served through Gravatar.com, which is operated by the same company, Automattic Inc., that owns WordPress.com. Your Gravatar and pop-up profile, or *Gravatar Hovercard*, appear with comments you make on WordPress.com blogs and on posts where you click **Like**. It is associated with your e-mail address.

I do not want my picture and information all over the place. Can I opt out?
Not exactly, because you automatically have a Gravatar account when you sign up with WordPress.com. However, you can leave your profile information blank, and only a symbol and your username appear when you comment or like a post.

Select Your General Settings

You can polish your site's title, add a tagline, and choose time formats, among other options, on the General Settings page. You can also upload an image to serve as a *favicon*, which appears in the address bar next to your blog's address. And if you do not like your choices, you can always change them later.

Select Your General Settings

① On the Dashboard, click **Settings** to open the settings list.

② If you want to modify your blog's title, type the new name in the Site Title box.

③ Type your blog's tagline in the Tagline box, which by default contains the tagline "Just another WordPress.com site." Or delete it and leave it blank.

④ In the Timezone box select a city in your time zone from the pop-up list or your time relative to UTC, or *coordinated universal time*.

Note: Scroll up in the pop-up list to find cities. If you choose a UTC setting, you must manually reset the zone for daylight saving time.

⑤ Review the date and time formats and click to choose one other than the default (○ changes to ⊙).

⑥ Click **Browse** to find an image on your computer for your Blog Picture/Icon.

⑦ Once you locate an image, click **Upload Image** to upload it.

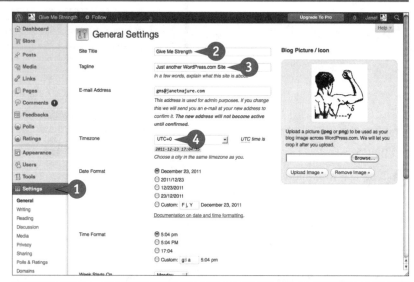

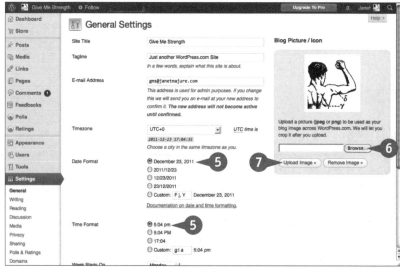

The image appears on a new screen.

⑧ Click and drag the white selection box to choose the area you want for your image.

Note: You can click the box's edge, and then drag it to stretch or shrink the selection.

⑨ Click **Crop Image**.

⑩ A confirmation screen opens with a Back to Blog Options link. Click it to return to General Settings.

⑪ Select the first day of the week you prefer for WordPress calendars from the drop-down menu.

⑫ If you plan to write in a language other than English, choose it from the drop-down menu.

⑬ Click **Save Changes**.

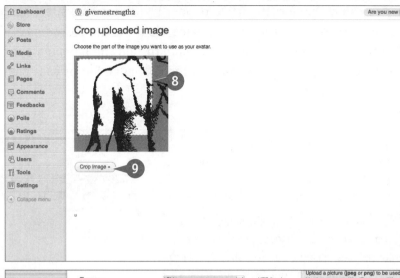

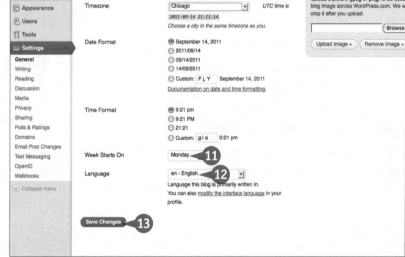

What is the difference between the Gravatar on the profile page and the Blog Picture/Icon on the General Settings page?
The Gravatar is an icon, also known as an *avatar*, associated with your e-mail address and appears with comments you make. The Blog Picture/Icon on this page — known as *blavatar* to indicate a *blog* avatar — is an icon specifically for your blog. It appears as the favicon in your blog's URL when people visit as well as in the WordPress.com Admin Bar.

Can I have the same image for both Gravatar and blavatar?
Absolutely. Many people prefer to use the same image for consistency, but you must upload the image twice — once for each purpose.

Consider Premium WordPress.com Options

You can do more customizing of your WordPress.com site when you buy premium features. These let you use your own domain name, do a custom *Cascading Style Sheet*, or CSS, and more. WordPress.com gives you many prompts to find the premium options, but the easiest and most consistent may be to click **Store** in the left menu bar of your blog's Dashboard. Your Dashboard also may display a Go Premium button.

The Premium Upgrades page at http://store.wordpress.com/ provides prices and links to more information about available premium features:

A Using your own domain name. Domain names, which are discussed in Chapter 1, can be purchased or, if you already own one, can be mapped to your WordPress.com site.

B Customizing your blog's color palette or editing the CSS if you know how.

C Using the WordPress.com VideoPress service to host your videos.

D Blocking ads that WordPress.com publishes occasionally on your blog.

E Getting personal help from WordPress.com staff to transfer your site to WordPress.org.

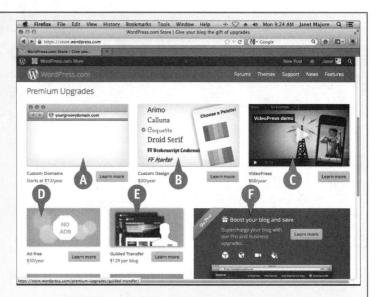

F Buying upgrade bundles, or sets of upgrades, at slightly reduced price.

G Letting WordPress.com send visitors from one WordPress.com address to another web address.

H Adding to the 3GB of storage that come with your WordPress.com blog.

I Getting a premium theme for added theme customization and support.

More about Upgrades

Custom Design

This upgrade lets you customize your site layout with Custom Fonts or with *Cascading Style Sheets*, or CSS. Try them for free before buying the upgrade by clicking **Custom Design** under Appearance in the Dashboard's left menu bar. Custom Fonts lets you choose from a selection of typefaces and sizes for your blog title, headings, and body type. CSS lets you create custom settings for the size, typeface, indention, color, and more, from headings to footers, posts to comments to links. CSS also gives the default style settings for images.

Adding Storage Space

Your free WordPress.com blog account includes 3GB of storage. You could blog for years and not use it up unless you use many big images. Because audio uses a lot of storage, however, WordPress.com requires a space upgrade if you want to upload audio or music to your blog. If you intend to host podcasts at WordPress.com, you need this upgrade.

VideoPress

VideoPress is a slick feature if you plan to use video, because it lets you host the video on your blog rather than on a separate site such as YouTube, and it makes your videos available as video podcasts. In addition, you can post video files up to 1GB, and there is no limit on video length. It supports all the major video file types, including the MP4 and Ogg formats.

Buy an Upgrade

To buy an upgrade, go to your site's Dashboard and click **Store** near the top of the left menu bar. Click the upgrade you want to buy, click the button, such as **Get more storage**, on the information page that appears, and follow the steps on the subsequent screens. Except for Guided Transfer and Premium Themes, all upgrades are for one year and must be renewed annually to maintain them. Most upgrades can be canceled and refunded within 30 days.

Buy a Domain at WordPress.com

When you buy a domain at WordPress.com, you can get the free hosting and support that WordPress.com offers while giving the world a web address that does not include the WordPress name. Although you can buy a domain at any number of domain registrars and use it with your WordPress.com site, buying the domain through WordPress.com keeps things simple. After you sign up to have a blog at WordPress.com, click **Store** and then **Domain** in your site's Dashboard to get started. WordPress leads you through the purchasing process. WordPress.com registers domains only with the .com, .org, .net, and .me extensions.

Buy a Domain at WordPress.com

① In your Dashboard, click **Store**.

The Store menu expands.

② Click **Domains**.

The Domains panel appears.

③ Type the domain you want.

④ Click **Add domain to blog**.

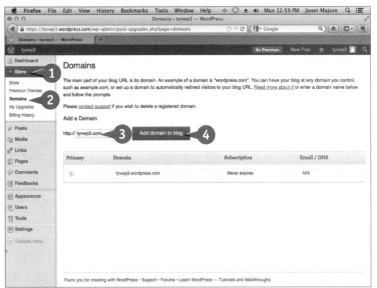

The Registrant details panel appears.

Note: If the domain name you typed is already registered, an alert appears.

⑤ Type your first name.

⑥ Type your last name.

⑦ Type an e-mail address.

⑧ Provide address information.

⑨ Scroll to bottom of the panel.

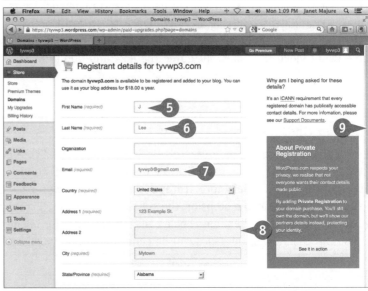

10 Type your postal code.

11 Type your telephone number.

12 Click **Register Domain**.

A dialog box appears that shows how your registration appears on the international registry.

13 Click **Just Normal Registration**.

A payment screen appears.

14 Complete the payment information and then click **Purchase**.

Ⓐ WordPress confirms your purchase.

Ⓑ After a few minutes the empty radio button (◯) changes to a selected button (◉).

15 Click **Update Primary Domain**.

Any web traffic to your previous WordPress.com address now goes to the newly registered domain.

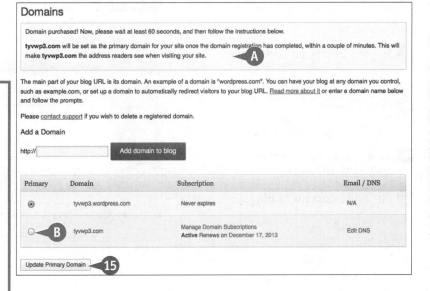

TIP

What is private registration?
Private registration lets you use a *proxy*, or substitute, for your personal registration information. That is, when you register a domain, your name and contact information appear on international registries. If you decide you want to make your information private after you register, go back to the Domain area of Store, click **Manage Domain Subscriptions**, and then click **Add Private Registration**.

Map a Domain to WordPress.com

If you own a domain that you did not register through WordPress.com, you can *map* that domain to WordPress.com. That means when someone types your domain address in a web browser, the browser opens the main domain page at WordPress.com just as if you had registered the domain at WordPress. Mapping a domain is a little more involved than most things you might do at WordPress.com. It is not difficult, though, and WordPress.com provides good documentation at http://support.wordpress.com/domains/map-existing-domain should you have difficulties. First, you need to find your registrar's *domain name servers* listing. Those servers help direct Internet traffic.

Map a Domain to WordPress.com

1 At your domain registrar, type the WordPress domain name servers into your current registrar's name server fields. The WordPress.com name servers are:

ns1.wordpress.com

ns2.wordpress.com

ns3.wordpress.com

2 Click **Save Nameserver Settings**.

Note: This example uses BlueHost.com.

3 In your Dashboard click **Store**.

The Store menu expands.

4 Click **Domains**.

The Domains panel appears.

5 Type the domain you want to map to WordPress.com.

6 Click **Add domain to blog**.

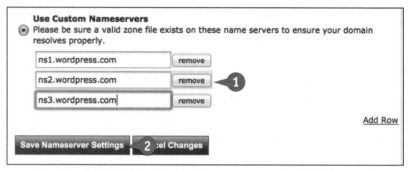

An alert screen appears.

7 Click **Yes! Start Mapping My Domain**.

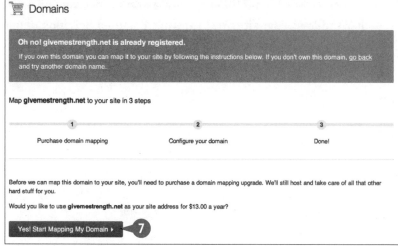

The screen changes.

8 Scroll down and complete payment information.

9 Click **Purchase**.

WordPress returns to the Domains page.

10 Click the radio button next to the domain you want to use for your WordPress.com blog address (⃝ changes to ⦿).

11 Click **Update Primary Domain**.

The new domain is the address for your blog.

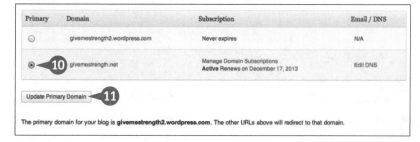

TIPS

Where can I find the place to change the domain name server for my domain?
The location depends on your registrar. The easiest and most reliable way is to contact support at your domain registrar and ask how to change your domain name servers.

When I try to change my domain name servers, my registrar says I need to provide a DNS Zone Record. Where do I get that?
Go to http://support.wordpress.com/domains/dns-zone-records. Type your domain name in the box, and click **Add DNS Zone**. When you do, WordPress.com will add the required record to its servers so that you can complete the task.

Choose Your Personal Settings

Your personal settings let you choose among numerous options that affect how you work on your WordPress.com site. You can find Personal Settings under Users in the left menu bar of the Dashboard.

Choose Your Personal Settings

① Click **Keyboard Shortcuts** (☐ changes to ☑) to enable keyboard shortcuts for comment moderation.

Ⓐ The More Information link leads to a keyboard shortcuts explanation.

② Click **Enable Geotagging** (☐ changes to ☑) to allow your site to use geotags.

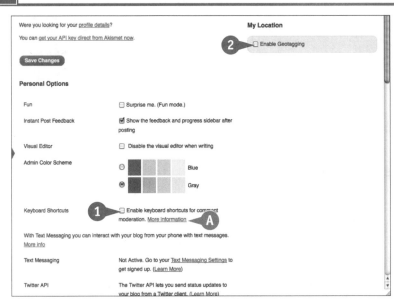

The geotagging box expands.

③ Type a ZIP code, city, or address.

④ Click **Find Address**.

Ⓑ WordPress shows a circle — not visible in some browsers — for an inexact address or a pointer for an exact address.

⑤ Review the privacy settings, which default to public geotags, and click to change them if you want.

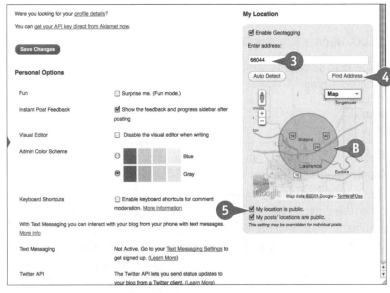

⑥ Scroll down the panel and click the check box in the **Browser Connection** area (☐ changes to ☑) if you access your blog via a public computer.

Note: This step helps protect your blog from hijacking by specifying use of a secure connection.

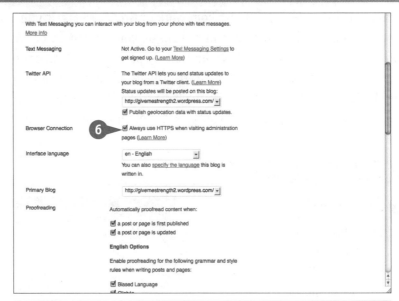

⑦ Confirm the e-mail address for notices from WordPress.com is correct.

ⓒ This is where you change your password if necessary.

⑧ Click **Save Changes**.

Your new Personal Settings are saved.

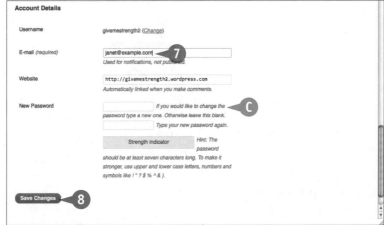

TIPS

What are all those other settings on this panel?
The Personal Settings are a catchall for assorted WordPress.com options. Most are covered in other chapters in this book. All are detailed at http://support.wordpress.com/personal-settings, but many, such as the Admin Color Scheme, are self-explanatory.

What about the Fun and Instant Post Feedback settings?
If you select **Fun** mode, you may occasionally see messages or even brief animations cheering you on. **Instant Post Feedback** produces a sidebar that appears as you publish each new post, telling you the post has loaded and making posting suggestions. It also keeps track of goals you may set.

Make Your Site Private

You can keep your WordPress.com work entirely private if you want. You may think doing so is a great idea until your site is in the shape you want it to be. A private blog can be seen only by you and readers whom you have invited — plus WordPress.com employees. If you think you might want a private blog, it is best to start private, because once things have been published publicly on the World Wide Web, it is very difficult to make them disappear. If you start out private, however, you can go public without difficulty. A middle ground is to discourage search engines.

Make Your Site Private

1 Click **Settings.**

The Settings menu list expands, and the General Settings panel opens.

2 Click **Reading.**

The Reading Settings panel appears.

3 Click the **I would like my site to be private** radio button (◯ changes to ◉).

4 Scroll down.

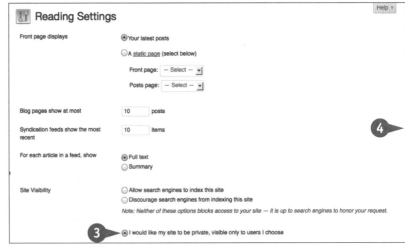

⑤ Click **Save Changes**.

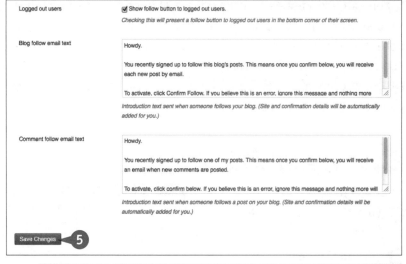

Ⓐ WordPress confirms the change.

Ⓑ Your blog is entirely private until you invite readers.

TIPS

How do I invite people to read my site?
After you save your private blog designation, an Invite viewers to access your blog button appears in the Site Visibility area of your Readings Settings. Clicking it opens a screen for inviting viewers. See the next section, "Add Viewers to Private Blogs," for details.

What is the search engine indexing about?
When search engines index your site, they make note of keywords that people might use to search the Internet. If your site is public, WordPress can ask search engines not to index your site, which should reduce odds of people finding the site by searching.

Add Viewers to Private Blogs

You can add Viewers to your private blog so that someone besides you and WordPress.com staff can access it. To do so, you must invite each person you want to have as a Viewer. Those potential Viewers must accept your invitation and get a WordPress.com username to see your site. You send the invitations from the Users panel in your blog's administration panels, where you also can keep track of the status of invitations. Unless you have discussed the matter with your invitees, you need to personalize the invitation so they understand why they need to sign up.

Add Viewers to Private Blogs

Your Actions

1 Click **Users** to expand the Users menu.

2 Click **Invite New**.

The Invite New Users to Your Private Blog panel opens.

3 Type up to 10 e-mail addresses or a WordPress.com member's usernames, separated by commas.

A Viewer is the default role.

4 Customize the invitation.

5 Click **Send Invitation**.

B WordPress sends an e-mail to the person or persons.

C The invitations are added to the Past Invitations list.

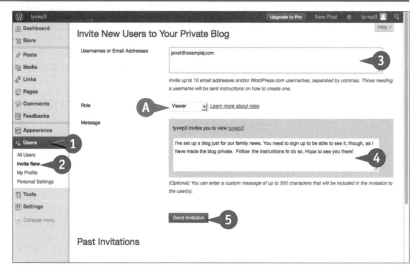

Invitee Actions

1 The invitee opens e-mail invitation.

2 The invitee clicks **Accept Invitation**.

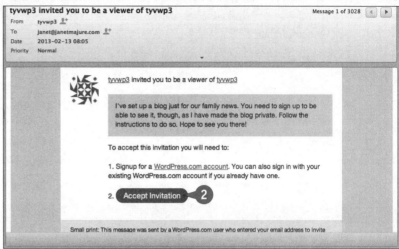

The WordPress.com logon screen appears in the invitee's web browser.

3 The invitee logs on or registers.

D WordPress.com members log on using their WordPress.com username and password.

E Viewers who are new to WordPress.com must register.

WordPress.com sends a confirmation e-mail to the contributor and updates your Users list.

TIPS

What if I want more than 10 Viewers?
You can have as many Viewers as you like, but you can only invite 10 at a time. That means after you send your first set of invitations, you need to type in the next 10 individuals' e-mail addresses or WordPress.com usernames.

Is there some way I can connect to my e-mail address book to make the invitations easier?
Not at this time. Most e-mail programs, whether online or on your desktop, do have the ability to export your address list. If you have many invitations you want to issue, check your e-mail program's Help to export addresses. That way, you can save time and avoid mistyping addresses at WordPress.com.

CHAPTER 3

Setting Up Your WordPress.org Blog

Your self-hosted WordPress.org blog requires a little more effort than a site at WordPress.com, but the payoff is in total control of the look, function, and content of your blog.

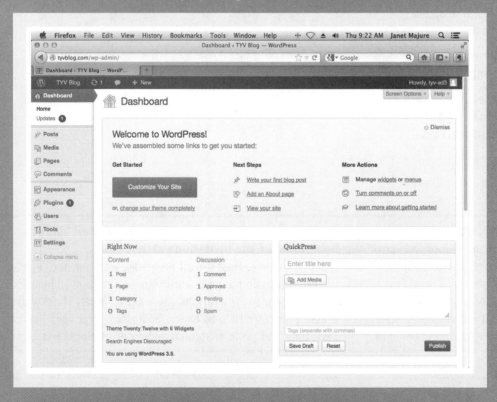

Choose a Host for Your Blog

When you choose a reliable and accessible web host, you can count on your WordPress.org blog staying online and available. You might even get some technical support for your WordPress installation. Countless web hosts are available, and some even provide free, one-click installation of the WordPress.org software. Many hosts offer modestly priced packages that do the job for small websites. The key is to select a host that meets your needs and the software requirements. Do a little research before you make your host decision.

What Web Hosts Do

A web host provides computer servers that store your blog's files and databases and make them available over the Internet. Web hosts usually offer a control panel to help you manage your files and low-cost domain registration options.

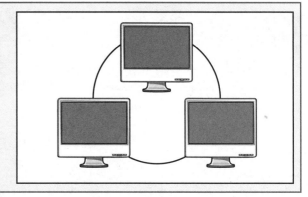

WordPress Requirements

Running WordPress 3.5 requires that the web host provide two basic software packages: PHP version 5.2.4 or greater and MySQL version 5.0 or greater. PHP is a scripting language, and MySQL is database software. WordPress also recommends, but does not require, Apache or Nginx as the server software.

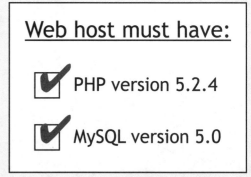

Web host must have:

☑ PHP version 5.2.4

☑ MySQL version 5.0

Your Requirements

Your computer needs to have Internet access. You also need to consider your blog's specific requirements, such as the amount of traffic you expect or hope for, and the type and quantity of media you expect to use. When you start from scratch, this information can be hard to determine, so make your best guess and, when contacting potential hosts, find out how they handle a surge in traffic or changing host packages if your needs change.

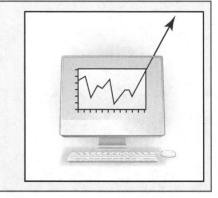

Shared or Dedicated Server?

A *shared server* means that the computer on which your website resides is also home to other websites. A *dedicated server* is reserved for your site alone and is naturally more expensive. A shared server is usually adequate for most small blogs.

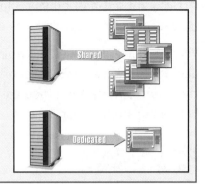

Options to Consider

Among the countless web hosts available are your Internet service provider, or ISP, and WordPress-recommended web hosts. Your own ISP may — or may not — be the least-expensive alternative. Some WordPress-recommended hosts, available at WordPress.org/hosting, provide one-click WordPress installations. For other host recommendations, ask

friends and read reviews at web-hosting-review.toptenreviews.com or reviewsignal.com/webhosting.

Checking Them Out

Once you have two or three web hosts to consider, check them out by reading reviews and by calling the host's support line — not the sales line — to see whether you are likely to be able to get help when you need it. Getting someone to talk on the sales line is easy, but a 10-minute wait when you call support may not be acceptable to you. Browse the host's support pages, too, to get a sense of the help they offer.

Take a Tour

Once you make a decision and sign up for web hosting, get familiar with your host's control panel. It makes managing your blog easier and most likely also provides access to helpful site data.

Stats	
Main Domain	yournewblog.com
Home Directory	/home/yournewblog
Last login from	183.88.68.42
Disk Space Usage	39.22 / – MB
Monthly Bandwidth Transfer	.57 / – MB
Hosting package	undefined

Buy a Domain

If you are self-hosting your blog, you likely will want to buy a domain name to make it easier for readers to find you. You may want to buy one for a WordPress.com blog, too.

You can buy a domain name from any number of *registrars* as a step independent of your hosting decision. However, web hosts often will register domains and give their customers a price break on the service. Therefore, if you are planning an independent blog, you may want to choose a web host before registering your domain.

Buy a Domain

1 Go to www.name.com in your web browser.

Note: This site is one of many where you can search for and buy domains. Your web host may give you a discounted price.

2 Type the name of your proposed domain in the box.

3 Click **Search** or press Enter.

A Domains with the name you searched appear at the top of the page. Those already registered are marked *Taken (Backorder)*. *Premium* domains are registered to someone else who is selling them at premium prices.

Choosing **Backorder** means Name.com will try to snag the domain for you when its registration expires.

Suggested alternative domain names appear farther down on the page.

If none of the available or suggested domain names satisfies you, repeat Steps 2 and 3 until you find one you want.

④ Click the domain name you want to register (☐ changes to ☑).

Ⓑ The domain also appears on the right side of the screen under Your Cart. You may select multiple domains if you want.

⑤ After you select all the domains you want to register, click **Checkout**.

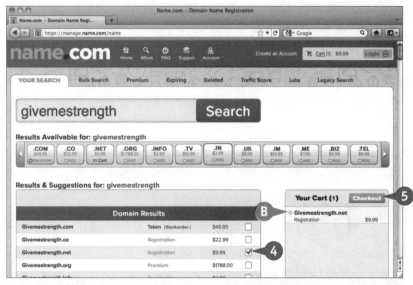

A new web page opens.

⑥ Review the information on the confirmation page.

⑦ If you are satisfied, click **Create an Account**.

The window expands to let you type registration information. Complete it, and then click **Continue**.

Proceed through the remaining screens until your registration and purchase are complete.

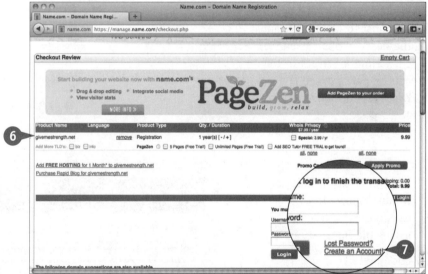

TIPS

Do I have to buy a domain name?
No. If you do not, however, your URL will be your web host's domain and directory listing, such as www.webhost.com/*myweblog*, or it could be a subdomain such as *myweblog*.webhost.com.

If the domain name I want is already taken, can I get a similar one, but as .info instead of .com?
Only you can decide. A *.info* domain should function just fine. You may need to make an extra effort to promote the site and make clear the address to avoid confusion with the *.com* domain. People in the future may be less likely to assume an address ends in *.com* with the launch in 2013 of a whole array of new domains.

Install WordPress via Your Host's Automatic Installation

If you chose a web host with automatic WordPress installation, you can have all the necessary WordPress files installed in the right spot on your directory in a minute or less. If you have trouble, the web host is there to help.

In this example, the host offers Simple Scripts installation. Other hosts may offer installation via Fantastico, Softaculous, or another service.

Install WordPress via Your Host's Automatic Installation

1 After you log on to your web host and go to its control panel, click its link for WordPress.

A If a WordPress link is not evident, you can call your web host for help, look on the host's support pages, or click **Simple Scripts** in the control panel to see if a WordPress option is available.

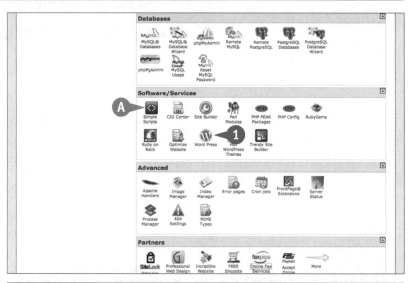

The WordPress installation window opens. In this example, Simple Scripts makes the installation.

2 Click **Install**.

3 Leave the WordPress version at the default setting.

4 Choose where to install WordPress.

5 Click the link to display Advanced Options.

Note: Simple Scripts sets **admin** as your logon name and gives you a random password unless you specify otherwise here.

6 Clear the check box (☑ changes to ☐) unless you want the plugin listed.

7 Review the license agreement.

8 Click the check box to agree (☐ changes to ☑).

9 Click **Complete**.

B The Simple Scripts Status window opens and shows the installation progress.

C Simple Scripts displays the URL for your new blog, the URL where you log on, and your username and password.

10 Click the site URL to see your new blog.

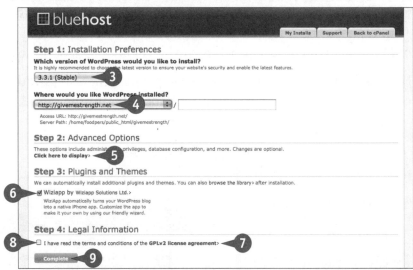

TIPS

How do I know where to install WordPress?
Your web host assigns you a home directory where it stores files for your website. Among them is a root directory, where your WordPress files go. It often is called public_html, web root, or something similar. If you are not sure which folder is your root directory, contact your web host and ask.

My web host does not list the domain I bought. How do I get my domain there?
If your host is not your domain registrar, you need to have the registrar point its nameservers — which translate domain names into IP addresses — to your host. Get the proper nameservers' names from your host and provide them to your registrar. The support pages of each will show you how.

Get an FTP Application for Manual Installation

An *FTP program*, or file transfer protocol program, lets you easily move files from your computer to your web host. You need it to do a manual WordPress installation. Your host may provide an FTP utility through its control panel, but using an FTP program on your computer may be faster.

FileZilla Client is a free, open-source FTP program that works with Windows, Mac, and Linux computers. You simply download it from the Internet and install it on your computer.

Get an FTP Application for Manual Installation

1 After starting your web browser, go to http://filezilla-project.org.

2 Click **Download FileZilla Client**.

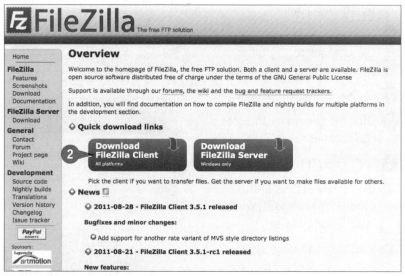

The FileZilla Client Download window opens.

3 Review the download options to find the version for your computer's operating system.

4 Click the link to the version you need.

A download window opens.

5 Follow the usual steps for your computer for program installation to install and launch FileZilla Client.

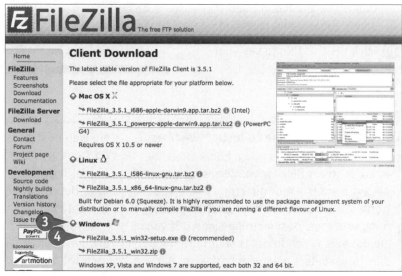

⑥ Type your FTP address.

⑦ Type your username at your web host.

⑧ Type your web host password.

Note: Your FTP address is probably *ftp://yourdomain.com*, where *yourdomain.com* stands in place of your regular web address. Check with your web host if you are not sure.

⑨ Click **Quickconnect**.

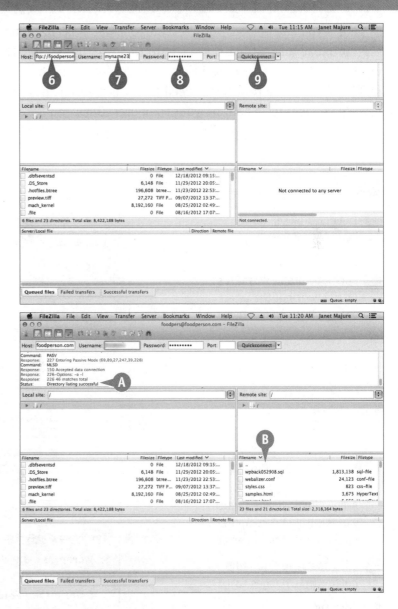

Ⓐ FileZilla confirms the connection.

Ⓑ FileZilla lists the files and folders, or *directories*, at your web host.

TIPS

What do I do if I cannot seem to connect?

Check with your web host to see whether you are entering the correct information. Among the possibilities is that your web host has assigned you a username that you are not aware of if you use your domain name to log on to your web host.

Do I have to type the connection information every time?

Probably not. If you click the drop-down list arrow next to Quickconnect (▾), you can click the last connection you made on FileZilla and the software will connect you. You also can save the connection in the FileZilla Site Manager, accessible via the File menu.

Download WordPress Software

Before you can upload WordPress to your web host for a manual installation, you first must download and extract the software from WordPress.org. This simple process is likely one you have used many times to download files from the Internet. The downloaded file is compressed, as a Zip or TAR.GZ file. As a result, you need to extract, or unzip, the file after the download and save it to a place you will remember on your computer. Once you do, you have the software you need to do a manual installation of the WordPress.org software.

Download WordPress Software

1 In your browser, go to http://wordpress.org/download.

2 Click **Download WordPress**. At this writing, the latest version is WordPress 3.5.

A download window, which varies with your computer's operating system, opens.

3 Click the **Save File** radio button (○ changes to ◉).

4 Click **OK**.

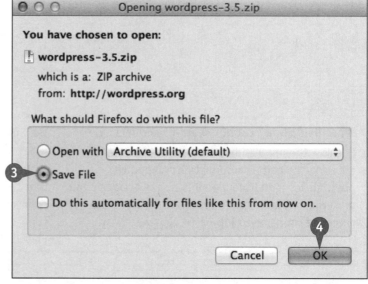

Your computer saves the file.

5 Double-click the filename.

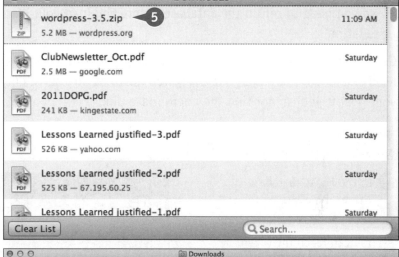

Your computer extracts the file.

Ⓐ Depending on the view you have chosen in your folder, the contents of the extracted WordPress folder may appear.

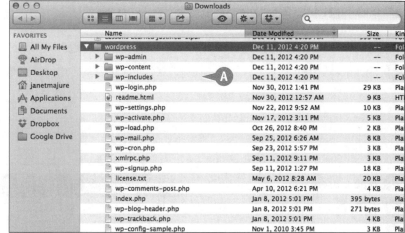

TIPS

How do I know whether to click the Download button or one of the links that appears under it?
You can use either one, but ZIP is the more widely used on personal computers. The TAR.GZ file is smaller, but not all personal computers have the software installed to extract it. But if the Zip file does not work for you, try the other.

Will the WordPress software work on my Mac?
Because WordPress software runs on your web host, not on your local computer, it does not matter whether your computer is a PC or a Mac. For the time being, your computer is merely storing the software.

Set Up the MySQL Database

You need a MySQL database to store all the content of your blog or site. No database, no blog, so you need to set up the database before you load your WordPress software for a manual installation.

Go to your web host and log on to its control panel to get started. This example shows the widely used cPanel control panel, but every web host has an equivalent. Check with technical support at your host if you cannot find the appropriate link.

Set Up the MySQL Database

1 In the MySQL Database Wizard, type a name for your database.

You can reach the wizard by clicking **MySQL Database Wizard** after you log in to cPanel.

2 Click **Next Step**.

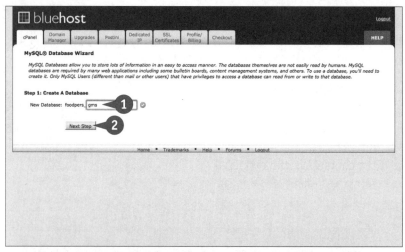

3 Type a username.

4 Type a password.

5 Retype the password.

Note: Be sure to record the username and password.

6 Click **Create User**.

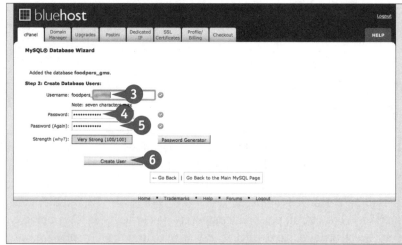

A The next window confirms the name and password.

7 To give the user you created — that is you, the administrator — all the privileges you require to set up and operate the database, click **All Privileges** (all ☐ change to ☑).

8 Click **Next Step**.

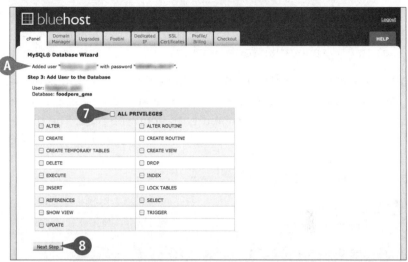

A new screen confirms the action.

9 Click **Return Home**.

You are back at the cPanel home.

TIPS

What should I name my database?

Give it a name that you readily associate with your blog so that you will recognize it now and in the future. You may find it helpful if you write it down for the installation process. If need be, you can find the database name and other configuration details in a file named wp-config.php. You can download that file from your host to your local computer and open it with a text program to get the information.

How do I set up the database if my web host does not use cPanel?

Many web hosts have phpMyAdmin available, which you also can use to set up the database. You can find instructions for using phpMyAdmin at http://codex.wordpress.org/Installing_WordPress#Using_phpMyAdmin. Another option is simply to contact your web host and ask.

Upload the WordPress Files

Uploading the WordPress files to your web host gives you all the files you need for your manual WordPress installation. Here is where you put your FTP client to work. Read how to install one in "Get an FTP Application for Manual Installation," earlier in this chapter.

After launching the FTP client, the upload process requires browsing to find the WordPress files you downloaded and extracted in "Download WordPress Software," earlier in this chapter, and then uploading them from your computer to your web host. The process is simple but may take several minutes for the uploading, depending on the speed of your Internet connection.

Upload the WordPress Files

1 Launch your FTP client and connect to your host.

Note: See details in "Get an FTP Application for Manual Installation," earlier in this chapter.

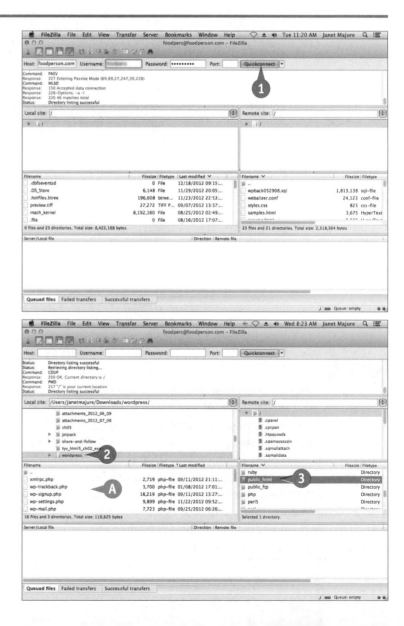

2 Navigate in the left panel until you find the folder containing the WordPress files you downloaded and extracted, and open that folder by double-clicking it.

Ⓐ The WordPress files appear in lower left pane.

3 In the right pane, navigate to the root directory, in this case public_html, and double-click to open it.

④ Select all the files and documents within the WordPress folder.

Note: Those files include three folders, or *directories*, starting with *wp-* and numerous other files.

⑤ Drag all files to your blog's root directory.

FileZilla uploads the files to your web host. This process probably will take several minutes.

Ⓑ The uploaded files appear in the right pane.

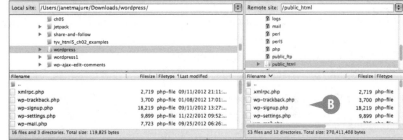

Complete the Configuration and Installation

Completing the configuration of your manual WordPress installation allows your MySQL database and WordPress files to communicate with each other. The WordPress software has a built-in script that does nearly all of the work for configuring your WordPress software on your web host. You, however, need to be ready with your database information, including database name, username, and password, so as to complete the installation.

To start, you need to open a web browser and connect to the Internet.

Complete the Configuration and Installation

① Type your blog's URL in your web browser address bar, followed by **/wp-admin/install.php**. So, if your site is mysite.com, type **http://mysite.com/wp-admin/install.php**. Press **Enter**.

Note: Skip to Step **10** if you created your own configuration file, as described in "Create the Configuration File," later in this chapter.

Ⓐ A WordPress message appears telling you that WordPress does not find the necessary wp-config.php file.

② Click **Create a Configuration File**.

A WordPress window opens and reminds you of the information you need to create your configuration file.

③ Review the list of needed information — which you created when you set up your MySQL database — and make sure you have it all available.

Ⓑ This example covers an individual blog installation, so you can ignore item 5 on the list.

④ Click **Let's go**.

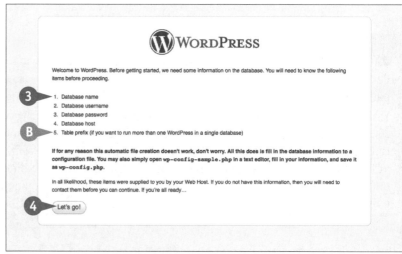

The Setup Configuration File window opens.

5 Type your MySQL database name.

6 Type your database username.

7 Type your database user password.

8 Click **Submit**.

9 If all went well, a confirmation screen appears. Click the **Run the install** button.

The Welcome window opens.

10 Type your blog title.

11 Type a username for your site.

12 Type and confirm a password.

Note: Record your username and password.

13 Type your e-mail address.

14 If you intend your blog to be somewhat private, click the check box to ask that search engines not index your blog (☑ changes to ☐).

15 Click **Install WordPress**.

The Success! window opens and shows your WordPress username. Click **Log In** if you are ready.

Note: WordPress e-mails your username to the e-mail address you provided.

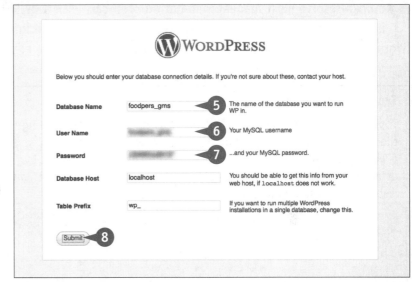

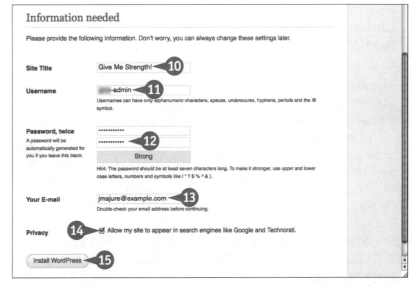

What if my installation did not work?

Although even the manual installation is fairly simple, occasionally things can go wrong. The error message or messages you see will guide you. See the next section of this chapter for troubleshooting. Be sure to read and take note of the message.

Troubleshoot Installation Errors

You can resolve most manual installation problems with a little troubleshooting. Typical problems include Internet connection issues or inaccurate database information. Fortunately, the large WordPress community is available to help with other occasional problems.

Trouble Uploading Files

If your Internet connection is slow, you may have trouble uploading the WordPress files to your host. If so, and if your web host uses cPanel, you can upload the WordPress Zip file and then extract it by using the cPanel File Manager. If you do not have cPanel, contact your web host and ask for advice.

Cannot Get to First Base

If you have uploaded your files and typed your site's URL, and you get a window saying the site cannot be found or is under construction, you may have uploaded the WordPress *folder* rather than its *contents*. If so, just move the files out of the folder using FileZilla or your host's file management utility.

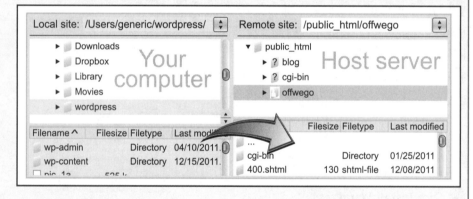

Error Messages

If you get an error message, the first step is to read it. Really. In its short life, WordPress has become very easy to install, and its error messages are one reason why. They provide brief but explicit information to help you fix the problem.

Error Establishing a Database Connection

This error message means you probably made a mistake in typing your database name, username, or user password in the Setup Configuration File window. These names are associated with the MySQL database that you created, as distinct from the username and password you may use to log on to your web host's control panel. Go back and confirm that you entered these correctly. Also, make sure that you have given the database user *all* privileges.

> **WordPress**
>
> **Error establishing a database connection**
> • Are you sure you have the correct username and password?
> • Are you sure you have typed the correct hostname?
> • Are you sure that the database server is running?
>
> If you still need help you can always visit <u>WordPress Support Forums</u>.

Other Installation Problems

For other problems, start at the beginning: Make sure that your host meets the minimum requirements as described in "Choose a Host for Your Blog," earlier in this chapter. Also, double-check that you do not need to use something other than Localhost in the Hostname box. Check with your host, or you can see a list of some popular hosts' hostnames at http://codex.wordpress.org/Editing_wp-config.php#Possible_DB_HOST_values.

Possible DB_HOST values

Hosting Company	DB_HOST Value Guess
1and1	db12345678
BlueHost	localhost
DreamHost	mysq1.example.com
HostGator	localhost
LaughingSquid	localhost
MediaTemple GridServer	internal-db.s44441.gridserver.com
pair Networks	dbnnnx.pair.com

Try a Fully Manual Installation

A fully manual configuration process involves entering your user information into the configuration file before running the installation script. The next section, "Create the Configuration File," explains how. For details, go to http://codex.wordpress.org/Installing_WordPress.

WORDPRESS.ORG

Codex

Installing WordPress

Languages: Español • **English** • 日本語 • Português do Brasil •

Forgotten Database Details

You misplaced your database details? The easiest solution is to simply create another empty database, and this time keep track of your username and password. The database name is always available via your host control panel.

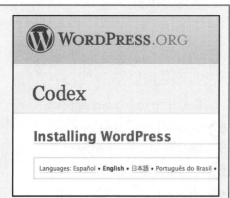

Username: Myname
Password: *&kuj19

Create the Configuration File

You can create your own WordPress configuration file, rather than entering the information in the screen WordPress presents. You might choose to do so because your installation did not work or because the WordPress installer and your web host do not work well together. You must use a text editor, such as Notepad for Windows or TextEdit for Mac, and not a word processing program.

To create the configuration file, you need to have downloaded and extracted the WordPress software and set up your MySQL database as described earlier in this chapter. You need the database name, username, and password.

Create the Configuration File

1 In your text editor, click **File**.

2 Click **Open**.

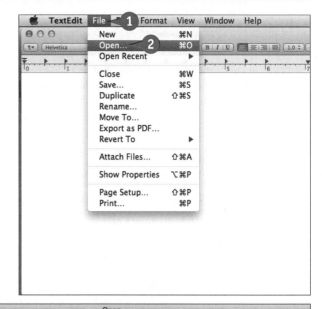

The Open dialog box appears.

3 Browse to the extracted WordPress software folder.

4 Click **wp-config-sample.php**.

5 Click **Open**.

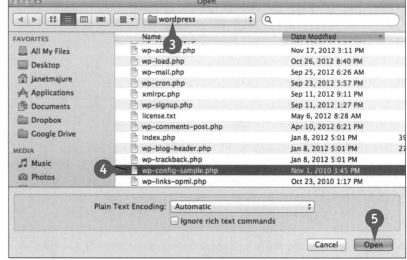

The file opens in the text editor.

⑥ Select database_name_here, and then type your database name.

Note: You are replacing database_name_here with the name of the MySQL database you created earlier.

⑦ Select username_here, and type your database username.

⑧ Select password_here, and type your database password.

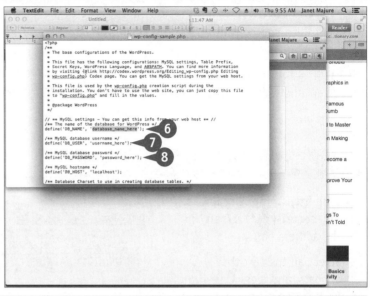

Ⓐ The most common hostname for your database is *localhost,* the default. You can be sure by contacting your web host or checking http://codex.wordpress.org/Editing_wp-config.php#Possible_DB_HOST_values.

⑨ Select the eight lines for authentication keys.

⑩ Launch a web browser.

Note: Do not close your text editor.

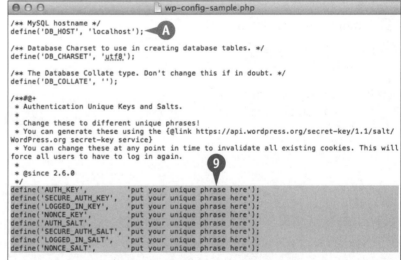

TIPS

Why can't I just use my word processor?
Word processors have behind-the-scenes coding that does not work for files that tell computers what to do. That can be a problem, even if you save your word-processed file as a TXT file and then rename it as PHP. Notepad, for Windows, and TextEdit, for Mac, are included in basic operating system installations.

Do I delete or leave in the single quotation marks around database_name_here and the others?
Leave the single quotation marks. What you are doing is creating a file readable in a programming language. The language recognizes single quotation marks as enclosing the needed information.

Create the Configuration File (continued)

After you open the configuration sample file and type your database information, you can complete the configuration file setup by using an authentication key generator that WordPress.org provides. You simply copy the keys that the generator provides and paste them into your configuration file. Once that is done, you save and rename the file and upload it to your web host. You then are ready to run the WordPress installation.

Create the Configuration File (continued)

⑪ Type **https://api.wordpress. org/secret-key/1.1/salt/** in the address bar.

⑫ Select all the text that appears, and press Ctrl+C (⌘+C on a Mac) to copy it.

⑬ Return to your text editor.

⑭ Press Ctrl+V (⌘+V on a Mac).

Ⓑ The secret keys appear in place of the text area you selected in Step **9**.

⑮ Click **File**.

⑯ Click **Save**.

Your text editor saves the file.

⑰ Using your operating system's usual method, make a copy of wp-config-sample.php and rename it wp-config.php.

⑱ Upload the new wp-config.php to your root directory. See "Upload the WordPress Files," earlier in this chapter, for more information.

You are ready to run the installer, which is described in "Complete the Configuration and Installation," earlier in this chapter.

TIPS

Should I do anything with any of the other define lines in the configuration file, such as the Charset or WordPress Database Table prefix?

Unless you are familiar with MySql or have some specific reason to do so, it is best to leave the rest of the configuration file as it is.

Is there some reason to copy the file after I make the changes, rather than before?

No. If you prefer, you can create a copy of wp-config-sample.php as your first step, make the necessary changes, and then save it. The critical thing is that you save the file with the name *wp-config.php*. The WordPress installer looks for a file with that exact name, so do not depart from that name in any way.

Log On to Your Blog's Dashboard

After you log on to your WordPress administrative interface, whose main page is called the Dashboard, you can do just about anything you want or need to do with your blog. Among the possibilities are writing or editing information, uploading media, and changing your site's appearance.

You do not need to log on to your web host to log on to your self-hosted WordPress Dashboard.

Log On to Your Blog's Dashboard

From the URL

1 After you start your browser, type your blog's URL, followed by **/wp-admin** into the address bar, and press `Enter`.

The browser takes you to your WordPress Log In page.

2 Type your WordPress username in the Username box.

3 Type your WordPress password in the Password box.

Ⓐ If you want WordPress to remember your computer so that you do not have to log on again, click the **Remember Me** check box (☐ changes to ☑).

Note: Do not use Remember Me if other people have access to your computer.

4 Click **Log In**.

The Dashboard opens.

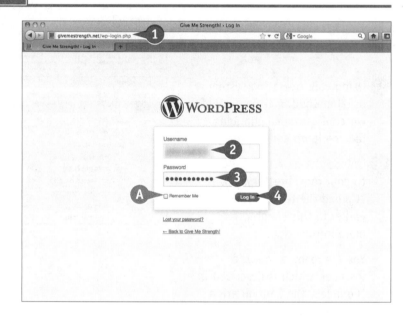

From Your Blog

1 Type your blog's URL in the address bar of your browser, and press **Enter** to open your blog's home page.

2 Click the **Log in** link.

WordPress takes you to the Log In page, where you type your information as explained previously, and then the Dashboard opens.

Note: If you later change the appearance of your blog, you may not necessarily have a Log In link, but you still can log on from the URL.

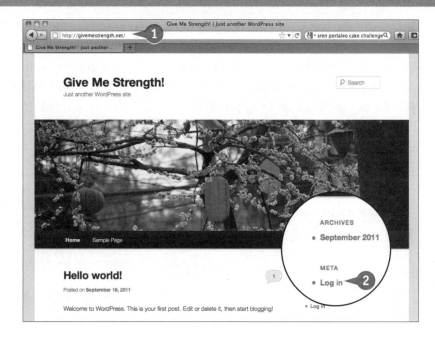

What if I cannot remember my password?

Click **Lost Your Password?** on the logon screen. The Lost Password window opens, where you type the e-mail address you used when you set up your blog, and then click **Get New Password.** Thus, keeping track of the information you used when creating your blog is important. WordPress sends your password to your e-mail address. Follow the directions in the e-mail.

I thought I typed my password right, but I am still having trouble logging in.

Your password is case sensitive, so be sure that you are typing capital or lowercase letters the same when you are logging in as you did when you created the password.

Review the Welcome Module

You can let WordPress introduce you to its functions through the Welcome module that appears in your WordPress Dashboard on your new WordPress.org site. That module provides links to support information, to a screen to customize the site's appearance, and to the panel for creating your first post. If you are the sort who likes to dive in and do it, you may like the Welcome module, even if you do not understand its options. Except for a link to a quick tutorial on WordPress, however, the Welcome module is not particularly educational, and you do not have to use it to use the software.

Review the Welcome Module

Ⓐ The Welcome module appears at the top of the Dashboard.

① Click **Customize Your Site**.

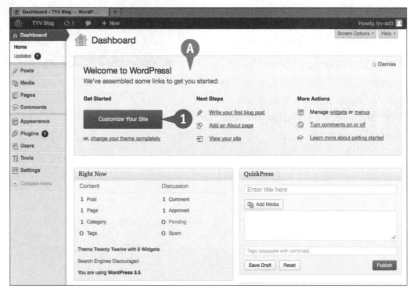

The customize screen appears, including a preview of your home page.

② Click **Site Title & Tagline**.

The title and tagline options appear.

③ Type your blog's title as you want it to appear on your site.

④ Type a *tagline,* or subtitle, for your site.

Ⓑ Your changes appear in the preview area as you type them.

⑤ Click **Save & Publish**.

C The Save & Publish button changes to Saved.

6 Click **1 Reply** to see a sample blog comment.

Note: You may want to click other links on the preview to see the sample content on your brand-new site.

7 Click **Close**.

The Dashboard returns.

D Click links to WordPress.org crash courses to learn more about operating your blog.

8 Click **Dismiss**.

The Welcome module disappears.

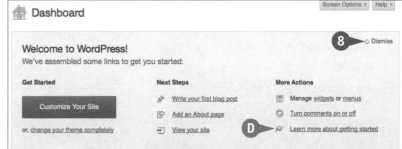

TIPS

How can I see my blog the way other people see it?
First, click your name in the Admin Bar and then click **Log Out**. The login screen appears. Click **Back to *Blogname*** at the bottom of the screen. The blog's front page then appears. "View Your New Blog" in Chapter 2 gives an overview of the contents. Some items there, such as the sharing buttons, are not immediately available in your self-hosted blog.

Can I get the Welcome module back once I dismiss it?
Yes. Simply click the **Screen Options** tab at the top of the screen, and then click the check box next to Welcome (☐ changes to ☑). The Welcome module returns to the Dashboard.

Get to Know the Dashboard

The Dashboard — the central administration panel for your self-hosted WordPress.org installation — puts links and tools at your fingertips to manage your blog or site. From the Dashboard, you can get a snapshot of the quantity of content on your site and read about WordPress and more. The Dashboard is composed of *modules*, or individual areas that serve a particular purpose. Each module has a descriptive title of the content within the module. Once you become familiar with the Dashboard modules, you can rearrange or eliminate them according to your preference.

Get to Know the Dashboard

Note: Most of the Dashboard's modules in this section are shown *collapsed*, meaning only their title bars appear. The default setting has the content *expanded*, as explained in "Customize and Navigate the Dashboard," later in this chapter.

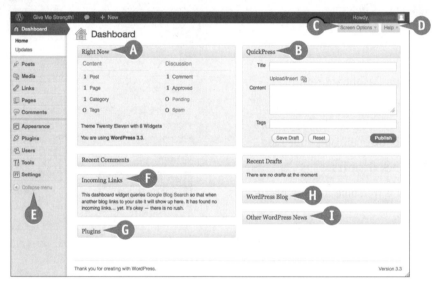

Ⓐ Gives a summary of your site's content, discussions, theme, widgets, and WordPress version.

Ⓑ Lets you make a quick posting.

Ⓒ Provides options for the modules you want to display. Every admin panel has different screen options.

Ⓓ Offers help information. Every admin panel has different help information.

Ⓔ Known as the left menu bar; contains links to the other admin panels.

Ⓕ Lists blogs that have linked to your blog.

Ⓖ Posts news about plugins, which are covered in Chapter 6.

Ⓗ Displays the latest news from the WordPress.org blog.

Ⓘ Displays the Planet WordPress news feed or other news feeds, which are described in Chapter 7.

Understanding the Admin Bar

The Admin Bar for self-hosted blogs, visible at the top of your site only when you are logged in, gives you quick access to the administrative functions you most need. You can remove the bar if you want, as explained in "Create Your Profile," later in this chapter. The content of the bar may vary depending on where you are on your site. It also may change as you develop your site by adding plugins, the little programming add-ons that give WordPress much of its flexibility.

Understanding the Admin Bar

Ⓐ Drop-down menu links to information about WordPress.org and to support.

Ⓑ Links to the Dashboard and frequently used administrative modules.

Note: When working within the admin panels, clicking the site name in the Admin Bar takes you to your site's home page.

Ⓒ Alerts you to any software updates that are available. The number tells how many.

Ⓓ Shows the number of comments awaiting approval, if any, and goes directly to the Comments panel to moderate them.

Ⓔ Gives quick access to the panels for creating or adding posts, media, pages, and users.

Ⓕ Shows the username — or that person's display name as set in the Profile — of the person logged on to the site. Drop-down menu links to the profile or lets you log out.

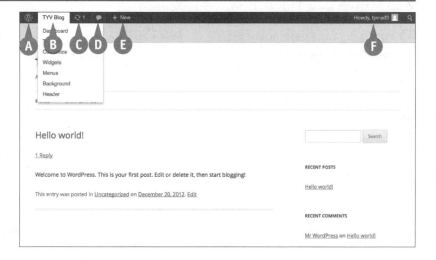

Customize and Navigate the Dashboard

You can adjust the Dashboard to fit the way you work and to show the information that is most important to you. What is important to you may not be the way the default Dashboard is set up. You can remove modules, rearrange modules, shrink modules, and even change the content of some modules. You may want to familiarize yourself with the content before you start changing things around too much, but the good news is that you always can change your changes.

Customize and Navigate the Dashboard

1 Position your mouse pointer over one of the content modules, such as Right Now.

An arrow (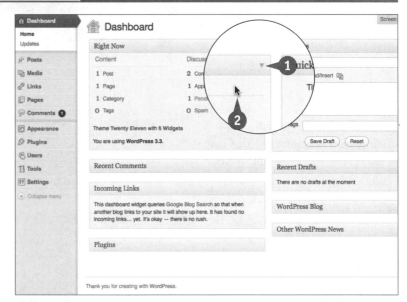) appears.

2 Click the arrow to collapse the module.

The module collapses, and only the heading appears.

3 Click the arrow again to expand the module.

Note: This technique works on all the WordPress Dashboard modules.

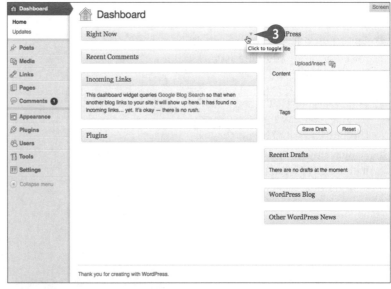

④ Position the mouse pointer over the Recent Comments module (► changes to 🖐).

The arrow appears, and a Configure link also appears.

⑤ Click **Configure**.

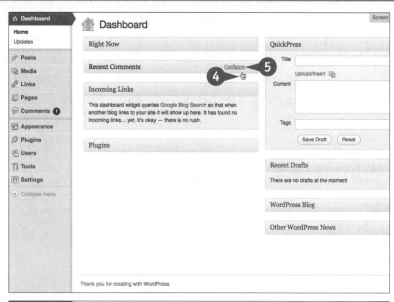

The Recent Comments module reveals a setting for how many comments you want to appear on your Dashboard.

⑥ Type the number of comments you want in the box.

⑦ Click **Submit**.

WordPress saves your comments preference and returns to the Recent Comments module.

Note: If you do not want to change the number, you can click **Cancel** to return to the comments list.

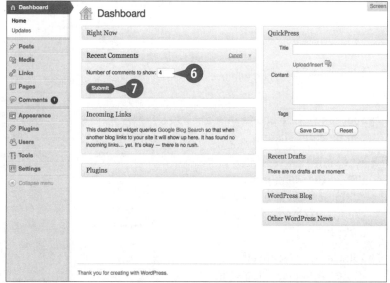

TIPS

How can I hide the left menu bar?
A left-pointing arrow appears next to the words Collapse Menu at the bottom of the menu. Click it, and the menu changes to a narrow band that lists icons with a right-pointing arrow at the bottom. Click it to expand the menu.

Are there other Dashboard options?
Click the **Screen Options** tab to reveal layout and content options for the page. Items that are checked (☑) are displayed. Those that are not checked (☐) do not appear on the Dashboard. Also, position your mouse pointer over the WordPress Blog and Other WordPress News modules and click **Configure** to change the content or display of those modules.

Set Your General Settings

The General Settings determine some of the basics about how your site appears to the public. Settings you need to review here include the time zone and the format of dates and times. These appear with each blog post you publish. You also can go to General Settings to edit or change your blog's title — the one that appears at the top of your blog, not the web address — and the site's tagline. Once you make the changes you want, be sure to save them. Changes apply to both new and previous posts, if any.

Set Your General Settings

1 From the Dashboard, click **Settings**.

The General Settings window opens.

A Your blog's title and tagline can be edited here.

2 Type or review your blog's URL in the WordPress Address (URL) box. Be sure to type the **http://** portion of the address.

B You can store your self-hosted WordPress blog's files and WordPress software files on different directories on your server. To do so, click the link after the Site Address (URL) box for instructions.

③ Choose a city in your time zone from the drop-down menu.

④ Click the radio button next to the date and time formats you prefer (◯ changes to ◉).

⑤ Click **Save Changes**.

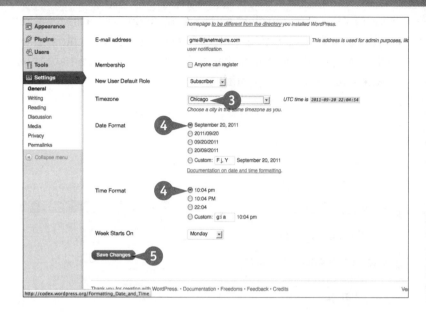

How do I create a custom time or date format?

Click the Custom radio button, and then type the following letters in any order you choose in the custom boxes. Other characters, such as hyphens or commas, appear exactly as you type them. Here are the most frequently used date and time codes.

Date codes	
l (lowercase L)	Full name for day, such as *Saturday*.
D	Three-letter abbreviation for day, such as *Mon* — without a period.
d	The number for the day without leading zeroes; use *j* if you want leading zeroes.
S	The ordinal number suffix for the day of the month, such as *st* in 1st or *th* in 5th.
F	Full name for the month, such as *March*.
M	Three-letter abbreviation for month, such as *Mar*.
n	The number of month, such as *4* for April; use *m* if you want leading zeroes, such as *01* for January.
Y	The year in four digits.
y	The year's last two digits.

Time codes	
a	Lowercase am or pm.
A	Uppercase AM or PM.
g	12-hour format for hour, without leading zeros.
h	12-hour format of hours, with leading zeros.
H	24-hour format of hours with leading zeros, 00 through 23.
i	Minutes with leading zeros.
s	Seconds with leading zeros.
T	Time zone, abbreviated.

Therefore, if you wanted the time on posts to appear as *Monday, December 03rd, 2013, 22:14 CST* you would type **l, F jS, Y,** in the custom date field and **H:i T** in the custom time format field.

Create Your Profile

Your profile lets you select settings for important aspects about how you want to work on your self-hosted WordPress.org blog. These include the color scheme of your administrative interface, whether you want the Admin Bar to be visible, and, perhaps most important, what name represents you when you write and publish articles.

Create Your Profile

① Click **Your Profile** under Users.

The Profile page opens.

② Click a color scheme for the administration pages
(○ changes to ◉).

③ Click the option to view the Admin Bar (☐ changes to ☑).

④ Type your first name in the First Name box.

⑤ Type your last name in the Last Name box.

⑥ Type a nickname in the Nickname box.

Note: The nickname defaults to your username. For security reasons, you should not make your username publicly available.

⑦ Click the arrow to reveal the drop-down menu.

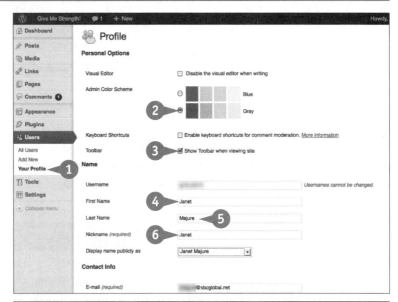

A menu lists options for how you will be identified publicly.

8 Click the public identity you prefer.

9 Scroll to the bottom part of the panel.

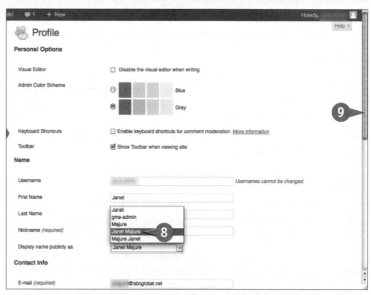

10 Confirm your e-mail address.

11 Add a website address if desired.

12 Type a little about yourself if desired.

13 Click **Update Profile**.

Your profile is saved, and WordPress gives you a confirmation message.

Your public identity appears in the WordPress greeting.

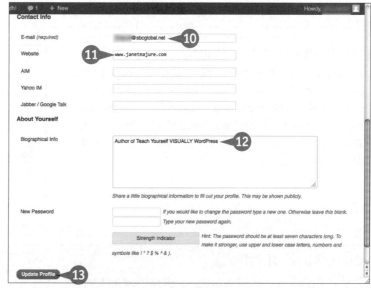

TIPS

Why not change the Visual Editor or Keyboard Shortcuts settings?

You can change the settings if you want by clicking the check box next to each item. First, though, you may want to read "Introducing the Visual Editor and Toolbar" in Chapter 4 and "Moderate Comments" in Chapter 7. Click **More Information** next to Keyboard Shortcuts on the Profile page for details on using those keyboard shortcuts.

Do I have to include contact information?

Only e-mail is required — which is not public and is only for receiving e-mail notices, such as when comments appear on your blog or when you forgot your password. You are free to add other contact information or biographical information if you understand it may become public, usually depending on your theme.

About Privacy Settings

The Internet may not be the place for you if you want to keep your thoughts secret. Still, you can limit what and where your blog posts are broadcast, and the WordPress privacy settings let you decide.

Limited Blog Privacy

On self-hosted WordPress blogs, only two settings are available to allow or discourage search engines such as Google to find your blog. Whichever setting you choose, anyone with the right URL can find your blog. If you do not link to other websites and do not give out your URL, however, your blog is not easily found.

| TYV blog | 🔍 |

TYV blog not found; showing *TV* blogs instead

What I'm watching
whatimwatching.blogspot.com/
12 hours ago - Whoa - I just discovered the 'RetroKids' channel! It's every single show I ever watched as a kid! I can't tell you how happy I am - I just curl up on the couch with some hot chocolate and I'm perfectly content. Now where's my teddy bear...?

WordPress.com Blog Privacy

WordPress.com offers the same privacy settings as self-hosted blogs as well as a third option, letting you specify a select group of people who can see your blog. The users must be registered at WordPress.com. WordPress.com employees can read your blog regardless of the settings.

○ Allow search engines to index this site.
○ Ask search engines not to index this site.
Note: Neither of these options blocks access to your site — it is up to

◉ I would like my site to be private, visible only to users I choose

Users allowed to access site:

(Invite viewers to your blog)

If you don't add anyone to your site, only you will have access.

Other Kinds of Privacy

If you are concerned about being identified as the writer of your blog, be sure to read the privacy policy of your web host as well as your domain registrar. Plugins such as Private Only provide reasonable privacy for your site. Plugins are discussed in Chapter 6. Additional privacy settings called *Visibility* are available on a per-post basis. These are discussed in the next section, "Select Your Search Engine Visibility."

AUT⊙MATTIC

Privacy Policy

Your privacy is critically important to us. At Aut

- We don't ask you for personal information unless we truly gender or income level for no apparent reason.)

Select Your Search Engine Visibility

You can choose whether you want the world to find your blog or to have relatively few viewers. You had a chance to address this matter during installation, and this setting can be changed later. Once your site is open to search engines, cached pages still may show up in search results. You may want to discourage search-engine indexing until you feel your site is ready for prime time. Although there is no guarantee that search engines will honor your do-not-index request, that setting should significantly reduce search-engine traffic. Just remember to change the setting later if you want that traffic.

Select Your Search Engine Visibility

① Position your mouse pointer over Settings in the left menu bar of the administrative interface.

The Settings flyout menu appears.

② Click **Reading.**

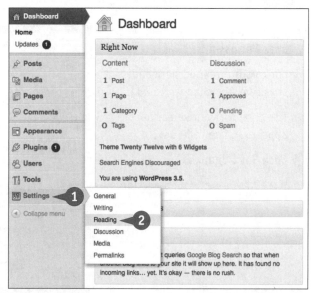

The Reading Settings panel appears.

③ Click **Discourage search engines from indexing this site** (☐ changes to ☑).

Note: Clicking the box asks search engines not to index your site, but does not make the site private.

④ Click **Save Changes**.

Set the Permalinks Structure

For the self-hosted site owner, the Permalinks setting lets you choose your posts' web addresses pattern. They can be taken from headlines of posts, typically requiring many characters but search-engine friendly, or they can be a relatively short ID that WordPress assigns. They also can be a combination of dates and headlines or something else altogether. Choose a setting that works best for you, and plan to stick with it for best site function. WordPress.com sets the Permalink structure for sites it hosts.

Set the Permalinks Structure

1 Expand the Settings menu, and click **Permalinks**.

2 Click your preferred permalink structure (○ changes to ◉).

A The code for your selection appears in the code box.

3 Click **Save Changes**.

WordPress saves your selection.

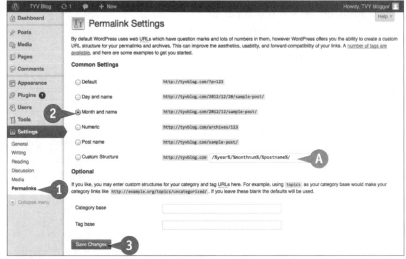

B WordPress confirms your Permalink structure change.

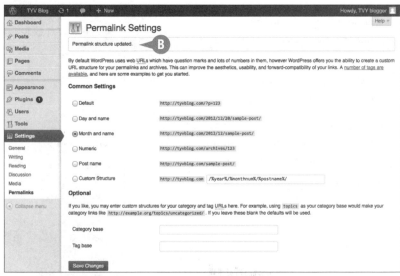

Understanding Other Settings

When you are just starting, you can ignore many of the settings panels. Still, knowing what they are about is useful as a frame of reference, but nothing to worry about. Some of the settings come into play later as you develop your site. You may never find a use for others.

Settings Options Evolve

The initial basic setup shows just six items under Settings. For the most part, the default settings work fine, but it is a good idea to consider the settings listed in this chapter. All can be changed, and you may want to try them out if you go through an experimentation phase with your blog. Otherwise, it generally is better to make decisions and stick with them to avoid confusing your readers — and maybe yourself. The number of settings items listed in the left menu bar may grow as you develop your blog. Plugins, discussed in Chapter 6, frequently add settings panels.

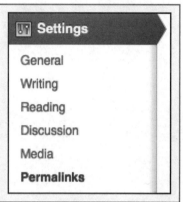

Writing and Discussion Settings

The default settings for these categories, apart from the ones previously discussed in this chapter, should work fine for when you are starting. You may want to scan Writing and Discussion settings panels to see what they contain. They are discussed in Chapters 4 and 7.

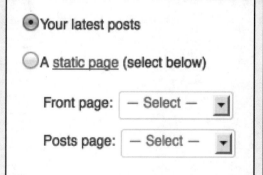

Reading and Media Settings

If you are hoping to use WordPress to operate a site where the home page is more or less fixed and the blog updates, if any, appear elsewhere, you will be interested in the front page displays area of the Reading settings. You may want to read "Using a Static Page as Your Home Page" in Chapter 13 before changing this setting. Media settings are discussed in Chapter 5. The media defaults may or may not work for you.

CHAPTER 4

Creating Written Content

WordPress lets you create written content — the heart of most blogs — with versatile tools that are easy to use. The basics covered in this chapter are enough for many people. They include writing, editing, publishing, and organizing your written material.

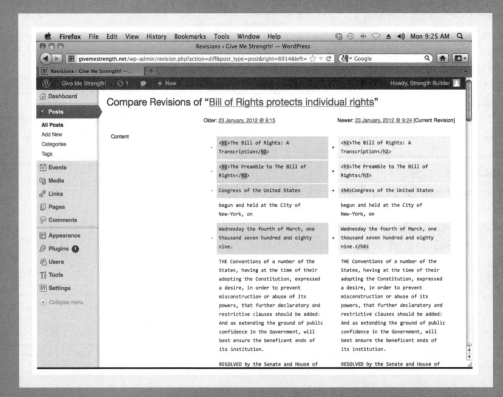

Understanding Pages and Posts

Wording Press provides two basic written content types for you to publish, *pages* and *posts*. The options let you present your content in reverse chronological order — that is, with the newest information appearing at the top of the home page — or let you have an unchanging home page. Generally, posts are for publishing new information, such as your latest blog post, and pages are best for regularly accessed but unchanging information, such as a Contact page or About page. The terms can be confusing, though, because WordPress behind the scenes by default includes pages for archives, categories, and more.

Posts

Individual posts — that is, one of the regular additions your WordPress site's content — have a few default traits that distinguish them from pages:

A They accumulate over time on your blog page, usually in reverse chronological order, and readers can browse through them.

B They are dated.

C You can assign them to categories.

D You can associate keywords, or *tags,* to them.

E You can show multiple posts at a time at your site's home page.

F You can split posts in two.

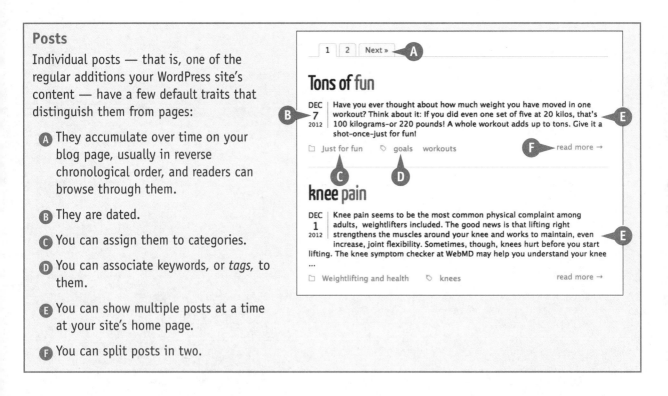

94

Individual Post Web Page

Besides accumulating on your blog page, each post also has its own individual web page.

A The individual post web page has a unique URL, also known as *permalink*.

B Individual post web pages typically include links to the next and previous posts in the blog's chronology.

C Post web pages typically include an area in which readers can reply or comment.

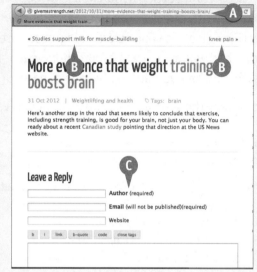

Page

A WordPress page lacks most of the items that make posts unique — dates, categories, tags, links to other pages, the option to split across multiple pages. Pages can have comment sections, although many times blog owners choose to turn them off, and pages do have unique Internet addresses.

A Pages by default appear as menu bar items in many WordPress design schemes, or *themes*.

Review the Writing Settings

The writing settings you choose affect the mechanics of how you write your blog posts, whether you write directly into your WordPress interface or post by e-mail or other means. Your writing settings also set your default blog post category. You may want to change a few of these settings now, but you may never need others, such as posting by e-mail. You can learn more about those settings when you are ready to expand your writing options in Chapter 11.

To access the Writing Settings page, click **Writing** under the Settings menu in the left menu bar.

Review the Writing Settings

Ⓐ Formatting

Lets you select whether WordPress automatically inserts graphic emoticons as you type, such as replacing :) with 😊. Also lets you decide whether WordPress automatically corrects certain XHTML errors. XHTML is a web page programming language. Selecting this is a good idea, although the occasional plugin will not work well with this option selected.

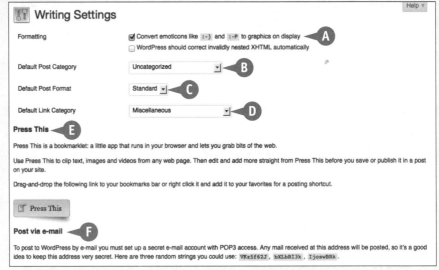

Ⓑ Default Post Category

Lets you choose what category to assign your posts to when you do not specify at the time you write the post. Until you create your own categories, as explained later in this chapter, the only option is Uncategorized.

Ⓒ Default Post Format

Lets you choose the default format for posts. Click the arrow (▾) to see the options, which may vary by theme.

Note: Some themes have only one post format and therefore do not offer this option.

Ⓓ Default Link Category

Lets you choose what link category your favorite links go to. The default and only option is Blogroll until you create more on the Link Categories page.

Note: This option, starting with WordPress 3.5, is not available with new WordPress.org installations. As of this writing, it is available for WordPress.com users. Link lists are discussed in Chapter 8.

Ⓔ Press This

Lets you instantly open a writing window with a link to the web page you are viewing. Just drag the Press This icon to your browser's bookmark or favorites bar.

Ⓕ Post via e-mail (or Post by E-Mail at WordPress.com)

Sets you up to post straight to your blog from e-mail. See Chapter 11 for details.

G Update Services, Inactive

Update service settings are available to WordPress.org users

but not to WordPress.com users. When your site is discouraging search engine traffic, as in this view, you have no change options here.

H Update Services, Active

When your visibility settings are open to search engine traffic, your WordPress.org installation by default notifies the update

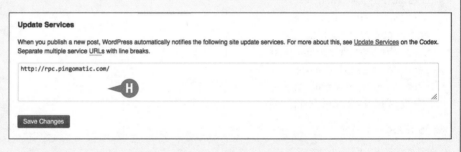

service Ping-O-Matic, which in turn notifies multiple search engines. You can add other update services if you want in this box. WordPress.com automatically notifies multiple services.

Get to Know the New Post Page

The Add New Post page provides the primary location for creating new posts. You can find everything you need to write, edit, and format your written content on the Add New Post page.

Find the Add New Post page by clicking **Add New** under Posts in the left menu bar as well as by using Admin Bar options. Note that the Add New Post page changes to Edit Post after you save or publish your post, but the modules and their functions stay the same.

A Headline Box

Where you type your post's headline.

B Add Media

Lets you upload or insert photos, videos, audio files, and documents such as PDF files. The WordPress.com post page has two other icons here: ● to add a poll, and ▦ to add a custom form.

C Toolbar

Provides tools to use as you write, edit, and format your post.

D Post Box

Gives you room to type your prose.

E Save Draft Button

Saves your post.

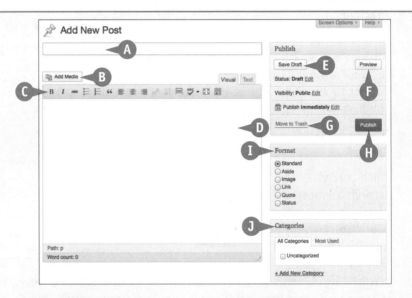

F Preview Button

Prompts browser to display how your draft post would look if published.

G Move to Trash Link

Puts an unwanted post into the Trash to hold or to eliminate later.

H Publish Button

Publishes your post to the Internet.

I Format Box

Lets you choose post format options. Options — and even the format box — may vary by theme.

J Categories Box

Lets you assign your post to a category of your blog.

A Writing Helper

Offers two tools to make writing easier, available at WordPress.com, but not on self-hosted installations. One makes it easy to get comments on your drafts before you publish, and the other lets you copy a post. A Duplicate Post plugin has similar functionality for WordPress.org users.

B Likes and Shares

Lets you choose whether to show *likes* on a WordPress.com post and to show buttons that make sharing your post easy via social media or e-mail. Plugins provide similar options at self-hosted blogs.

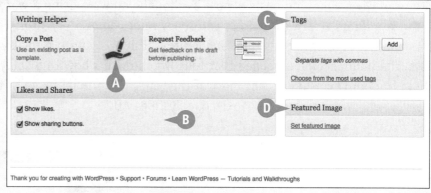

C Tags Box

Lets you assign tags, which are like keywords, to your posts.

D Featured Image

If your theme uses this option, lets you choose images to be featured on particular posts.

A Screen Options

Lists modules that you can display (as indicated by ☑) or not (☐) on the Add New Post — and Edit Post — panel.

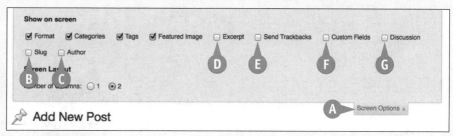

B Slug

Specifies editable portion of the post's permalink but generally is not needed for most users.

C Author

Presents a drop-down list of authors, which is helpful for multiauthor sites.

D Excerpt

Provides a space to write abstracts or teasers for your post that may appear in search results, RSS feeds, and on the front page of some themes.

E Send Trackbacks

Lets you notify non-WordPress blogs when your post links to them.

F Custom Fields

Allows you to add extra information to your post. That information may be data to help search engines find your post or to make a special feature of your theme work. Not available at WordPress.com.

G Discussion

The discussion module lets you choose whether to allow comments on an individual post. Overrides default selection under Discussion Settings.

Introducing the Visual Editor and Toolbar

You can write your blog posts almost as though you were using a word processor when you use the WordPress WYSIWYG — *what you see is what you get* — editor. The panels where you write posts and pages refer to it as the *visual* editor. It allows you to format your entries without knowing HTML, the programming language that tells web browsers how to display web pages. The visual editor should fit your composing needs most of the time. The official name of the WYSIWYG editor is TinyMCE, which was created by Moxiecode Systems AB.

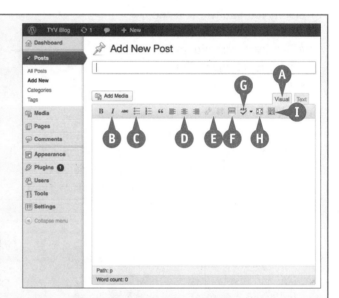

A Visual Tab

Is dark gray when active, which means you can use the WYSIWYG editor to write or edit your post.

B Text Formats

Change text you select in the post box to bold, italic, or strikethrough, as shown on the formatting buttons.

C Paragraph Formats

Assigns special paragraph formats as indicated on the buttons: bulleted list, numbered list, and block quote, a style format intended for use when quoting others.

D Text Alignment

Aligns selected text to the left, center, or right.

E Links

Lets you insert or remove links to other web locations. The option is dim except when you select text.

F Post Break

Inserts a More tag in a spot you choose within your blog post so that only part of the post appears on the front page of your blog.

G Spell-Checker

Checks the spelling on the post.

H Full Screen

Toggles your post box to and from a full screen to make it easy to see more or less of your post.

I Extra Buttons

Shows or hides a second row of buttons.

A Styles Menu

Lets you assign an HTML tag to selected text. Read more about HTML in the next section, "Introducing the Text Editor and Toolbar."

B More Formats

Adds underlined text and justified alignment as WYSIWYG formats.

C Text Color

Lets you add color to text you select.

D Pasting Tools

Lets you paste text from browsers or other applications without formatting errors.

E Format Eraser

Removes formatting from selected text.

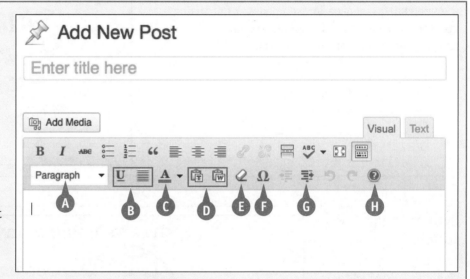

F Special Characters

Opens a pop-up window in which you can choose special characters such as mathematical operators; bullets; letters with accents, or *diacritics*; and dashes.

G More Indentions

Changes the indention on paragraphs you select but does not add bullets or block quote formats.

H Help

Provides added information about the visual editor, including keyboard shortcuts.

Introducing the Text Editor and Toolbar

If you are a veteran HTML user, you may prefer to write in the text editor window of the post box. Even if you are not an HTML vet, you need to know about it when things do not go as expected with the visual editor because the visual editor occasionally misunderstands your intentions or lacks the tools to do what you want. You can find the text editor on the New Post Page by clicking the **Text** tab at the top of the post box.

What Is HTML?

HTML, which is short for *Hypertext Markup Language*, is the publishing language for web pages. HTML, using instructions called *tags*, tells browsers how to display text and other content on a web page.

Benefit of the Text Editor

As handy as the WordPress visual editor is, it sometimes makes mistakes, particularly when you make a lot of formatting changes or paste text from other applications. The text editor helps you clean up the problems. Also, at some stage you may need the text editor to insert special advertising links or *shortcodes*, which are a sort of coding shortcut.

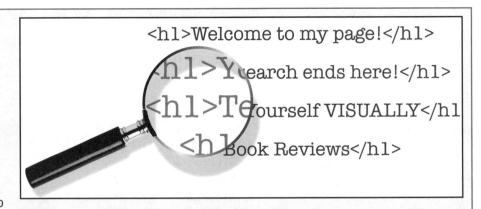

The Text Editor

A Text Editor Tab

Tells you that you are in the text, or HTML, editor.

B Quicktag Buttons

Inserts HTML tags individually or as opening and closing HTML tags if you select text before clicking a button.

C Post Box

Displays post text with its HTML tags instead of as it appears in a web browser. Shows most HTML tags, as indicated by angle brackets, with a starting tag and an ending tag for each instruction.

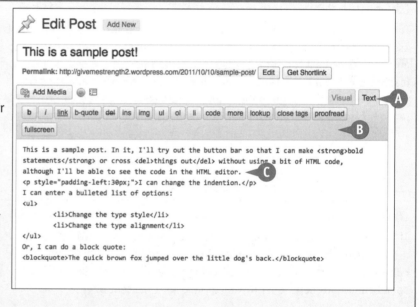

Getting the Hang of the Editor

You do not have to be an HTML pro to use the text editor, but take a moment to get a little familiar with HTML conventions. When you write your first few blog posts, compare the visual versions and the HTML versions simply by clicking the **Visual** and the **Text** tabs at the top of the post box.

Advanced HTML

If, on the other hand, you *are* an HTML whiz, you may love the text editor because you can use any HTML tags that you want and thereby do more with your posts than what the visual editor allows. If you want, you can even disable the visual editor with your Personal Options on the Profile panel for WordPress.org installations. WordPress.com users must switch to the Text tab every time.

Understanding Categories and Tags

Well-thought-out categories and tags make a convenient way for readers to navigate through your blog. That is because readers can click a category or tag associated with a blog post, and WordPress displays a list of all your posts within the same category or tag. Although you can add categories and tags as you go along in your blog, doing a little planning makes them more useful. Each blog post's categories and tags appear above, below, or alongside the post, depending on the theme.

Categories versus Tags

If you think of your blog as a book, think of categories as chapters and tags as index items. In other words, categories work best for bigger concepts, and tags work best for details. Also, every blog post must be assigned to at least one category, but tags are optional. Both categories and tags help search engines find your content, and WordPress.com uses them to help readers find your content through the WordPress.com Topics.

Default Category

If you do not specify a category when you create a post, WordPress assigns it to the default category, which initially is *Uncategorized*. You can name and choose your default category, and probably come up with something more pertinent to your topic than Uncategorized.

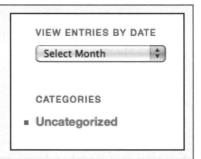

Category Display

Most blog themes include an option for displaying a category list in a sidebar, and the category of a post also may appear at the end or beginning of each post. Sidebar display options include a simple list and a drop-down list. These links take readers to an archive-type page that shows post headlines and, often, excerpts in the selected category (Ⓐ).

Category Archives: *Cooking Italian*

Summer Minestrone
September 20, 2011

Summer Minestrone 3 TBSP olive oil 1 large onion, finely chopped 1 paste 1 lb ripe plum tomatoes, peeled and finely chopped (or use ca chopped 3 waxy new potatoes, chopped 2 cloves garlic, finely chopp vegetable stock or water 1 15-oz can cannellini or other white beans 1/5 cup chopped basil 1/2 cup shaved Parmesan cheese salt and pe large saucepan and add the onion. Cook until softened. Add the tom zucchini, potatoes, and garlic. Cook 10 minutes. Add ... Continue rea

Cooking Italian Leave a comment

Preserving the herb garden
September 15, 2011

Categories and Subcategories

You have the option of creating subcategories, or *child* categories, as well as categories. For example, if you have a gardening blog, you might have Flowers as a category with Annuals, Perennials, and Biennials as subcategories. You might also want a Vegetables category and From the Garden as your default category's name. Tags have no hierarchy.

- Food in the news
- Food preparation
  - Cooking for one
  - Cooking tips
- recipes
- Tools

Why Use Tags

Although tags are optional, tags are useful because they provide another means to help and encourage readers to view more of your blog, and because they provide another means for search engines to find your blog posts.

Popular Tags

apples baking beef cherries chicken CSA desserts eggs family Farmers markets Food for change challenge foodperson.com food politics food preservation food safety foraging free food freezing fruits gardening herbs Kansas Lawrence Farmers Market Local Burger local food meat movies mushrooms Nina Planck pasta potlucks raspberries rBGH Real Food recipes restaurants Rolling Prairie Farmers Alliance Roundup salads soup spring spring produce summer produce tomatoes wheat

Best Practices

Your blog will look more professional and be easier to understand if you decide on and apply some rules to provide consistency for category and tag names. For example, you may want to

☐	**farmers market**	farmers-market	2
☐	**Farmers markets**	farmers-markets	13

make your categories nouns and capitalize them and your tags verbs and lowercase. Doing so also reduces odds that you will accidentally create both *Seeds* and *seeds* tags.

Create and Edit Categories

You can create categories to help organize your site's content in two places, the Categories panel and on the posting panel. The Categories panel lets you create, edit, and delete categories, one at a time or in multiples. The posting panel lets you create categories on the fly, if you will, although you cannot edit or delete categories there. WordPress has a built-in template for displaying posts by category, so that readers can easily view all your posts in a single category, such as My Dog's Tricks.

Create and Edit Categories

Create a Category in the Categories Panel

1. After clicking **Posts** in the left menu bar, click **Categories**.

   The Categories panel opens.

2. Type a category name.

3. Type a description.

4. Click **Add New Category**.

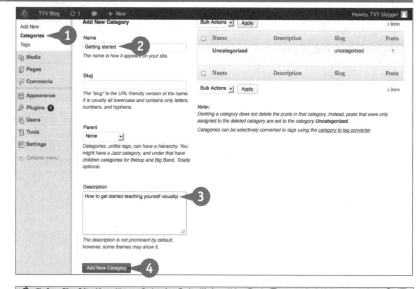

A. The category appears in the list at right on the Categories panel.

Create a Subcategory

1 Type a subcategory name.

2 Click the drop-down menu under Parent.

3 Click the category that you want as the *parent,* or the category that your subcategory falls under.

4 Type a description if desired.

5 Click **Add New Category**.

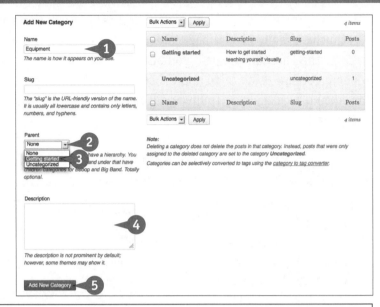

B The subcategory, preceded by a dash, appears under the parent category in the list at right on the Categories panel.

	Name	Description	Slug	Posts
☐	**Getting started**	How to get started teaching yourself visually	getting-started	0
☐	**— Equipment**	The kind of computers and connection you need	equipment	0
☐	**Uncategorized**		uncategorized	1
☐	Name	Description	Slug	Posts

TIP

What is a category slug?

The slug appears in the URL for a page that lists posts by category. If you do not enter a slug, WordPress converts the category name to a slug by making it all lowercase, stripping it of punctuation, and inserting hyphens where you had spaces. Thus, in this example the Getting Started category page's URL becomes www.tyvblog.com/category/getting-started. WordPress.com does this by default. With a self-hosted blog, you can create user-friendly URLs. For example, if your category name is *Best Popular Music of the 1920s*, you could rename it *20s-pop-music*.

> Slug
>
> 20s-pop-music|
>
> *The "slug" is the URL-friendly version of the name. It is usually all lowercase and contains only letters, numbers, and hyphens.*

continued ▶   **107**

Although it is a good idea to plan your categories, sometimes you may realize as you are writing that you really need a new category. WordPress lets you do so right from the New Post panel. Back at the Categories panel, you also can edit categories, such as to change the capitalization scheme you are using or to apply a consistent type of phrasing to category names. A common reason for editing a category is to give your default category a name that fits your blog topic, rather than the generic Uncategorized.

Create and Edit Categories (continued)

Create a Category in the Post Panel

1 On the New Post or Edit Post panel, click **+ Add New Category** at the bottom of the Categories module.

New boxes appear under Add New Category.

2 Type the new category in the first box.

3 If desired, choose a parent category from the drop-down menu.

4 Click **Add New Category**.

⊙ The new category appears in the Categories box as checked, meaning the post is assigned to that category.

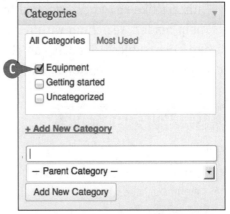

Edit Categories

① In the Categories list, click the name of a category you want to edit.

The Edit Category subpanel opens.

② Add or change information for the category.

This example adds a category description.

③ Click **Update**.

The changes are saved, and WordPress returns to the Categories panel.

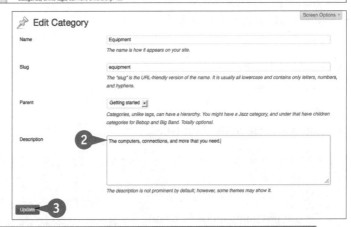

TIPS

How do I change the default category?

Click **Uncategorized** in the list on the Categories panel to open the Edit Category panel. Then, change *Uncategorized* to the name you prefer. Alternatively, click **Writing** under Settings in the left menu bar and then choose the default category from the Default Post Category drop-down list.

How do I delete a category?

You can position your mouse pointer over the category name and click the **Delete** link. To delete more than one category, click the check box next to the unwanted categories in the Categories panel (☐ changes to ☑). Then, click the Bulk Actions drop-down list, click **Delete**, and click **Apply**. Posts in the deleted categories move to your default category.

Create and Edit Tags

Tags are like keywords attached to individual blog posts. When you assign tags to posts, you can help readers searching within your blog and those using search engines to find information on a particular subject. Readers can click a tag next to your post to see all posts with that tag. Unlike categories, tags are optional, and they are not hierarchical, so you cannot have child and parent tags.

Create and Edit Tags

Create a Tag in the Tags Panel

1 After clicking **Posts** in the left menu bar, click **Tags**.

The Tags panel opens.

Ⓐ The panel shows tags you have used most often.

2 Type a tag name.

Ⓑ Slug is optional on WordPress.org blogs and does not appear on WordPress.com blogs. If you leave the Slug box blank, WordPress creates an all-lowercase slug based on the tag name.

3 Type a description.

4 Click **Add New Tag**.

Ⓒ The tag appears in the list on the right side of the Tags panel.

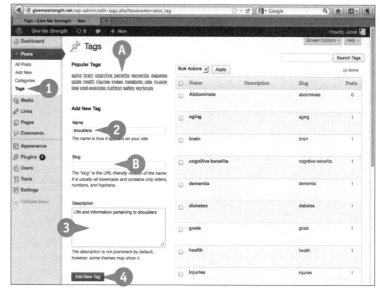

Create a Tag in the Post Panel

1 On the posting panel, click **Add** in the Tags module, and type the desired tag or tags, using a comma between tags.

2 Click **Add**.

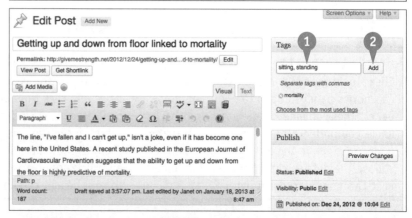

110

D The new tags appear below the Add box and are attached to the post.

Edit Tags

1 In the Tags panel, click a tag you want to edit.

E You can click a tag in the list or under Popular Tags.

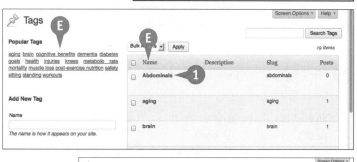

The Edit Tag subpanel appears.

2 Make your changes.

3 Click **Update**.

WordPress saves your changes and returns to the Tags panel.

TIP

What are the links that appear under a tag name when I rest my mouse pointer there?

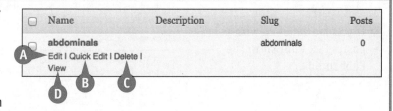

Edit (**A**) opens the Edit Tag page for that tag, just as clicking the tag name does. *Quick Edit* (**B**) expands a pane in the Tags list where you can change the name and slug — or name only at WordPress.com — and update it without leaving the Tags panel. *Delete* (**C**) opens a confirmation dialog box to delete the tag, and *View* (**D**) opens a page showing posts that use the tag.

Write and Publish Your First Blog Post

Whehen you write and publish your first blog post, you are a real blogger; no better time to start than now. You can do it in more than one way, but this section covers the most basic method, using the posting panel accessible from your Dashboard. To get there, click **Posts** in the left menu bar, and then click **Add New**. The Add New Post panel appears. You may notice that the panel title changes to Edit Post after you save your work, but it is the same place as far as function is concerned.

Write and Publish Your First Blog Post

Write a Blog Post

1. Click in the headline box and start typing.

A. WordPress displays your post's permalink. If your permalink structure uses the blog post headline (as all WordPress.com blogs do), WordPress inserts hyphens between the words.

B. WordPress automatically saves your post as a draft and displays the time saved.

2. Press Tab to move to the post box, and start typing.

3. Click **Save Draft** periodically as you work and when you are done.

Publish Now

1. If you are satisfied with your post, click **Publish** in the Publish box.

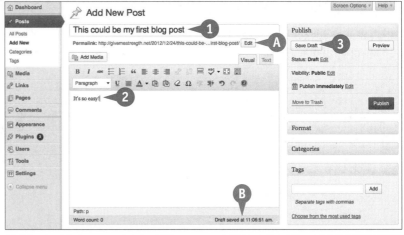

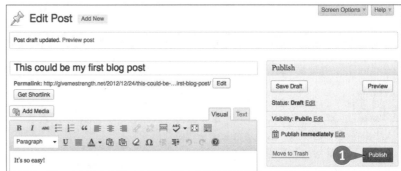

⊙ WordPress publishes your post, and notifies you of that fact. You can click **View Post** next to the notice to see your newly published blog post.

Publish Later

1 To schedule your post to publish at a different time, click **Edit**.

The current date and time appear.

2 Change the date and time to when you want the post to publish to the web.

3 Click **OK**.

The Publish box shows the scheduled time, and the Publish button now reads Schedule.

4 Click **Schedule** to confirm that you want the post to be published at the specified time.

WordPress confirms the scheduled publication time, and the Schedule button changes to Update.

TIPS

What is the Get Shortlink button next to the permalink in the post window?

Clicking that button opens a box that displays a short, alternate link that you may copy for use in places such as Twitter, where a long link might not work well. It does not change the actual permalink.

Can you explain the settings that appear when you click Edit next to Visibility in the Publish box?

The settings determine who can see the post. The default is *Public*, so any reader can see the post. The *Stick this post...* check box keeps that post at the top of your blog page. *Password protected* lets you assign a password so only people with the password can read the post content. *Private* posts are visible only to editors or administrators on your site. Read more on user capabilities in Chapter 14.

Apply Categories to Posts

You can assign categories to your posts as you write your post or after the fact. After the fact, you can assign categories to one post or several at a time. If you are smart, you planned and created categories as described earlier in this chapter that fit your blog's purpose. Those are the categories you are most likely to use as you compose your posts. If you add a category or two later, you can assign old posts to the new categories if you want.

Apply Categories to Posts

In the Posting Panel

1 Click the box next to the category you want to assign (☐ changes to ☑).

Ⓐ Categories are required, so if you do not choose a category, your post is assigned to the default category. In this example, *Other weightlifting information* is the default.

2 Click **Save Draft**.

WordPress saves your post draft and assigns the post to the designated category.

Note: The process is the same for a published post, except that you would click **Update** where the Publish button (Ⓑ) is for new posts.

On the Posts List

1 Position your mouse pointer over the post of interest, and when the links appear, click **Quick Edit**.

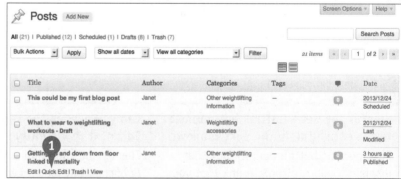

The Quick Edit pane appears.

2 Click the check boxes
(☐ changes to ☑) next to
any category you want to
apply to the post.

3 Click **Update**.

WordPress saves your
changes and closes the Quick
Edit Pane.

Multiple Posts in the Posts List

1 Click the check box next to
each post in the group you
want to assign to a category
(☐ changes to ☑).

2 Click the **Bulk Actions** down
arrow (▾).

3 Click **Edit**.

4 Click **Apply**.

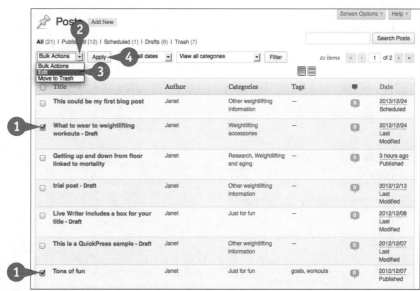

TIPS

Is there a limit to the number of categories I can have?

No, but it is good practice not to attach too many to a single post. A large number may confuse readers and search engines. Aim for two or three categories at most. Again, it helps to think of categories as chapters in a book and perhaps chapter subtitles as subcategories.

Can I use the Bulk Edit box to remove a category from a group of posts?

Not without a plugin. You must individually edit or QuickEdit each post to remove it from a category or delete the entire category on the Categories panel. If you do, and the posts do not have another category assignment, they go to the default category. However, a plugin, Bulk Delete, lets you delete groups of posts from selected categories or tags.

continued ▶

The longer you operate your blog, the more you may need to adjust your category assignments, and you can do so by using the Bulk Edit function in the Posts Panel, which is always available by clicking **Posts** in the Dashboard's left menu bar. WordPress lets you filter your posts, which makes it easier to apply categories to a group of posts. Without a plugin, however, you cannot remove a category assignment from a group of posts and must remove category assignments one post at a time.

Apply Categories to Posts (continued)

The Bulk Edit pane appears.

⑤ Click the check box next to the category or categories you want to apply (☐ changes to ☑).

⑥ Click **Update**.

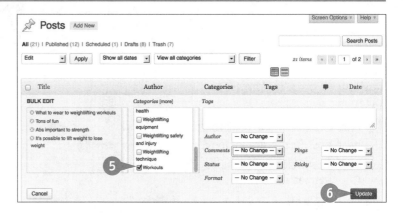

Ⓑ WordPress confirms the change.

Ⓒ The new category assignment appears with each updated post in the posts list.

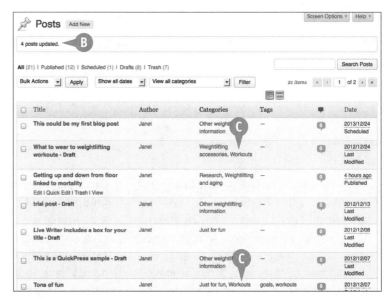

A Select Group in the Posts List

1 Click the **View all categories** down arrow (▾).

2 Click the category you want to assign to another category.

3 Click **Filter**.

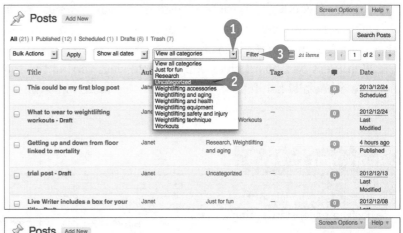

WordPress applies the filter and shows only the category selected.

4 Click the check box next to Title.

☐ changes to ☑ next to Title and next to every post in the list.

5 Follow Steps **2** to **6** in "Multiple Posts in the Posts List," earlier in this section.

Note: You also can filter your posts by date, or by date and category together.

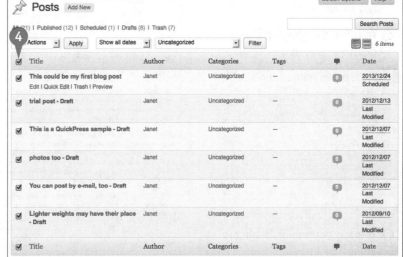

TIP

What if I want to add a category assignment to all but one of a group of posts I wrote last month?

You can filter the posts as described in this section, and when the Bulk Edit pane appears, click the dot with an X (⊗) next to the post that you want to exclude from your group category assignment. When you click ⊗ , the post disappears from the list.

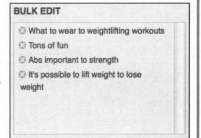

Apply Tags to Posts

As with categories, you can assign tags to your posts as you write them or after the fact. After the fact, you can assign tags to one post or several at a time. Just do your best to assign tags, as they help search engines identify your content for possible readers. If you apply tags as you write, the WordPress Dashboard gives you multiple ways to find the tags you already created. Those tools become especially helpful as your tags become more numerous.

Apply Tags to Posts

1 In the Tags module of the posting page, start typing a tag name.

A WordPress displays a list of possible tags as you type.

2 Click a tag name from the list and press **Enter** (**Return** on a Mac).

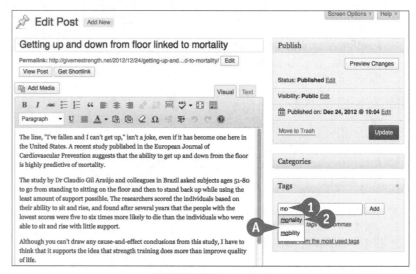

B The tag you applied appears under the tag entry box.

3 Click **Choose from the most used tags**.

The Tags box expands to display a word *cloud,* wherein the most frequently used tags appear largest.

4 Click a tag.

C The tag immediately appears.

5 Click **Update**.

The tags are saved with the post.

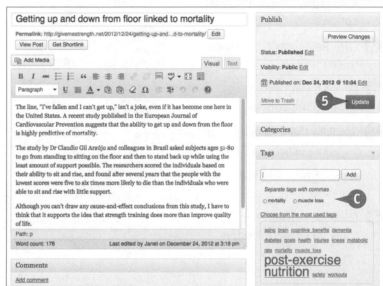

How do I assign tags to multiple posts?

You follow the same procedure as for categories, where you select a group of posts in the Posts list as explained in the preceding section of this book. The only difference is that for tags, you type tags in the Tags box rather than click check boxes next to categories. As with assigning tags while composing your post, the Tags box displays a drop-down list of possible tags as you type. The Bulk Edit box, however, does not offer a word cloud as does the Tags module where you write or edit a post.

Recall an Earlier Version of Your Blog Post

Uh-oh. You have writer's remorse and wish you could change your post back to the way you wrote it earlier. Post Revisions to the rescue! This revision-saving feature of WordPress lets you view and restore earlier versions of a post. What a relief.

Once you save your post, even if you have not published it, a simple *undo* command does not undo the changes.

Recall an Earlier Version of Your Blog Post

1 Click **Screen Options** to expand the Show on Screen options.

2 Click **Revisions** (☐ changes to ☑).

3 Click **Screen Options** to collapse the options.

4 Scroll to the bottom of your Edit Post page.

A list of post revisions appears.

5 Click the version that you think you want to restore.

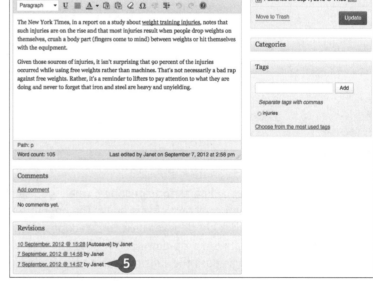

WordPress opens a new page that displays that version in the HTML format and at the bottom of that page, the list of revisions that you can compare.

6 Click the radio button next to the revisions that you want to compare (◯ changes to ◉).

Note: One button must be in the left column of buttons, and the other must be in the right column.

7 Click **Compare Revisions**.

WordPress displays the two versions side by side, and it highlights places in which the two versions are different.

Ⓐ The older version appears on the left.

Ⓑ The newer version appears on the right.

Ⓒ Specific changes are highlighted.

8 When you identify the desired previous version, click **Restore**.

WordPress restores the desired version and returns you to the Edit Post page.

9 Make any changes you want, and then click **Update** if the post already has been published (or **Save Draft** if the post has not been published).

TIPS

Can I compare one old version with another old version?

Yes. Just click the radio buttons beside the versions you want to compare, and then click **Compare Revisions**. You can compare only two versions at a time. Each time you click a new comparison revision, you need to click **Compare Revisions** to refresh the display.

I relied on WordPress automatically saving my post as I worked, but I see only one Autosave version in the list. How can I get an earlier Autosave version?

You cannot. WordPress keeps only the most recently automatically saved version. Hence, you need to click **Save Draft** (or **Update Post**) as you work if you want to have access to multiple older versions.

Write and Publish a Page

Unlike many blog platforms, WordPress allows you to write and publish *pages*. Pages are *static*, meaning they do not change as you add posts. Most themes make pages always accessible from your blog's home page.

The initial installation of the WordPress software (or blog registration at WordPress.com) by default includes one page. WordPress also lets you make *child* pages, or subpages of pages.

Write and Publish a Page

1. Under Pages in the left menu bar, click **Add New**.

   The Add New Page panel opens.

2. Type a headline or label in the headline box.

Note: If your theme displays your pages as tabs on your home page, use a short label.

3. Type your text in the page text box.

4. Click **Save Draft**.

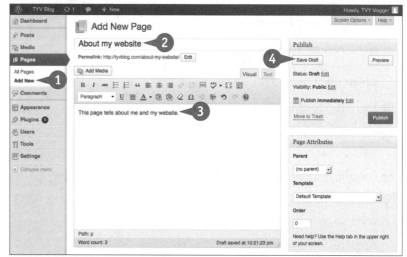

A. WordPress saves your work.

Note: Click **Save Draft** periodically as you work and when you are done.

B. A permalink appears, which you can edit if desired.

Note: Unlike post permalinks, page default permalinks have no reference to dates or numbers.

C. The panel title changes to Edit Page.

5. Click the drop-down menu under Parent, the ▾ next to (no parent).

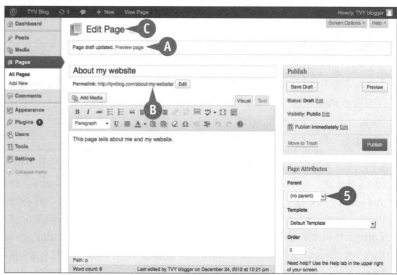

6 Click **Sample Page** (or **About** at WordPress.com) to make that page the parent of the new page you just made.

If you prefer to keep your page as a main page rather than a subpage, simply collapse the menu and proceed.

D Pages usually appear in alphabetical order, but you can assign each page a number to specify the order in which your home page lists your other pages.

E Some themes include more than one page template or standard page layout. Those themes have a Template section in the Page Attributes module, and you can choose a template from this list.

7 When you are done, click **Save Draft**.

8 When you are ready to publish your page to your website, click **Publish**.

Note: The Publish module works the same for pages as it does for posts. See "Write and Publish Your First Blog Post," earlier in this chapter, for more.

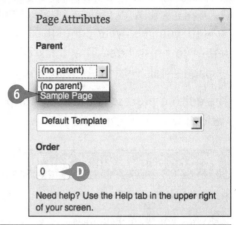

TIPS

What can I use pages for?
You can use one as the home page for your blog by selecting it in the Reading Settings. You can use a page or pages to display products or family photos or link lists or *FAQs*, frequently asked questions. Essentially, you can use them for just about anything you would use a web page for. See Chapter 13 for more ideas.

I do not understand the parent and child pages.
Parent pages are main pages and their names generally appear on your home page's menu bar. *Child* pages are like subpages; that is, they are secondary to the parent pages, which can be helpful to avoid cluttering your main page menus or for creating a hierarchy of pages.

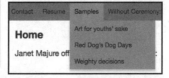

Edit or Delete What You Write

Knowing how to edit or delete a post or a page after you have published it or saved it as a draft lets you keep your content current. It also lets you write and edit at your convenience and then return to finish later. The Quick Edit feature lets you edit just about everything but the text in a post or page — all without leaving the main Posts or Pages panel.

The editing process is the same for posts and pages. This section uses a post as an example of the various ways you can edit your work.

Edit or Delete What You Write

Basic Editing

1 Click **Posts** (or **Pages**).

The Posts (or Pages) panel opens and lists all your posts. You can:

Ⓐ Filter posts by date or category or both.

Ⓑ Search posts.

Ⓒ View posts in a list, as shown, or with the headline and *excerpt*, which is either a summary you wrote on the Edit Post page or the first 55 words of your post if you did not write an excerpt.

Ⓓ Browse the Posts list.

2 Click the title on the post (or page) you want to edit.

The Edit Post (or Edit Page) window opens. You can edit and update as you did when you first wrote a new post or page.

Basic Deletion of Post or Page

1 Position the mouse pointer over the post (or page) you want to delete.

2 Click **Trash**.

Quick Edit Posts or Pages

1 Position the mouse pointer over the post (or page) you want to edit.

2 Click **Quick Edit**.

The Quick Edit panel opens.

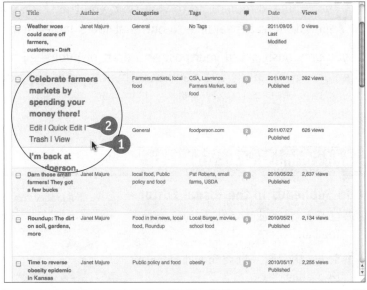

E The Quick Edit panel lets you edit the post or page title, slug — the editable part of the URL — categories, and more. Options are slightly different on the Quick Edit page screen.

3 After you make your changes, click **Update** to save.

WordPress collapses the Quick Edit panel and returns you to the list of posts or pages.

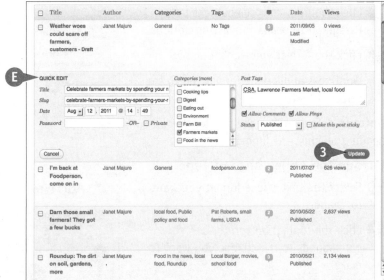

TIPS

Can I recover a post or page I sent to Trash?

Yes, for up to 30 days. At the top of the Posts or Pages panel is a count of your current posts or pages. If you have any items in Trash, a Trash link appears. Click it to find your trashed items.

Position your mouse pointer over the item you want to keep until you see the Recover link, and click it.

Is the Edit link that appears under the post or page title different from clicking on the title?

No, it is just another way to arrive at the same destination, the Edit Post (or Edit Page) panel.

Add Formatting to Your Text

Wh…hen you add formatting to your text, you transform your post from one with a rather monotonous appearance to one that looks more inviting and may be easier to skim.

If you previously saved your post as a draft or published it, you can find it by clicking **Edit** under the Posts menu in the left menu bar. This task uses the expanded visual editor toolbar.

Add Formatting to Your Text

Add Subheads in the Visual Editor

Ⓐ Click here to expand the visual editor toolbar.

① Select the text whose format you want to change.

② Click the drop-down menu next to Paragraph to reveal formatting options.

③ Click the format you want to apply.

WordPress applies the formatting to the selected text.

Note: In default HTML, the smaller the heading number, the bigger the type.

Change the Appearance of Type

① Select the text whose format you want to change.

② Click the toolbar button that corresponds to the change you want to make.

WordPress changes the text as you directed.

Note: B (**B**) is for bold, *I* (*I*) for italic, ABC (~~ABC~~) for strikethrough, and U (U) for underline.

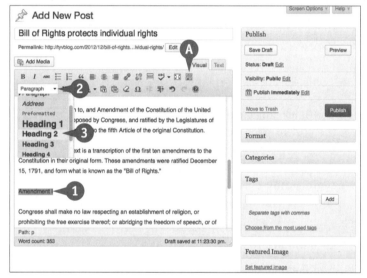

Change Paragraph Formatting

1. Click anywhere within the paragraph you want to change.

Note: Click and drag to select multiple paragraphs.

2. Click a paragraph formatting button to apply.

   WordPress changes the paragraph format as you specified. In this example, it indents a paragraph.

3. Click **Save Draft** to save your changes.

Note: If you are formatting a published post, click **Update** instead.

4. Click **Preview** to see how your changes look.

Note: If you are formatting a published post, click **Preview Changes** instead.

   WordPress opens the blog post preview.

View Your Changes

Ⓐ An example of boldface.

Ⓑ An example of a Heading 2.

Ⓒ An example of an indented paragraph.

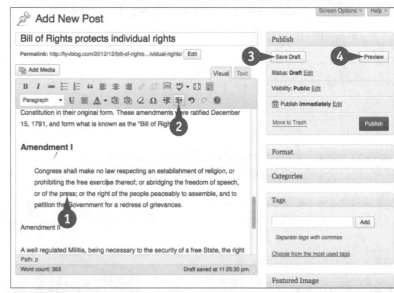

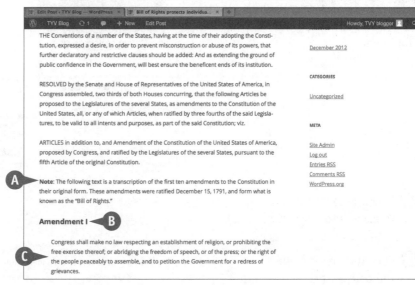

TIPS

How do I change the text color?
Select the text you want to change, click the color formatting button (Ⓐ), and then click the color of your choice. If you do not like the options shown, you can click **More colors** and get just about any color you might want.

Is there a quicker way to change the formatting?
Yes. Press Ctrl on a PC (⌘ on a Mac) plus the following letters to change the text using keystrokes only:

Ⓑ Bold		② Heading 2
Ⓘ Italic		③ Heading 3
Ⓤ Underline		④ Heading 4
① Heading 1		

Add Text Hyperlinks to Your Post or Page

When you add hyperlinks, you can give others credit for ideas you mention or quote, lead readers to additional pertinent information, and reach out to fellow bloggers, who love it when you link to them.

A hyperlink is a reference to another location on the web — including elsewhere on your site.

Add Text Hyperlinks to Your Post or Page

1 Select the URL on the page you want to link to and copy it.

Note: With most browsers, you can copy the URL by pressing `Ctrl`+`C` (`⌘`+`C` on a Mac). Or, you can click **Copy** from the Edit menu.

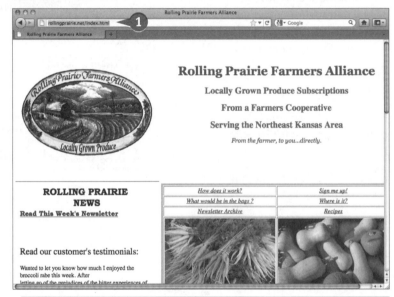

2 Click the text that you want to make into a hyperlink within your post or page.

3 Click the link icon on the toolbar (🔗).

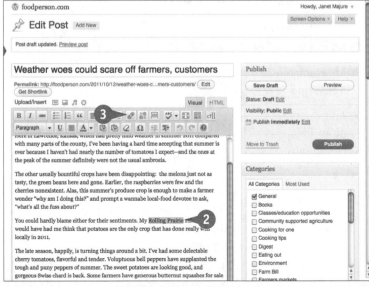

④ In the Insert/edit link window, paste the URL in the URL box.

Note: The URL needs to include the *protocol*, or http:// portion, of the web address, and WordPress automatically includes it.

⑤ Type the name of the page.

Note: The Title text is optional. Readers see it when they position their mouse pointer over a link. If you do not type anything in the Title box, readers see the URL.

⑥ Click **Add Link**.

WordPress returns to the Edit Post page.

Ⓐ The text you selected appears as a hyperlink, and the Title text appears when you position your mouse pointer over the link. The link is active when you preview the page or publish it.

⑦ Click **Save Draft**.

The link is saved to your site.

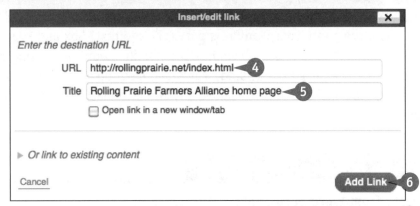

Paste Text from Other Sources

You can write blog posts in Microsoft Word — even do considerable formatting — and then paste them into your WordPress post (or page text) box and keep the formatting, as long as you know how. Doing so lets you compose in a familiar word-processing program and then eliminate the word processor's extra coding, which can mess up web pages. Conversely, the special WordPress pasting tools make it easy to remove unwanted formatting when you copy and paste text from word processors or web pages.

Paste Text from Other Sources

Paste from Word Documents

1. After copying the text in a Word document that you want to use in your blog, go to the New Post or Edit Post page where you want to paste the text in WordPress. Click the **Word Paste** button (📋).

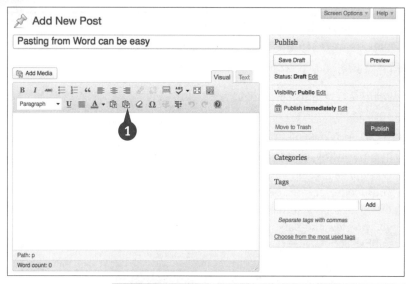

The Paste from Word window opens.

2. Press Ctrl+V (⌘+V on a Mac) to insert the copied Word text.

   WordPress pastes the text without extraneous coding.

3. Click **Insert**.

   Your copy, as written in Word, appears in the post (or page text) box.

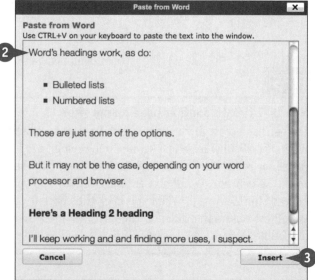

Paste Formatted Type as Text

1 After copying the text, such as from another web page, that you want to put in your post or page, click the **Paste Text** button (📋).

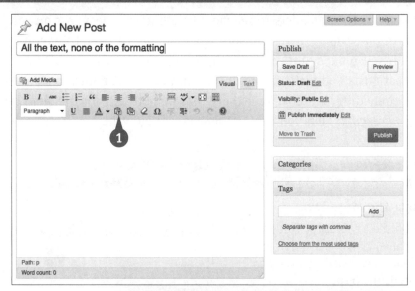

The Paste as Plain Text window opens.

2 Press **Ctrl**+**V** (**⌘**+**V** on a Mac) to insert the copied text.

WordPress pastes the text without formatting.

A You may choose not to retain line breaks by clicking **Keep linebreaks** (☑ changes to ☐).

3 Click **Insert**.

Your copy appears as plain text in the post (or page text) box.

TIPS

Why would I want to paste text without formatting?

Pasting copied material from other websites as plain text and then adding formatting is often easier than removing and reformatting text that you copied. If you are skeptical, paste something from another web page straight into the Visual blog post window. Then click the **Text** tab to see the coding. Chances are you will see a lot of code.

I pasted a table from Word, which looks fine, but I cannot seem to type anything below it. What should I do?

Click the **Text** tab at the top of the post or page text entry window. You will see `</table>` at the end of the table. Click after that HTML tag and start typing. Then, return to the visual editor and proceed as usual. Switching to the Text editor can solve similar problems whenever you have trouble adding or formatting text.

Using the More Option to Break Your Posts in Two

If you want your readers to see more headlines and less text on your blog's front page, you can make that happen with the More tag. That can be useful if you have written an especially long post. It's also handy for changing the appearance of your blog's front page. If you use the More tag on most posts and increase the number of posts that appear on the blog front page, your blog has an entirely different look. Your theme has default text for the More tag, typically something like *continue reading,* but you can customize it if you want.

Using the More Option to Break Your Posts in Two

Insert the More Tag

1. On the New Post or Edit Post panel, click the location in your post where you want to split the post.

2. Click the **Insert More Tag** button (▭).

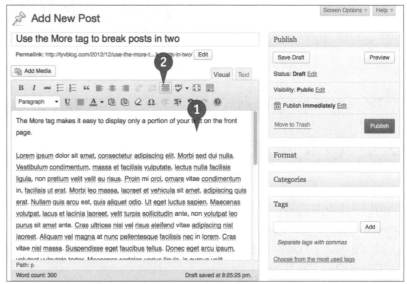

Ⓐ The More marker appears in the post.

3. Click **Publish**.

   The post is published to your blog.

Note: Clicking **Preview** or **View Post** does not reveal the More tag, as it appears only on the blog front page.

4. Click your site name.

The home page of the blog opens, with only part of the divided post showing.

⑤ Click **Continue reading**, which appears at the location where you inserted the More tag.

The post page opens, revealing the full text of the post.

Note: The wording that refers readers to the full post varies from theme to theme.

Change Number of Posts Displayed

① Click **Settings** and then **Reading** in the Dashboard's left menu bar.

The Reading Settings appear.

② Type the number of items you want to appear on your blog's front page.

Note: The default is 10.

③ Click **Save Changes**.

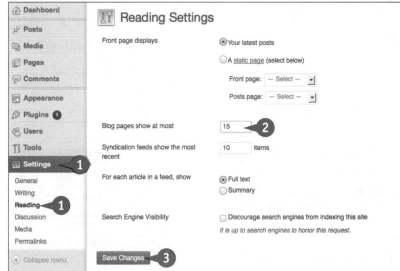

Why am I seeing odd formatting after I insert the More tag, and how do I fix it?

You probably accidentally inserted the tag between a pair of HTML formatting tags. Click the Text tab of the post composing box to see the HTML. If you see something like <em> and then some text followed by <!--more--> and then </em>, move the </em> in front of the More tag, <!--more-->.

Is it possible to change the text that the More tag displays?

On an individual post, go to the Text editor and find the More tag, <!--more-->. Click after more, type a space, and then type the text you want, such as <!--more Please keep reading-->, which inserts the text *Please keep reading*. To change your theme's standard More text at self-hosted blogs, use a plugin such as More Link Modifier, or do it yourself with detailed instructions at http://codex.wordpress.org/Customizing_the_Read_More.

Convert Categories and Tags

You can change categories to tags and vice versa, as a group or a few at a time, if you change your mind about how you organize your post identifiers. Also, if you import your blog to WordPress from another blogging platform, you may find that all your old tags are now categories. Fortunately, WordPress has a tool that lets you convert categories to tags and vice versa.

Convert Categories and Tags

1 Click **Tools** and then **Import** in the left menu bar.

2 Click **Categories and Tags Converter**.

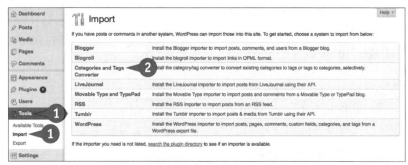

At WordPress.com, the Convert Categories to Tags panel opens. At self-hosted blogs, a plugin screen opens.

3 Click **Install Now**.

Note: WordPress.com users skip Steps 3 and 4.

WordPress installs the plugin.

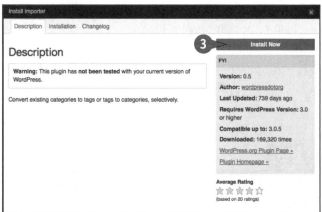

4 Click **Activate Plugin & Run Importer**.

The Convert Categories (*n*) to Tags panel opens, where *n* represents the number of categories available to convert.

5. Click the check box for each category that you want to convert to a tag (☐ changes to ☑).

6. Click **Convert Categories to Tags**.

Ⓐ WordPress displays the progress and confirms the conversions.

7. Click **Tags to Categories**.

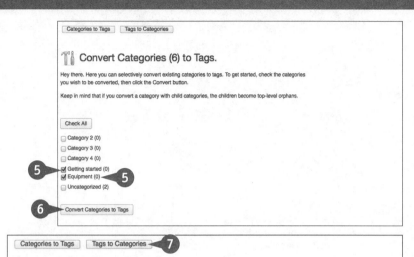

The Convert Tags (*n*) to Categories panel opens, with *n* as the available tags.

8. Click the check box next to the tag or tags you want to convert to a category (☐ changes to ☑).

9. Click **Convert Tags to Categories**.

WordPress displays the conversion progress and converts the selected tags to categories.

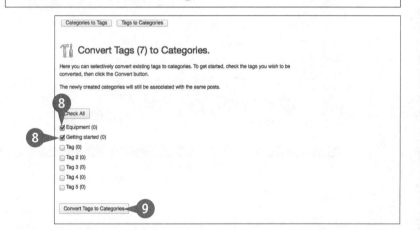

TIPS

What happens to the posts when I convert categories and tags?

The names are still attached to the posts to which they were previously assigned, but as categories instead of tags, or vice versa. Because categories are required, though, if you change all categories assigned to a particular post, the post automatically is assigned to the default category, such as *Uncategorized*.

What happens if I convert a parent category to a tag but do not convert its child, or subcategory?

The subcategory becomes a top-level category. Incidentally, if you convert a parent and its child, both become tags, but without the parent-child relationship. As you may recall, you cannot create a hierarchy with tags.

CHAPTER 5

Creating Visual and Audio Content

Just because the program is called WordPress does not mean pictures and sounds are not welcome. In fact, WordPress provides all the tools you need to use images, audio, and video files with your blog.

Consider Media Issues

A blog rarely includes words and only words. You, too, can enrich your readers' blog experience by including images, sounds, and even video — your own or those created by others, if you have the proper permission. For best results, it helps to understand a bit about how the Internet handles your media. You also are smart to remember that while media can enhance your site, poorly executed images, videos, and podcasts can detract or make your site look decidedly amateurish.

Images and Dimensions

Web browsers display images according to the number of pixels specified for them. If you upload an image 1600 pixels wide, but you have room only for a 500-pixel image, the browser reduces the 1600-pixel image to display it at 500 pixels. The large image causes the page to load more slowly than if you had uploaded a 500-pixel image.

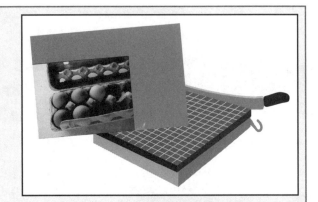

Media Selection

Well-chosen media enhances a blog, but too much or poorly chosen media can be a distraction. Well-chosen media includes a map that shows a location you recommend, a photograph that illustrates a point you have made, or a video clip that demonstrates a process you describe. A poor choice might include a fuzzy photo that fails to make the desired point.

Media and Memory

One picture may be worth *more* than a thousand words in terms of computer storage. Sound and video files use even more storage space. In fact, WordPress.com requires you to pay for increased storage if you want to upload sound and video. If your blog is self-hosted, make sure you have enough space with your host to store sound and video files.

Off-Site Image and Video Storage

Instead of storing your image, sound, and video files with your web host, you can store them with a hosting service and then link to your files. Flickr, Photobucket, and Picasa are among the free image-storing services available. Video hosts include the well-known YouTube and Vimeo. You

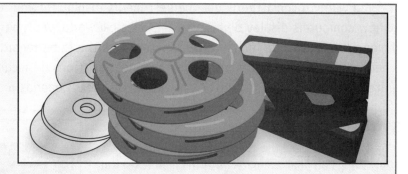

also can take advantage of the hosts' audience to build traffic to your blog. If you embed the work of others, make sure you have their permission.

Off-Site Music and Podcast Storage

You can store and link to your audio files at SoundCloud and podcasts at Liberated Syndication, also known as *Libsyn*, among others. At WordPress.org sites, the Blubrry PowerPress plugin comes as a recommended and easy way to host your podcasts. You also can link to

other people's sound files, such as those at BandPage and Spotify. Yes, you also can embed slide shows and store and serve documents from your WordPress blog, both the self-hosted and the WordPress.com varieties.

Where to Begin

The media options can seem a bit overwhelming. As with so many aspects of your blog, you are wise to step back and do some thoughtful planning about how media can tie in to your blog's purpose. Displaying every media type possible not only requires lots of work on your part but it also stands a good chance of

making for a confusing site. Thus, the best place to begin is by choosing the medium that best advances your purpose, learn it well, and use it. Then add another medium only when you are sure it benefits your blog and when you have the time to learn and use it.

Understanding Display and Image Dimensions

If you want to consistently get the best media display for your needs, you first need to understand how computers display objects. In the physical world, we tend to think of a dimension as a dimension. That is, an inch or a centimeter looks the same regardless of where you measure or whether you use a metal ruler or a plastic one, variations of accuracy aside. A pixel does not work quite that way. A pixel is a pixel, but the way it *looks* depends on your screen resolution.

Screen Resolution

You can understand the concept better if you view a few things on your computer with the monitor set at different screen resolutions. First, open a web page or any window on your machine. Then, on a Windows 7 or Windows 8 computer, right-click in the desktop background and click **Screen resolution** in the pop-up menu. In the box that appears, click the **Resolution** drop-down arrow, and move the slider to a lower resolution. Click **Apply**, and then look at

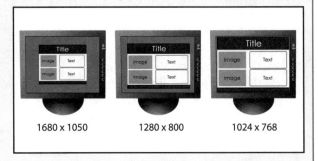

how the windows change appearance. The pixel settings of the content are the same, but they *look* different because the lower-resolution display makes things look larger but less clear. Mac users go to System Preferences and Display.

Image Resolution

The concept of *image resolution*, by comparison, is entirely a physical concern when you want to print digital images. With printed images, the more pixels you pack into an inch, the sharper and smaller the image is. But for online display, you can take an image of 400 by 600 pixels and save it as three separate files with three different image resolutions,

such as 300 pixels per inch, or *ppi*, 200 ppi, and 72 ppi. All three images appear exactly the same when you upload them to the Internet.

Take-Away Message

If you remain confused, just remember one thing: The image you upload displays online according to the image's dimensions stated in pixels. Therefore, uploading an image that is 3200 pixels wide makes no sense if you never intend to display it any wider than 800 pixels. Uploading a large image will, however, take longer, use more storage space, and make it possible for others to make a good print of your image, which you may not want them to do.

Review Media Settings

The Media settings let you set standard image sizes for a consistent look. These settings can save you time and trouble in the long run. Until you settle on a permanent theme, however, you may want to stick to the default settings, as the maximum width may vary from theme to theme. If you are not sure how wide your blog is, you may be able to find out from the theme developer, from the WordPress.com theme showcase, or by using one of the developer toolbars discussed in Chapter 13.

Review Media Settings

At WordPress.org

1. Click **Media** under the Settings menu in the left menu bar.

   The Media Settings panel opens.

2. Review the thumbnail, medium, and large dimensions to make sure they are appropriate for your blog and theme.

Note: You can use the Information button in the Web Developer Toolbar introduced in Chapter 13 to determine your blog theme's dimensions.

3. Click **Crop thumbnail** (□ changes to ☑) unless you want thumbnails to display to an exact size that you specify. (This option is unavailable at WordPress.com.)

4. Click **Save Changes**.

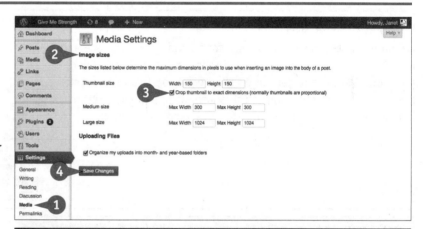

At WordPress.com

1. Review settings as for WordPress.org above.

2. Deselect the Enable carousel check box (☑ changes to □).

3. Ignore the Video Player setting for now.

Note: This setting applies only if you purchase the VideoPress add-on discussed later in this chapter.

4. Click **Save Changes**.

Prepare Images for Uploading

W hen you take the time to edit and resize images before you post them on your blog, you assure that your images look their best and do not slow down your site. Although WordPress provides some online editing tools, you may do better with an image editor to prepare your photos and other images. It can be a simple and free program, such as GIMP or Picasa or Preview for Mac, or the do-it-all Adobe Photoshop. If you have a digital camera, it may provide a basic editing program, too. Online image editors, such as Pixlr and PicMonkey, are other options.

Crop to Focus Interest

Crop is the term that editors use for trimming images. Use your editor's cropping tool to eliminate distracting activity, objects, or blank areas or to zero in on the item of particular interest. Save an unedited version of the photo, although your editor may do so automatically, in case you change your mind.

Adjust the Image

Take advantage of the editor's tools to eliminate red eye in flash photos, to straighten out sloping horizons, and to correct poorly rendered color, contrast, and other image flaws. You want people to see the image, not be put off by its shortcomings.

Annotate the Image

Add arrows, labels, and other notations to your image if they would help readers. For example, a simple Start here and an arrow can make a map much more meaningful to your readers than a large amount of text. Similarly, clear labels on graphs aid in understanding.

Save the Image

After you finish editing, you need to save your image in a file format that web browsers can display properly. The acceptable formats are JPEG, which stands for Joint Photographic Experts Group; GIF, or Graphics Interchange Format; and PNG, for Portable Network Graphics.

Choose a File Format

GIF is best for images with few colors because it retains quality and creates a small file. GIF often is good for logos. JPEG supports millions of colors and thus is good for photographs, but it creates bigger files unless you increase compression, which reduces JPEG image quality. PNG is the newest format and shares many GIF advantages, but a few old browsers may not support it.

Resize the Image

Chances are reasonably good that your image is bigger than you want on your blog, especially if you downloaded it full size from a digital camera. View the image at 100 percent size in your image editor to see how big the image *really* is. Use your editor's resizing tools to reduce it to the largest size you would want it to appear on your site.

Upload and Insert an Image While Posting

By using the tools that WordPress provides, you can upload your images from your computer in a batch or one at a time. Then you can insert them into your blog posts to add some visual pizzazz to your site. As you insert them, you need to add some information to help readers and search engines understand your image. You can upload and insert images as part of your post-writing process or as a separate operation, and WordPress offers multiple upload methods. One is sure to follow your preferred way of working.

Upload and Insert an Image While Posting

① From the Add New Post or Edit Post page, click in your post at the location where you want to insert your image.

② Click the **Add Media** button (□ Add Media).

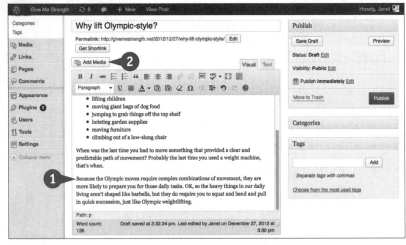

The Insert Media window opens.

③ Click **Upload Files**.

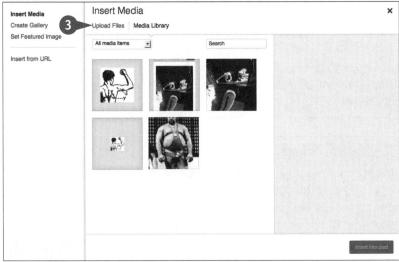

The Upload Files panel appears.

④ Drag an image from a folder on your computer to the upload window, and release the mouse button when the border of the drop-files area changes color.

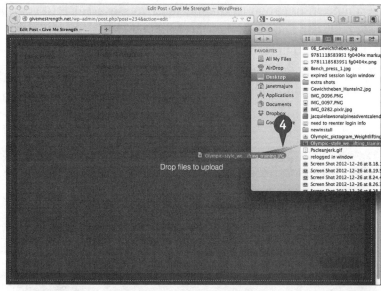

Ⓐ Bars appear, showing the upload progress.

TIP

Do I have to drag and drop? I find it awkward.
No. If you prefer, you can click **Select Files** in the middle of the Upload Files panel. Doing so opens an upload window by way of your web browser, and then you can browse your computer files for the image or images you want to upload. Click the filename, click **Open**, and you get the same result as drag and drop.

dding information to the image as you insert it into your post lets you give readers information about the image. It also can help you keep track of images in the Media Library you add to every time you upload an image. If you want to reuse an image, it is easier to find one named *green_apples.jpg* than to figure out that the one named *DSC123_456* is the image that you want. The information in the Title field is what appears in the Media Library image list.

Upload and Insert an Image While Posting (continued)

The upload finishes.

B A thumbnail of the image with a checkmark confirms that the image is selected for insertion.

C The Attachment Details pane shows the filename, upload date, and size.

5 In the Title box, type a name for the image's listing in the Media Library.

Note: The default is the image's filename.

6 Type alternate text to describe the image.

7 Scroll down to the Attachment Display Settings.

8 Choose a size from the Size drop-down list.

9 Click **Insert into post**.

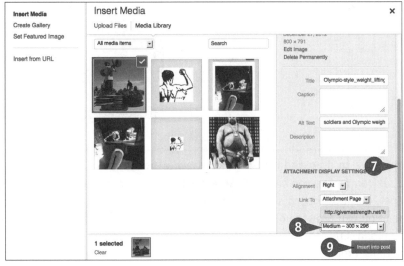

The Add Media window disappears, and the Edit Post window displays the image at the cursor location.

⑩ Click **Save Draft/Update Post**, depending on whether the post is a new draft or an existing post, to save the change.

⑪ Click **Preview**.

A preview of the post's individual page appears with the image inserted.

Can I upload more than one image at a time?
Yes. Simply select multiple files on your computer and drag them to the upload window. It helps if all the images you want to upload are in the same folder on your computer. You also can upload multiple images when you use the Select Files option to browse for images.

My image took forever to upload, and I have a high-speed connection. What is going on?
First, Internet upload speeds typically are far slower than download speeds. The bigger issue, however, probably is that your image file is too large. Try to keep it less than 200 kilobytes or so for fast uploads and space conservation. Although 200 kilobytes is an arbitrary limit, it can help you recognize when you have larger files than you need.

Edit an Image While Uploading

You can edit an image as you upload it, a handy feature should you belatedly realize you overlooked some needed changes. Perhaps you should have cropped out a portion of the picture or realize that you need to rotate the image. Easy-to-use tools allow you to correct those problems as part of the posting process. Start by clicking **Add Media** on the post-writing panel as described in the preceding task and uploading an image. The editing task occurs within the Insert Media window. WordPress retains your original image.

Edit an Image While Uploading

1 Click **Edit Image**.

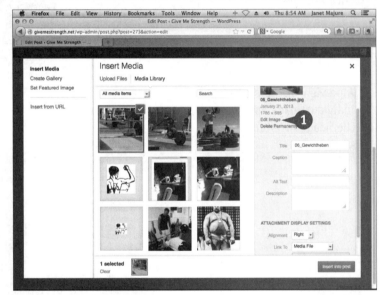

The Edit Media panel appears.

2 Click **Scale Image**.

The scaling area expands.

3 Type the desired maximum display width.

Ⓐ WordPress automatically adjusts image height proportionally.

4 Click **Scale**.

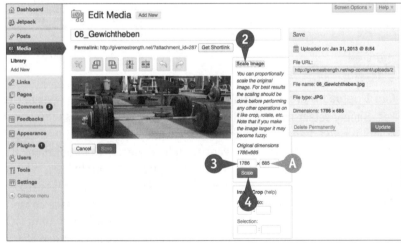

WordPress saves the change.

⑤ Click and drag your mouse pointer within the image to define an area to crop.

⑥ Click the **Crop** button ( ).

WordPress crops the image.

Ⓑ You can use these buttons to rotate the image to the left or right and flip it vertically or horizontally.

⑦ Click **Save**.

⑧ Click **Update.**

⑨ Click **X** to close the Edit Media tab.

⑩ Click **Refresh**.

The dimensions and cropping update on-screen, and Refresh changes to Edit.

⑪ Add information if desired.

⑫ Click **Insert into post**.

The edited image is inserted into your post.

The Edit Media window behaved differently for me on my WordPress.com blog.
Yes, some details may be slightly different. At this writing, WordPress.com displays a new Edit button after you save an edit. The procedure is essentially the same, though.

How can I undo changes?
You can click the **Undo** button ( ) as you are editing. You also can click **Restore Original Image** to eliminate all changes you may have made. You then click **Restore Image** to confirm your intention. Once you insert the image and save the post, however, these options are not available.

Format an Image from the Edit Image Window

Once an image is inserted into a post, you can move it around, adjust its size, alter or add borders, and more. It all starts by clicking the image in the Edit Post window. When you do, size handles appear around the image, which you can drag to change size. You also can click in the middle of the picture and drag it to the location you prefer. Or you can click a button to edit image properties such as the wrap settings, size, and link.

A Image Handles

Click and drag corner handles to resize an image proportionally. Click and drag a side handle to stretch or squeeze an image. You can click anywhere within the image and drag it to a new location in the post.

B Edit Image

Click to open the Edit Image window to edit size, link, caption, and alignment settings and Advanced Settings, as explained on the next page.

C Delete Image

Click to delete an image from its location in a post, but not from the Media Library.

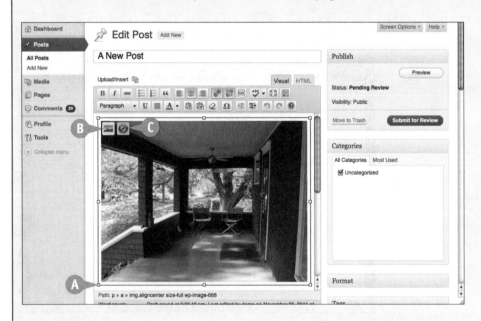

Ⓐ Size Scale

Click to resize an image display to a percentage of the inserted size.

Ⓑ Alignment

Click to specify whether image is in line with text via the None setting or whether the image aligns to the left, right, or center relative to the text.

Ⓒ Edit Options

Click to enter or change the information you provided when you uploaded your image.

Ⓓ Update/Cancel

Click to save or cancel changes you made in the Edit Image window and then return to the Edit Post window.

Ⓔ Advanced Settings Tab

Click to open the Advanced Settings window.

Ⓐ Original Size

Click to reset the image to the uploaded size.

Ⓑ Image Properties

Click to add or alter borders and spacing around the image.

Ⓒ Advanced Link Settings

Click to edit characteristics of links associated with the image. These are useful if you are familiar with HTML and CSS.

Ⓓ Update/Cancel

Click to save or cancel changes you made in the Advanced Image Settings window and return to the Edit Post window.

Add Images to the Media Library

Depending on how you work, you may find it more convenient to upload your images without worrying about where they go in your blog posts. You can do that by adding them to the Media Library with the multi-file uploader. The Media Library also provides a searchable repository for your images and other media. When you add images to the library this way, they are not associated with any posts until you add them to a post.

Add Images to the Media Library

① Click **Media** in the left menu bar.

The Media menu expands, and the Media Library window opens.

② Click **Add New**.

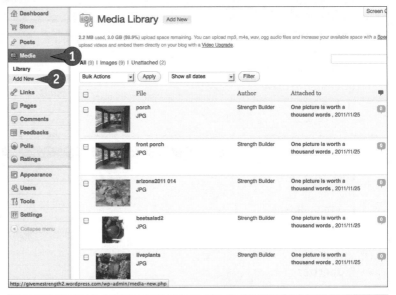

The Upload New Media panel opens.

③ Click **Select Files**.

Note: You also can drag and drop images, as described in "Upload and Insert an Image While Posting," earlier in this chapter.

A file selection window opens.

④ Select the file or files you want to upload.

Note: Press Ctrl (⌘ on a Mac) to select multiple files.

⑤ Click **Open**.

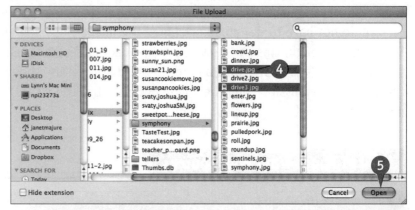

WordPress uploads the files to your server and stores them in your Media Library.

⑥ If desired, click **Edit** to edit image properties, as described in "Edit an Image While Uploading," earlier in this chapter.

⑦ Click **Media** to return to the Media Library.

TIPS

Can I just upload images with my FTP client?
Yes, if you have a self-hosted blog. Simply upload the images from your computer to the correct folder, or directory, or your server. See your Miscellaneous Settings if you are unsure where to upload your files.

How do I insert images from the Media Library into my posts or pages?
When writing a post or page, click **Add Media**, and then click the **Media Library** tab in the Insert Media window. Click the image you want to use, which reveals its settings and other details, and click **Insert into post**. The Insert Media window closes, and the image appears in the post or page.

Insert Images from Web Sources

You can save storage space on your web host when you insert images based on other websites. You do not have to download or upload the image files; you embed, or *link*, them with a URL. Sometimes, though, this can slow your page loading time because your page must retrieve the image from the other site or set the stage for a future broken link should that site's owner change or delete the URL. Get permission from the image owner to use the image, unless the image is in the public domain or the website gives copyright permission.

Insert Images from Web Sources

1 Right-click the image to which you want to link (or ⌘+click on a Mac).

2 Click **Copy Image Location**.

The link is saved to your computer's clipboard.

3 Go to your blog, and click **Add Media** at the top of the post- or page-writing panel where you want the image to appear.

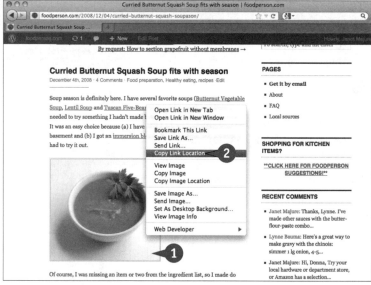

The Insert Media window opens.

4 Click **Insert from URL**.

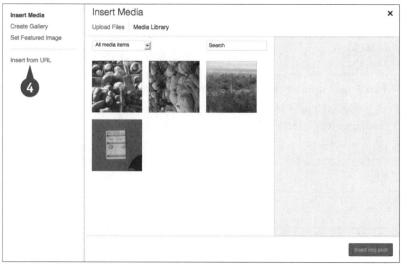

The Insert from URL view appears.

5 Paste a copied image URL in the URL box.

A The image to insert appears.

6 Type alternate text describing the image.

7 Click **Insert into post**.

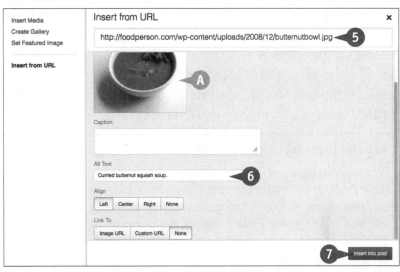

B The Insert Media window disappears, and the writing panel displays the image where your cursor was.

8 Click **Save Draft**.

9 Click **Publish** to publish the post on your website.

Note: Media embedded into your blog through the URLs of other websites are not saved to your Media Library.

Where can I find images in the public domain?
A favorite location for finding images is Wikimedia Commons at http://commons.wikimedia.org. Click the public domain category. Also, images on U.S. government websites almost always are available copyright-free.

I found photos that say they are subject to the Creative Commons Share Alike license. What does that mean?
Numerous licensing and copyright options exist. The most common seem to be standard copyrights, which means you must get permission before using the photo, and Creative Commons licenses, of which there are several versions. To understand the restrictions of the Creative Commons licenses, read the information at http://creativecommons.org/licenses.

Using Images to Enhance Posts

You can get the best results from your well-chosen images when you use them not just for color but also to enhance the content of your posts. After all, if one picture is worth a thousand words, one picture *plus* a thousand words must be worth five thousand words, as long as the words and pictures complement each other. Earlier sections provided various ways to insert images. Now consider the best ways to use those images. Remember also that using a reasonably consistent pattern improves your blog's visual identity.

Art for Interest

As with headings, you can use images to break up a large block of uninterrupted text. If you do not have a suitable image, you can consider microstock images in addition to the public domain images mentioned in the preceding section. Two popular microstock sites are iStockPhoto.com and Shutterstock.com.

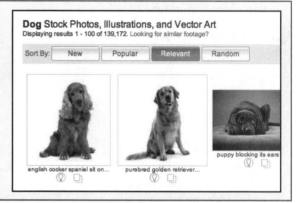

Take Advantage of Images' Words

Besides providing information for visitors using screen readers or other assistive devices, the alternate text for your images also leads search engines to your photos. The image title, which defaults to the filename, appears in some browsers when the mouse pointer rests over the image. The filename also can lead searchers your way. So, name it autumnleaves.jpg rather than img0235.jpg.

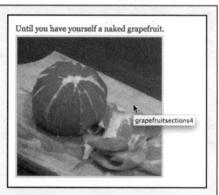

Captions Not Required

Just because your WordPress image-inserting window allows you to type a caption does not mean you must use that option (A). The caption feature generally puts a border around the image with the caption included. You may not like that look. The next section provides some options. And some images require no captions at all.

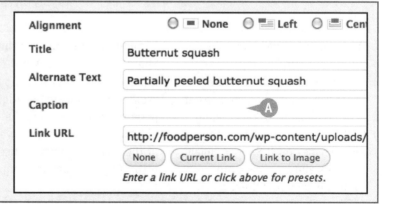

156

Consider Wrapping Text

You may want a powerful image to stand alone on a line using the None or Center format. An image that mainly illustrates your words, however, might work better with text wrapping around it, using the left or right alignment. Learn how in "Wrap Text Around an Image," later in this chapter. Make sure the photo is small enough to allow at least three or so words to fit on every line beside it.

Get yer farm-fresh produce here. The Kansas City Star provides a detailed list of farmers markets in the Kansas City region, both in Kansas and Missouri. (KC Star) Of course, other market lists are available that capture most markets in the United States. They include Local Harvest and the USDA's Agricultural Marketing Service lists. The AMS list currently shows 81 markets in Kansas. For fellow Kansans, don't forget the KS Farmers Markets site.

Offer Two Display Options

You can upload a large photo, say one that is 800 × 1200 pixels, but insert it in your post using the Thumbnail option or a percentage display. That represents the size that the image appears in the post, but readers can click the small image and see its larger version in another window. It does not hurt to tell them so ().

quilt patterns, a vineyard, fruit tree plazas and the children's Fun Food Farm. It is a feast for the eyes as well as the ... ... (Click below for larger images of, from left, a portion of parterre, vineyard and Fun Food Farm sign.)

Give Credit

Crediting the source of your images () is useful to readers — as well as to artists and photographers, perhaps including you. You can do it in alternate text, but doing it on-screen is nicer. Some people recommend doing it in both places. Also, if you do not want others to use your photos, declare your copyrights with each image.

Hot beans! Read a profile of Alan Townsend, head of the J. Hawkens Bean Co. in Goodland, Kansas. Growing edible dry beans makes sense in western Kansas. Maybe more growers will follow his lead and quit depleting the Ogallala Aquifer. (Profile by Ron Wilson, at Kansas State University.) Did I mention I love beans? You can read about the aquifer at Scientific American, among other places. (*Map: U.S. Geological Survey*)

Add a Caption to an Image

Captions provide added information to your readers about images that you post on your site. You can add a caption when you upload an image, or you can add it after the fact as part of your post. When you use the Caption field in the Media panels, WordPress includes the caption in the image's display and uses the style specified in your theme's style sheet. That is the easiest way to add a caption. If you want a caption but not the styling, you can add caption information in other ways.

Add a Caption to an Image

1 Click the posted image in the post-writing panel.

2 Click the **Edit Image** button (🖼) that appears.

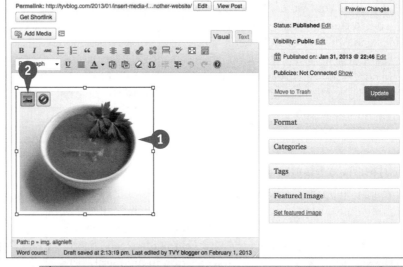

The Edit Image window appears.

3 Type a caption.

4 Click **Update**.

The posting panel returns and shows the caption.

5 Click **Update**.

6 Click **View Post**.

WordPress opens the post, where you can view the caption as the world sees it.

TIPS

Can I just add a caption when I upload an image?

Yes, by typing your caption in the Caption field in the Insert Media screen. Some people prefer to do it after the fact, however, especially if they upload several images at a time. It is a matter of your preferred workflow.

How can I add a caption without my theme's styling?

Two good options exist if you do not want to edit the theme's Cascading Style Sheet, or CSS. One is to type the caption as a separate paragraph to appear under the image or beside it, if you wrap text as described in the next section. The other is to provide image information at the bottom of the post, which may look good but probably is less desirable from a reader's perspective.

Wrap Text Around an Image

Wrapping text around an image lets the image be integrated into the text. You can set up the text wrap as part of your image-inserting process while writing a page or post. Place your cursor in the text where you want the image to appear, and click **Add Media**. After you choose the image you want to upload, you click the appropriate alignment setting. When you insert the image, the text wraps around it.

Wrap Text Around an Image

1 With an image selected in the Insert Media panel, click the Alignment box down arrow (▾).

2 Click **Right**.

3 Click **Insert into post**.

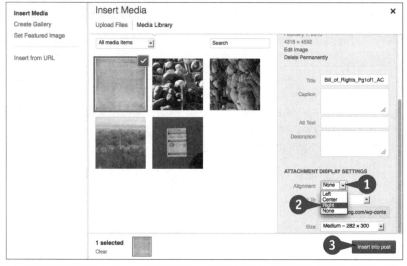

Ⓐ The image appears, aligned right, in the post panel.

4 Click **Save Draft**.

5 Click **Preview**.

A preview of the post with the inserted image appears in a new tab.

⑥ Click **X** to close the tab.

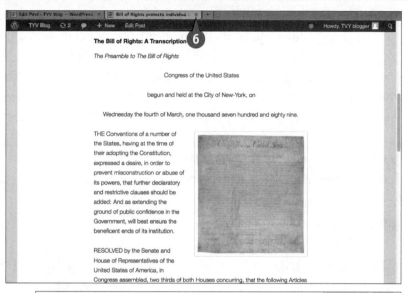

The Edit Post page returns. You can click **Publish** (Ⓑ) if you are satisfied, or click the image and then the **Edit Image** button (▣) to make additional changes.

Why does more text appear to the side of the image on one computer than on another?

The answer goes back to differences in screen size and resolution as explained in "Understanding Display and Image Dimensions," earlier in this chapter. If you are concerned about how much text appears, try viewing the post using different resolutions on your computer.

How can I adjust the amount of space between the image and the text?

Click the image in your post, and then the **Edit Image** button (▣). Click the **Advanced Settings** tab. Type values, in pixels, for the amount of vertical space, which is the space above and below the image, and horizontal space, which is the space beside the image, that you want. Then click **Update**.

Determine the Image Target

You can determine what happens when someone clicks an image on your site. The options include displaying the image by itself on an otherwise blank web page, opening a totally different web page, and displaying the image as an *attachment page*. An attachment page displays the image in the same format as a blog post. You also can set it so that a click on the image does nothing. At this writing, the WordPress interface makes the attachment page option a bit confusing, but you can work it out. Start by clicking the **Insert Media** button in the posting panel.

Determine the Image Target

When Inserting the Image

1 In the Insert Media window, click the **Link To** down arrow (▾).

2 Click **Custom URL**.

Ⓐ Click here to open a blank web page displaying only the full-size image.

Ⓑ Click here to open the image in an attachment page.

Ⓒ Click here to cause no action when the image is clicked.

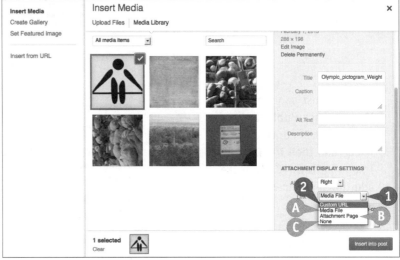

3 Type a target URL.

4 Click **Insert into post**.

WordPress inserts the image and associated URL. You then need to save or update the post. When you publish or preview the post, you can click the image, and it causes your browser to open the specified web page.

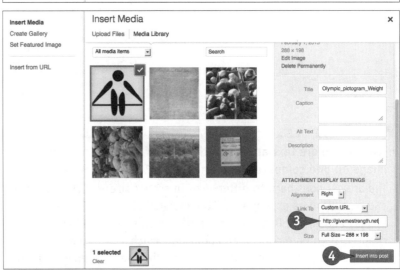

When Editing the Image

1 Click the image.

2 Click the **Edit Image** button (🖼).

The Edit Image window appears.

D The current link target appears.

Note: In this case, the target is the image upload location, the equivalent of the Media File target option in the Insert Image window.

3 Click **None**.

The link target disappears, which means that clicking on the image creates no action.

E This is the equivalent of the Media File option in the Insert Media window, which causes the image to open in a blank web page.

4 Type a target URL in the Link URL box, the equivalent of the Custom URL in the Insert Image window.

5 Click **Update**.

WordPress updates image and associated URL. You then need to save or update the post. When you publish or preview the post, you can click the image, and it causes your browser to open the specified web page.

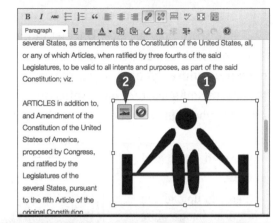

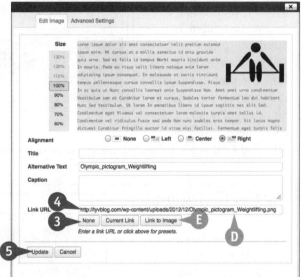

Understanding Unattached Images

WordPress developers continue to work with how the software manages the images you upload and store on your site. Understanding a little of the background may help to avoid potential problems such as accidentally deleting images in use on your site or filling your server storage with numerous unused photos if you run a self-hosted site. The WordPress ways of media handling have simplified some matters but confusion still occurs. The question of unattached images may never arise for you, but if it does, a little knowledge will prepare you.

What an Attached Image Is

When you upload and insert an image while posting, that image is forever associated, or *attached*, to that post. You can delete the image from the post or include it in another post, but as far as WordPress is concerned, it remains attached to the original post unless that post is deleted.

What an Unattached Image Is

An *unattached* image, unsurprisingly, is one that is not attached to a post. An image could be unattached for several reasons. A formerly attached image could become unattached if you delete the post to which it was originally added. An image could be unattached if you upload it directly to the Media Library without ever attaching it to a post. Similarly, images you upload via FTP to your site remain unattached until they are inserted into a post.

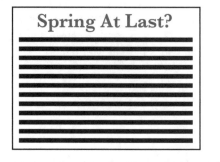

Images and Galleries

You may not think attachment matters, but it does. If you want to add a slide show to your post, for example, the images in the show generally need to be attached to the post. If your post reuses an image attached to another post, that image will not show up in your slide show. The same thing is true for galleries, or collections of images, as described in "Insert an Image Gallery," later in this chapter.

Unattached Does Not Mean Unused

It is important to remember that unattached does not mean unused. As you maintain your blog, you may decide to reduce the load on your server or simply to eliminate clutter in your Media Library by deleting unused photos. Do not make the mistake of identifying and deleting all unattached photos. Here is what can happen. You have a post with an attached photo or two. Meanwhile, you create a new post and insert the same images, using the Media Library. Then you decide to delete the first post. The post goes away, but the images stay in the library as *unattached*. If you delete them from the Media Library based on their being unattached, you in effect delete them from the second post. Also, an image you use for your site's background or header may be unattached even though in use.

Attached Does Not Mean Used

WordPress may create multiple versions of an image when you upload it. These versions fit the thumbnail, medium, and other size options. You do not see each version listed in the Media Library, but they are there, and most probably are attached to a post but not used. At this writing, however, there is no convenient way and no established plugin to identify and delete these extras.

Getting Attached

WordPress provides an easy way to identify unattached images and attach them to posts. The next section in this chapter explains how. You also can use the filter for unattached images to try to identify unused images if you want to delete them. Not all unused images appear in the Media Library, however. You may need to view the contents of the wp-content/uploads folder on your server to see all images stored there.

Attach Images to a Post

When you attach images to a post, you make them readily available for use in galleries and slide shows. WordPress has a convenient way for you to identify unattached photos. You can select the ones that you want to attach, identify the post to which you want to attach them, and soon the images are attached. This technique can be especially useful for you if you prefer to upload images in batches directly to the Media Library or to your host using FTP. WordPress lets you attach media individually or in batches.

Attach Images to a Post

Attach a Single Image

1 Click **Media**.

The Media Library panel opens.

2 Click **Unattached**.

The library filters for unattached images.

3 Position your mouse pointer over an image you want to attach and click the Attach link that appears.

The Find Posts or Pages dialog box appears.

4 Type a search term.

5 Click **Search**.

A list of posts containing the term appears.

6 Click the radio button next to the post to which you want the image attached (○ changes to ◉).

7 Click **Select**.

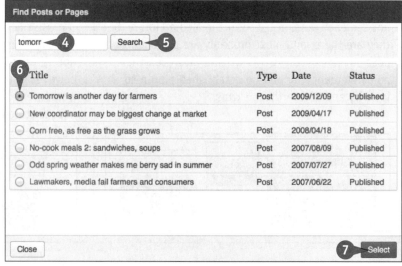

WordPress confirms the attachment, removes the item from the Unattached list, and reduces the number of unattached media.

Attach Multiple Images

1 Click **Media**.

The Media Library panel opens.

2 Click **Unattached**.

The library filters for unattached images.

3 Click the check box next to the images you want to attach to a post (☐ changes to ☑).

4 Click the Bulk Actions drop-down menu, and click **Attach to a post**.

5 Click **Apply**.

The Find Posts or Pages dialog box appears.

6 Type a search term.

7 Click **Search**.

A list of posts containing the term appears.

8 Click the radio button next to the post to which you want the image attached (◯ changes to ◉).

9 Click **Select**.

WordPress confirms the attachment, removes the item from the Unattached list, and reduces the number of unattached media.

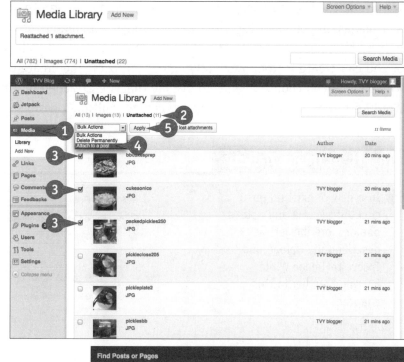

TIP

Once I attach an image, does that mean it appears in the post?

No. Attaching an image associates it with the post in the WordPress software. If you want it to appear in the post, you need to insert it. When you do, you choose the Media Library tab in the Insert Media window. You can choose Uploaded to this post from the drop-down menu to see only media attached to that post.

Insert an Image Gallery

A WordPress image gallery gives you a quick and easy way to display a set of photos or other images on your website. The gallery displays thumbnails of the images, and then you can click individual images to view larger versions. You can create a gallery as you upload images to a post, or you can create it from previously uploaded posts. The Create Gallery option in the Insert Media window lets you choose images to display that are attached or not attached to your post. The WordPress.com version lets you choose among multiple possible gallery views.

Insert an Image Gallery

1 In a new or existing post, click **Add Media** and upload one or more images, as described in "Upload and Insert an Image While Posting," earlier in this chapter.

2 After the images are uploaded, click **Create Gallery**.

A Newly uploaded images have check marks and will be added to gallery.

B Clicking on an image with a check mark changes the mark to a minus sign. Click it if you do not want that image in the gallery.

3 Confirm images for the gallery, and then click **Create a new gallery**.

④ Click and drag images to change their order.

⑤ Click here and type a caption if desired.

⑥ Click **Insert gallery**.

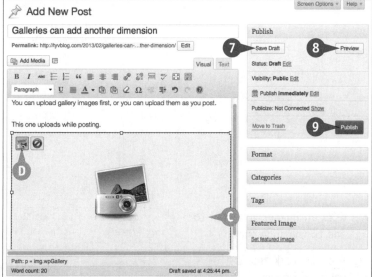

WordPress inserts a gallery placeholder.

ⓒ The gallery placeholder indicates gallery location in your post.

ⓓ The Edit gallery button, visible when you click the gallery placeholder, opens the Edit Gallery window.

⑦ Click **Save Draft**.

⑧ Click **Preview** to view the gallery.

⑨ Click **Publish** when satisfied.

The post with the gallery appears live on your site.

TIPS

What are the WordPress.com display options?
In addition to the default layout, you can choose tiled, square tiled, or circles from the Type drop-down menu in the Edit Gallery window. You can try one, look at the preview, and then change your mind if you like.

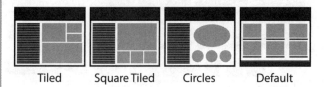

What is the difference in the two Link To gallery settings?
This setting determines how individual images appear when you click them in the gallery. The Attachment Page option opens the image in a separate page using your theme's image attachment template. The Image File option opens the image alone on a blank browser page.

Add a Slide Show to Your Posts

Why limit yourself to an image or two, or even a gallery, if you can have a slide show simply and easily? WordPress recently integrated a slide show option in with its gallery interface, so the setup could not be easier. Self-hosted site owners also have numerous plugins to choose from to create and manage slide shows. The plugins typically provide more options than the built-in slide show, although the built-in version is likely to satisfy the average user. To create a slide show, you start out as you would to create a gallery, and then you choose the Slideshow display option.

Add a Slide Show to Your Posts

1 In a new or existing post, click **Add Media**.

2 Click all images you want to add to the slide show.

A A check mark appears in selected images.

3 Click **Create a new gallery**.

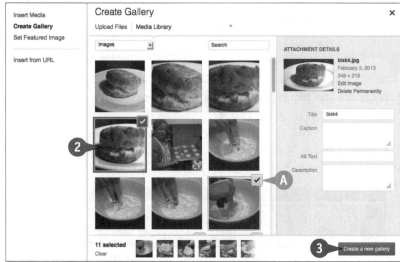

The Edit Gallery window appears.

④ Add captions if desired.

⑤ Click **Slideshow** in the Type drop-down list.

⑥ Click **Insert Gallery**.

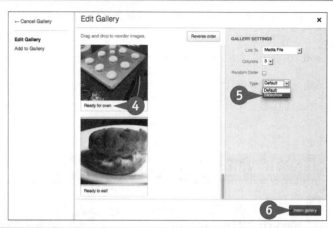

The post window returns with a placeholder (Ⓑ) for the slide show.

⑦ Click **Save Draft**.

⑧ Click **Preview**.

The post preview appears with the active slide show in new tab.

⑨ Click **X** to close the tab.

⑩ Publish or edit the post for future publication.

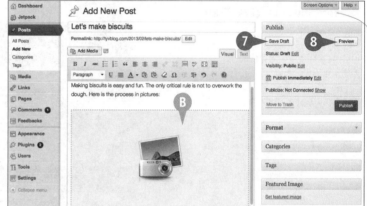

TIPS

How can I change the way the slide show frame looks?

You need to edit the slide show properties on your theme's Cascading Style Sheet, or CSS. At WordPress.com, that requires the Custom Design add-on. Or you can create your show at SlideShare.net, which has other display options, and use the code provided to embed your show on your self-hosted or WordPress.com site.

Can I use a plugin or embed my picture at Picasa or Flickr on my site?

Self-hosted WordPress users have many slide show options. Some plugins provide innumerable options, including timing, display size and color, type styles, and more or are designed specifically to work with photo-sharing sites such as Picasa, Flickr, or Instagram. Go to wordpress.org/extend/plugins and search to find the one that suits your needs.

Link to YouTube and Other Videos

Videos are a little more trouble to deal with than images, but they can add a lot of visual energy to your blog posts. Using embedded videos through links may be the easiest way to get them up and running, and you do not have to use your own host space to store the videos.

You can link to most videos hosted at YouTube.com and at Vimeo.com, and you can upload your own videos there, too.

Link to YouTube and Other Videos

1 After you find the video you want to post on your blog at YouTube.com, click **Share**.

The linking box appears.

2 Click **Embed**.

Ⓐ The embed code appears.

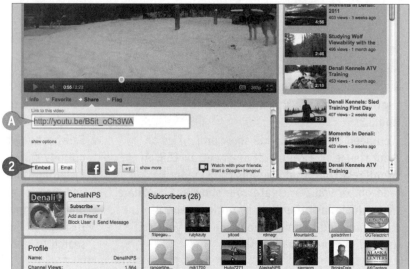

③ Scroll down to see embed options, and make any selections you want.

④ Scroll back up and copy the code.

⑤ Back at your WordPress Dashboard, start a new post, and click the **HTML** tab.

⑥ Click in the post where you want the video to appear, and paste the code you copied from YouTube.com.

⑦ Click **Save Draft** for a new post or **Update** for an existing post.

WordPress saves the post and inserts a placeholder for the video in the visual editor.

⑧ Click **Preview** to see how the video appears on your site.

A preview of your post appears in a new window, where you can click a Play button to view the video.

⑨ Click **Publish** to publish the post on your site.

Note: You can use the same process to embed a video on a page or an existing post.

Do I have to pay for the video add-on to post YouTube videos with WordPress.com?

No, because you are embedding the video rather than hosting the video on your WordPress.com account. The video add-on is required only if WordPress.com is storing and serving your videos.

Is there any other way to link to videos?

You can simply put the video's URL in a separate line in the HTML editor and save it, which is the best bet at WordPress. com. To customize it at WordPress.com, see the instructions at http://en.support.wordpress.com/videos/youtube. Self-hosted bloggers can check for YouTube plugins, explained in Chapter 6, at WordPress.org. Chapter 13 explains more options.

Upload Video Files to Your Host

You have more control over the look and performance of your videos when you host them yourself. Doing so takes a few more steps than when you link to videos posted elsewhere. But, unlike most videos at YouTube, for example, you can show your videos without advertisements appearing along with them.

If your blog is hosted on WordPress.com, your first step is to buy the VideoPress upgrade. That upgrade allows you to upload and store your videos at WordPress.com.

Upload Video Files to Your Host

Basic Installation on a Self-Hosted Blog

1 On the New Post or Edit Post page, click **Add Media**.

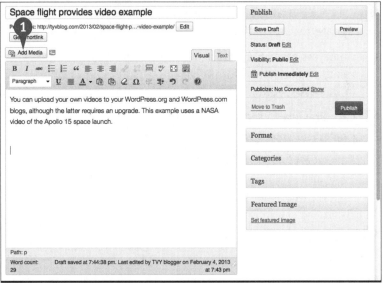

The Insert Media window opens.

2 Click **Upload Files**.

3 Click **Select Files**.

Note: You can drag a file to the upload window if you prefer.

Your browser opens a file selection window, from which you select the video you want to upload and then click **Open**.

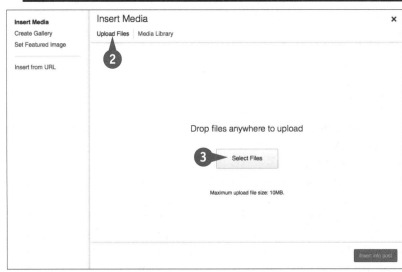

The Insert Media window returns and shows the progress of the upload.

Ⓐ When the upload is complete, details about the video appear.

④ Type a title, which is the text that appears for a link to the video.

⑤ Click **Insert into Post**.

A link to the video file — but no image — appears in your post box.

Full-Featured Installation on WordPress.com

① After clicking **Store** in the left menu panel and then buying the VideoPress upgrade, go to a New Post or Edit Post page, and upload as described in Steps **1** to **5** above for installing video on a self-hosted blog.

A message appears, informing you that your video is being processed and will be ready in a few minutes.

Note: If you use many videos you may also need to purchase a space upgrade.

② While you wait for the video to be processed, go to http://en.support. wordpress.com/videopress to read detailed instructions on setting up your video.

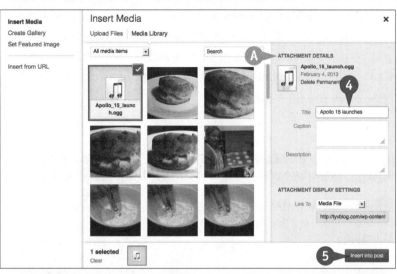

TIPS

Is a link the best I can do for video I store and post on my self-hosted blog?

You can do much better, actually, but it requires use of a plugin. See Chapter 6 for information about plugins, and then search for a video plugin that suits your needs.

I get a message saying that my upload is too big on most videos. On other videos, they take forever to upload. What can I do?

With your self-hosted blog, you can speed things up and avoid that upload limit by uploading files directly to your uploads folder on your web host via FTP, as described in Chapter 3. Unless you have customized your upload folder in your Miscellaneous settings panel, the default uploads folder is wp-content/uploads.

Link to a Podcast or Sound File from Your Blog

With audio files, you can give your readers the sound of your voice, of bird calls, of music. Linking to such files is much like linking to videos, and you also can host them on your site if you do not want to embed or link to audio files. First, you need to find the audio file to which you want to link. Then you upload it, and a very basic audio player appears. Your readers can click it to hear what you have to say.

Link to a Podcast or Sound File from Your Blog

1 From the New Post or Edit Post window, click **Add Media**.

2 The Insert Media window opens, where you click **Insert from URL**.

The window changes to Insert from URL.

3 Type or paste the URL of your chosen audio file into the URL box.

4 Click here and type a title for the audio file. The title provides the link text.

5 Click **Insert into post**.

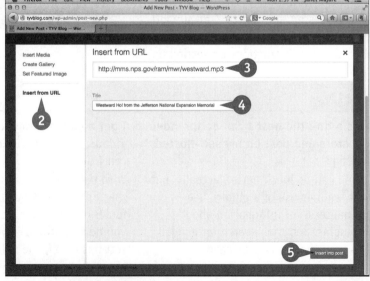

The Insert Media window closes, and a link to the audio file appears in the post box.

6 Click **Save Draft**.

7 Click **Preview**.

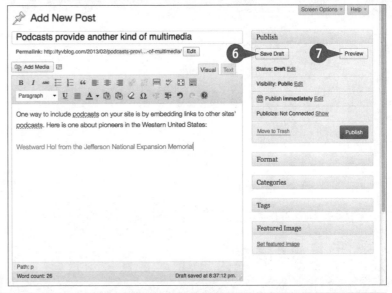

WordPress displays the post in your browser, where you can click the link to hear the sound file.

The sound file opens at its URL and begins playing.

TIPS

Can I host files on my blog so that people do not get transferred to another location?

If your blog is self-hosted, the steps are the same as for uploading a video file described in the previous section, "Upload Video Files to Your Host." Again, you may want to get a plugin, as explained in Chapter 6, so that the player appears on your site rather than a link to the sound file. On a WordPress.com blog, you need to buy an upgrade if you want to upload an audio file or embed music from SoundCloud. See http://en.support. wordpress.com/audio for the options.

Can I make music automatically play in the background?

It is not a good idea; many people object to that audio intrusion. Much better to make the file available and let people choose to listen or not.

CHAPTER 6

Changing a Site's Look and Function

Through the use of themes, or format packages, you can give your WordPress site a look you like and probably can adjust. When you use plugins and widgets, you also get to choose many aspects of how your blog works. The options range from simple to complex.

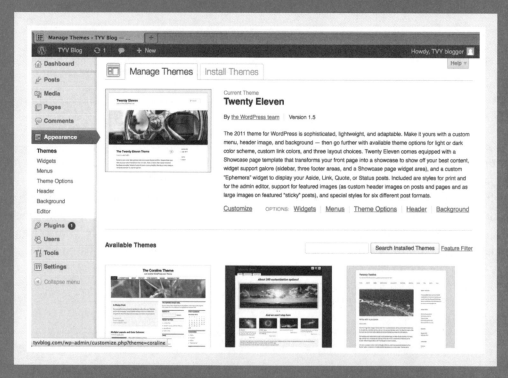

Understanding Themes

Themes dress up your WordPress installation in the visual style that makes it unique. The theme, a sort of visual template, sets your site's color scheme, choice of typeface, and its general layout. Some of the more complex themes may specify added functions, such as automatically creating thumbnail images to display on a front page. You probably can find a theme that looks and behaves exactly as you want it, and you may very well be able to adjust it to your taste. WordPress.org installations come with two basic themes guaranteed to work. At WordPress.com, you chose a theme during the setup process.

Importance of Appearance

Before anyone reads a word on your blog, a reader first notices its overall appearance. Also, once people associate a certain look with your site, the look helps build the blog's identity. Choosing your theme carefully is worthwhile for these two reasons, keeping in mind what kind of first impression you want your blog to make.

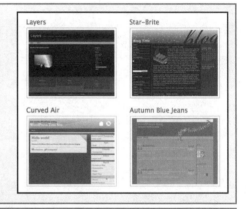

Theme Organization

Consider the purpose and content of your blog. A standard, latest-post-at-the-top blog can use any basic theme that pleases you. If, however, you want to show off artwork, you might search for *portfolio* themes. If you want to highlight multiple posts on your blog's front page, consider *magazine* or *news* themes. Social-network-type blogs need a front-page posting option.

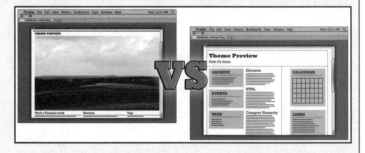

Free Themes

Perhaps the best way to review hundreds of free themes is to go to the Themes Directory at http://wordpress.org/extend/themes. The directory includes users' ratings and comments on free themes, notes about the themes, and theme preview. You can also search from your WordPress Dashboard by clicking **Appearance** in the left menu bar and then using the search function on the Manage Themes page.

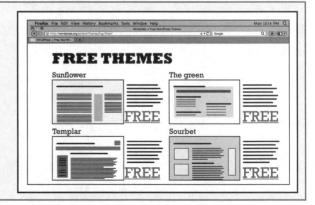

Commercial Themes

Commercial or *premium* themes refer to themes you pay for. The expected advantage of premium themes is that, unlike many free themes, they include ongoing support for theme users, and they keep their themes aligned with updated WordPress versions, although there is rarely a guarantee. These themes do not appear on a self-hosted site's Appearance/Install Themes search, although they do at WordPress.com. If your site is self-hosted you can find links to such commercial themes at http://wordpress.org/extend/themes/commercial or by doing a Google search on *premium themes*.

Custom Themes

In addition to using free and premium themes, you can pay someone to design a theme entirely to your specifications if you have a self-hosted site. If you want a custom theme, it is a good idea to get a designer experienced with WordPress themes. It is also a good idea to get a clear understanding up front as to what you get and what it costs.

Codex

Theme Development

Languages: **English** • 日本語 • Português do Brasil • Русский • 中文(简体) • 中文(繁體)

This article is about developing WordPress Themes. If you wish to learn more a to install and use Themes, review Using Themes. This topic differs from Using because it discusses the technical aspects of writing code to build your own Th rather than how to activate Themes or where to obtain new Themes.

Customize a Theme

Many, if not most, free and premium themes allow you to make at least limited adjustments to them simply by making selections in the theme's options panel within the Dashboard's Appearance menu. Those adjustments often include color changes or custom header images. Some of the basics are covered in this chapter. See Chapter 13 for more.

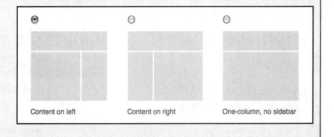

Content on left　　Content on right　　One-column, no sidebar

Try Out Your Theme

As exciting as it is to get your site running, you probably will not have a lot of readers at first. That situation lets you try out a theme or two without upsetting your audience. In this initial phase, get a few posts up and ask people whose opinion you value to comment on your blog's theme. Also, try out its options. If your site is established, you can use a test-drive plugin for WordPress.org users to try out a theme on your site. Look for one at http://wordpress.org/extend/plugins/theme-test-drive.

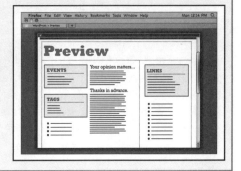

Find and Activate a WordPress.com Theme

You can give your blog a meaningful look by choosing a theme that corresponds with your purpose or personality. WordPress.com gives you more than 200 options, including themes for photo galleries and for social networking blogs. Although you probably chose a theme when you signed up for your WordPress.com blog, it is a good idea early on to revisit your selection. If you are not happy with it, try to find one you like before promoting your site. Consider what first impression you want your site to give: light or dark? Stark or busy? Fixed or *responsive,* meaning it adjusts to the viewer's device? Then find and activate your theme.

Find and Activate a WordPress.com Theme

Find by Browsing

1 Click **Appearance** in the left menu bar.

WordPress opens the Manage Themes page.

A The Manage Themes page lists the current theme and its options.

B A selection of themes appears at the bottom of the page.

C WordPress gives you six ways to browse themes.

2 Scroll down to view the currently displayed themes.

3 Click **Details**.

D A description of the theme appears under the image.

4 Click **Live Preview**.

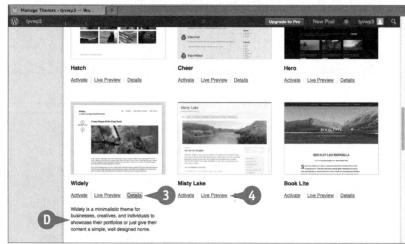

A preview with customization options appears.

Ⓔ Clicking  in any sidebar area expands options to try.

⑤ Click **Try Now**.

The Custom Design area expands.

⑥ Click a palette.

Ⓕ The preview shows the palette in action.

Note: Such changes do not appear on your blog until you purchase the Custom Design upgrade.

⑦ Click **Cancel**.

continued ▶ 183

TIPS

Why do I not see Custom Design in the menu bar of the preview screen?

The options in the preview screen vary according to theme. Not all variables are addressed in the live preview, and some themes offer more options than others do. The preview provides a *general* idea of the possibilities. Sometimes a theme's description gives added clues.

What do the browsing links mean?

They provide different modes of browsing. If you click on each, WordPress displays an explanation of that browsing mode as the top of the themes displayed, say A-Z, or alphabetically. *Trending* indicates themes whose use is growing fast, whereas *Popular* shows the most-used themes. *Friends of WP.com* themes are developed with outside partners.

Find and Activate a WordPress.com Theme (continued)

You can find a WordPress.com theme by browsing or by searching, and WordPress.com offers two ways to search. You can search by keywords, or you can use the Feature Filter to home in on a theme to your liking. When you search by way of your site's Dashboard, WordPress lets you see a preview of your site themes that catch your eye. If you are less interested in a preview and more interested in greater detail, you can go to the WordPress.com themes page, click a theme, and read more information about the theme than is available via your Dashboard.

Find and Activate a WordPress.com Theme (continued)

WordPress returns to the Manage Themes page.

Find by Searching

1 Type a search terms.

2 Click **Search**.

Ⓖ WordPress displays themes that have your keyword assigned to them.

3 Repeat Steps 3 to 7 on the previous page for themes of interest.

4 Click **Feature Filter**.

The theme filters appear at the top of the page.

5 Click the check boxes next to features you want (☐ changes to ☑).

6 Click **Apply Filters**.

WordPress displays themes that meet all the traits you checked.

Note: You may need to scroll down to see the filtered themes.

7 Repeat Steps 4 to 6 for themes of interest.

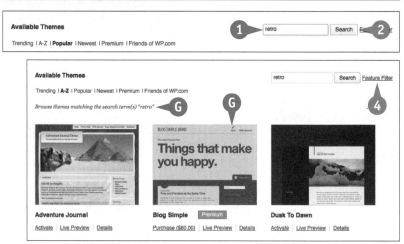

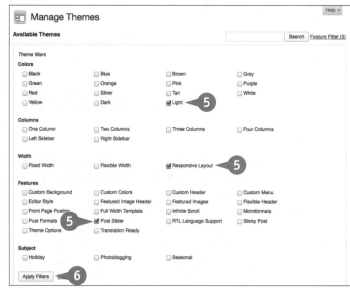

Activate Your Theme

1 Click **Activate** below the theme of your choice.

WordPress activates the theme you chose.

TIPS

Where can I get more details about a theme?
At http://theme.wordpress.com. Although you also can browse and search themes there, a good approach may be to do your initial hunting via the Dashboard, and then go to the WordPress theme page and read the in-depth description of your final picks. The Live Demo there also shows themes in action using all types of headings, pages, and so on.

Do I have to get the Custom Design upgrade?
No. This book mentions it because the upgrade is so prominent in the preview window. If you do like a theme but in a palette available only via the upgrade, then you must buy it to use it. Note that you can activate a theme and then get the Custom Design upgrade later.

Find a WordPress.org Theme

When you seek a theme for your WordPress.org blog, you can choose among more than 1,600 free themes that meet WordPress.org criteria and are searchable from your blog and at WordPress.org. In addition, WordPress.org lists more than 60 commercial theme developers whose themes you must pay for, and uncounted other developers have created WordPress themes. You get more information more easily by finding your theme via the WordPress.org themes pages at http://wordpress.org/extend/themes. Then you can install your chosen theme from your administration panels.

Find a WordPress.org Theme

① Type **http://wordpress.org/extend/themes/browse/popular** in your web browser address bar, and then press **Enter** (**Return** on a Mac).

② Scroll down to see the most popular themes as determined by download numbers.

Ⓐ The average user rating appears here.

③ Click a theme thumbnail.

The theme's page opens.

Ⓑ The number of ratings at each rating level appears here.

Ⓒ You can click here to link to forum where you can see questions and answers about the theme.

④ Click **Preview**.

The theme preview window appears.

5 Scroll down to see a sample of how the theme's main page appears with some sample posts.

6 Click tabs to view other display aspects of the theme.

7 Click the **X** (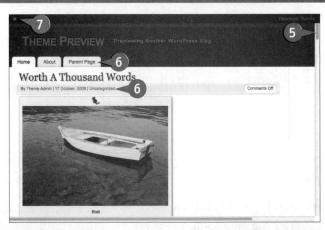).

The theme's page reappears.

8 Go to http://wordpress.org/ extend/themes.

9 Type a search term.

10 Click **Search Themes**.

Themes appear that use the term either in their name or descriptions.

11 Repeat Steps 3 to 7.

12 Record the names of two or three themes you want to try.

TIPS

With so many theme sources, how do I know what is best?

It is hard to know. For free themes, stick with themes listed at WordPress.org, read user reviews there, see whether the theme is up to date, and view the WordPress.org forums and the theme's home page to see what problems arise and how well the developer or community addresses them. For commercial themes, their acceptance at WordPress.com is a good recommendation.

Are there other ways to find themes?

You can use the filter interface, at http:// extend.wordpress.org/themes/tag-filter. The Commercial link on the Themes Directory page shows providers of *commercial*, or paid, themes. You also can find themes from your Dashboard. Click **Appearance** and then click the **Install Themes** tab at the top of the themes panel.

Install and Activate a WordPress.org Theme

You can install and activate most free themes more easily than you can change your clothes. Installing commercial themes is only slightly more involved. With your new theme, you are ready to make your first impression. This section assumes you have already chosen a theme by following the guidance in the preceding section.

Install and Activate a WordPress.org Theme

Automatic Installation

1 Click **Appearance** in the left menu bar.

The Manage Themes panel opens and displays the two standard WordPress themes.

A Twenty Twelve is installed by default.

B Twenty Eleven is also available in the standard installation.

2 Click **Install Themes**.

The Install Themes panel opens.

3 Type the name of your chosen theme in the search box.

4 Click **Search**.

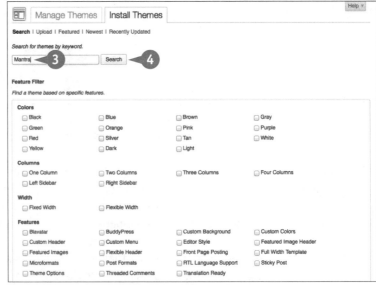

The Install Theme panel displays the designated theme.

5 Click **Install Now**.

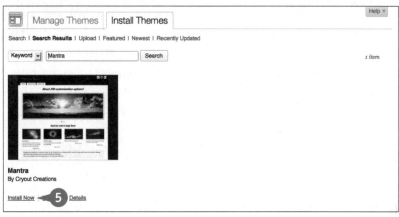

WordPress displays installation progress as it installs the theme.

6 Click **Activate** to make the theme active.

WordPress activates the theme.

C Your newly active theme appears at the top of the Manage Themes panel.

D Depending on the theme, you may have an options panel, and WordPress may display it rather than the Manage Themes panel.

TIPS

My theme does not look the way I expected. Why is that?

You may need to have more content. Or, as themes have become more complex, they may require you to select various theme options to get the expected look. Read the theme's home page for guidance. Find it by going to Wordpress.org/extend/themes for free themes, or to the vendor's home page for premium themes.

What if I have questions about my theme?

The first place to check is the theme designer's website. Designers usually include a link to their site in the footer of their themes, and, if you got the theme at Wordpress.org, you will find a link on the theme's page there. If you have no luck, try the WordPress Codex or the forums at WordPress.org, discussed in Chapter 10.

continued ▶

You can have a broader array of theme options if you get a theme, such as a commercial theme, available outside of WordPress.org. One of the many attractive themes available may be closer to the look you want, but themes not listed at WordPress.org may require manual installation. The manual installation method works for all themes. You may prefer to use it if you have a slow Internet connection, or if you just like to be in control of every step of the process. Perhaps you downloaded a theme or two when you reviewed it at WordPress.org. In any case, the process is straightforward.

Install and Activate a WordPress.org Theme (continued)

Manual Installation

① Download the theme you have chosen from the Wordpress.org or the developer's site, and save it to your computer.

ⓔ Do not extract it; leave it as a Zip file.

② Click **OK** in the download window.

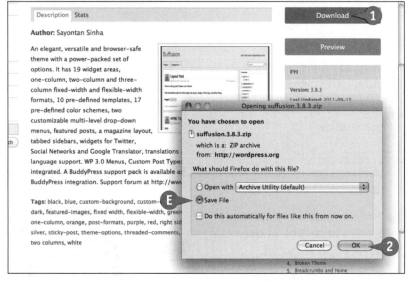

③ On the Install Themes panel — which you reach by clicking **Appearance** in the Dashboard's left menu bar and clicking the **Install Themes** tab — click **Upload**.

A new version of the Install Themes panel opens.

④ Click **Browse**, and find the theme on your computer.

Your computer's File Upload window, or the equivalent, opens. When you locate the theme's Zip file, click **Open**.

The file location appears in the box next to Browse.

⑤ Click **Install Now**.

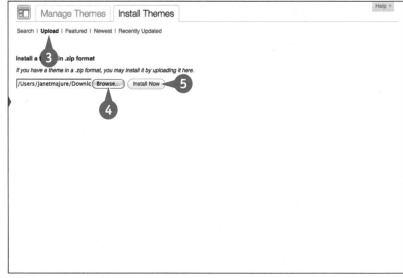

WordPress lists the progress of your installation.

⑥ When the theme is successfully installed, click **Activate**.

The Manage Themes panel opens with the new theme activated, or it may take you directly to the theme's options panel.

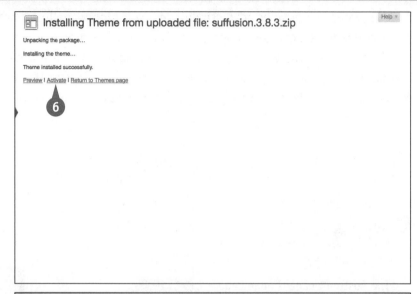

When Uploading from Install Themes Panel Does Not Work

① After downloading your theme, extract the file, and upload the extracted folder with your FTP software to the themes folder inside the wp-content folder at your web host. Then go to the Manage Themes panel to activate it.

Note: Check inside the extracted theme folder for a ReadMe.txt file, which may have additional installation instructions.

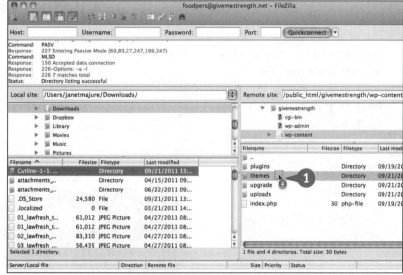

TIPS

A bunch of gibberish appears on my screen when I click Activate. What happened?
There is a good chance the theme was activated anyway. Click **Themes** in the left menu bar and see if your theme appears as the current theme. If not, try clicking **Preview** under the theme image, and then **Activate** in the preview window.

Can I install more than one theme at a time?
Yes. To do so, follow the directions for installation when your WordPress site's Upload feature did not work. Use your FTP software to upload the extracted theme folder for each of them to the wp-content folder at your host. Then go to your WordPress administration panels to activate one.

Customize Your Header Art with a Built-in Tool

Using your own header art distinguishes your blog visually from others that use the same theme. The header art can be a photo, drawing, or other graphic. You can find themes with a built-in tool by using the Custom Header option when searching for a theme. Using your own header art may be one of the easiest ways to make your site unique. This example uses the Twenty Eleven theme for WordPress.com or WordPress.org blogs. The process is basically the same, though, for most themes.

Customize Your Header Art with a Built-in Tool

Use Your Own Header Art

1 With your theme activated, click **Header** under Appearance in the left menu bar.

The Custom Header Image page opens.

2 In the Upload Image section, click **Browse** to find the image on your computer that you want in your header, and click **Open** in your browser's window to choose it.

A The file location appears in the box.

3 Click **Upload**.

The image is uploaded to your web host.

4 Stretch, shrink, or drag the crop box to crop the image.

5 Click **Crop and Publish** when you are satisfied.

Note: You can repeat Steps 2 to 4 and upload multiple header images.

WordPress confirms the update, and the new header image is published to your blog.

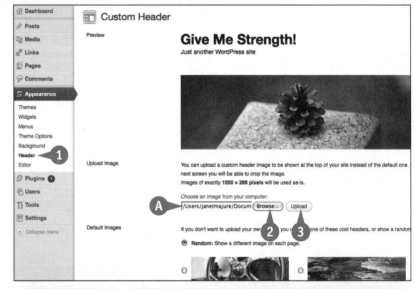

Choose Display Options

1 On the Custom Header panel, scroll down to reveal all available images.

B A selected radio button (◉) indicates the active header image.

2 Click the **Random** radio button (○ changes to ◉) to have WordPress display a different image on different pages.

3 Scroll to the bottom of the page.

4 Click **Select Color**.

A color selection tool opens.

5 Click a color.

C The range of colors with and without black added to them appears.

6 Click and drag the slider to adjust the hue's *tint* or *tone* — that is, the amount of white or gray added.

7 Click and drag the circle to adjust hue or to change the *shade*, or the amount of black.

Note: Scrolling to the top of the page reveals a preview of the text color.

8 Click **Save Changes** to save the text color to your site.

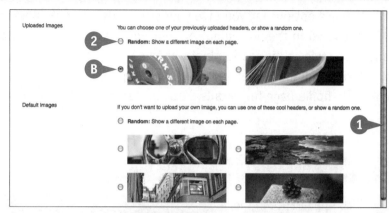

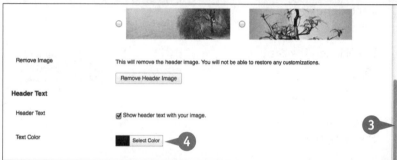

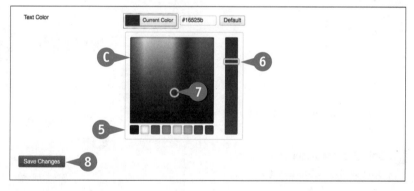

TIPS

I do not like the way my image looks after it was resized for the header. Any suggestions?
To get the results you want, use a paint program or image editor to create your header image, and make it the size specified on the custom header page. You have more control that way.

I do not see a Header or Custom Header option under Appearance.
Different themes use different terminology, but the process is essentially the same. The popular Suffusion theme, for example, does not have a Header panel under Appearance, but if you click **Suffusion Options**, **Skinning**, and then **Header**, you will find more than a dozen options for your custom header. You may need to experiment, or go to your theme's home page for help.

Identify and Use Your Theme's Options

A theme's options let you give your site a custom look. Besides simple header image changes discussed in the preceding section, options may include changing colors, sidebar arrangements, and type styles. This section looks at the Twenty Eleven theme, available on both WordPress.com and WordPress.org and one of the WordPress.org default themes. Your theme may vary in its approach; check its home page for details. You can learn about more complex theme options in Chapter 13.

Identify and Use Your Theme's Options

1 Click **Appearance** in the left menu bar of your administration panels.

The Manage Themes panel appears.

2 Click **Theme Options**.

A Here is another link to the Theme Options panel.

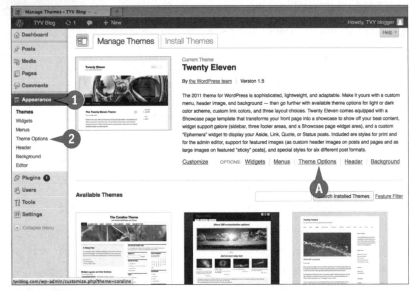

The Theme Options panel opens.

3 Select a color scheme radio button (⦾ changes to ⦿).

4 Click **Select a Color** to change the Link Color from the default.

A color selector pops up.

5 Click in the circle to choose the hue; click in the square to choose the intensity.

6 When you are satisfied, click in the main window.

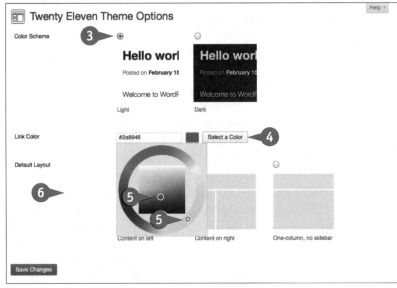

The color selector disappears.

B You can click the **Default color** link if you want to restore the default color.

7 Click a radio button to select a layout (○ changes to ●).

8 Click **Save Changes**.

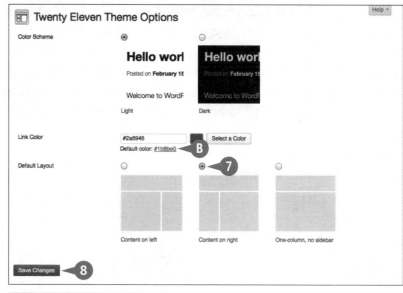

WordPress confirms that the changes have been saved.

Can I use the Customize link on the Manage Themes panel to do the same thing?

Yes. When you click **Customize**, the preview panel opens. You can click **Colors** (**C**) to change the color scheme, link color, and background color and image, which are discussed in the next section, "Change the Background." Under the Layout portion (**D**), you can choose the content configuration. Click **Save & Publish** when you are done. The Customize panel lets you see the effects of changes as you try them and puts many options in one location. The panel is not especially helpful for all themes, however.

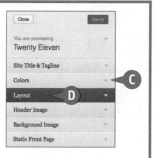

Change the Background

You can change the background color or even place an image or pattern in the background of most WordPress themes. In most cases, the *background* is the area around or behind the posts and sidebars of your theme. Although it is possible in many cases to change the background color or image through the Customize screen available from the Manage Themes panel, using the Background panel arguably has an easier interface. This example uses the Twenty Eleven theme, which is available for both WordPress.com and WordPress.org installations.

Change the Background

Change the Background Color

1 Click **Background** under Appearance in the left menu bar.

The Custom Background panel appears.

2 Click **Select Color**.

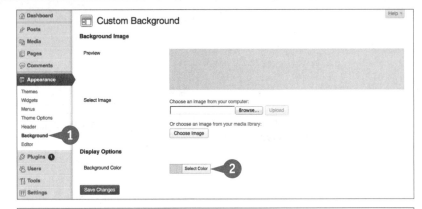

A color selector appears.

3 Click and drag the circle to the desired hue and *shade*, which is the hue plus black.

4 Click and drag the slider to adjust the *tint* or *tone*, the amount of white or gray in the hue.

Ⓐ The new color appears here.

5 Click **Save Changes**.

WordPress saves the new background color.

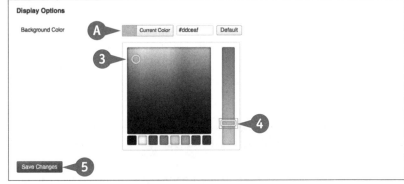

Place a Background Image

1. Click **Browse**.

   A File Upload window appears.

2. Click the image you want.

3. Click **Open**.

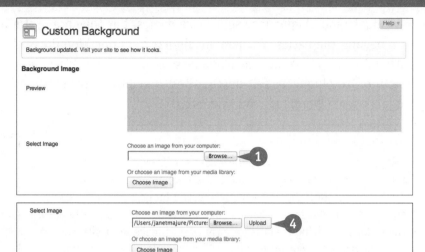

The file location appears in the box.

4. Click **Upload**.

   WordPress uploads the image and updates the background.

Ⓑ A repeating, or *tiled,* pattern of your uploaded image appears.

5. Click **Visit your site** to see the background live on the page.

Ⓒ A Remove Background Image button appears, which you can click to remove the background.

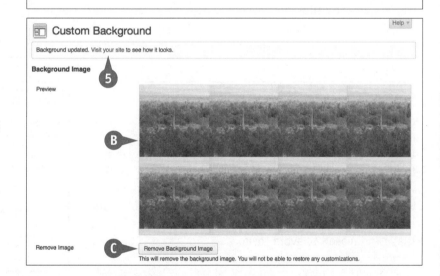

TIPS

My background image looks terrible and I cannot read the text. Can I have a background that goes around the text?

You can choose a theme that, in effect, puts the background around the content areas, as does Twenty Eleven. If you do not want to change the theme, edit your image and significantly reduce the opacity of the background.

What are the display options — Position, Repeat, and Attachment — that appeared after I uploaded my background image?

Those control how your background image *tiling,* or background piecing, works. The Customization panel — click **Customize** under the theme on the Manage Themes panel — works well to try the Position and Repeat settings. The Attachment setting determines whether the background remains *fixed,* or unmoving, or whether it *scrolls,* or moves, as you scroll the page.

Introducing Widgets and Plugins

Widgets and plugins may sound like games, but they are useful bits of code that extend your blog beyond the basics. Widgets are similar from one WordPress blog to the next, but plugins are optional and not available at WordPress.com. However, WordPress.com offers certain widgets that function like plugins at self-hosted sites. Similarly, a set of plugins called *Jetpack* give self-hosted bloggers some WordPress.com widgets.

Widgets for Sidebars

Widget is the term that WordPress uses for items that appear in the sidebars of your blog — and sometimes in other locations such as the footer. Both hosted and self-hosted blogs come with a few standard widgets. If your theme supports widgets, and nearly all of them do, organizing them is an easy way to make your site easier to navigate and more informative. Plan to make setting up your widgets an early site-improvement task.

Plugins for Everything

Plugins, available only on self-hosted blogs, are like miniprograms that do lots of things, from adding buttons to your post box interface to installing a media player so that you can play your own photo gallery, podcasts, and videos. Plugins can serve ads, increase your search-engine visibility, point out frequent commenters, and do lots, lots more. Now and then, though, they can cause problems, but that is no reason to avoid them.

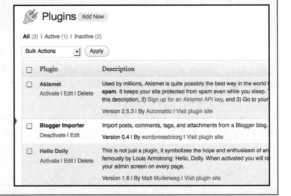

Standard Widgets at Self-Hosted Blogs

At this writing, self-hosted blogs generally have widgets to display a monthly archive of posts, a calendar, blog categories, a custom menu, a *meta* section for logging in and other tasks, a list of static pages, a display of recent comments, a list of recent posts, the RSS feed of your choice, a search box, a tag cloud, and text widgets, which give lots of options, such as for images and HTML. Sometimes, a theme adds another widget or two.

Standard Widgets for WordPress.com Blogs

WordPress.com does not allow users to upload and install plugins, but the host makes up for it in large part by having numerous widgets in addition to most of those included on self-hosted blogs. You can add any of the widgets to your sidebar just by following some simple directions, which the next section describes.

Related
Akismet Widget
Archives Widget
Author Grid Widget
Authors Widget
Blog Stats Widget
Box.net Widget
Calendar Widget
Categories Widget
Custom Menu Widget
Custom Theme Widgets
Delicious Widget
Flickr Widget

WordPress.com Widgets and What They Do

The following WordPress.com widgets are in addition to those that are standard on self-hosted blog installations. At http://en.support.wordpress.com/widgets/ you can find links to full descriptions and configuration instructions.

WordPress.com Added Widgets	
Widget	**What It Does**
Akismet	Displays how many comments spam catcher caught.
Author Grid	Shows a grid filled with author avatars.
Authors	Shows capsule information about all authors on your blog.
Blogs I Follow	Highlights blogs in your WordPress.com Reader.
Delicious	Displays your Delicious bookmarks according to your settings.
Flickr	Displays photos based at Flickr.com.
Follow Blog	Lets readers sign up to get your posts by e-mail.
Gravatar	Shows your Gravatar image plus text.
Image	Lets you easily display an image in a sidebar.
Links	Displays your favorite links.
RSS Links	Provides links for readers to sign up for your RSS feed or feeds.
Top Clicks	Lists blog links that get the most clicks.
Top Posts & Pages	Lists posts that get the most views.
Top Rated	Lists posts or pages that have the highest reader ratings.
Twitter	Displays your tweets.
Other	Others change periodically but include About.me, Blog Stats, GoodReads, Milestone for a date countdown, My Community showing your blog users, Posts I Like, BandPage, Box.net File Sharing, and Gravatar Profile.

Choose and Insert Widgets

You can add or remove widgets any time you want after you have your blog running. Widgets make it easy to add sidebar features on your blog. Take advantage of them! Depending on the theme you have in place, you may have widget areas above or below your site's main content area, not just in sidebars. The process for adding widgets to those areas is the same regardless of where the widget area appears on the page. If you change themes, your old widgets become inactive, and you will need to place them in the desired widget areas.

Choose and Insert Widgets

1 In the left menu bar, click **Appearance** to expand the Appearance menu.

2 Click **Widgets** to open the Widget panel, which lists available widgets in alphabetical order.

Ⓐ This is the primary widgets module.

Ⓑ These modules are for each available widget area.

3 Use the scroll bar or page-down until you see a widget you want to add, such as the Search widget.

4 Click and hold on the **Search** widget until ꕥ changes to ✊.

5 Drag the Search widget to the sidebar list.

When the widget reaches the list, a dotted line appears under the sidebar label indicating that you can release the mouse button.

Note: The sidebar area needs to be expanded, not collapsed, to accept the widget. Click the arrow (▼) to expand the sidebar area.

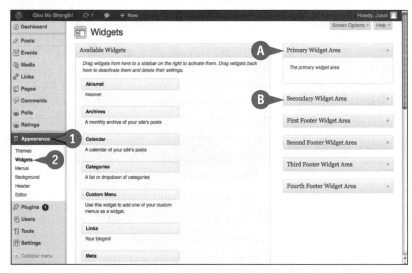

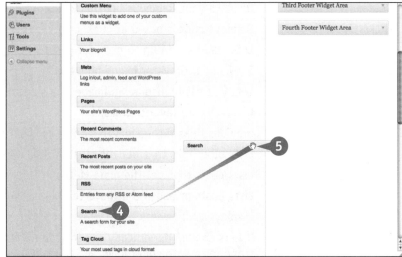

C You can type a title for your Search widget in the title box.

Note: Widget titles are usually optional.

6 Click **Save**.

Note: Options for each widget may vary from one theme to the next. If your widget has no options, simply dragging it to the sidebar is all you need to do.

7 Click your blog's name to see your widget in action.

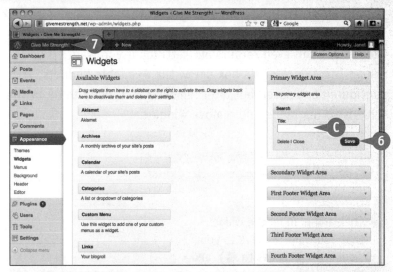

D The Search widget appears in the sidebar.

8 Click the **Back** button (◀) to return to the Widgets panel, where you can add more widgets to your sidebars.

TIPS

After I installed my first widget and looked at it on the site, the archives box that appeared when I installed my theme was no longer there. What did I do wrong?

Not a thing. Themes may display widgets as part of their installation. Those widgets probably are not listed as active on your Widgets panel, however. Once you configure your first widget, the default widgets may go away. You replace them the same way you installed your first widget.

Why do I have more widgets than the standard ones?

Many themes have additional widgets. It just means your theme's developer automated more functions for you. Try them out. If you install plugins, as discussed later in this chapter, they also may add widgets.

Rearrange and Remove Widgets

Another great thing about widgets is that they are as easy to remove as they are to add, which makes experimenting with different arrangements a simple task. You can rearrange and remove widgets — and even retain your settings if you want. If you scroll down the Widgets panel, you can see an Inactive Widgets box below the Available Widgets. That is where you can find widgets you configured and saved but later removed. You need to be in the Widgets panel of your administrative screens to rearrange and remove widgets.

Rearrange and Remove Widgets

Rearrange Widgets

1. Click and hold on the widget that you want to move to your sidebar (⬆ changes to ✊), and then drag the widget to the position you want it to have in your sidebar.

2. When a rectangle with a dotted line appears at the desired location, release the mouse button.

   The widget appears in its new position in the sidebar.

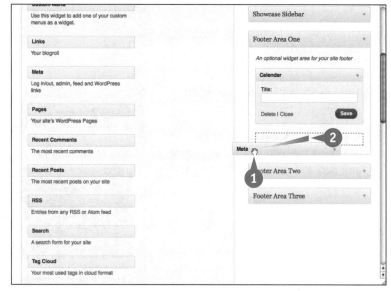

Remove a Widget and Retain Its Settings

1. Click the widget you want to deactivate, and drag it to the Inactive Widgets module in the lower portion of the Widgets panel.

2. Release the mouse button when the dotted box appears. WordPress keeps the title you assigned to the widget.

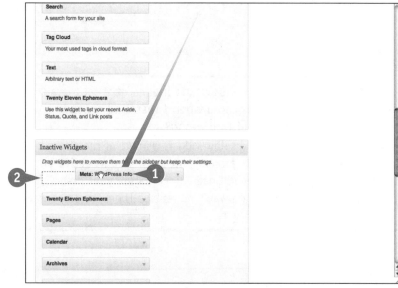

Remove a Widget without Retaining Its Settings

1. Click and hold the widget you want to remove (➤ changes to ✋). Drag the widget to the Available Widgets box of the Widgets panel and release the mouse button.

Ⓐ A deactivate message appears at the top of the Available Widgets box, and the widget disappears from the Sidebar box.

Reactivate a Saved Widget

1. Click and hold the mouse button on the widget you want to reactivate (➤ changes to ✋).

2. Drag the widget to the widget module, and then release the mouse button when a dotted-line rectangle appears in the location where you want the widget.

The widget reappears in the module's widget list.

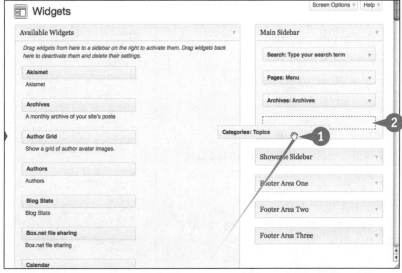

TIPS

I am having trouble dragging the widgets around. Any suggestions?
Yes. Expand the Screen Options on the Widgets panel, and click the **Enable accessibility mode** link. After you do, each Available widget has an Add link, and each Active and Inactive widget has an Edit link. Click those links to open subpanels to add, configure, edit, or reorganize your widgets.

Why do my widgets appear only on my front page?
Different themes vary in their widget displays. Some limit them to the front page or static pages. Others have some, but not all, widgets appear on individual post pages. If you want them to appear on every screen of your blog, you may need to search for a theme that uses widgets in that way.

Add Sidebar Items Using HTML in a Text Widget

Among the many widgets WordPress themes offer is one innocuously titled Text. And, yes, you can use it to show, say, a favorite quote or a bio about yourself in a sidebar. But you also can use it to insert more complex additions that use HTML. Note that you cannot use Javascript and similar code at WordPress.com, however. You can use multiple Text widgets.

Add Sidebar Items Using HTML in a Text Widget

Add a Basic Text Widget

Ⓐ After you click and drag a Text widget to a sidebar, a large configuration box appears.

① Type a title in the Title box.

② Type text in the text box.

③ Click **Save**.

The text appears in the sidebar location you selected, using the formatting specified in your theme's style sheet.

④ Click **Close** to collapse the configuration box.

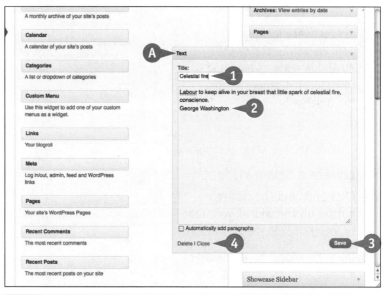

Change Text Widget Format

① Type simple HTML tags around text you want to format, in this case `<em>` and `</em>` around the text to put it in italics and `<p style="text-align: right;">` to align the last line right.

② Click **Automatically add paragraphs** (☐ changes to ☑) to have WordPress start a new paragraph when you press Enter.

③ Click **Save**.

Your formatting is saved and appears on the blog's sidebar.

Note: Your theme's style sheet may override some HTML styling.

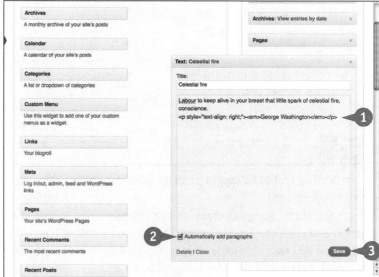

Add Functional Content via Text Widgets

① Go to http://yowindow.com/ weatherwidget.php in your web browser.

② Provide the information requested.

Note: If you do not know the desired window size, use the default and change it later.

③ Scroll or page-down to complete all the requested information.

④ Choose a publishing option (○ changes to ⦿), using **Any website or blog** for self-hosted sites, or **WordPress** if your site is at WordPress.com.

Ⓑ YoWindow supplies code that fits your information.

⑤ Click in the code box, which selects the code, and copy the code using your browser's Edit menu or by pressing Ctrl+C (⌘+C on a Mac).

Paste that code into your Text widget and save. The Weather widget for your blog appears in your sidebar.

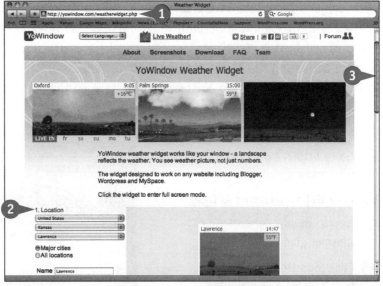

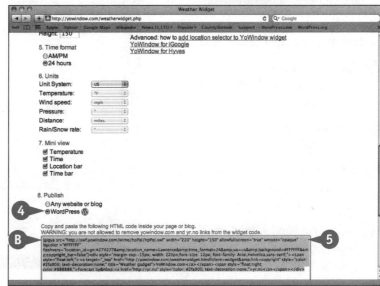

Get a Key and Activate Akismet

adly, junk producers have created junk comments just like junk e-mail. Happily, WordPress has the
Akismet antispam feature built in. WordPress.com bloggers have the service running by default.
Users of self-hosted WordPress blogs must take an extra steps for Akismet to work for them. Those steps
involve activating the Akismet plugin and getting an API, or *application programming interface,* key.
Activating and configuring Akismet is definitely worth the trouble to avoid a deluge of spam comments.

Get a Key and Activate Akismet

1. Go to http://Akismet.com/
wordpress in your browser.

2. Click **Get an Akismet API** key.

   A new window opens listing
   Akismet plan options.

3. Click **Sign Up** under Personal,
   which opens a new window.

   Note: Click one of the other Sign Up
   buttons if you have a commercial site.

4. Type your first name and last
   name in the First Name and Last
   Name boxes.

5. Type your e-mail address in the
   two e-mail boxes.

6. Move the slider to show how much
   you want to pay for the service;
   zero is an option for personal sites.

   Ⓐ Links take you to the service's
   terms and conditions and privacy
   policy.

7. Click **Continue**.

   Akismet sends an API key to your
   e-mail address. A confirmation
   screen appears if you made a
   contribution of zero. Otherwise,
   you first see and complete a
   payment screen before getting
   confirmation.

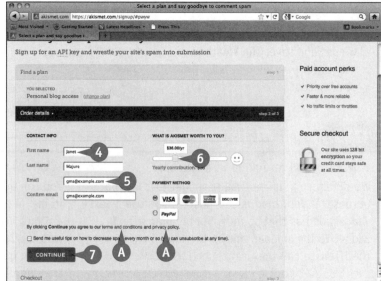

8 After getting your API key from your e-mail, log on to your blog's Dashboard, and click **Plugins**.

The Plugins menu expands, and the Manage Plugins panel opens to reveal installed plugins.

9 Click **Activate** in the Akismet section.

The Plugins panel alerts you that the plugin is activated and prompts you to enter your API key.

10 Click **enter your Akismet API key**.

The Akismet Configuration panel opens.

Ⓑ The Akismet Configuration panel includes instructions on how Akismet works.

11 Paste or type your API key in the API Key box.

12 If desired, click here to discard spam comments after a month (☐ changes to ☑).

13 Click **Update options**.

WordPress confirms that your options are saved.

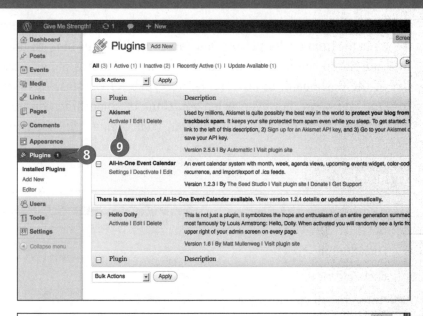

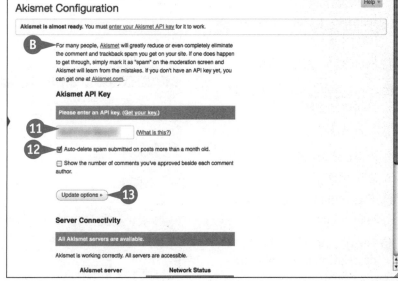

TIPS

How will I know if Akismet has caught any spam comments?
A count of comments in the spam comment queue appears at the top of the Edit Comments panel, which you reach by clicking **Comments** in the left menu bar of the Dashboard. You can see the comments by clicking the Spam link there. You also can click **Akismet Stats** under the Dashboard item in the left menu bar to see charts and tables about the spam that has been captured.

Does Akismet ever catch comments that are not spam?
Rarely, but it does happen, which is why checking the junk comments listing periodically is a good practice.

Find Plugins

Plugins provide all sorts of functions for your self-hosted WordPress blog besides those that are built in, from media players you can embed in your blog to post and comment rating systems and lots more. You can investigate plugins from the Plugins panel, accessible via Plugins in the left menu bar of the Dashboard, or at WordPress.org/extend/plugins. At first, you may not know what to search for. You will know, however, when you think of something you do on your blog that you want to automate or think of some function that your theme does not handle well.

Find Plugins

Find Plugins via the Plugins Panel

1. Click **Plugins**.

2. Click **Add New**.

Ⓐ In the Install Plugins panel, you can find plugins that are featured, popular, new, or your favorites at WordPress.org.

Ⓑ Search for plugins here.

Ⓒ A tag cloud reveals popular plugin tags.

3. Click a link or do a search.

A list of the plugins that fit your selection appears.

Ⓓ The rating from plugin users appears here.

Ⓔ The list includes a brief description of the plugin.

Ⓕ A link to the plugin developer's home page appears here.

4. Click **Details**.

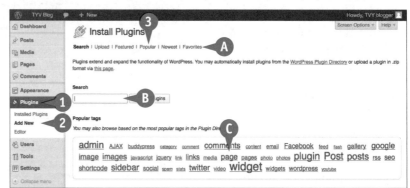

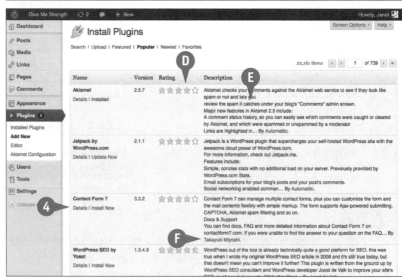

An information window opens.

5 Read the detailed description.

G More information is available on other tabs.

6 Click the **WordPress.org Plugin Page** link.

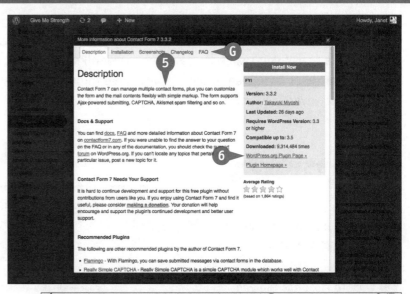

The WordPress.org Plugin Directory opens in a new tab to the plugin page you selected.

7 Scroll down to the Support area.

8 Click **View support forum**.

H In the Compatibility area, you can see whether the plugin works with the current version of WordPress.

TIPS

What should I look for, exactly, on the plugin page?

Look at the number of downloads, the ratings, and the number of ratings. A plugin that has been downloaded 400 times and has an average rating of 5 stars — but has only been rated once — may be great, but there is no way of knowing based on so little data.

Should I worry if only very few plugin forum topics are marked as resolved?

Probably not. The original creator of a forum topic is the only one who can mark a topic as resolved, and many forum users forget to do so even when they get good answers. You are better off to read a few of the forum threads to see if questions get answered promptly.

You can find plugins from your site or at WordPress.org. The two search approaches are slightly different. You may prefer one or the other, or you may like to use a combination of both. One difference is that if you search by a keyword at WordPress.org, you can sort the result by relevance, age, popularity, or rating, an option not available through your installations plugin page. Searching via your site, however, may make for quicker browsing. Try them both, and see which works best for you.

Find Plugins (continued)

9 Click a topic or two and read what problems and praise others have made about the plugin.

10 Click to close the tab and return to the information window.

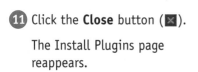

11 Click the **Close** button ( ).

The Install Plugins page reappears.

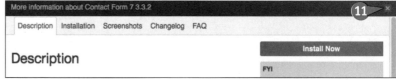

Find Plugins via the WordPress.org Directory

1 In your browser, go to http://wordpress.org/extend/plugins.

I Click **More** to open the tags cloud.

J Click **Most Popular** to browse the most popular plugins.

2 Type a search term.

3 Click **Search Plugins**.

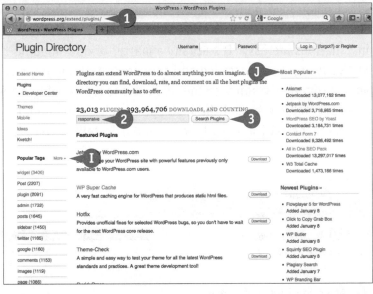

Search results appear.

K Click a radio button (○ changes to ◉) to sort the results by relevance or other options.

4 Click a plugin title.

The plugin page opens.

5 Repeat Steps 7 to 9 to review.

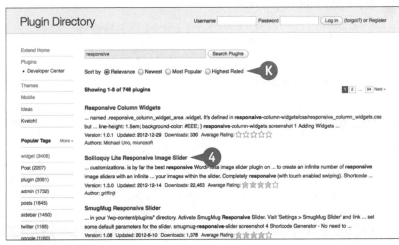

TIPS

Why do I need to read plugin details before I install a plugin?

As helpful as plugins are, they also can cause problems. Some plugins may conflict with other plugins, for example, or a plugin may not work on the version of WordPress that you are running. By doing a little research first, you can avoid headaches.

Where can I read plugin reviews?

On the plugin's page at WordPress.org, you can click the **Reviews** tab to see a listing of all reviews. You also can click the rating in the ratings area — click **5 stars**, for example, to read what people said who rated the plugin with 5 stars.

Install and Activate a Plugin

Once you identify the plugins that you need — or simply want — installing them is easy. Most plugins can be installed with a few clicks from the Add Plugins panel, but even manual installations are easy. It's usually a matter of downloading the plugin and uploading it using your FTP software. Once installed and activated, each plugin may have other settings and operations that you configure according to the instructions on the plugin's information screens. It is a good idea before installing to read the Installation tab on the plugin page at WordPress.org to see if there is anything special you need to know about installing that plugin.

Install and Activate a Plugin

Install and Activate a Plugin from the Add Plugins Panel

① After you find your chosen plugin in the Add Plugins panel, click **Install Now**.

A confirmation window appears.

② Click **OK**.

The Installing Plugin panel appears.

③ After Successfully installed appears in the Installing Plugin panel, click **Activate Plugin**.

Ⓐ The Plugins panel appears and confirms the activation. You now can use or configure the plugin according to the instructions provided on the plugin information pages.

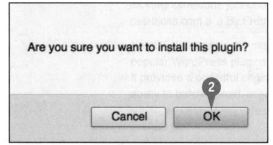

Install a Plugin Manually

1 After you find the plugin's page in the WordPress Plugin Directory, click **Download Version**.

A download window appears.

2 Click **Save File**.

Your browser downloads and saves the Zip file, which you need to extract.

3 After extracting the Zip file, connect to your site using your FTP client or web host FTP panel, and click the extracted plugin folder on your computer.

4 Drag or copy that folder to the plugins folder, or directory, in your blog's wp-content directory.

The plugin is installed.

5 Go to the Plugins panel, and click **Activate** under the plugin name. If you had the panel open during the upload, refresh the page for the plugin to appear.

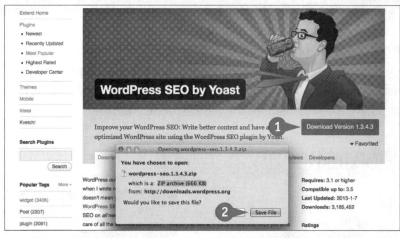

TIPS

I installed my plugin, but it does not seem to be working. What do I do?

First, make sure you activated it on the Plugins panel. If you have, then click **Visit plugin site** in the plugin's listing on the Manage Plugins panel for more information. The plugin also may have added items to your Dashboard's left menu bar. Check to see if it has any settings there you need to address.

The plugin I installed has a notice and link about donating money for the plugin. What is that about?

Individuals develop plugins and make them available for free to WordPress users, and many developers ask for donations. Giving money is optional, but it is a good way to ensure that developers maintain their plugins and develop new ones as the need arises.

Deactivate and Delete a Plugin

You can easily deactivate or delete a plugin that gives you trouble, no longer serves your purpose, or turns out to be something different from what you expect. The process could not be easier. You simply identify the plugin on your Plugins panel, and click **Delete**. You can delete multiple plugins at one time if you want. If you delete a plugin, you lose any settings you may have done with the plugin should you change your mind and want to reinstall it. Therefore, before you delete a plugin entirely, be certain you no longer want it.

Deactivate and Delete a Plugin

1 Click **Plugins**.

The Plugins panel opens.

2 Click **Deactivate** under a plugin you want to deactivate.

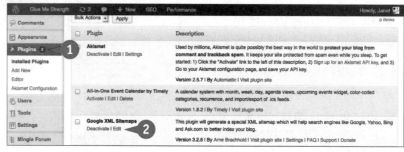

A WordPress confirms the deactivation.

B The Deactivate link changes to Activate.

3 Click **Delete**.

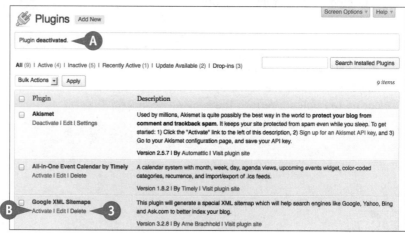

The Delete Plugin panel appears.

④ Click **Yes, Delete these files**.

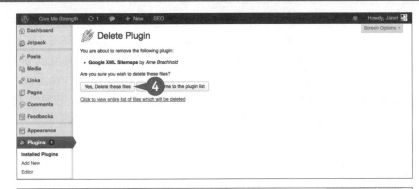

WordPress deletes the plugin.

C A deletion confirmation appears.

D The deleted plugin disappears from the plugin list.

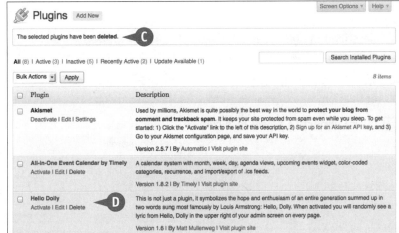

TIPS

How can I restore a deleted plugin?
Once you delete a plugin, the only way to restore it is to find the plugin and install it as if for the very first time. That is why it is best simply to deactivate, and not delete, a plugin for which you have created settings until you are certain you do not want it.

How do I delete multiple plugins?
Click the check boxes beside the plugins you want to delete (☐ changes to ☑). Next, choose Delete from the Bulk Actions drop-down list at the top of the page, and then click **Apply**. Note that you cannot delete an active plugin. You must deactivate it first. You also can deactivate groups using the Bulk Actions list.

Understanding and Using Jetpack

J etpack lets you use a collection of plugins at WordPress.org blogs that generally are available as widgets or other tools at WordPress.com. Jetpack is a bit of an oddity, in that it bridges the WordPress.com and WordPress.org divide. Among the implications is that you can keep an eye on blogs you may keep at WordPress.com and at WordPress.org from one location. At this writing, Jetpack is a package of two dozen plugins. You can install and activate Jetpack and then choose which of the specific plugins you want. You must connect with WordPress.com to use Jetpack.

Understanding and Using Jetpack

1 Install and activate Jetpack as described in "Install and Activate a Plugin," earlier in this chapter.

A WordPress confirms the activation.

2 Click **Connect to WordPress.com**.

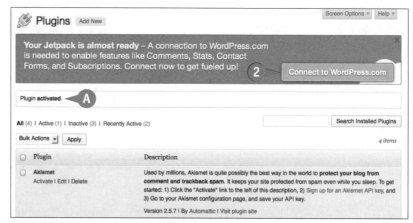

The Jetpack authorization screen appears.

3 Type your WordPress.com username.

4 Type your WordPress.com password.

5 Click **Authorize Jetpack**.

B Click this link to create a WordPress.com account if you do not have one.

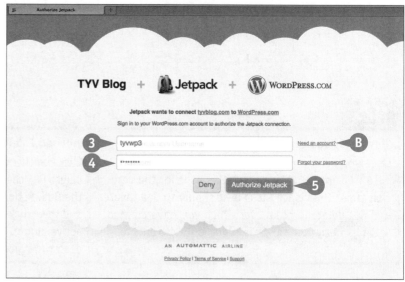

Your WordPress.org site connects to WordPress.com and opens the Jetpack screen.

C A message appears that the activation is confirmed.

D A Jetpack area is added to the left menu bar.

E The WordPress.com connection status appears here.

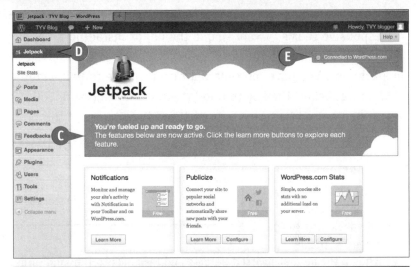

6 Click **Learn More** under the WordPress.com Stats module.

F An information panel opens.

G The Configure button changes to Deactivate.

7 Read about the module, and then click ⊠ to close information panel.

8 Scroll down to review other modules.

TIPS

Why do some modules have an Activate or Configure button and others do not?

The modules without Activate buttons are activated by default. You can deactivate them by clicking **Learn More** and then click the **Deactivate** button that appears. The exception is VaultPress, a backup utility. It requires a monthly subscription to use. Clicking **Learn More** gives you a link to buy one if you want. Modules with Configure ask you to provide information or choose options.

Can I get just the modules I want without connecting to WordPress.com?

Probably. You could install Jetpack Lite for the statistics module. Slim Jetpack, brand new at this writing, holds promise. You also can search for plugins that provide the specific function you seek.

Optimize Your Site for Mobile Devices

You can make your WordPress blog more easily viewable on handheld devices. By selecting a responsive theme, a very simple theme, or installing an appropriate plugin, your content appears in a way that will keep readers reading, even when they have access to your site only on their smartphones. You have multiple options available to you, whether you have a self-hosted site or one at WordPress.com. The key to good results is making sure your site has a way to detect the type of device being used to access your site and then to adapt the presentation to that device.

Responsive Themes

Perhaps the easiest way to optimize your site for mobile devices is to use a *responsive* theme,

Width

☐ Fixed Width   ☐ Flexible Width   ☑ Responsive Layout

which is a theme that in itself detects and responds to the kind of device on which it is being viewed. To find one, type **responsive** in the theme search box at either WordPress.com or WordPress.org. The Feature Filter found via your WordPress.com Manage Themes has a Responsive Layout filter option. The themes you find maintain their general look regardless of the device used to view your site.

WordPress.com Mobile Options

WordPress.com makes available a basic mobile theme that it displays when it detects that your site is being viewed on a mobile device. It is easy to enable. To do so, click **Appearance** in the left menu bar, and then click **Mobile** to open the Mobile Options panel. Click the radio button next to Yes (◯ changes to ◉) (**A**) to enable the mobile theme, and then click **Update** (**B**). The drawback is that the mobile theme is the same regardless of your overall theme choice. You also have the option of showing full posts or excerpts on your front page and archive pages.

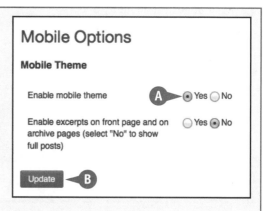

Plugins for Self-Hosted Sites

You have multiple options for plugins to adapt your site to mobile devices. The one that has the longest track record is WPtouch, which has free and paid versions. Other plugins that are coming on the scene that generally have favorable ratings include Any Mobile Theme Switcher and WordPress Mobile Pack. These plugins may work better with some themes than for others or may allow you to choose among theme options. Your best bet is to try one out and choose the one that you like most.

Jetpack Mobile Theme Module

If you have Jetpack installed and activated on your self-hosted site, you probably have the Mobile Theme module activated. It is among those that are automatically activated when you activate Jetpack. Like the WordPress.com Mobile Options, it presents your site in a sort of generic, but highly readable, format when it is viewed on a mobile device. You may want to click the **Configure** button (Ⓐ) in the Mobile Theme module to confirm the settings.

Mobile Theme

Automatically optimize your site for mobile devices.

Free

Learn More   Configure ◀Ⓐ

Create an App

If you want to get serious about having a mobile audience, you may want a mobile app that readers can install on their mobile devices. For most of us, creating a custom mobile app means paying someone to do it. The apps, generally in conjunction with a plugin, present your nicely styled content, and readers do not have to use their browser to access it. This sector is quite new for average WordPress users. Among the options you may want to look at are UppSite and MoPublication.

Create Custom Menus

You can choose what appears on your site's menus to help readers find their way around the site. Custom menus give you lots of flexibility to do so, either in the main menu or as a menu widget. You can use custom menus to call attention to portions of your site that you want to highlight. The default navigation menu for most themes lists your site's pages. With custom menus, you can have a menu item that opens a *category archive* — that is, a page that lists past posts that fit a particular category — a tag archive, or even a link to a particular post.

Create Custom Menus

1 Click **Menus** under Appearance in the left menu bar.

The Menus panel opens.

Note: If your theme does not support custom menus, the Menus panel allows you to create a custom menu for a widget.

2 Type a menu name.

3 Click **Create Menu**.

WordPress creates the menu, adds a Theme Locations module, and activates content modules.

4 Click the drop-down list ⊡.

5 Click your new menu.

Note: You may have more options if your theme displays multiple menus.

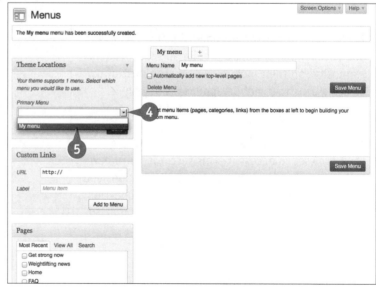

6 In the content modules, click the check boxes for items you want to appear on your custom menu (☐ changes to ☑).

7 Click **Add to Menu**.

Ⓐ WordPress adds the items to your custom menu.

Ⓑ The Screen Options panel lets you reveal selection modules for tags, posts, and more.

8 Repeat Steps **6** and **7** for each content module you use.

Note: You can drag the items within the module to rearrange their order or drag them to the right to create submenu items.

9 Click the module expansion arrow next to a menu item (▼).

10 Type a screen tip if you want.

Note: This text appears when a reader rests the mouse pointer over the menu item.

11 Click **Save Menu**.

Your custom menu replaces the default navigation menu on your site.

12 Click the blog title to view your new menu.

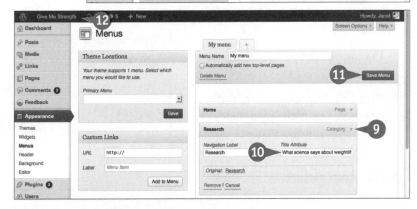

TIP

There seem to be a lot of options for these menus. What do I do with them all?
You can add a link to a menu, create submenus, edit menu item titles, and more. For details, check out the support for custom menus at http://codex.wordpress.org/Appearance_Menus_Screen for self-hosted blogs, or at http://en.support.wordpress.com/menus for blogs hosted at WordPress.com.

Create and Install a Favicon for a Self-Hosted Blog

You can add to your brand by displaying a favicon, the tiny icon that appears next to a web address in many browsers. The favicon also may appear in a browser's Favorites or Bookmarks list. See Chapter 2 for information about icons related to your WordPress.com blog.

Do not worry about pronouncing favicon correctly. There is no definitive pronunciation. Options include FAVE-icon, from the word's root as *favorite icon*, and FAVV-uh-con, with a short *a*, as in *hat*.

Create and Install a Favicon for a Self-Hosted Blog

① Go to www.degraeve.com/favicon and click **Browse**.

A file selection window opens, where you browse for an image that you want to convert to a favicon.

② Click **Open**.

③ When the path to your image appears in the Upload this Image box, click **upload image**.

Note: Alternatively, you can click **Clear All**, click a color in the palette, and then move your mouse pointer to the square editing area at the left to draw a favicon.

The image appears in a new window.

④ Click and drag, even stretch, the selection box until it surrounds the part of your image that you want to make into your icon.

⑤ Click **Crop picture**.

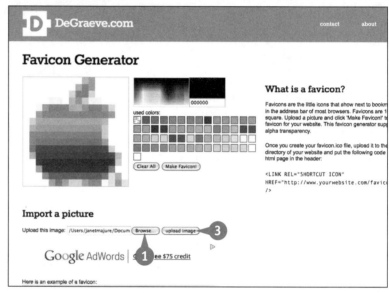

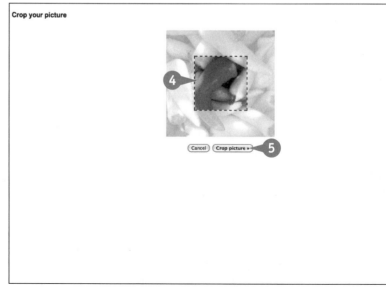

Note: The DeGraeve icon generator lets you crop from a larger image. Many icon generators, such as the one at Dynamicdrive.com, simply reduce an entire image to create a favicon.

The browser returns to the Favicon Generator window and shows your pixilated favicon.

⑥ Click **Make Favicon!**.

The favicon appears on the screen. Follow the directions for saving the favicon, named favicon.ico, to your hard drive.

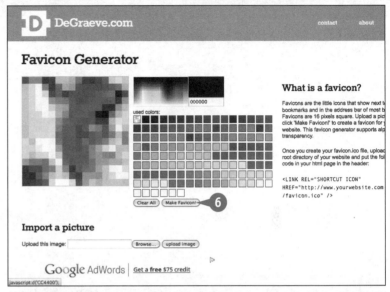

⑦ Using your FTP client, such as FileZilla, upload favicon.ico to the root of your blog site, as in /public_html.

Ⓐ The file appears in the directory listing.

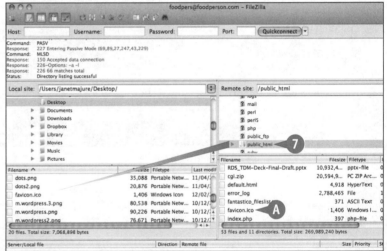

TIPS

Is there some other way to make a favicon?

You can make your own custom favicon with a paint or image-editing program. Just make sure the favicon is 16 × 16 pixels (although some browsers support 32 × 32 pixels) and then name it favicon.ico.

I followed the directions, but the favicon is not appearing. Why?

Most likely, it will not appear until your browser's cache has been cleared; go to your browser's Help menu to learn how. Or it should appear in a couple of hours. If you have waited two days or so and it still does not appear, your theme may need to be modified to support favicons. Search the WordPress.org forums for help.

CHAPTER 7

Engaging Your Readers

When you take advantage of the interactive aspects of WordPress, you can develop relationships with your readers and build a loyal audience. Those relationships develop as you let your readers participate in your blogs through comments, ratings, and more.

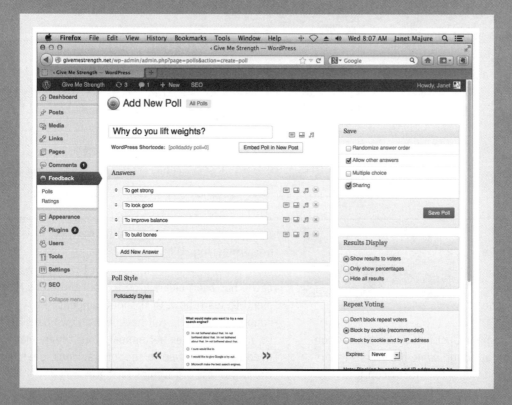

Write an About Page

The About page usually is the most frequently visited address on a blog after the home page, and you need to make yours worth visiting. People like to know who is behind the blog and to get a snapshot of what the site is about. Developing a good About page makes so much sense, in fact, that many themes have an About page by default, and WordPress may send reminders to you to update your About page. If you do not have an About page, first create a page, as described in Chapter 4, and then name it *About* or something similar.

The Five Ws

The five Ws — who, what, when, where, and why (and maybe, how) — are always a good place to start. In a brief paragraph, tell readers your name, what they gain by reading your site, when or how often you post, where you live, and why you created your site. You can use a pseudonym if you are not comfortable using your real name, and your location can be general, such as "the West Coast." Just make sure readers can put you in some context and know what to expect when they go to your site.

Include a Photograph of Yourself

Adding a picture of yourself makes you more human and familiar in the vast Internet world of strangers. Although the best images for that purpose are clear, recognizable portraits, you can hedge and still fulfill readers' need to see you. You can have a photo, for example, of you peeking from behind a door or in dramatic shadows or looking over your shoulder at the camera from your desk, garden, or stove, as appropriate to your blog's topic. Or you can edit your photo so that it is less distinct.

Remember the Reader

A hallmark of good marketing is to focus on how your product or service — or in this case, your blog — benefits the reader. Keep that idea in mind as you write your About page. That means, try to write things like *As you read this blog, you will read tips on how to save money on your grocery bills* instead of *I'm going to tell you how I save money on my grocery bills*. What would you want to know if you were visiting your site for the first time? Include answers to that question on your About page.

Be Brief

Remember, your readers probably just want a nutshell idea of who you are and what you are trying to do with your site. That means make it brief. If you want to write a long explanation of your philosophy or your reasons for creating the blog, go ahead and do so — but link to your long explanation from your About page. If you want to write more than a couple of paragraphs, you might try a question-and-answer format to let readers skim your page for the information they most want.

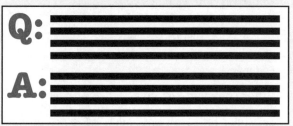

Encourage Engagement

The About page is a good place also to encourage readers to get involved, so consider adding a call to action. In other words, ask readers to *do* something, such as add a comment on the About page telling you what they hope to get out of your blog or encouraging them to sign up to receive your new posts in an RSS feed or by e-mail, as discussed later in this chapter.

NO COMMENTS SO FAR ↓
There are no comments yet...Kick things off by filling out the form below.

LEAVE A COMMENT

Janet Majure	**Name**
janet@foodperson.com	**Mail**
http://www.foodperson.com	**Website**

Stay Up to Date

Plan to update your About page regularly. Depending on how fast your life and blog change, you might schedule an About page update monthly or quarterly. As you are regularly updating your content through your blog posts, it is easy to forget that new readers are going to go to your About page early on. They will not be impressed if it is clear that your About page hasn't been updated in a year or two.

Choose the Discussion Settings

Your choices of Discussion Settings determine how you and your readers interact, and it is good to remember that interacting is a key to the success of most blogs. Among the options, you can choose the order in which comments appear, set some rules for when you want to review comments for approval, and decide whether and what kind of avatar to show with comments. Your choices can help you avoid comment spam and block inflammatory comments. Many settings create defaults that can be overridden on individual posts if you choose.

A Default Article Settings

Lets you make the default choice as to whether WordPress notifies blogs you link to, accepts notice of links to your site from other blogs, and allows readers to comment.

B Other Comment Settings

Sets rules for conditions under which you allow comments.

C Threaded Comments

Allows readers and you to respond directly to other comments.

D Comment Display Order

Lets you choose whether readers see the newest comment first — or last.

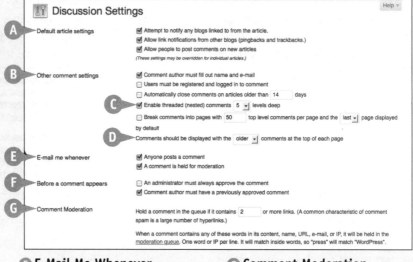

E E-Mail Me Whenever

Specifies whether you receive e-mail notification of comments posted or held for moderation. WordPress.com also offers e-mail notifications when someone likes a post, reblogs a post — essentially quoting and commenting on your post — or chooses to follow the blog.

F Before a Comment Appears

Lets you choose to review all comments or automatically accept comments from a previously approved commenter.

G Comment Moderation

Sets parameters under which comments are held for your review before posting. Options include a box to specify the minimum number of links that provoke moderation and a box in which you can list terms that may be signs of spam comments. A second box, Comment Blacklist, lets you list terms that automatically identify comments as spam. WordPress.com also lets you choose to keep old comment spam and to include a Follow Comments option or a Follow Blog option in the comment form.

A Avatar Display

Indicates whether to show *avatars*, which are like personal logos associated with comment writers.

Note: WordPress.com sites and self-hosted sites running Jetpack also have a setting on this panel for Gravatar Hovercards. It lets you choose whether to allow Hovercards to pop up when you place your mouse pointer over a person's Gravatar. See "Sign Up at Gravatar.com" in Chapter 1 for more information.

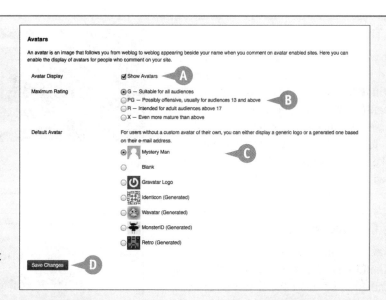

Avatars

An avatar is an image that follows you from weblog to weblog appearing beside your name when you comment on avatar enabled sites. Here you can enable the display of avatars for people who comment on your site.

Avatar Display ☑ Show Avatars — A

Maximum Rating
- ◉ G — Suitable for all audiences
- ○ PG — Possibly offensive, usually for audiences 13 and above — B
- ○ R — Intended for adult audiences above 17
- ○ X — Even more mature than above

Default Avatar For users without a custom avatar of their own, you can either display a generic logo or a generated one based on their e-mail address.
- ◉ Mystery Man — C
- ○ Blank
- ○ Gravatar Logo
- ○ Identicon (Generated)
- ○ Wavatar (Generated)
- ○ MonsterID (Generated)
- ○ Retro (Generated)

Save Changes — D

B Maximum Rating

Lets you choose which avatar ratings you allow, using the ratings that users provide when they create avatars at Gravatar.com, the avatar service that WordPress uses.

C Default Avatar

Allows you to pick a default image for commenters who do not have an avatar. The generated options change slightly from one person to the next.

D Save Changes

Click to retain choices on the Comment Settings page.

Note: At the bottom of the Discussion Settings page, WordPress.com lets you change the default text that viewers see in the comment box, and Jetpack users see the options to include Follow Comments or Follow Blog in the comment form.

Create a Comment Policy

WordPress gives you the power to decide who can and cannot comment on your blog and under what conditions. You can even choose on a post-by-post basis whether people can comment on your blog. In other words, you can be the lone voice or the leader of a free-for-all. The choice is yours. Several considerations need to be taken into account as you contemplate what kind of comments you want. Once you decide, create a policy that you announce clearly to your readers. It will make life easier for everyone.

How Thick Is Your Skin?

Sharing opinions with readers sounds like a good idea until you get your first flame, a searingly critical comment, or troll, a commenter whose remarks are aimed at provoking argument, often by being nasty. If you love the kind of debate that those provoke, you may not need a comment policy. Otherwise, give it some thought.

Time Considerations

Moderating comments can be a time-consuming task, especially if you attract a lot of comments. Do you have time to manage that? Your WordPress Discussion Settings that give a pass to previous commenters, that ban words you specify, or that hold comments with numerous hyperlinks can reduce the load while making your blog somewhat less vulnerable to trolls.

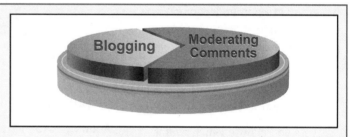

Consider Your Audience

Your policy should take into consideration not only your preferences but also those of your readers. If you are aiming at members of your church, you may want to block profanity. If you are aiming at American teens, you probably need to allow abbreviations commonly used in instant messaging and texting.

Aim for a Balance

Keep in mind that a major appeal of blogs for readers and publishers alike is the ability to interact by way of comments. Commenting that is too restricted or delayed, as when waiting for the moderator, can be frustrating for readers, but frequent malicious comments are a turnoff for lots of people. Try to strike a balance with your policy.

What to Include in Your Policy

Make your policy clear and concise. It is a good idea to state who can comment — anyone or registered users only, for example — what you consider acceptable and unacceptable, and what your expected response is to unacceptable comments. Your response could be to edit or delete the comment or even to ban the writer via the Discussion settings. Your policy also might state if you close comments after a set number of days.

State Your Policy

Having a written comment policy is good for two reasons. First, creating it causes you to think about what is and is not acceptable to you. Second, it gives you something to point to when people complain about comments being deleted, edited, or excluded. Let your readers know where you stand.

Put It Where People Will Find It

Create a separate Comment Policy page, or put your policy on your About page. If you have a self-hosted blog and are comfortable making a few adjustments with your theme, you could put your policy next to your comment form on your blog pages. That way, anyone who wants to comment and has questions will have immediate access to your policy.

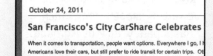

Enforce Your Policy

If your policy says you do not allow profanity, then be consistent about deleting or editing profanity-laced comments, as you stated you would do in your policy. To have a policy and not enforce it opens you up to complaints, which may well be publicly aired, that you have been unfair in your enforcement. You do not need that kind of conflict.

Moderate Comments

Chances are you will need to moderate, or review, comments occasionally, even if you have a fairly wide-open comment policy. Doing so reduces comment spam and keeps the commentary within your comments policy. Remember, you can choose which comments need to be moderated and how and whether you are notified with the Discussion Settings, as explained in "Choose the Discussion Settings," earlier in this chapter.

Moderate Comments

Moderate an Individual Comment

1 Click **Comments** in the left menu bar of the administrative interface or Comments in the Dashboard's Right Now module.

The Comments panel opens.

A The number of comments awaiting moderation appears here.

B Comments awaiting moderation appear in the Recent Comments module with a note, *[Pending]*, and a pale yellow background.

2 Position your mouse pointer over the area of a comment awaiting moderation, which has a pale yellow background.

A set of options appears.

Note: Typos and lots of links are common in spam comments.

3 Click **Approve** to approve the comment.

The comment is published to your blog, and the background turns white.

Note: The other options are discussed later in this chapter.

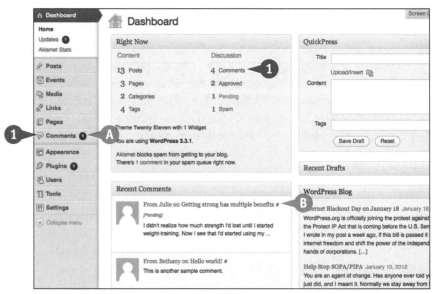

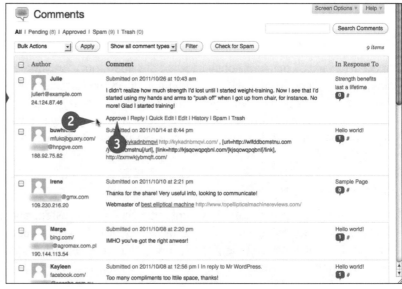

Moderate Multiple Comments

1 Click the comments you want to moderate (☐ changes to ☑).

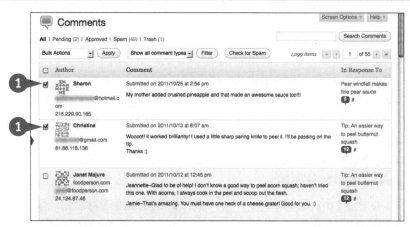

2 Click the drop-down menu next to Bulk Actions.

The Bulk Actions menu expands.

3 Click **Approve**.

4 Click **Apply**.

All checked comments are approved and published.

What do I do about the e-mail I got asking me to moderate a comment?

Just click the appropriate link to approve the comment, delete it, or mark it as spam. Your browser then opens to a screen where you confirm your action. Or, you can click the fourth link, which takes you to the moderation panel, otherwise known as the Edit Comments panel.

What is that information under In Response To on the Comments panel?

Ⓐ This shows the name of the post associated with the comment and links to the Edit Post panel for that post.

Ⓑ This applies a filter to show only those comments made on the post listed.

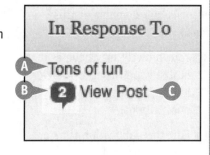

Ⓒ This links to the published post associated with the comment.

Edit a Comment

Editing comments lets you correct typos, tone down rhetoric, or make comments conform to your comment policy. Editing often is a nicer alternative to approving or deleting troublesome comments. From the Comments panel, you can open the Edit Comment panel or expand the Quick Edit mode. Many themes have an Edit link on your site's comment display when you are logged in. You can click that link to go straight to the Edit Comment panel. If you want to add formatting, though, you must use HTML. There is no WYSIWYG editor for comments.

Edit a Comment

From the Edit Comment Panel

1. In the Comments panel, position the mouse pointer over the comment you want to edit, and click **Edit**.

The Edit Comment panel opens.

2. Make any changes you want, including spelling, grammar, and HTML formatting, in the HTML editing box.

Note: A WYSIWYG comment editor is not available at this time.

Ⓐ Your browser may have a built-in spell-checker that highlights possible misspellings.

3. Edit the publication time or status if desired.

4. Click **Update**.

WordPress saves the changes and returns to the Comments panel.

From the Quick Edit Pane

1 Position your mouse pointer over the comment you want to edit, and click the **Quick Edit** link that appears.

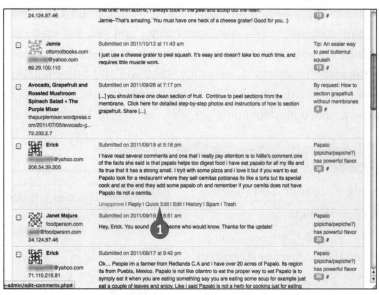

The Quick Edit pane expands.

2 Make any changes you want, including spelling, grammar, and HTML formatting, in the HTML editing box.

Note: Editing options in this pane are limited to the comment text, author, e-mail, and URL.

3 Click **Update Comment** when you are done.

The changes are saved, and the Quick Edit pane closes.

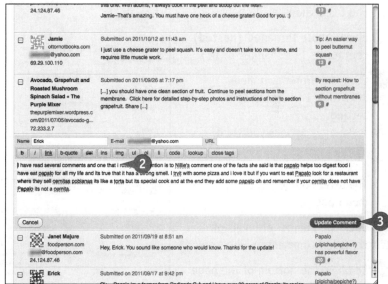

TIPS

Why would I want to edit the published time or status?

You may have occasions where you want to change the order in which comments appear. Editing the times can change the order. Among reasons you might want to change the status is if you belatedly realize an approved comment is spam.

Is there a way that commenters can edit their own comments?

If you have a self-hosted blog, you can use the WP Ajax Edit Comments plugin to make that happen. See Chapter 6 for information about plugins. If you blog at WordPress.com, however, there currently is no way for your readers to edit their comments.

Allow and Use Threaded Comments

You can reply — and let readers reply — directly to specific comments on your blog. The result is stair-stepped, or *threaded*, comments, and you can make them several levels deep. The Discussion Settings let you allow threaded comments and determine how many levels you want. The advantage of threaded comments is, naturally, that you and other readers can comment and read related comments. The drawback is that the newest comments on your site do not necessarily appear at the top — or bottom, depending on your Discussion Settings — of your comments list.

Allow and Use Threaded Comments

Enable Threaded Comments

1 Click **Settings**.

The General Settings panel opens and the Settings menu expands.

2 Click **Discussion**.

The Discussion panel opens.

3 Click **Enable threaded (nested) comments** (☐ changes to ☑).

4 Click the drop-down menu ▾ next to 5, the default level setting.

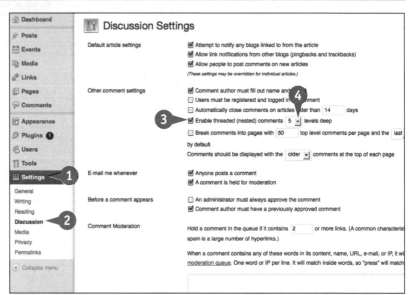

The level number drop-down menu opens.

5 Click the number of levels of threaded commentary you want.

6 Scroll to the bottom of the page and click **Save Changes**.

A confirmation message appears.

7 After saving changes, click your blog name to visit the site.

Your blog opens for you to check the comments, and a Reply link appears with each comment in addition to with the post.

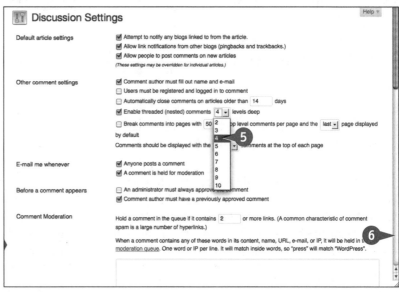

Reply to a Specific Comment from Post

1 After going to the comments on a post, click **Reply** next to the comment that you want to reply to.

The regular Reply box disappears, and a Reply box that combines with the comment appears.

2 Type your reply in the Leave a Reply box.

3 Click **Submit Comment** when done.

Ⓐ The comment appears as a subcomment of the selected comment.

Ⓑ Subcomments become threaded or nested.

Ⓒ Comments made by clicking the **Reply** link in the post are top-level comments.

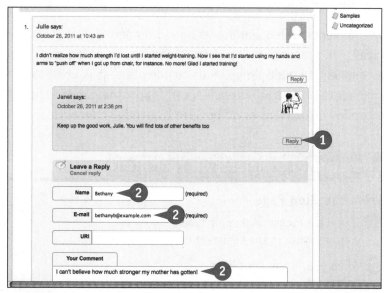

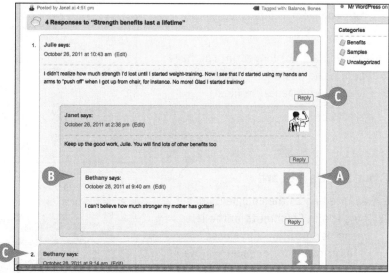

TIPS

Can I create a threaded comment by clicking Reply on a comment in the Edit Comments panel?

Yes. Just click **Reply** under the appropriate comment. Note that if you want to add a top-level comment — a comment that is *not* threaded — you need to go to the blog post on the site and click **Comment** directly under the post. Your readers use the same processes.

Is there a way to number comments, as I have seen on some websites, so people can refer to other comments by number?

Yes, if your blog is self-hosted. A plugin, Greg's Threaded Comment Numbering, at http://wordpress.org/extend/plugins/gregs-threaded-comment-numbering/, assigns numbers to comments, and includes a system for numbering threaded comments.

Respond to Comments on Your Blog

If you think blogs are all about conversation, then you will want to respond to your readers' comments. When you do, you build readers' sense of involvement in your blog, which can increase loyalty and readership. You can respond on the blog page or from the Dashboard. If you address a comment to multiple previous commenters, it is good to address them by name or link to their comments so that other readers can follow the conversation. This especially is true when you create a top-level comment or do not use threaded comments.

Respond to Comments on Your Blog

From the Blog Page

① If you are logged in, simply type your response in the comment box.

② When you finish, click **Post Comment**.

Your comment is published to the site.

Note: If you are not logged in, you have to type a name and e-mail address just as any other commenter would.

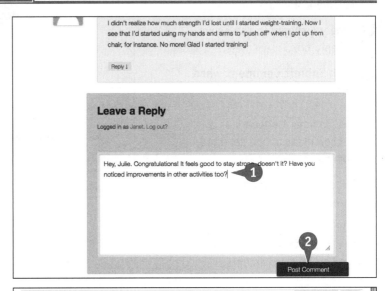

From the Dashboard

① After going to the Comments panel by clicking **Comments** in the left menu bar, position the mouse pointer over the comment you want to respond to, and click **Reply**.

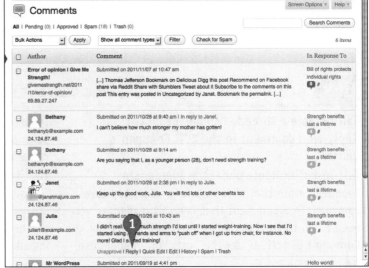

The Reply to Comment pane opens.

② Type your response in the space provided.

③ Click **Reply**.

The Reply to Comment pane closes.

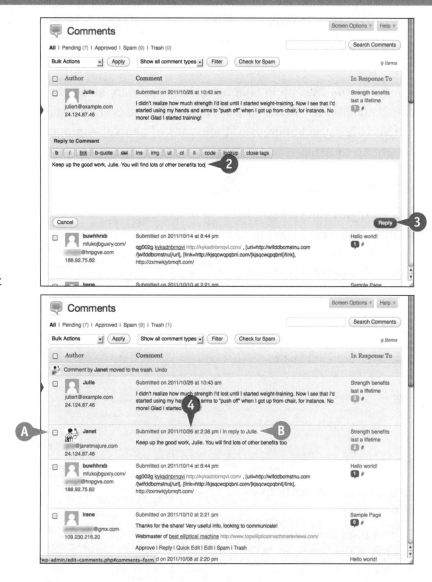

Ⓐ The Comments panel lists the reply, which also is published to your blog site.

Ⓑ The Comment details note that the comment is in reply to *Name,* where *Name* represents the commenter. If you have allowed threaded comments, as discussed in "Allow and Use Threaded Comments" later in this chapter, the comment appears under that particular comment rather than as the newest comment.

④ Click the date and time display.

The link takes you to the published comment.

Can I respond to several comments at once?
If you are looking for a bulk response option, none exists. What most bloggers do is to write one comment but refer to previous comments by the writers' names as shown on their comments. For example, you might write, "Susan, I agree with you. Bill, you make a good point, but I think . . ."

How do I link to a particular comment?
The date and time display with each comment on the Edit Comments panel has a permalink to the comment embedded in it. You can right-click the link and choose **Copy Link Location** to copy the comment's permalink. Then use that permalink as needed. Or, click the date and time display, which takes you to the comment, and the permalink for that comment appears in your browser address bar.

Deal with Comment Spam

Even after setting hurdles for commenters to clear, comment spam still gets through. Your blog will look better and be more appealing if you make sure that spam comments are zapped as soon as possible.

The Akismet tool, set up in Chapter 6, is the primary means by which WordPress bloggers handle spam comments. It catches lots of spam before it ever gets published, and one reason it is so effective is because hundreds of thousands of people — bloggers like you — keep the Akismet spam database up to date.

Deal with Comment Spam

Spam that Got Published

1 After clicking **Comments** in the left menu bar to open the Edit Comments panel, find the offending comment in the list, position your mouse pointer over the comment to reveal the options, and click **Spam**.

The comment moves to the spam queue.

Ⓐ The marked comment is noted in the Comments list, along with an Undo link to click if you made a mistake.

Note: Spam comments do not otherwise appear in the ordinary Comments list after you click the **All** option under the Comments title.

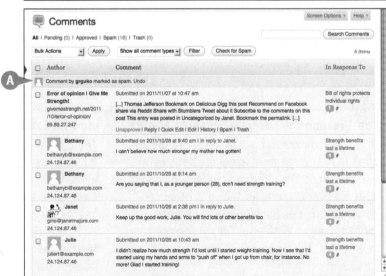

From an E-Mail Notice

1 After getting an e-mail notice to moderate a comment and clicking the link to spam it at a WordPress.org blog or Mark as Spam on WordPress.com, click **Spam Comment** in the Moderate Comment screen to confirm the item is spam.

WordPress sends the item to the spam comment list and notifies the Akismet database, which aids its spam-catching ability.

B You can click **No** if you realize the comment is not spam.

Review Spam Comments

1 Click **Comments**.

2 Click **Spam**.

The Comments panel reveals comments marked as spam. Review to make sure no valid comments are incorrectly identified as spam. You can position the mouse pointer over any valid comments and click the **Not Spam** link that appears, sending it to the regular comments list.

3 Click **Empty Spam**.

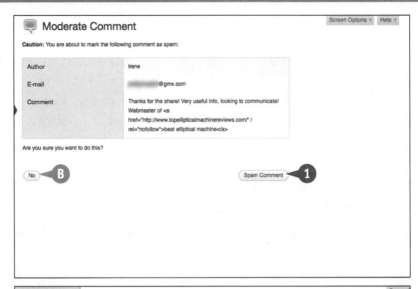

TIPS

How often do I need to review the spam list?
You need to check it periodically to make sure that your spam queue is not eating up the space on your web host and to make sure valid comments are not getting caught. Akismet automatically deletes comment spam after a month. Akismet Stats under Dashboard in the left menu bar show how many spam comments have been caught.

Why not just click Trash when a spam comment shows up in the Comments panel?
When you click **Trash** rather than **Spam**, you are not letting Akismet learn what senders and IP addresses are sending you spam comments. So, click **Spam** when you get a spam comment, and Akismet will start catching that sender for other WordPress users, too.

Review Notifications

You can get a snapshot of your blog's activity through the Notifications feature at WordPress.com and in Jetpack, the WordPress.org plugin bridge to some WordPress.com features. When you click the **Notifications** button (■), you see a list of the latest comments made on your blog or blogs as well as the instances where someone has indicated that he or she liked a post or decided to follow your blog. You can even moderate and reply to comments via the Notifications drop-down, or you can click **View All** to open the Notifications panel at WordPress.com. The panel allows you to filter the notices in various ways.

Review Notifications

1 Click the **Notifications** button in the menu bar (■).

Ⓐ The latest notifications appear.

2 Click an item.

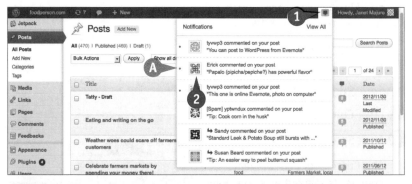

Ⓑ A fly-out pane lets you read more about the item.

Ⓒ Click here to link to the pertinent post.

Ⓓ Click links to take various actions.

3 Click **View All**.

The Notifications panel at WordPress.com opens in a new tab.

④ Click a pending comment.

The comment appears in the right pane.

⑤ Click an option.

Reply opens a pane for replying. Spam and Trash comments are marked in the list as such. Approved comments appear in the list without symbol or notation.

ⓔ The arrow indicates comments to which you have replied.

⑥ Click **Unread**.

ⓕ WordPress displays only unread comments.

ⓖ The column on the left shows other filter options.

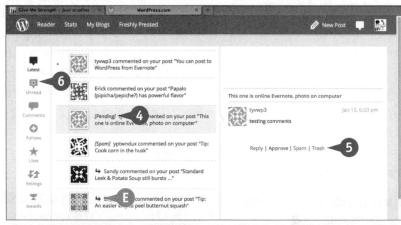

TIPS

What other kinds of notifications might I receive?

WordPress notifies you if new people have chosen to follow your blog, have said they like a post, or have *reblogged,* or used your post as a basis for their posts. You also receive notices of *awards,* which are notes about achieving new milestones with your blog. Corresponding filters appear on the Notifications panel at WordPress.com.

- January 15: Your best day for follows on "Give Me Strength"

- Strength Builder and janetm and 2 others followed your blog "Give Me Strength"

- janetm liked your post "Embedded images add more options"

Why do I see both my self-hosted blog activity and my WordPress.com activity in Notifications?

Because you have activated Jetpack on your self-hosted blog and used the same e-mail address when you activated it as you use for your WordPress.com blog. It's handy, but can be confusing.

Include Avatars with Comments

When you include avatars with comments, you let readers share a bit of their identity with your audience. An *avatar* is a small image that a person chooses as his or her online visual identifier. It may be a photo, drawing, logo, or other symbol. WordPress uses the Gravatar avatar service, which associates a person's avatar with an e-mail address. If you authorize avatars through your Discussion settings, the avatars of those who have signed up at Gravatar.com appear because they have to provide an e-mail address to comment. You can choose a generic symbol to display for those who do not have Gravatar avatars.

Include Avatars with Comments

① Click **Settings** in the left menu bar.

② Click **Discussion**.

The Discussion Settings panel appears.

③ Scroll to the bottom of the page.

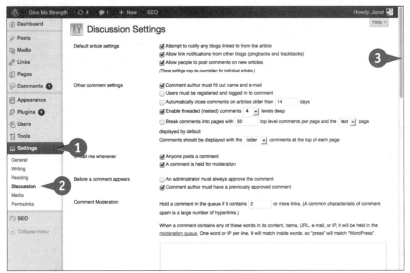

④ Click the check box next to Show Avatars (☐ changes to ☑).

⑤ Click the radio button next to the default avatar type to appear when a commenter does not have a Gravatar avatar (○ changes to ●).

Ⓐ The Blank option shows no image when a commenter does not have an avatar.

⑥ Click **Save Changes**.

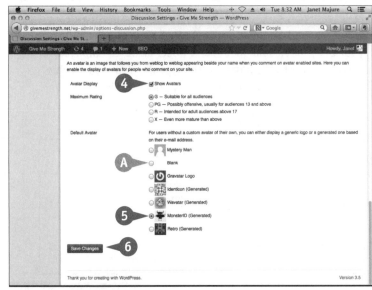

B WordPress confirms the changes.

7 Click **Comments**.

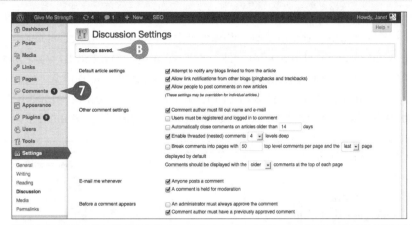

The Comments list appears.

C Gravatar and default avatars appear.

Note: These also appear with comments on published posts.

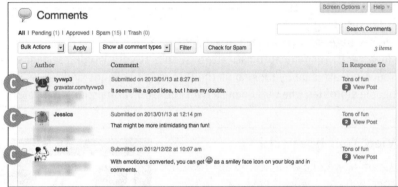

What does *generated* mean next to some of the default avatars?

Those defaults automatically generate avatar images that are random, but consistent for each user on your site. Many people think they are more fun than the Mystery Man, blank, or Gravatar logo options, which are the same for every user who lacks a Gravatar.

What are the Maximum Rating options about?

They let you exclude Gravatars whose creators deem them offensive at various levels. When a person creates a Gravatar, as described in Chapter 1, she is asked to rate her Gravatar according to suitability for various audiences. The default rating is G, suitable for all.

Understanding Gravatar Hovercards

You can give your commenters even more of an identity if you choose to include Gravatar Hovercards. The hovercard option is available and active by default at WordPress.com sites. Self-hosted sites must have Jetpack installed and activated to make Gravatar Hovercards available. When hovercards are enabled, readers can rest their mouse pointer over a commenter's Gravatar avatar, and a pop-up window shows a brief bio of the avatar's owner along with a link to his complete Gravatar profile. Readers who do not like the pop-ups can turn them off with a click.

Your Publisher Settings

It is important to remember that your Gravatar settings as a WordPress blog publisher

are separate from your Gravatar settings as a blog reader. If you think your readers would like Gravatar Hovercards, they are automatically available at your WordPress.com site or Jetpack-enabled self-hosted site. You can make sure by looking at the Discussion settings under Gravatar Avatars. The check box next to View people's profiles when you mouse over their Gravatars should be selected (☑).

View Your Hovercard

Assuming you have signed up at Gravatar.com, you can see your hovercard in the Gravatar section of your Discussion Settings by resting your mouse over your Gravatar. It has the display name you chose at Gravatar.com and, if you provided them, your location and a brief bio. It also has a link to your complete Hovercard profile.

Your Preference as a Reader

Your preference as a reader may be different from your preference as a publisher. If, as a reader, you do not want to see hovercards when you move your mouse over a Gravatar, then you can turn them off by clicking the **Turn off hovercards** link within any hovercard. Here's the really tricky part, however — clicking that link creates a cookie in your browser that prevents you from seeing any hovercards. That *cookie*, a little piece of data, must be removed from your browser if you want to start seeing hovercards again.

Change Hovercard Settings

If you have a WordPress.com blog or a Jetpack-enabled self-hosted site, you have hovercards enabled by default. You can change the hovercard visibility for your site in the Discussion Settings. To change your setting as a viewer, you used a link in a hovercard to quit setting the cards, but you must delete a cookie to restore your viewing.

Change Hovercard Settings

To Disable Hovercards on Your Site

1 In the Avatars section of the Discussion Settings, click the check box to turn off hovercards (☑ changes to ☐).

Your Gravatar image disappears.

Note: To restore hovercards, click the check box again (☐ changes to ☑).

To Disable Your Ability to See Hovercards

1 When a hovercard appears, click **Turn off hovercards**.

The card — and your ability to see any Gravatar hovercards — disappears.

To Restore Card-Viewing Ability

1 Select the **nohovercard** cookie in your browser's cookies list.

Note: Search your browser's Help to learn how to delete a cookie. This example uses Firefox.

2 Click **Remove Cookie**.

The cookie is removed, and you can view hovercards in your browser again.

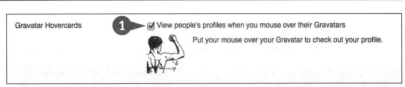

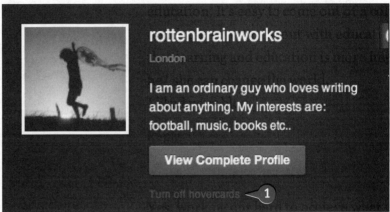

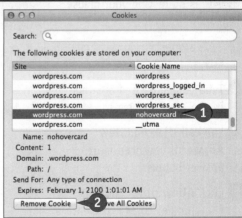

Create a User Poll

Polls get readers involved in your blog, and when readers feel involved, they want to come back for more. WordPress.com has a Polldaddy tool built in, and self-hosted blogs can get similar functions with a Polldaddy plugin. *Polldaddy* is an online polls and surveys service that lets you create a simple, one-question poll. Other poll and ratings plugins are available for self-hosted sites. If your blog is self-hosted, first go to Polldaddy.com and register, then install the Polldaddy Polls & Ratings plugin. If your blog is at WordPress.com, click **Polls** and then auto-create an account at Polldaddy.

Create a User Poll

1 Click **Feedback** in the left menu of your Dashboard.

The Feedback menu expands, and the Polldaddy Polls panel opens.

Note: At WordPress.com, you also must click **Polls** in the left menu bar.

2 Click **Create a Poll Now**.

Ⓐ After your first poll, click **Add New** instead.

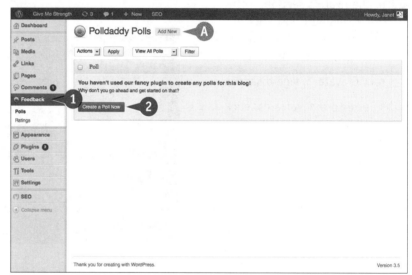

3 Type a question in the first box.

4 Type your proposed answers in the Answers boxes.

Ⓑ You can click **Add New Answer** if you need more answer blanks.

5 Click **Allow other answers** (☐ changes to ☑) to create an answer called Other that has a box for users to type more information.

6 Scroll down to reveal the Poll Style module.

7 Click the double arrows on either side of the sample poll until you find a design you like.

Note: Positioning your mouse pointer over the sample reveals the companion design for poll results.

8 Click the width of your choice.

9 After you are satisfied, click **Save Poll**.

The window name changes to Edit Poll and confirms a poll has been created. It is available for later editing in the Polldaddy Polls panel.

10 Click **Embed Poll in New Post**.

WordPress opens an Add New Post panel with your poll embedded in the text area. When you save and publish your post, the poll appears, too. It includes a link to the results view.

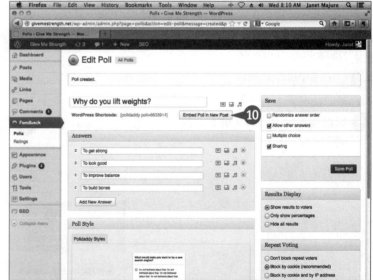

TIPS

What is the WordPress shortcode about?

Shortcodes are WordPress *macros*, or a compacted sequence of commands. In this case, you can copy the Polldaddy shortcode from the top of the Polldaddy Polls panel and then paste the code wherever you want your poll to appear on your blog. Chapter 12 discusses shortcodes in more detail. For example, you can paste it in a text widget in a sidebar of your site. Be sure to choose the narrow width option for better display.

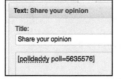

What difference does it make to click the multiple choice button?

Multiple choice lets poll-takers choose more than one answer. Polldaddy has lots of options. You can learn more about the many options by going to http://support.polldaddy.com and browsing the support articles.

Create a User Survey

With a reader survey, you can elicit even more information than with a poll. Unlike a simple, one-question poll, a survey lets you seek rankings, ratings, and open-ended commentary. You can use Polldaddy as described in the preceding task, but you must create your survey at http://polldaddy.com. Start by logging in there.

Create a User Survey

1 Click **Create a new....**

A drop-down list appears.

2 Click **Survey**.

3 Type a title in the Survey name box.

4 Click a style you like (○ changes to ◉).

5 Scroll to the bottom of the page.

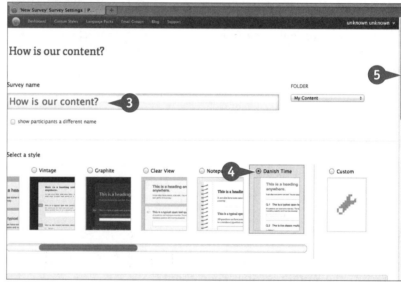

6 Review the survey options and make selections as desired.

7 Click **Save Settings**.

8 Click your choice of question type, and drag to the question area.

A box appears where you type your survey question information.

9 Type a question or statement.

10 Type answers.

11 Click **Done**.

12 Repeat Steps **8** to **11** for each survey question.

13 Click **Finish & Share** when you are done with your questions.

A Share Survey window appears.

14 Copy the WordPress.com shortcode.

15 Paste the shortcode in a text widget, post, or page at your blog.

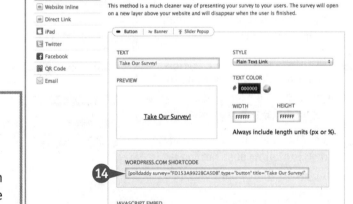

TIPS

How do I see the results of the survey?
Log in at http:// polldaddy.com. When your Dashboard appears, click **Reports** beside the survey in your list of surveys. A results screen appears that shows response numbers, percentages, and graphic illustrations of the results.

How do I share the results?
Of course, you may just want to survey readers for your own information, but the best way to share results is to write a post describing key findings. You can learn about other ways to share survey results at http://support. polldaddy.com.

Let Readers Rate Content

With your account at Polldaddy, as explained in "Create a User Poll," earlier in this chapter, you also can let readers rate your posts, pages, and even comments. When readers are involved, they are more likely to stay and to return. Self-hosted bloggers can choose a different plugin, such as WP-Post Ratings, if they want to offer ratings but do not want to include polls. This section covers only Polldaddy ratings and assumes you have installed the Polldaddy plugin or are blogging at WordPress.com.

Let Readers Rate Content

1 Click **Feedback** (**Feedbacks** at WordPress.com) in the left menu bar.

The menu area expands.

2 Click **Ratings**.

The Ratings Results panel opens.

3 Click **Settings**.

The Rating Settings panel opens to the Posts tab.

4 Click the check box (☐ changes to ☑) to allow post ratings to appear on the front page, archive lists, and search results.

5 Click the check box (☐ changes to ☑) to allow post ratings to appear on individual blog post pages.

6 If desired, click the drop-down menu and choose **Below each blog post**.

Note: The default ratings location is above the post.

7 Click **Save Changes**.

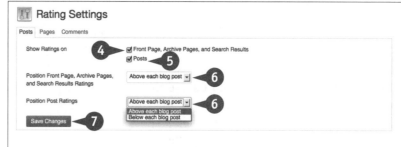

The selections are saved, and an Advanced Settings link appears at the bottom of the panel.

8 Click **Advanced Settings**.

The Advanced Settings subpanel expands.

Ⓐ Click here to choose between 5-star ratings and a Nero rating (for thumbs-up or thumbs-down ratings).

Ⓑ Click here to change the size, color, and more for ratings graphics.

Ⓒ Click here to change the display of ratings graphics and text.

Ⓓ Click here to allow for the disabling of results popups and to provide a ratings number, which you can use to identify posts to exclude from ratings.

Ⓔ Click here to preview display selections, including rating text and results popups if you move your mouse pointer over the preview module.

Ⓕ Click here to change or eliminate text that accompanies the ratings.

9 After making display selections, click **Save Changes**.

10 Return to the top of the page, and repeat Steps **4** to **9** to allow ratings on pages and comments if desired.

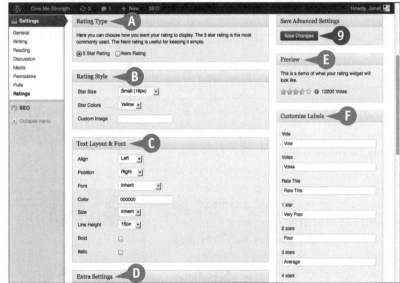

TIPS

How does the Custom Image option under Rating Style work?

It lets you select an image to use rather than stars for the ratings. Upload an image to your site, as explained in Chapter 5, and then paste the image's URL in the Custom Image box. Now your ratings will show the flowers, birds, dots, or whatever else you choose. Make sure the image is scaled to the size you choose under Star Size.

What are the ratings reports?

After you have some ratings, the Rating Results panel lets you see which posts, pages, and comments have the top ratings — and you can filter the report to see which are the best of all time or the best for the current month, among the many options.

Understanding and Joining RSS Feeds

By providing an RSS feed from your blog — which WordPress creates automatically — you give people who use feed readers ready access to your new content. Feed readers let someone read the updates of all of his or her favorite websites by going to a single location. When you read feeds, you too can keep up with your favorites. After you view the new content, the feed reader typically removes it from the reader unless you tell it to keep an item. The net effect is easy, consistent access to updates from favorite sites.

What Is RSS?

RSS stands for *Really Simple Syndication*, and it really is simple to use. All it takes is a feed reader and feeds from your favorite sites. Blogs and news sites typically provide feeds. When you open your feed reader, you see content from each site that has been added since you last read that site's feed.

Feed Readers

Feed readers, also called aggregators, may be web-based, such as Feedly and Bloglines. Some, such as FeedDemon for Windows, are *client* programs based on your local computer that download your feeds. Internet Explorer has a built-in reader capability as does WordPress.com. Other readers are browser extensions. There also are mobile feed reader apps, such as News360. You can find a comparison list at http://en.wikipedia.org/wiki/Comparison_of_feed_aggregators.

Identify Feeds

Not all browsers display an icon when they detect a feed on a web page. Internet Explorer shows the standard orange RSS logo in its toolbar when it detects an available feed, but Firefox and Chrome do not. Also, many web pages display text or logo or both, inviting you to subscribe. Make sure your site displays an RSS invitation.

Subscribe to Feeds

Choose a feed reader for yourself, and then start subscribing to feeds. Subscribing to a few blogs in your topic area is a good way to see what others are saying. Sign up for your feed, too, so that you can make sure it is functioning properly. If you do not see an RSS icon or subscription link for the site you are interested in, you can subscribe by following these steps:

Subscribe Now!

...with web-based news readers. Click your choice below:

MY YAHOO! | newsgator | MY AOL
SUB BLOGLINES | netvibes
Google™ | Pageflakes

...with other readers:

(Choose Your Reader)

1 Right-click on the web page, and then click **Page Source** or **View Page Source**.

A window of code appears.

2 Press `Ctrl` (`⌘` on a Mac)+`F` and type **/feed** in the search box that appears.

3 Press `Enter` (`Return` on a Mac).

4 Copy the URL ending in /feed. There may be more than one.

5 Paste the URL in your browser's address bar, and press `Enter` (`Return` on a Mac).

A list of recent posts appears along with a button you can click to subscribe to the feed.

Logged-on WordPress.com users can go to http://wordpress.com/#!/read/edit and type a URL to subscribe to, or *follow*, a blog or news site.

Decide Feed Settings

Your blog's Reading Settings under Settings in the left menu bar specify whether your feed includes an entire post or a summary. If you choose Summary, the feed sends an Excerpt if you wrote one on the Posts panel. If you did not, it sends a *teaser* — the words before a More tag. If there is no More tag, the feed sends the first 55 words of your post.

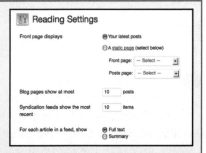

Reading Settings

Front page displays	○ Your latest posts
	○ A static page (select below)
	Front page: — Select —
	Posts page: — Select —
Blog pages show at most	10 posts
Syndication feeds show the most recent	10 items
For each article in a feed, show	○ Full text
	○ Summary

Invite Your Readers to Subscribe

You can do more to promote your blog's feed than rely on the RSS logos in browsers and perhaps within your theme. Consider writing a post from time to time specifically about your feeds — WordPress comes with one for your new posts and one for comments — or adding a line at the end of each post encouraging subscriptions or mentioning it in a sidebar.

Subscribe to my RSS feed!

Click here and start reading!

Add an RSS Feed to Your Sidebar

You can continue to build community or keep your readers up to date with blogs or news sites that you read by posting that blog's RSS feed on your blog's sidebar. A WordPress widget simplifies this task once you choose what feeds to feature. Your theme may automatically include a feed link in the header, footer, or elsewhere, but it never hurts to give your audience multiple ways to get access to your site. Adding an RSS notice to your sidebar is a simple matter of identifying the feed, as described in the previous section, and using a widget to display it.

Add an RSS Feed to Your Sidebar

1 After you identify a feed you want to subscribe to, paste the URL in the address box and press **Enter** (**Return** for Mac).

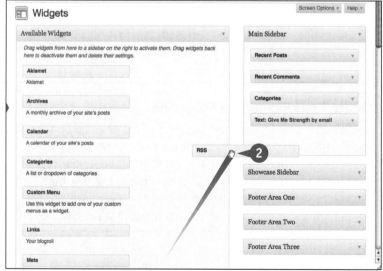

2 After clicking **Widgets** under Appearance in the left menu of your Dashboard, scroll to the RSS widget, and click and drag the widget to the widget area where you want the feed to appear.

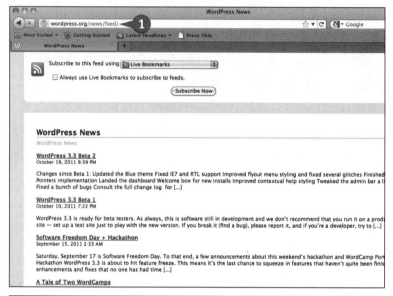

The widget opens.

3 Paste the URL of the feed in the first box.

Note: Be sure to include the protocol, http://.

4 Type a name for the feed.

5 Click the drop-down menu next to How many items and click to choose the number of feed items you want to display.

A You can select check boxes to add content, author, or date to the RSS display on your page.

6 Click **Save**.

7 Click **Close**.

The feed is published to your sidebar.

8 Click your blog title to go to your site.

9 Scroll down to view your RSS feed display.

10 Position your mouse pointer over one of the headlines to read the first part of that item's content.

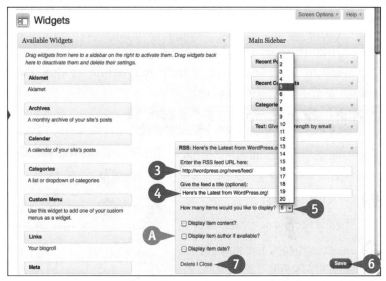

TIPS

Can I publish my own feed this way on my blog?
No, you need to use the Recent Posts widget instead. Like the RSS widget, it lets you choose how many recent posts to show in the widget and to give the widget a title. You also can choose whether to show the post's date.

> **Recent Posts**
>
> The most recent posts on your site

What is the difference between the RSS widget and the RSS Links widget?
The RSS Links widget, available as a default on WordPress.com and with the Jetpack plugin package, lets you promote your own feeds in your sidebar. You can choose whether the links are text only, RSS image only, or text plus image. If you use image only, you can choose the color of the RSS logo. Similar plugins are available for self-hosted WordPress blogs.

Create a Category RSS Feed Link

If your blog has categories that may appeal to different audiences, you can set up separate feeds for those audiences. For example, you may have a needlework blog. You can create separate feeds for your knitting, needlepoint, crewel, and crochet categories. WordPress has the code built in; you just need to point your readers to it by providing a link and promoting it on your site. Sidebars are always a good location for such links.

Create a Category RSS Feed Link

1. From your blog's administration pages, click **Posts**.

2. Click **Categories**.

   The Categories panel opens.

3. Select and copy the slug of the category to which you want to provide a feed link.

4. Click **Appearance**.

5. Click **Widgets**.

   The Widgets page opens.

6. Drag a Text widget to a sidebar.

   The widget pops open.

7. Give your widget a title.

8. Type an HTML link to the category feed, like so: **<a href= "http://www.yourblog. com/category/category_ slug/feed">link name</ a>**, where *www.yourblog.com* (*yourblog*.wordpress.com) is your blog's URL; *category_slug* is the slug for the desired category; and *link name* is what you want your link to say.

Note: At WordPress.com the feed link would be `<a href="category/ category_slug/feed">link name</a>`.

9. Scroll down and click **Save**.

258

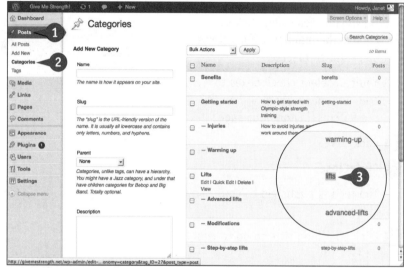

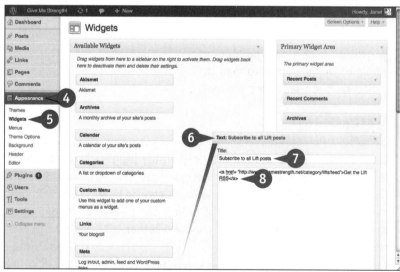

The widget is published to your website.

10 On your blog's front page, find the new sidebar widget, and click the new subscription link.

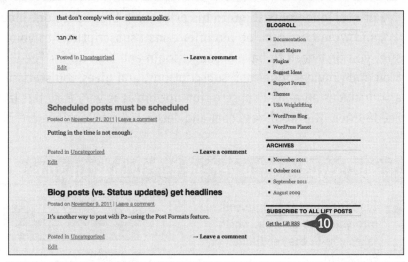

A feed subscription window opens.

11 Click **Subscribe Now** to subscribe to your own feed.

A subscription window appears and leads you through the steps.

TIPS

Can I do this with tags too?
Yes. WordPress has feeds built in that you can use at any time. In addition to the main content, comments, and categories feeds discussed in this chapter, standard feeds are available for authors and for tags. Use the format described in Step **8**, except rather than `category/category-slug/`, type `tag/tag_name/` or **`author/author_name/`**.

Do I have to do anything to maintain the feed?
No. Again, WordPress has the feed code built in. In fact, savvy readers could even subscribe to any feed, including category, tag, and author feeds, without your knowing it by typing the appropriate URL in their browsers and subscribing.

Sign Up with FeedBurner and E-Mail Subscriptions

Not everyone wants to go to his or her web browser to get blog updates. Fortunately, FeedBurner and WordPress.com let you offer e-mail subscriptions to your posts. If you have a self-hosted site, you first need to have a Google login and sign up for FeedBurner. That service tracks your RSS feed and provides for e-mail subscriptions, and gives you statistics on both. The Jetpack plugin set also includes an e-mail subscription option. It is very easy but lacks the statistics information of FeedBurner. The WordPress.com and Jetpack e-mail options are discussed in the next section.

Sign Up with FeedBurner and E-Mail Subscriptions

1 Type **feedburner.google.com** into your web browser, which takes you to the FeedBurner My Feeds page.

Note: If you are not already logged in to your Google account, you are first asked to sign in.

2 Type your blog's URL into the Burn a Feed box.

3 Click **Next**.

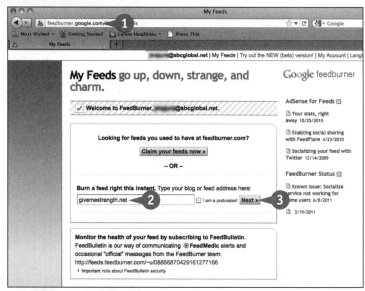

The Identify Feed Source page opens. It lists feeds available at your home page URL.

4 Click the feed you want to track (○ changes to ◉).

5 Click **Next**.

FeedBurner gives a confirmation message. Click **Skip directly to feed management**, which opens a page saying that your feed is ready.

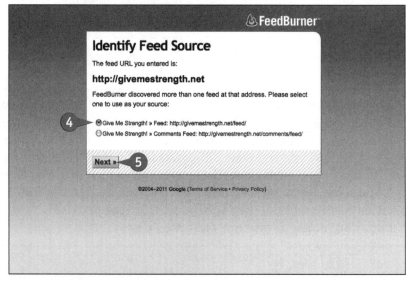

FeedBurner confirms your feed and its new feed address.

6 Click **Next**.

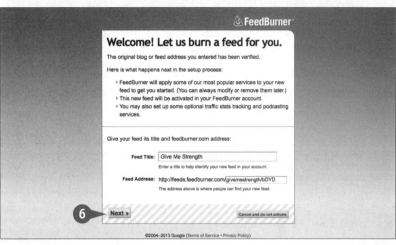

Your feed is now ready.

7 Click **Publicize**.

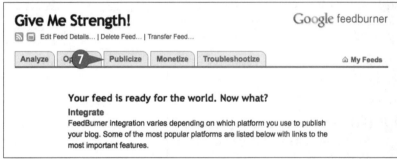

The Publicize Your Feed page opens.

8 Click **Email Subscriptions**.

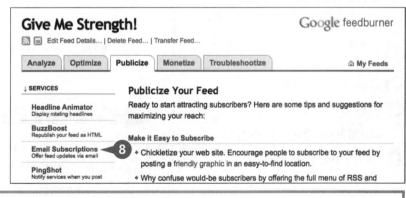

What do feeds have to do with e-mail subscriptions?
FeedBurner takes advantage of your site's RSS feeds to create e-mail notices. It provides you a link or code for a signup so that people can subscribe to get your posts in a daily e-mail when you post new content. When you sign up, though, it does mean that you can direct your RSS feed to go through FeedBurner, which then provides statistics about your feed traffic. Those aspects of FeedBurner, plus how to track your e-mail subscriptions, are discussed in Chapter 9.

Can I use FeedBurner with my WordPress.com blog?
You can, but you cannot publish the FeedBurner signup form. Still, you can post a signup link in a widget that readers can click to sign up for a FeedBurner e-mail subscription.

With the code that FeedBurner supplies, you can add an e-mail subscription signup form to your site. You copy the code from FeedBurner, and then paste it in a new text widget at your blog. Once you do that, you need to do nothing more to see that your e-mail subscribers get your new content delivered to their e-mail inboxes. You can make adjustments if you like as to how often your subscribers get their e-mail and at what time of day. New subscribers will first get an e-mail to confirm their intent to subscribe.

Sign Up with FeedBurner and E-Mail Subscriptions (continued)

The Email Subscriptions page opens.

⑨ Scroll down to the code box.

⑩ Copy all the code in the top code box to create a signup form for your site.

Note: You can use the code in the second box to create a signup link rather than a form.

⑪ Click **Send me an email whenever people unsubscribe** if you want notification when people unsubscribe (☐ changes to ☑).

⑫ Log in to your blog's dashboard.

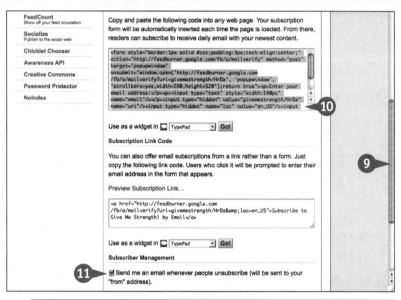

⑬ Click **Appearance**.

⑭ Click **Widgets**.

The Widgets panel appears.

⑮ Drag a Text widget to a sidebar.

16 Type a title.

17 Type introductory text, and then paste the FeedBurner code.

18 Click **Save**.

The widget is published to your sidebar.

19 Click your site name.

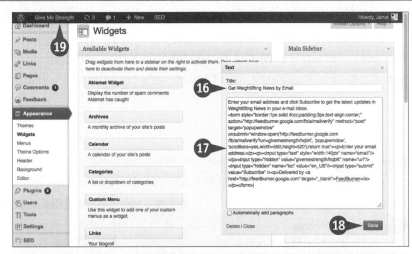

A The widget appears in your sidebar.

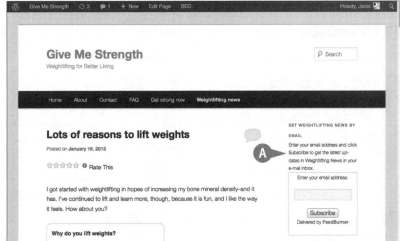

Whose e-mail address shows as the sender from my FeedBurner-managed e-mail?

The e-mail address you used to sign up at FeedBurner appears, unless you prefer something else. If you want to change the "from" e-mail, click **Communication Preferences** under Email Subscriptions on the Publicize tab at FeedBurner. You also can change the standard confirmation e-mail text and subject line on that page. Remember to save changes.

After I set up the link and subscribed to my own feed, I put up a new post, but I have not received it in my e-mail. Did I do something wrong?

It may be a matter of timing. At FeedBurner, click **Delivery Options** under Email Subscriptions in the Publicize panel, choose the time for your daily e-mail, and click **Save**.

Offer E-Mail Updates at WordPress.com and Jetpack

The simplest of e-mail subscription options is available to WordPress.com users and self-hosted site publishers who have the Jetpack plugin package. In both cases, creating a signup option is as easy as dragging a widget to a sidebar location and configuring it. At WordPress.com, the e-mail subscription is integrated with the service's blog following feature.

Offer E-Mail Updates at WordPress.com and Jetpack

At WordPress.com

1. From your blog's administration pages, click **Appearance**.

2. Click **Widgets**.

   The Widgets panel appears.

3. Drag the Follow Blog widget to a sidebar.

The widget expands.

4. Make any changes you want in the widget box.

5. Click **Save**.

6. Click the blog title to view the site.

Ⓐ The Follow widget appears in the designated widget area.

Using Jetpack

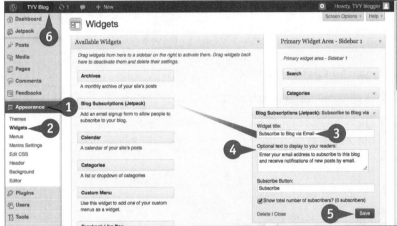

① From your blog's administration pages, click **Appearance**.

② Click **Widgets**.

The Widgets panel appears.

③ Drag the Blog Subscriptions widget to a sidebar.

④ Make any changes you want in the widget box.

⑤ Click **Save**.

⑥ Click the blog title to view the site.

The subscription e-mail appears in the designated sidebar.

TIPS

What happens when someone clicks the Follow or Subscribe button?

At WordPress.com, those signed in at WordPress.com have the site added to their Reader with the setting to get e-mail updates immediately. At self-hosted sites — or WordPress.com if the person is not logged in — the widget sends an e-mail to the address provided to confirm the subscription, and the widget tells the reader it is doing so.

How do I get a Follow button to appear on my front page?

That Follow button appears to viewers who are not logged in at WordPress.com. You need to do nothing to make it show up on your blog. If you do not want it to appear, however, you can go to the Reading Settings under Settings in the left menu bar, and deselect the check box in the Follower Settings area next to Show follow button to logged out users (☑ changes to ☐).

Add a Contact Page and Form

You can let readers get in touch with you privately, via a contact form. While you probably do not want to publish your e-mail address — unless you want it to be a giant target for spam — providing some form of private communication for your audience tells readers that you want to hear from them. You can use a plugin, the Jetpack contact form features, or the WordPress.com contact form function. Several good contact form plugins are available for self-hosted blogs, including the well-established and popular Fast Secure Contact Form. This example uses the WordPress.com/Jetpack contact form.

Add a Contact Page and Form

1. Click **Pages**.
2. Click **Add New**.

   The page-writing panel appears.

3. Type **Contact** as the title.
4. Type some introductory text.
5. Click the **Custom Form** button (⊞).

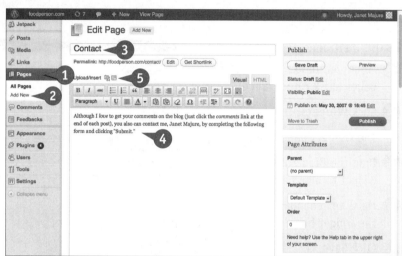

   The form builder dialog box appears.

6. Position your mouse pointer over an area you want to edit, and click the edit link that appears.

Ⓐ An editing area appears.

7. Make your change.
8. Click **Save this field**.
9. Repeat Steps 6 to 8 for any other fields you want to edit.
10. Click **Add this form to my post**.

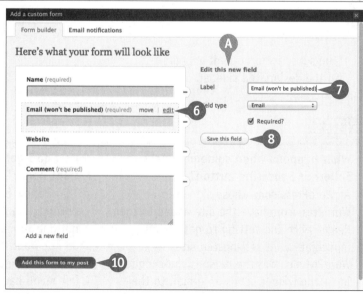

The form builder disappears, and the code for your contact form appears in your page.

⑪ Click **Publish**.

WordPress publishes your Contact page.

⑫ Click **View Page**.

Your Contact page with the response form appears.

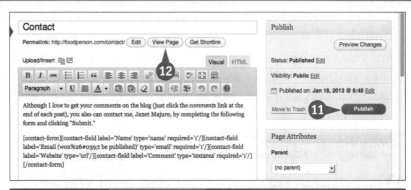

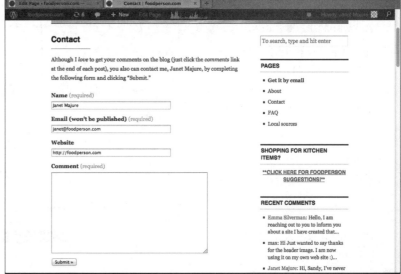

TIPS

How can I add more fields to the form?
When the form builder first appears, click the link under Can I add more fields? A new field appears in the preview at the left, and the right area displays the edit field boxes. There, you add a label and choose the field type from the drop-down list.

How can I add an image or different colors to the form?
To make that kind of change, you need to use a plugin such as Fast Secure Contact Form or BigContact Contact Page. They offer many more customization options but, as you might expect, are more complicated to set up than the WordPress.com/Jetpack forms.

Add Cross References to Your Posts

You get your readers interested and more involved in your site when you add cross references within your posts to other content you have written. To do so, you create a link in your post. The WordPress link dialog box makes it extra easy to find previous pages and posts that you may want to link to. Once you insert and save your link, readers can click it to go to another page or post. It gives readers another reason to stay or return to your site. You can even link to a list of posts by category or tag if you like.

Add Cross References to Your Posts

1. On an Edit Post page, highlight the text to which you want to add a link.

2. Click the **Insert/edit link** button (🔗 ✂️).

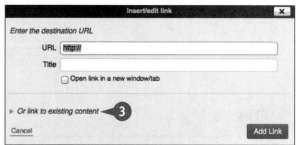

The Insert/edit link dialog box appears.

3. Click **Or link to existing content**.

4. Scroll to find the desired page or post, and click it.

Ⓐ You can use the search box to find previous contact.

5. Click **Add Link**.

Add Link changes to Update.

6. Click **Update**.

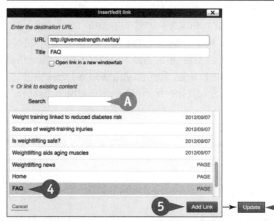

The Insert/edit link dialog box disappears, and the post box returns with the new link in place.

⑦ Click **Update**.

WordPress confirms you have saved the changes.

⑧ Click **View Post**.

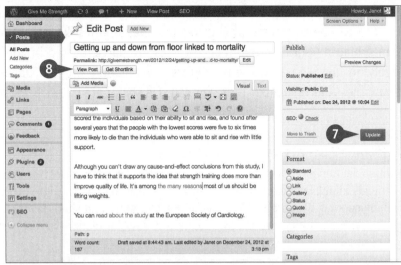

Ⓑ WordPress updates the post to include the internal link.

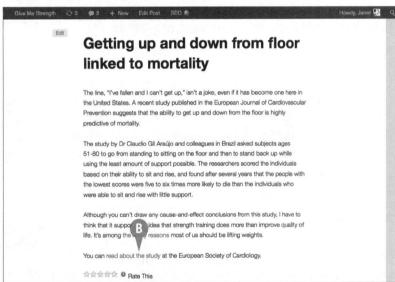

How can I search for a previous post on a topic that is not stated explicitly in the title, categories, or tags?

Simply type your search term in the Insert/edit link search box, and WordPress searches your entire blog database for the term as you type. It filters your content and displays only those posts and pages that include your search term anywhere.

How do I link to a list of posts in a particular category?

The easiest way is to click a category on your blog to open the category archive display, copy the hyperlink you see, and then paste it in the URL box that appears when you click the **Insert/edit link** button.

Let Readers Share Your Posts

Even if you are not a member of Facebook, LinkedIn, Twitter, Digg, or other online communities, you can be sure some of your readers are. If you take advantage of that situation, your readers can promote your blog and feel like they are participating in your site. These social networks are evolving fast, so watch the WordPress news module on your Dashboard to see what new options are available. And remember that you can use social media both for incoming and outgoing content.

Social Networks and Bookmarks

At social networks such as Facebook and LinkedIn, people post personal updates and photos — and tell friends about favorite web pages they have read. Delicious, Digg, StumbleUpon, and other social bookmarking sites are specifically for users to store and share favorite links. All these sites can boost traffic to your blog, so it is worthwhile to make it easy for readers to recommend your post to their social networks.

Let Readers Promote WordPress.org Posts

Numerous plugins are available that let your readers recommend your posts by clicking buttons that go to their social networking sites, such as Facebook, or their social bookmarking sites, such as StumbleUpon. Favorite plugins include Sociable, Share Buttons by Lockerz/AddToAny, Social Sharing Toolkit, and Social Media Widget. They have similar functions but different looks. You also can use the Publicize module of Jetpack.

- improves balance
- maintains strong bones
- makes everyday tasks easier

Posted in **Benefits** | Tagged **Balance, Bones** | **4 Replies**

The Publicize Tool at WordPress.com and Jetpack

The Publicize settings — available on the Sharing Settings panel under Settings in the left menu bar at WordPress.com and Jetpack-enabled self-hosted sites — provide links to connect with and publish to Facebook, Twitter, Linked In, Tumblr, and Yahoo! Updates. Clicking the **Add new...** link for each service takes you through a series of screens that tells those services to publish an update with your latest WordPress post. These are discussed in more detail in Chapter 8.

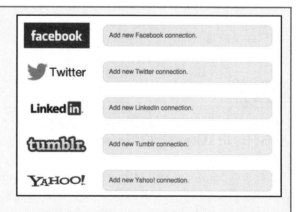

Add Share Buttons

One of the best ways to encourage your readers to spread the word about your site or particular posts is to add social sharing buttons to your site. One way that is available to both WordPress.com and self-hosted WordPress bloggers with the Jetpack plugin pack is the Publicize feature. It is enabled by default, but you need to choose what services you want to use. Once you do, your readers can click a sharing button or two and let their networks know you have written a great post.

Add Share Buttons

1. Click **Settings** and then **Sharing** in the left menu bar.

   The Sharing Settings panel opens.

2. Scroll down to the Sharing Buttons section.

3. Click and drag a service button to the Enabled Services area.

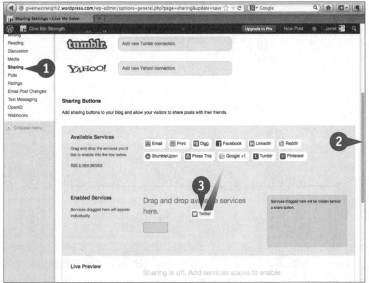

A. The button appears in the Live Preview area as it will appear on your blog.

4. Repeat Steps 1 to 3 for each service button you want to add.

5. If desired, make changes to button display style, the buttons' label text, where to open links, and where to display the buttons.

6. Click **Save Changes**.

   WordPress publishes the buttons to your site.

CHAPTER 8

Building Traffic to Your Blog

Building traffic to your blog starts with great content, and it takes a while to accumulate enough good content to get much search engine attention. You have many other tools, however, from social networks to search engine optimization strategies, to gain more readers.

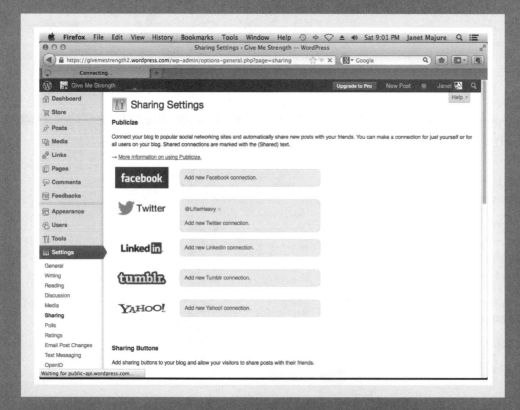

Understanding Blog Traffic

You can have an active, stimulating blog — or a quiet one, if you prefer — if you take advantage of — or avoid — the various means to boost traffic to your site. It is easier to do so if you understand more about how your blog may attract traffic. Apart from *bots* — programs that automatically scan sites for information — your visitors find your site or particular posts through search engines, through directly typing in your address or using a bookmark, or by way of links in e-mail messages, social networks, and other outside websites. You can take steps to raise your blog profile in all these venues.

Great Content

The number one way to generate high traffic to your site is to provide great content. To a large extent, publishing great content in itself helps search engines find your site and prompt individuals to bookmark your site, recommend it to their friends, or link to it from their sites. Although there is no single definition of great content, you are on the right path if it benefits your intended audience. To do so, make sure your content answers readers' questions, addresses their needs, is stimulating or entertaining, and is visually appealing. Edit your copy so that it is understandable and follows standard spelling and grammar conventions.

Attract Search Engines

Search engines such as Google can direct considerable traffic to your site. See "Optimize Your Blog for Search Engines," later in this chapter, for steps you can take to raise your site's rankings in search engine searches. Again, great content is a critical aspect of improving your site's ranking. In time, you can see what search terms people use when they find your site via a search engine, and those results can give you clues for further content.

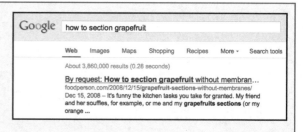

Encourage Bookmarks

Chapter 7 discusses making it easy for your visitors to participate in your site by providing buttons to social networking sites, such as Facebook, and bookmarking sites, such as StumbleUpon. Those options provide a double benefit for you by engaging readers and by attracting more traffic to your site. Use them!

Add It to E-Mail

Adding your site's URL to your e-mail is such a simple thing, and yet many people overlook this step. Set up an automatic signature with your e-mail program. The steps vary from one program to another, but if you search your online or computer-based e-mail software Help for *signature* you are sure to find the steps to do so. You

Signature

Signature: ○ Do not use a signature
● Show a signature on all outgoing messages

Keep up with my xeriscape updates:
http://myxeriscapeblog.com

can add a line of encouragement or just list the address as you prefer, but make it a part of your routine e-mail practices.

Link Out

When you *link out,* you link to other sites. Some people worry that linking out takes readers away from their sites. Although that is true, two other actions also are likely to result. First, the reader who clicks the link to another site very well may back up

Here locally, informal discussions with market producers indicate that sales are down. And Lynn Byczynski, editor of Growing for Market newsletter for growers, noted in her 2011 Trends special edition that the increase in markets is cutting into sales for some established farms.

and return to your site. Second, the owners of the site may very well notice that you linked to their site, prompting them to visit your site — and maybe return the favor. You can link out in posts, pages, and through a links list.

Post to Social Networks

You also build traffic when you repost your material to your social networks. The web gets very weblike indeed with these networks. When you repost your material or at least links to your Facebook or Twitter accounts, for example, you are telling your friends and perhaps your friends' friends as well. How to do so is discussed in the next four sections of this chapter.

Participate in Other Blogs

Read and make useful comments on other blogs — and include your blog address. If you blog at WordPress.com, make sure you follow blogs that you appreciate and click the Like button on

posts you like. Doing so alerts the owners of the blogs that you are out there, and they just might check your site out. If they like yours, too, you may have gained yourself a regular reader.

Create a Links List

You can share the love by including other websites and blogs in your *blogroll*, otherwise known as a links list. Adding others to your blogroll also lets them know that your blog exists. Everybody wins!

You can find the Links panel to set up your list via the left menu bar at WordPress.com. WordPress developers, however, removed the Links panel as a standard part of new WordPress installations starting with version 3.5. If you have a self-hosted site, you need to install the Link Manager plugin.

Create a Links List

Create Your List

1. Click **Links** in the Dashboard's left menu bar.

   The Links panel opens.

   Note: New WordPress.com blogs come with a few links already listed.

2. Click **Add New**.

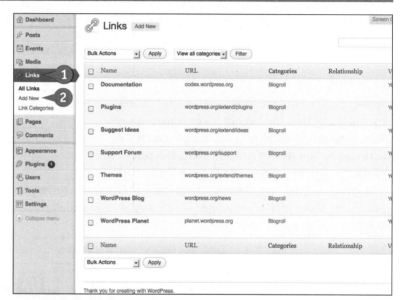

The Add New Link window opens.

3. In the Name module, type the name of the link as you want it to appear in your blogroll.

4. Type the complete URL of the site in the Web Address module.

5. If you want, type a brief — as in four or five words — description of the site in the Description module.

6. Click **Blogroll** (☐ changes to ☑).

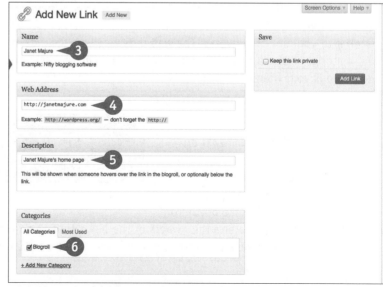

7 Scroll down to the Target module.

8 Click **_none** (◯ changes to ◉), which makes the target URL open in the same browser window or tab as your links list.

9 If desired, complete the relationship information.

10 Return to the top of the page and click **Add Link**.

WordPress saves the link and returns a new Add New Link screen.

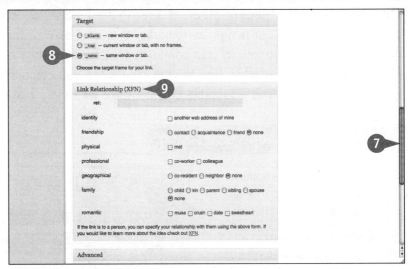

Display Your Blogroll

1 After expanding the Appearance menu, click **Widgets**.

2 Drag the Links widget to one of the active widget areas on the right side of the Widgets panel.

3 Click your preferred display options (☐ changes to ☑).

4 Click **Save**.

WordPress saves your selections and displays your blogroll on your site.

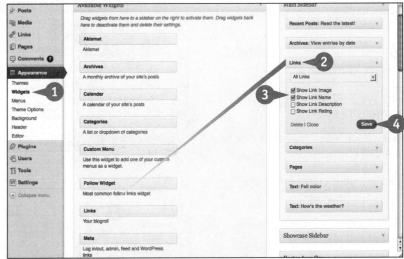

TIPS

What are the Link Relationship and Advanced modules about?

The Link Relationship lets your links relay information about your relationship to the party you linked to. The Advanced options allow you to display an image along with the link or add other information for your own use, such as RSS address, notes, and rating.

How do I organize my links into link categories?

You can create link categories on the Add New Link, Edit Link, or Link Categories panels. Then, when you edit individual links, you can assign the link to a category or categories. From the Link Categories panel, you also can edit category names, so that you can call yours Favorite Links rather than Blogroll and still have just one category.

Comment on Someone Else's Blog

Commenting on the blogs of others is a recognized means of attracting people to your blog. How? When others read your insightful remarks, they cannot wait to read what else you have to say. They therefore click the link in your comment that leads to your blog. As a result, make sure to take every opportunity to include a link to your blog when you comment on someone else's blog. You also can create a reputation as a valuable commentator when you make regular and useful comments.

Comment on Someone Else's Blog

1 On the post that you want to comment about, click the link to the comments form.

Note: Comment link location and text vary from one blog to another.

2 Type your name in the Name box.

3 Type your e-mail in the Email box, if required.

4 Type your blog's URL in the Website box.

Note: Most blogs provide a link to your website with your comment.

5 Type your comment in the space provided.

A Some blogs let you preview your post.

6 Type the words or letters of the *captcha* (or in this case, ReCaptcha) box, if present.

Note: Captcha is a spam-avoidance tool that you can add to self-hosted blogs with a plugin. See Chapter 6 to learn about using plugins.

7 Click **Submit Comment**.

Your comment is published or submitted for moderation.

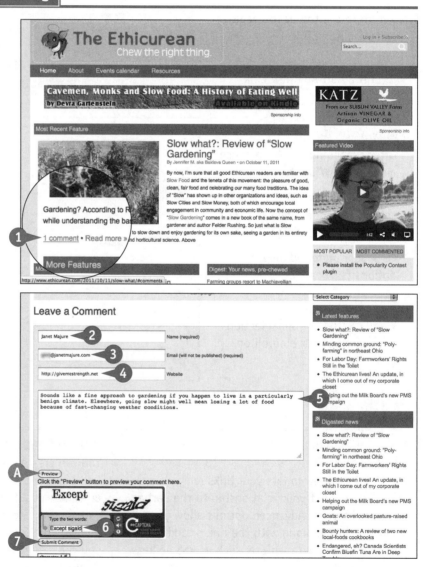

278

What to Say on Someone Else's Blog

Well-placed and considered comments prompt readers of other people's blogs to click to your website to read what else you have to say. Reading and commenting contributes to the blogging community and adds to your standing. Of course, leaving useless or annoying remarks can have the opposite effect. Remember, too, that you probably cannot delete or edit your comment once you submit it, so review it carefully before clicking **Submit** or **Post Comment**.

What to Say

Add something *useful* to the conversation. Useful might be anything from adding a bit of helpful advice based on your experience with the subject to sharing the good resources you know about. Useful also may mean to pose a question related to the blog post; pertinent questions expand the conversation. Also, you should see if the site has a comments policy and read it before commenting.

How to Say It

Whatever you say, keep it relevant to the topic of the blog post, keep it brief, and keep it polite. Break any of those rules and you lose most if not all the benefits that you might accrue by commenting. If you can provide a link to a useful resource, add it to your comment, too. As always, proofread what you write; you may not be able to change it.

What Not to Say

New bloggers, eager to attract readers, often are tempted to visit numerous blogs and comment, "Great post!" or "Thanks for writing this!" Although such comments do little harm, they rarely have the desired effect — and they might be identified as spam. Self-promotional comments are rarely welcome, unless you really do have *the* solution to the problem being discussed.

Connect with Facebook

Facebook, with its ocean of users, provides a useful means of spreading the word about your blog posts to your Facebook connections. To add those posts to your Facebook feed with a minimum of effort, you need to connect WordPress with your Facebook account. You need to have a Facebook account, and self-hosted bloggers need to use a plugin. A popular one is Add Link to Facebook. This section uses the Sharing tool in Jetpack for WordPress.org users. WordPress.com users likewise can connect with Facebook using the WordPress.com Sharing tool.

Connect with Facebook

Make the Connection

1. Click **Settings**.

2. Click **Sharing**.

   The Sharing Settings panel opens.

3. Click **Add new Facebook connection**.

   Facebook opens an authorization window.

4. Click **Friends**.

5. Confirm or change who you want to have access to your posts on your Wall.

6. Click **Go to App**.

Facebook shows a dialog box.

7 Click **Allow**.

WordPress confirms the connection.

8 Click **OK**.

WordPress returns to the Sharing Settings page, where it lists your connection.

Use the App

A The Publish module on the Edit Post panel shows the link to Facebook.

1 Click **Edit Settings**.

The Publicize area expands.

2 Edit the message if desired. The default is to use the post title.

B Click ☑ to change it to ☐ if you do not want the post published to Facebook.

3 Click **Publish**.

Your post is published to your blog, and the message with a link to the post appears on your Facebook Wall.

TIPS

Why does the app ask if WordPress.com can publish to Facebook when my site is self-hosted?

Because the Jetpack functions operate through the WordPress.com servers. You need to authorize the connection if you want to use Jetpack to connect to Facebook.

My blog's connection to Facebook does not seem to be working anymore. What should I do?

Essentially, you need to start over. On your blog site, click the **X** next to the Facebook profile you previously connected, which removes the connection. At Facebook, go to your Account Settings and then to Apps. If you see a WordPress.com app, click the **X** next to it and then confirm your intent to remove the app. Then go back and reconnect as you did in the first place.

Connect with Twitter

WordPress and Twitter let you communicate more than ever. Your blog readers can keep up with your Twitter feed right on your blog, and you can inform your Twitter followers of your new WordPress posts. You also can display other Twitter feeds of interest to your readers. To post to Twitter, you need a Twitter account, available at http://twitter.com, to get started. Then you need to connect using a plugin for a self-hosted site or the Publicize Twitter connection for WordPress.com blogs. One popular plugin is WP to Twitter. This example uses Publicize, available at WordPress.com and through the Jetpack plugin pack.

Connect with Twitter

Make the Connection

1. Click **Settings**.

2. Click **Sharing**.

   The Sharing Settings panel opens.

3. Click **Add new Twitter connection**.

Twitter opens an authorization window.

4. Type your Twitter username.

5. Type your Twitter password.

6. Click **Authorize app**.

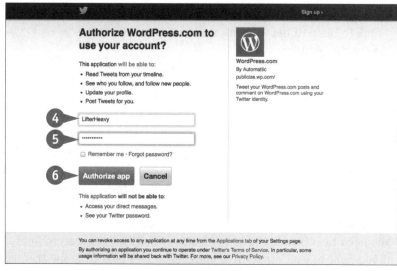

WordPress confirms the connection.

7 Click **OK**.

> You have successfully connected your blog with your Twitter account.
>
> ☐ Make this connection available to all users of this blog?
>
> OK ◄ **7**

The Publicize panel reappears, with the connection listed next to Twitter.

🐦 **Twitter**   @LifterHeavy ✕

Add new Twitter connection.

Use the App

Ⓐ The Publish module on the Edit Post panel shows the link to Twitter.

1 Click **Publish**.

WordPress publishes your post to your blog, and your Twitter feed adds a message with a link to the post.

Ⓑ The Edit link lets you alter the Twitter message, which defaults to the post title.

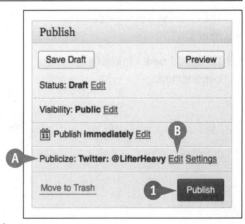

Publish

Save Draft   Preview

Status: **Draft** Edit

Visibility: **Public** Edit

📅 Publish **immediately** Edit   **B**

A Publicize: **Twitter: @LifterHeavy** Edit Settings

Move to Trash   **1** Publish

TIPS

How do I display my Twitter feed on my blog?
If you have Jetpack or blog at WordPress.com, go to your Widgets page under Appearance in the left menu bar, and drag a Twitter widget to a sidebar. Add your Twitter username — or someone else's feed if you like — and choose among the options, then click **Save**, and your feed soon appears. Note that it must be a public feed.

Can I publish my Twitter feed on my self-hosted site without Jetpack?
Yes. Several plugins are available. Twitter Tools is among the most popular. You also can create the code for a custom Twitter widget by going to http://twitter.com/widgets. Click **Create New**, provide the requested information, click **Create Widget**, and then copy the code that appears. Paste the code in a Text widget at your blog, and you are set.

Connect with LinkedIn

Connecting your blog with your LinkedIn account is a great way to share your business-related or career-related posts. When you connect the two, your WordPress posts automatically appear as updates, using your post title plus its web address. Jetpack at self-hosted blogs and WordPress.com have a built-in tool on the Publicize page to connect your accounts. Other plugins are available to bloggers who do not want to use Jetpack. NextScripts: Social Networks Auto-Poster is a good one. In fact, it links to more than a dozen networks.

Connect with LinkedIn

① Click **Settings**.

② Click **Sharing**.

The Sharing Settings panel opens.

③ Click **Add new LinkedIn connection**.

LinkedIn opens an authorization window.

④ Type the e-mail address you use at LinkedIn.

⑤ Type your LinkedIn password.

⑥ Click **Ok, I'll Allow It**.

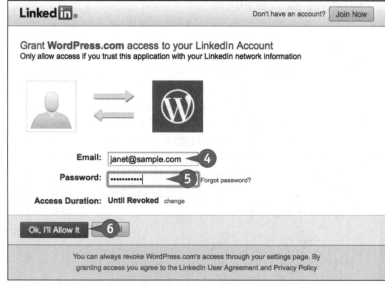

WordPress confirms the connection.

7 Click **OK**.

The Publicize panel reappears, with the connection listed next to Twitter.

TIPS

Now that the blog and LinkedIn are connected, how do I publish my blog posts to LinkedIn?

It works just as described in the previous sections, "Connect with Facebook" and "Connect with Twitter." You can be connected to multiple networks and post automatically to all of them, or you can disable the connection on a per-post basis.

Why does the confirmation box ask whether to make LinkedIn available to all the blog users?

If your blog has multiple authors, as discussed in Chapter 14, selecting this check box means their posts also are published to your LinkedIn updates. They do not otherwise have access to your LinkedIn account. You also can create a separate connection for each user to connect to his or her LinkedIn account. These options also are available for Facebook and Twitter.

Auto-Post to Other Networks

You can post to more networks than Facebook, Twitter, and LinkedIn, but it is not always easy. At this writing, for example, Google+ does not offer access to WordPress or other developers to automatically write to your Google+ account. At WordPress.com and Jetpack-enabled self-hosted blogs, you can add automatic publishing to Yahoo updates and your Tumblr blog. At this writing, those are the only added possibilities for WordPress.com users. Other plugins for self-hosted blogs publish to 20 or more networks. You need to have a logon at each one where you want to publish.

Connect to Yahoo and Tumblr

The easiest way to automatically post to Yahoo updates and Tumblr blogs is to use the Publicize page at WordPress.com and Jetpack. You follow essentially the same steps as explained in the preceding sections on connecting to Facebook and others via the Sharing Settings page. Each requires an account. You log on, and then authorize the service to allow WordPress.com — and Jetpack by way of WordPress.com — to publish there. At Yahoo, you also can choose whether to make your updates available to anyone or just your connections.

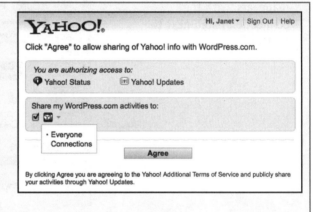

Connect to Google+

At this writing, Google+ does not allow anyone to write directly to a Google+ account from a WordPress blog. Until that changes, you can try NextScripts: Social Networks Auto-Poster Pro, which requires $50 for a script that lets you publish but that may not be secure. A workaround exists if you want to try it: Add your site's RSS feed to your Google Reader page. Then, use the +1 icon at Google Reader to add posts to your Google+ page. However, Google plans to discontinue Google Reader.

Pin Post Images at Pinterest

Like Google+, Pinterest at this time does not have an *application programming interface*, or API, that allows outside publishers, such as WordPress, to publish to its site. As a result, you need to install the Pinterest bookmarklet on your browser and use it to post images from your WordPress site. It is available at http://pinterest.com/about/goodies. Alternatively, you can use a Pinterest sharing button from WordPress.com, Jetpack, or any number of social sharing plugins. Then click the button on your site to pin your image to your Pinterest page.

Plug In to Many Networks — or One

Plugins are available that let you publish to a dozen or more networks. Among them are Network Publisher, which includes MySpace, Plurk, Foursquare, and more among the more than 26 networks to which it links. Another is NextScripts: Social Networks Auto-Poster. If you have a particular network that you want to link to, such as MySpace, you might be better off to find a plugin just for that network.

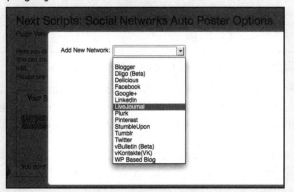

Social Network Managers

If you are serious about getting your posts to the largest number of networks, another option is a separate social media dashboard. Such providers tend to provide reports and monitoring tools as well as publishing tools. One widely respected and accessible manager is HootSuite, which has both free and paid versions.

The Need to Cross-Post

You may wonder whether you need to cross-post your WordPress entries to a dozen social networks. The truth is no one can say for certain whether doing so is worthwhile. If you decide to spread your posts across numerous networks, you probably should be committed to keeping up with those networks in terms of responding to comments and otherwise maintaining your presence. Many argue that the payoff in added blog traffic is enough to justify the time required.

Understanding Trackbacks and Pingbacks

Trackbacks and pingbacks automatically alert blogs when other bloggers have linked to them. When you publish trackbacks and pingbacks as miniature comments, you also let readers see that your blog has credibility elsewhere. If you publish pingbacks within your blog — that is, from one of your posts to another — you also provide another means of navigation for your readers. The most important thing about them, though, is that they foster greater traffic to your site.

Why Send Trackbacks and Pingbacks?

Sending trackbacks and pingbacks to blogs that you have referred to builds community among bloggers and promotes your blog to the sites to which you link. It is a nice way to give credit and to let others know you exist.

Why Publish Trackbacks and Pingbacks?

Publishing the trackbacks and pingbacks that other blogs have sent to your site similarly encourages community. It lets you and your readers discover other sites and is a way of saying thank you to the blogs that have linked to your site. They also may link back to you, and links to your site help raise your ranking at search engines.

How Trackbacks and Pingbacks Look

The appearance of trackbacks and pingbacks depends on the theme, but most themes style them a little differently than they do other comments. Typically, a theme displays a link to the post that links to yours and an excerpt from the pingback post, often framed by ellipses inside square brackets like so, [...]. Some themes may allow you to publish pingbacks and trackbacks separately from other comments.

Ruby Red Grapefruit: Jewels in my Kitchen // Nov 21, 2010 at 10:03 pm (Edit)

[...] help sectioning a grapefruit? Here's a great step by step pictorial that is really [...]

Reply

Avocado, Grapefruit and Roasted Mushroom Spinach Salad « The Purple Mixer // Sep 26, 2011 at 7:17 pm (Edit)

[...] you should have one clean section of fruit. Continue to peel sections from the membrane. Click here for detailed step-by-step photos and instructions of how to section grapefruit. Share [...]

Reply

Trackbacks versus Pingbacks

Trackbacks are manual, and pingbacks are automatic if you have enabled them. With pingbacks, that means that if you link to another site, WordPress automatically sends a sort of mini-comment to the other site showing that you have linked to the site.

How to Enable Trackbacks and Pingbacks

Whether to routinely allow trackbacks and pingbacks is part of the default article settings

Discussion Settings

Default article settings

☑ Attempt to notify any blogs linked to from the article
☑ Allow link notifications from other blogs (pingbacks and trackbacks)
☑ Allow people to post comments on new articles
(These settings may be overridden for individual articles.)

mentioned in Chapter 4. The Attempt To Notify setting is for sending pingbacks, and the Allow Link Notifications setting is for publishing them on your site. You can change settings for individual posts, instead of site wide, in the Discussion module of the Edit Post panel. You may need to go to Screen Options on the post panel to reveal the Discussion module.

Why and How to Send a Trackback

You may want to send a trackback when you mention or give credit to a blog but do not specifically link to it. To do so, type the URL of the blog or blog post in the Send Trackbacks module of the Edit Post/ New Post panel.

Send Trackbacks

Send trackbacks to:

(Separate multiple URLs with spaces)

Trackbacks are a way to notify legacy blog systems that you've linked to them. If you link other WordPress sites they'll be notified automatically using pingbacks, no other action necessary.

Stop Unwanted Self-Pingbacks

To prevent a pingback from appearing on an old post that you link to in a newer post, type only the part of the previous post's URL that comes after the domain as your link. For example, instead of using http://www.myblog.com/2012/

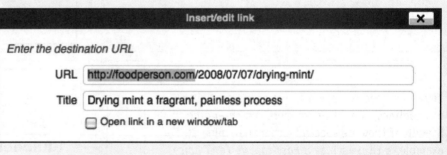

Insert/edit link   ✕

Enter the destination URL

URL   http://foodperson.com/2008/07/07/drying-mint/

Title   Drying mint a fragrant, painless process

☐ Open link in a new window/tab

03/12/oldpost/ as the link, use /2012/03/12/oldpost/. If that fails, use the HTML editor to enter the link.

Optimize Your Blog for Search Engines

You draw more readers to your blog when they are able to find it through search engines such as Google and Yahoo!. *Search engine optimization*, or SEO, means taking steps to help search engines do just that. Search engine operators are constantly refining their techniques as they try to serve the best search results and avoid sites that are not helpful. Generally, having good content, descriptive post titles, and somewhat regular activity are helpful. Entire books have been written about SEO, so consider these pages an introduction.

How SEO Works

Search engine companies do not reveal exactly the process they use to rank web pages found in their searches — and they change them periodically. Whatever their specific algorithm, you can be sure it is based primarily on words. WordPress gives multiple opportunities for you to feature words that highlight your blog and specific posts. Go to www.google.com/webmasters/docs/search-engine-optimization-starter-guide.pdf to read the SEO suggestions straight from the leading search engine.

Use Keywords

Keywords are key to SEO. Think of keywords as words or phrases that people might use when searching for information that you have in your blog post. Therefore, if you have a post with great information about health problems in golden retrievers, use the term *golden retrievers* frequently, and not just your dog's name, *Bruno*.

Use Meaningful Blog Post Titles

Keywords need to appear in your blog post titles, or headlines, too. They are more search-engine friendly if they are specific rather than general. For example, a title such as *8 Easy-to-Care-For Tropical House Plants* is likely to get more search engine traffic than a title like *My Favorite Plants*.

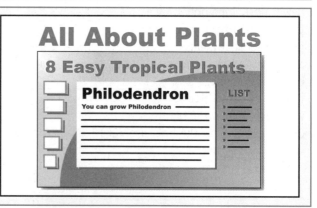

Choose Custom Permalinks

If you have a self-hosted blog, choose a post permalink structure that includes the post title or headline. You can do that on the Permalinks panel available under Settings in the left menu bar. (WordPress.com blogs automatically include the post title.) You can shorten the permalink when you create a post if you think it is too long.

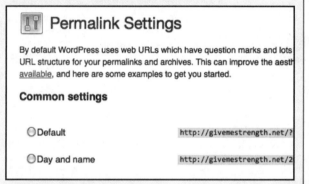

Select Meaningful Category Names

Category names also provide words that search engines scan, or *crawl*. Again, specific names are better than general ones. Naming a category *Pet Care Books* is better than naming it simply *Books*, even if your blog topic clearly is pet care. The same thing is true for tags. Assign them sparingly to posts; using dozens looks like a spam site.

Other SEO Opportunities

Provide lots of high-quality content and update often, and your SEO will be fine. Still, you can and should use keywords in the alternate text of your images (see Chapter 5). At a self-hosted blog, you might consider an SEO plugin such as All in One SEO Pack or Yoast WordPress SEO. Provide opportunities for users to recommend your site as noted in Chapter 7 in "Let Readers Share Your Posts" and "Add Share Buttons." Encourage visitors to stay on your site longer and click through to other pages and posts. Site mapping, available via a plugin, also can be helpful.

SEO No-No's

Although incoming links to your site help SEO, do not waste your money paying someone to build links to your site. Ignore outdated recommendations to stuff your site with lots of metadata and extra keywords. Search engines have become wise to those techniques.

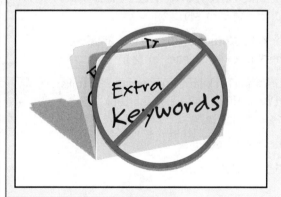

Using an SEO Plugin

Using a plugin that aids in search engine optimization can help build blog traffic. Two popular ones are All in One SEO and Yoast WordPress SEO. These plugins augment the built-in WordPress search engine optimization features. Having plenty of good content that search engines can index, or *crawl*, should remain your first priority in attracting search engines, however. Plugins are not available at WordPress.com. This section introduces Yoast WordPress SEO, a comprehensive and complex plugin, and some recommended settings. You can start with the default settings, however, and change others later if you like.

Using an SEO Plugin

1. Install and activate Yoast WordPress SEO, as described in "Install and Activate a Plugin" in Chapter 6.

2. Click the new SEO item in the left menu bar.

   The WordPress SEO General Settings panel opens, and other SEO settings appear in the menu list.

3. Deselect the check box to disable the Advanced part of the WordPress SEO meta box (☑ change to ☐).

   Note: Step 3 is optional. Disabling the Advanced section is important only if you have untrustworthy co-authors and editors.

4. Click **Save Settings**.

5. Click **Titles & Metas**.

   The Titles & Metas panel opens.

6. Click the **Force rewrite titles** check box (☐ changes to ☑).

7. Click the **Noindex subpages of archives** check box (☐ changes to ☑).

8. Click the check boxes for hiding RSD links, WLW manifest links, and shortlink (☐ changes to ☑).

9. Click **Save Settings**.

10. Click **XML Sitemaps**.

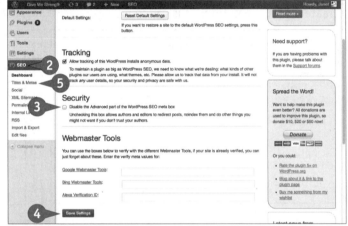

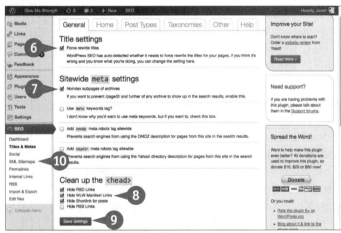

The XML Sitemaps panel appears.

11 Click the **Ping Yahoo!** check box and the **Ping Ask.com** check box (☐ changes to ☑).

12 Click **Save Settings**.

13 Click **+ New**, and choose **Post**.

Note: Alternatively, you can open a previous draft or post.

A post page appears, where you can write a brief draft.

Note: Steps 14, 16, and 17 are not illustrated.

14 Scroll down to the Yoast WordPress SEO module.

Ⓐ This shows how your post would appear in search results.

15 Type a keyword or phrase that is the focus of your post.

Note: The module displays a list of possibilities as you type.

16 Press `Tab`.

Ⓑ A checklist of where your term appears in the post emerges.

17 Click **Save Draft** at the top of the post panel.

18 Click **Page Analysis**.

A page analysis appears. Review it for ideas on how to help your search engine ranking.

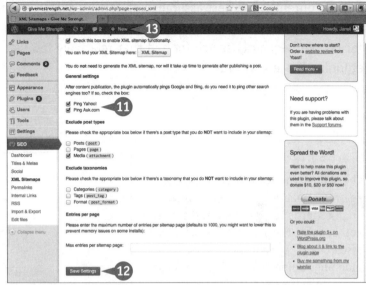

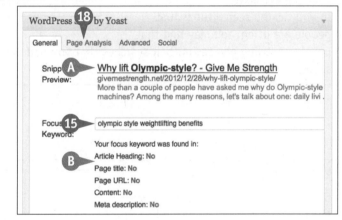

What do I do with all those other settings?
The default settings generally are adequate to start with this comprehensive plugin. To learn more about it, you can read an article that goes into greater depth. Try www.coolestguyplanettech.com/how-to-set-up-wordpress-seo-plugin-by-yoast-for-wordpress-3-31. The plugin's home page is pretty tough to understand, unfortunately.

Research Keywords

Good content is the best assurance of getting search engine attention, and using good keywords is an important factor. The best keywords for building the best rankings in searches are those that people frequently search for and that relatively few websites address. Tools exist to help you determine those keywords.

Start Early

The sooner you start discovering the keywords that will help send search engine traffic to your blog, the sooner you benefit. Many experts recommend researching keywords before you begin blogging. Doing so can help you focus your subject matter. It also points out to you related search terms that people are using. You may find that people are using phrases in their searches that you had not thought of but that are well-suited to your subject.

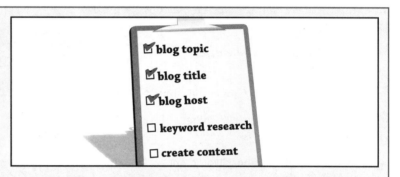

☑ blog topic
☑ blog title
☑ blog host
☐ keyword research
☐ create content

Think First

Before you can do good research, you need to have a clear understanding of the central focus of your site. The object of keyword research is to find terms related to your topic, not to find topics and then blog about them. To that end, write down your blog's focus and a half-dozen or so closely related terms. Maybe your focus is *being a Suzuki violin parent*. Related topics, which could well be your category names, might be *making violin practice fun*, *avoiding practice power struggles*, and *tips for encouraging good violin technique*, among others.

Suzuki violin parent

- **making violin practice fun**
- **avoiding practice power struggles**
- **tips for encouraging good violin technique**

Try One or More Tools

Several free research tools are available. Among them are the Google AdWords tool, available at https://adwords.google.com/select/KeywordToolExternal/ and the Google Trends page, www.google.com/trends/, which takes in the former Google Insights. Free tools that require registration include Bing Keyword Research, at www.bing.com/toolbox/keywords, and SEO Book Keyword Tool, at http://tools.seobook.com/keyword-tools/seobook. You also can try www.freekeywords.wordtracker.com and www.keyworddiscovery.com/search.html.

What the Tools Tell You

Each tool provides slightly different results, and some for-pay tools give detailed analyses of findings. As you begin, however, keep an eye out for frequently sought terms that relatively few websites use. The Google Keyword Tool, for example, lists an estimate of the total monthly number of searches for your term and for related terms, and it provides a general rating for how strong the competition among websites is for being discovered when someone searches for that term. Researching a focus of *Suzuki violin parent* with the Google tool reveals no searches for that term — hence, not a great keyword phrase — but the phrase *learn violin* has a decent number of searches and low competition. The phrase *violin for kids*, meanwhile, has high competition and fewer than half as many searches.

What to Do with Your Findings

Your research should help you come up with a list of useful terms to attract readers to your site. Remember, the point is not to fit your subject to the terms but to incorporate the terms as you write about your subject. If you only like the terms you find that have high competition, you certainly can continue to use those terms, but you will have a harder time rising in the search engine rankings.

Check in Often

As you add posts and develop your site, continue to do keyword research periodically. Doing so keeps you and your posts focused and up to date on search term trends. If you installed the Yoast WordPress SEO plugin, it provides links in the post panel to the keyword search tools at Google and at SEO Book. Take advantage of them. Refine your keyword lists and try out new ideas as you become more comfortable with your blog.

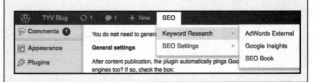

CHAPTER 9

Tracking Blog Statistics

If you are serious about your site, you soon will become serious about your site's statistics. After all, they probably are the best way to gauge how much traffic you are getting, where it is coming from, and how it got there. Knowing that information can help you increase your audience.

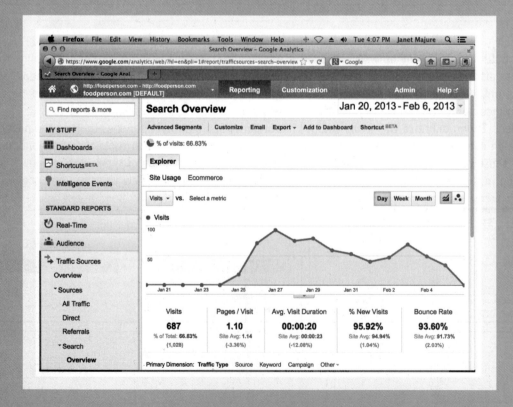

Understanding What Statistics Offer

You can get seemingly endless information about your website traffic thanks to the web's constant flow of data. By using one or more statistics trackers or analyzers, you can learn where site visitors come from geographically, what browsers they use, which of your posts gets viewed most, what search terms people use to arrive at your site, and much more. Checking that information periodically can help you see trends and refine your blog content. First, though, it helps to understand some of the possibilities.

Visitor Counts

Whatever tool you use, your statistics tracker undoubtedly shows numbers of visitors, visits, and page views. *Visitors* (or *unique visitors*) is a count of visits from a unique IP address (an ID assigned to everything connected to the Internet) to your blog. *Visits* is a count of uninterrupted sessions on your site, and *page views* indicates the number of pages viewed.

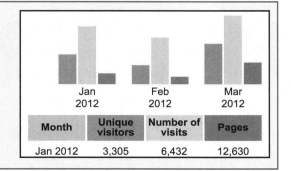

Month	Unique visitors	Number of visits	Pages
Jan 2012	3,305	6,432	12,630

Traffic Sources

You also may receive information on your tracker about where your visitors came from, both geographically and *virtually*. That is, it tells you the page from which visitors clicked to arrive on your site, the search engine that pointed to your site, and how many visitors entered your URL directly into their web browser. It also tells you how many times automated programs checked on your site.

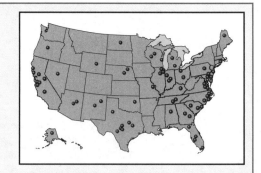

Content Popularity

Do you want to know what posts or pages get read the most? Your tracker tells you. It also tells you at which pages visitors arrived, or *landed*, and from which pages visitors left. It also tells you what search terms people used to find your content.

Pages-URL (Top 25)

152 different pages-url	Viewed	Average size	Entry	Exit	
drying-mint	1,404	67.84 KB	749	711	
tuscan-bread	1,264	35.50 KB	761	710	
butternut-squash	1,028	47.63 KB	916	731	
papalo-power	658	59.05 KB	251	169	
vegetable-dish	168	45.70 KB	81	93	

More Statistics

Most statistics trackers provide more information than you know what to do with. They tell you what browser people used, for example, and what links visitors clicked on. They tell you how long visitors stayed on your site and how many pages they viewed on average.

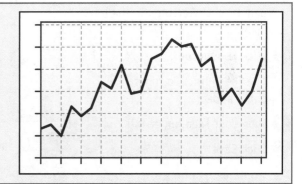

Look for Trends

What do you do with all those statistics? If you are blogging for pleasure, you can ignore them entirely. If you want popularity, you may aim for an ongoing traffic increase as judged by statistics trends. You might gauge whether a particular *type* of content draws traffic or if certain search terms work for you, and then use that knowledge to shape content.

A Cautionary Note

The truth is that website statistics are imperfect. None can give you an exact count of much of anything, and one tracker may give different information from another. Your time is far better spent creating great blog content than in watching your statistics. In other words, keep an eye on what is happening with your site's traffic, but do not put too much credence in any particular statistic.

Track Feed Traffic with FeedBurner

I f you wonder how many people are subscribed to your RSS feed, you can get a pretty good idea by opening an account with FeedBurner, a service that Google acquired in 2007. When you direct your feed to go through FeedBurner, it keeps count of your subscriptions and provides other statistics. To check your traffic, you first need to sign up for a FeedBurner account and ask it to track, or *burn*, your feed. Doing so is detailed in "Sign Up with FeedBurner and E-Mail Subscriptions" in Chapter 7.

Track Feed Traffic with FeedBurner

1 Install and activate the FD Feedburner plugin.

Note: For details on installing this plugin, see "Install and Activate a Plugin" in Chapter 6.

The plugin is active, and a new item appears under Settings.

2 In your blog's administrative panels, click **Settings** in the left menu bar.

3 Click **Feedburner**.

The Feedburner Configuration panel appears.

4 Type your FeedBurner URL.

5 Click **Save**.

WordPress confirms the configuration.

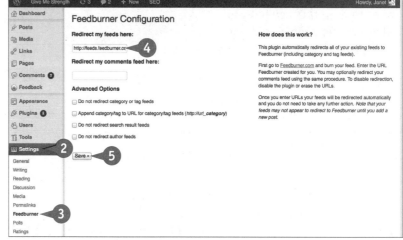

6 Go to feedburner.google.com in your web browser.

The My Feeds page appears.

Note: If you are not already logged in to your Google account, you first are asked to sign in.

A Your feed or feeds appear along with the number of subscribers.

7 Click the feed whose statistics you want to examine.

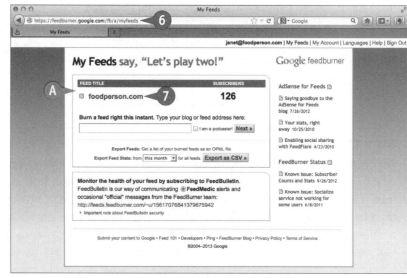

The Feeds Stats Dashboard appears, giving an overview of the previous day's feed activity.

B You can click here to select a different time period.

C The number of feed subscribers is shown here, with the scale on the left.

D This indicates the *reach,* or the number of interactions with the feed by readers, with the scale on the right.

E This shows the popular feed items.

F Click here to open the panel showing clicks and views over time.

8 Click **Subscribers**.

The Feed Subscribers panel opens.

9 Scroll down to view statistics.

G This section shows details on feed readers your subscribers use.

H This section shows the number of e-mail subscribers. Click it to find a link to e-mail subscriber list details, including addresses and whether a subscription is active.

TIPS

What do I do with these statistics now that I have them?

Feed use does not show up in general site traffic statistics, so knowing how many subscribers you have and having an idea of whether they are reading the feed gives you a better idea of how many readers you have and what posts get their attention. Viewed over time, these numbers also help you gauge whether feed and e-mail traffic is growing.

Is there an alternative to FeedBurner? I have heard that Google may drop it.

Yes, that subject has been talked about for some time, but FeedBurner remains the chief RSS service. Still, alternatives include a simple plugin that involves no outside service. Among them are Feed Statistics and Simple Feed Stats, which is quite new but looks promising. FeedBlitz, as described in the next section, is an alternative service.

Track Feed Traffic with FeedBlitz

Y̶ou can get more statistics, particularly about e-mail subscribers, than you may care to know about your feed when you use FeedBlitz, a paid service. Like FeedBurner, it provides for e-mail subscriptions and RSS feed tracking. It also has added features, such as providing for e-mail newsletters and interaction with social media. The price is based on the number of active e-mail subscribers you have. FeedBlitz offers a free trial for new users, and if you already are using FeedBurner, it provides a guide to move your FeedBurner data to FeedBlitz. In short, FeedBlitz offers more services and better support, but it is not free.

Track Feed Traffic with FeedBlitz

1 In your web browser, go to http://feedblitz.com.

2 Click **Get your FREE TRIAL**.

A payment screen appears.

3 Type your credit card information.

4 Scroll down to complete billing information.

5 Click **Review Order**.

6 Click **Continue**.

A welcome screen appears.

7 Click **RSS Services**.

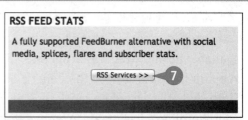

RSS FEED STATS

A fully supported FeedBurner alternative with social media, splices, flares and subscriber stats.

RSS Services >> **7**

A new screen appears.

8 Type your blog address.

9 Click **Add Site to FeedBlitz**.

FeedBlitz takes a few minutes to set up your feed or feeds and e-mail subscription options.

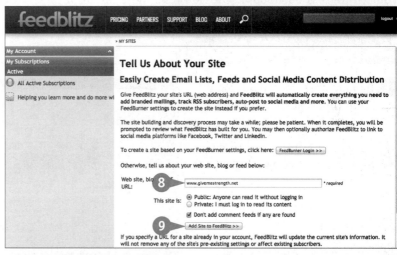

The account dashboard for your site appears.

10 Click **Finish Setup** in the RSS box.

An information screen appears.

11 Click **Set It Up Now**.

FeedBlitz presents a series of screens to add social media options and more. Continue through the screens.

12 Click **Account Dashboard**.

The Account Dashboard refreshes, and you can click **Site Dashboard** under your new site to see your site statistics.

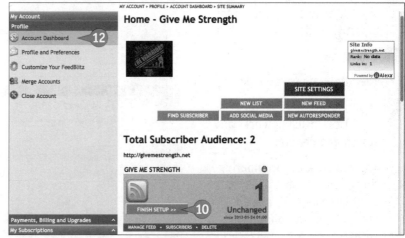

TIP

What kind of statistics can I get?

FeedBlitz reports subscribers to both RSS and e-mail updates, of course. In addition, it tells whether e-mail subscriptions are working and whether recipients are opening their e-mail. FeedBlitz also tracks links within feeds and provides a link on the feed's dashboard to the Alexa data service.

Access WordPress Site Stats

Bloggers at WordPress.com and self-hosted bloggers using the Jetpack plugin have the easiest possible access to statistics about their websites. The WordPress.com Site Stats are immediately available at any WordPress.com site. Jetpack users have to connect to WordPress.com, whose servers keep up the data, to get the benefit of the numerous statistics that WordPress.com Site Stats keeps. Those benefits include a quick look at your traffic statistics in your WordPress Admin Bar and from your WordPress Dashboard. You can read more about Jetpack in Chapter 6.

Access WordPress Site Stats

1 In your site's Dashboard, scroll down to reveal the Site Stats module.

A This graph displays site traffic for the preceding two weeks.

B This list shows top posts and top searches for the preceding two weeks.

2 Position your mouse pointer over a bar to see the stats for a particular day.

3 Click **View All**.

The Site Stats panel appears.

4 Scroll down to see more statistics, including clicks and search engine terms.

C You can click the **Summaries** link to show cumulative statistics since the start of your blog or its connection with WordPress.com via Jetpack.

5 Click **Check it out now**.

The statistics panel at WordPress.com appears.

D This graphic now shows both *views* and *visitors*.

6 Position your mouse pointer over a specific day.

E The views, visitors, and average number of page views per visitor appear.

F Click these links to view stats by weeks or months.

7 Scroll down.

G You can view a list and graphic of visitors by geographic location.

H You can view the top posts and pages.

I You can view the top sites for sending traffic to your site.

J You can view the links on your site that visitors clicked.

K Click here to see search terms that brought search engine traffic to your site.

8 Click the **Back** button on your browser (◀) to return to your Dashboard.

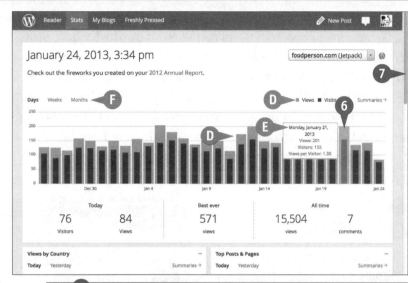

TIPS

How accurate are the statistics?
They are as accurate as any site statistics. Do not concern yourself too much with raw numbers. Pay more attention to changes over time and to those that show something received a lot of attention — or hardly any attention.

How deeply can I view the statistics?
On the main stats page, you can see only the current day and the previous day, except for the visit graphic across the top of the page. Subsequent sections of this book go into the what and how of these statistics, but rest assured, you can look at the previous weeks, months, and years, even on specific posts.

Track Feed Traffic with WordPress Site Stats

WordPress.com users have access to a sort of feed traffic tracking that self-hosted bloggers do not. WordPress.com users can keep track of who gets posts by e-mail, who gets feeds using the WordPress.com Follow feature, and who is following comments. That information is a standard part of the WordPress.com installation. WordPress.com Site Stats, however, mostly do not give information about RSS subscriptions. If you promote your RSS feed, you need a service like FeedBurner or FeedBlitz. If you are using Jetpack, you do not get the follow-blog feature, although you can provide and track e-mail subscriptions operated through Jetpack.

Track Feed Traffic with WordPress Site Stats

1 Click **Dashboard**.

2 Click **Site Stats**.

The site statistics panel opens.

3 Scroll down to the Totals, Followers & Shares module.

4 Click **Blog**.

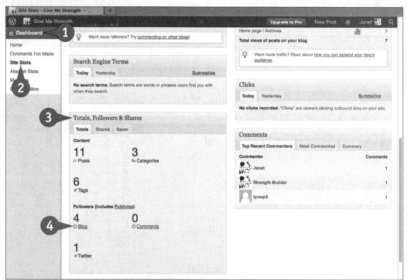

The My Followers panel appears.

A You can see WordPress.com members who follow your blog.

B This indicator shows that you are following that person's blog.

5 Position your mouse pointer over a follower.

C The Gravatar hovercard appears, telling a little about the reader and linking to his Gravatar profile.

Note: The hovercard disappears when you move the mouse.

6 Click **Email Followers**.

The My Followers panel displays e-mail subscribers and their e-mail addresses, if any.

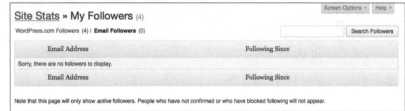

Find Popular Posts with Site Stats

When you are on your WordPress.com Site Stats panel through your Dashboard or at WordPress.com, you can get a quick look at the most popular posts and pages on your site. The Top Posts & Pages module of WordPress.com Site Stats for your WordPress.com or Jetpack-enabled self-hosted site gives you details by the day, week, month, and beyond. Thus, you can readily determine which posts have staying power, and which, perhaps, are more forgettable. You may be able to see what works best at different times of year. Start from your Site Stats panel.

Find Popular Posts with Site Stats

1 Scroll to the Top Posts & Pages module.

A This is a list of the day's most-viewed posts.

B These are post titles, which link to the post.

2 Click the **Statistics** icon (▥) next to a post of interest.

Note: If viewing Site Stats at the WordPress.com home page, the icon is a magnifying glass (🔍).

The statistics panel for the post appears.

C This is a graphic of daily post views.

D This shows views by months and years.

E This shows average daily views by month.

F The color highlights the highest traffic.

Note: Views by day and by week for preceding six weeks appear at the bottom of the screen, with links to traffic for each specific day.

3 Click **Return to Stats**.

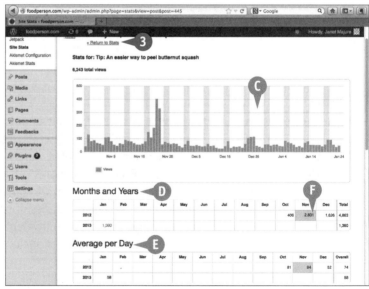

The Site Stats panel appears.

④ Click **Summaries** in the Top Posts & Pages module.

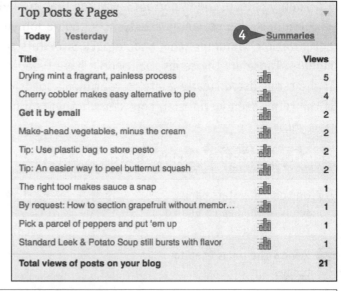

The Top Posts summary of the preceding seven days appears.

⑤ Review the list.

⑥ Click **Quarter**.

The Top Posts for the most recent 90 days appear.

⑦ Review the list.

⑧ Repeat Steps 6 and 7 for other time periods.

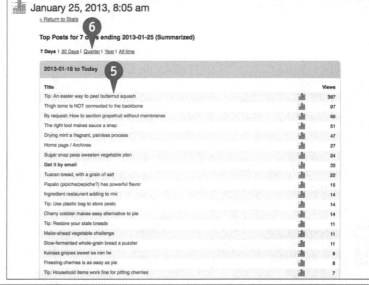

TIPS

Is there a way to compare the Top Posts lists from different time periods?

Site Stats does not have a built-in comparison tool. However, you can copy the lists by selecting them with your mouse and pressing Ctrl + C (⌘+C on a Mac) and then pasting them in a spreadsheet program. If you have the option, paste the list as plain text to eliminate the graphics. Paste the lists from different time periods side by side in your spreadsheet to compare.

I have had my blog for a year, so why do the Top Posts numbers only go back four months?

You must have installed and activated Jetpack at that time. With Jetpack installed, activated, and connected to WordPress.com, the WordPress.com servers can track your traffic, but they cannot record activity before the connection occurred.

Find Important Keywords with Site Stats

When you learn the important keywords that are helping people find your site through search engines, you get an idea as to how good a job you are doing with your search engine optimization. WordPress.com and Jetpack Site Stats show keywords in the Search Engine Terms module. Those are the terms that people have typed in to search engines that led them to your site. If the terms listed clearly relate to your blog's focus or subtopics, then you are doing a good job. If the terms seem peripheral, consider whether you need to do a better job of helping searchers to find you.

Find Important Keywords with Site Stats

1 On your Site Stats panel, scroll to the Search Engine Terms module.

2 Review the terms used for today.

3 Click **Summaries**.

The Search Terms summary for the preceding seven days appears.

4 Review the list.

5 Click **All time**.

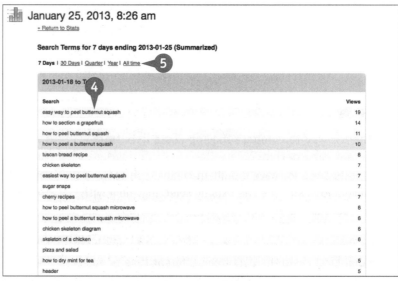

The Search Terms since you started blog or activated and connected Jetpack appear.

6 Review the list.

Ⓐ Note the similar search terms that helped people find your site.

7 Click **Return to Stats**.

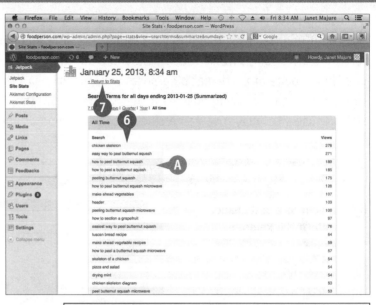

8 Click **Yesterday**.

The top search terms for the previous day appear.

9 Click **Other search terms**.

The Search Terms summary panel appears with the complete list of search terms leading to your site the previous day.

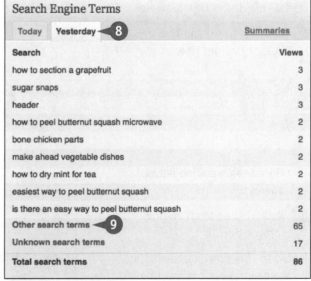

TIPS

Why do the Search Terms summaries list unknown search terms?

Occasionally, Internet users may have their browsers set up so as not to record their searches. These lead to unknown terms at your site. The number nevertheless may be interesting to you.

What does it mean when many similar search terms show up in the search terms summaries?

If those terms are related to your most popular posts, it means that those posts do a good job of using multiple words or phrases that people use to search when they want more information about the topic. If the terms do not point to popular posts, it probably means that most of your traffic comes from sources besides search engines.

Find Major Referral Sources with Site Stats

Getting links to your site from other sites is a wonderful way to boost traffic as well as to learn about your readers. Happily, your WordPress.com and Jetpack Site Stats show you where your referral traffic comes from. That is, they list the links on other sites that people click to arrive at your home page or particular blog post. You, in turn, can thank the sites for the mention, perhaps comment on the referring post — if the referrer is another blog — and generally take a look at the sites. Those sites may give you a clue as to what type of audience you are attracting.

Find Major Referral Sources with Site Stats

① On your Site Stats panel, scroll to the Referrers module.

② Review the list.

Note: There is not much referral traffic this day in this example!

③ Click ⊞ to expand the Search Engines line.

More search engine detail appears.

④ Review the search engine information.

Note: In this example, almost as many searches are coming from the Google image search engine as the regular search engine.

Ⓐ Clicking ⊟ closes the search engine details.

Ⓑ Clicking ⊞ shows the many Google search engines in use, mostly according to country.

⑤ Click **Summaries**.

The Referrer summary for the preceding seven days appears.

6 Click ⊞ to expand the Pinterest line (⊞ changes to ⊟).

C Referring Pinterest pins appear. You can click the link to see the appearance at Pinterest.

7 Click a link from another website.

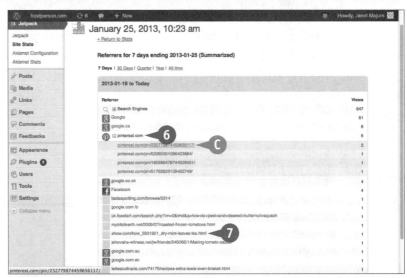

The page with your link opens.

D This is the link that leads to your site.

Note: You may have to search or scroll the page to find the link.

8 Click ◄ to return to the summary page.

9 Repeat Steps **6** to **8** to investigate other referrers and other time periods.

TIPS

What do I do with this information?
It is up to you, of course, but here are some ideas. If you do not see many referrers besides search engines, you may want to increase efforts to increase referral traffic by including social media sharing buttons on your posts, by linking to other websites, and by commenting at sites that have referred traffic to you.

Does the Referrers module show all links to my site, or just the ones people have clicked?
Just the ones people have clicked for the day on the Site Stats overview page or the time period you choose on the Referrers Summaries page. You know the referring sites listed have enough traffic to prompt readers to click. You may want to pay special attention to sites that have multiple active links to your site.

Find Popular Links with Site Stats

When your readers click on links you include on your site, they give you an idea of the depth of their interest in a topic while alerting that link target site owner that your site exists. It is all part of the interrelated aspect of the Internet. WordPress.com and Jetpack Site Stats let you see which links readers click in your posts, pages, and widgets. They do not show links from one place on your blog to another place, however. Site Stats has a module called Clicks that shows the link activity for the day while also linking to summaries by other time periods.

Find Popular Links with Site Stats

1 On your Site Stats panel, scroll to the Clicks module.

2 Review the list.

3 Click **Summaries**.

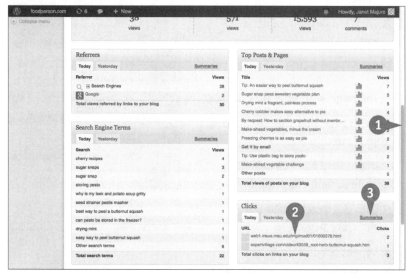

The Clicks summary for the preceding seven days appears.

4 Review the list, watching for the proportion of smaller sites relative to major sites.

5 Click a link if you are not sure where it might go.

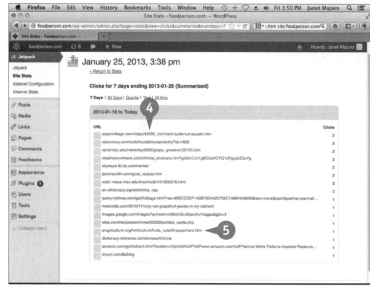

The link target opens.

6 Click ◄.

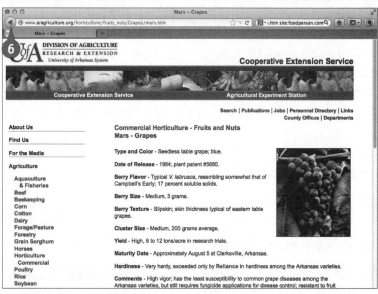

The summaries page returns.

7 Click **Quarter**.

Clicks for the preceding 90 days appear.

8 Review the list.

A Large commercial or reference sites may be good for readers, but probably do not yield return attention to your site from the large commercial site.

TIPS

How can I tell which post a link appears on?
Alas, WordPress.com/Jetpack Site Stats does not provide a convenient way for you to find out. It probably does not matter, however. The point of looking at your links is to see that you are providing links that people use. See Chapter 10 to learn how to find outdated links.

Why should I care if people click links leading away from my site?
Because each credible link you provide adds to your credibility while also helping readers to understand your sources and giving credit when credit is due. If readers are not clicking links, however, it could be a sign that you either do not have many links or that readers do not find them relevant.

Sign Up with Google Analytics

When you track your site's statistics with Google Analytics, you get more detail and more ways to look at the data than you can with most free statistics programs. Google Analytics works by giving you a piece of code that you insert into your website in a location that appears with every page view. Each time someone lands on a page, the code lets Google Analytics track that person's activity. Many themes and some plugins have built-in tools for inserting the Google Analytics code, however, if you do not want to get into your site's code. Also, you cannot use it at WordPress.com.

Sign Up with Google Analytics

1. In your browser, go to www.google.com/analytics.

2. Click **Create an account**.

3. A new page opens, where you can sign in with existing Google account information or, if you do not have a Google account, you can sign up for one.

4. Proceed through the pages until you agree to terms and conditions, then click **Create Account**.

The tracking instructions page opens to the Tracking Code tab of your account.

5. Make sure the radio button is selected (●) next to your domain or domains to be tracked.

6. Click in the box to select the code, and then press Ctrl + C (⌘ + C on a Mac) to copy the code.

7. Click **Save** at the bottom of the page.

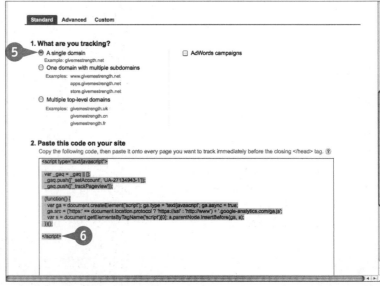

8 In your blog's administrative pages, click **Appearance**.

The Appearance menu expands and the Manage Themes page opens.

9 Click **Editor**.

The Edit Themes panel opens.

10 Click **Footer (footer.php)**.

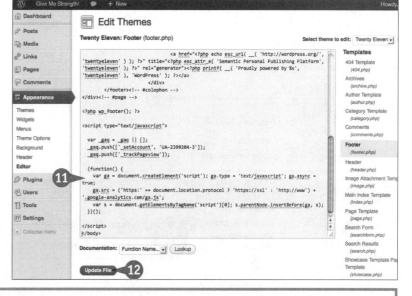

The footer template opens.

11 Scroll to the bottom of the Edit Themes box, click to insert your cursor in front of </body>, and then press Ctrl + V (⌘ + V on a Mac) to insert the analytics code.

The code appears in the box just before </body>.

12 Click **Update File**.

The Google Analytics code is inserted.

TIPS

I cannot find </body> in my footer.php file. Where do I put the code?

You can put it just before the </head> tag, usually found in header.php. Or you can check your other template files for the </body> code. Look for a template that you know appears on every page, and it likely has the </body> tag.

Is there another way to insert the code?

You can find a theme that provides easy integration of the Google Analytics code. Among those are Catch Box and Magazine Basic. You can get a plugin, of which there are several, at http://wordpress.org/extend/plugins. Or you can skip Google and use a tool from your web host, such as AWStats.

Get to Know Google Analytics

As soon as you insert the Google Analytics code on your site, Google starts recording every visit to your site. It takes a few days or longer to get meaningful data. Then, after you sign in, you can view results in the Audience Overview and elsewhere. Audience Overview and other pages show the number of visitors, time on the site, the average number of pages viewed, and more, and provide links to other kinds of data. To reach the Audience Overview, log in to Google Analytics and click your site in the accounts list.

Ⓐ Statistics shown are for dates listed here, and the drop-down ▼ allows you to select other time periods.

Ⓑ This line graph shows visit numbers. This example has an abrupt uptick of visits, which corresponds with the date that the tracking code was inserted on this site.

Ⓒ Click the drop-down ▾ to select other statistics to graph.

Ⓓ You can choose the time interval for statistics viewed.

Ⓔ Visits refers to the raw number of visits during the selected time period.

Ⓕ Link goes to alerts that show when Google Analytics notes a marked change in traffic.

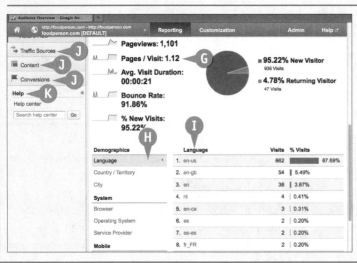

Ⓖ Google Analytics shows more raw numbers regarding visits and visitors.

Ⓗ Select an item in this list, and details appear in (**Ⓘ**).

Ⓘ Panel shows details panel of item chosen in (**Ⓗ**).

Ⓙ Menu bar links to reports for other data types.

Ⓚ Click to view Google Analytics Help.

Identify Traffic Patterns

Peak Times for Views

A click of the time period arrow opens a panel where you can select the time range you want to view and compare it to other time periods. By choosing a short period, you can easily identify hour-by-hour traffic to see peak times of day. By choosing a week and

clicking the **Compare to** check box (☐ changes to ☑) to compare it to another week, you can see whether, as you suspected, you get your best traffic on Sundays. The time periods, by the way, correspond to the time in your Profile Settings under the Admin button at the top of the Google Analytics page.

Mobile or Computer Viewers

When you click on the Operating System item under System at the bottom of your Audience Overview panel, Google Analytics displays the operating systems of visitors during the selected time period. If you see many views from the iOS, Android, or Blackberry iOS, it means readers are accessing your site from their mobile

devices. If you have not yet done so, such information might be a signal that you need to take advantage of options to make your site mobile-friendly, as discussed in Chapter 6.

Massage the Numbers

Google Analytics lets you set up regular export of your data. It will send you an e-mail with the Audience Overview data in several data formats, including comma-separated values and tab-separated values for use with your database or spreadsheet program. It even will send it as an Excel or Google Spreadsheets document. With the data on your computer, you can sort, analyze, and otherwise organize your Google Analytics data to your heart's content.

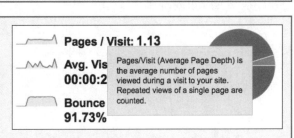

Understanding the Terms

Google Analytics puts out many terms that may not be familiar to you. Fortunately, it makes the understanding easier by displaying a quick definition when you position your mouse pointer over a term. The definition then disappears when you move the pointer again. See "Understanding Your Statistics," later in this chapter, for more information.

Find Popular Posts with Google

When you know which posts get the most views, you can further promote those posts, learn what kind of content attracts readers to your site, and take action to encourage them to stay longer on your site. You can use a plugin to identify your popular posts, but as long as you have Google Analytics working, you might as well take advantage of its data. To find your popular posts, you first need to log in at www.google.com/analytics/ and click your site name.

Find Popular Posts with Google

1 Click **Content** in the left menu bar.

2 Click **Overview**.

The Content Overview panel opens.

Ⓐ You can click here to determine the time period to be viewed.

Ⓑ A graph of total page views is displayed here.

3 Scroll to bottom of page.

Ⓒ A list of most-viewed pages during the timeframe appears.

4 Click **view full report**.

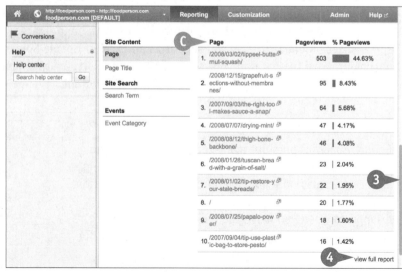

The panel displays details of page views, with the most-viewed pages at the top.

D You can click here to open a page in a new window.

E This column shows the average time in minutes that a viewer spent reading a page. More is better than less.

F This shows the percentage of viewers that left the site without viewing more content. Less is better than more.

5 Click **Landing Pages**.

The Landing Page data appears, with the most common landing page at the top.

G The average number of pages viewed by a visitor who entered your site at this page is shown here. More is generally better than less.

H This shows the average time visitors who arrived at the page stayed on your site. If a visitor arrived and left from the same page, the time spent on the page does not count toward the average time spent on the site for visitors who arrived at this page.

I Landing page information for your home page is displayed here.

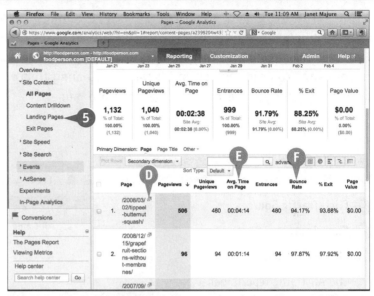

TIP

Why do I care which posts are most popular, and what do I do with the information?

In this example, one post has received most of the traffic, but most people who land there read it and leave. That indicates a need to add to the site, and especially to that post, something to encourage visitors to stay. Including links to related content on your site or asking visitors to sign up for your feed are two ways to turn drop-in visitors into regular readers.

Review Traffic Sources with Google

Y ou get traffic to your site via *direct entry*, meaning someone typed a URL into his or her browser, and by *referrals*, which means a person clicked a link at another site or in an e-mail message. The Traffic Sources reports of Google Analytics help you see which sources are bringing the most traffic to your site. You can see how much traffic is coming from which sources. You first need to log in at www.google.com/analytics/ and click your site name.

Review Traffic Sources with Google

1 Click **Traffic Sources**.

2 Click **Sources**.

3 Click **All Traffic**.

The All Traffic reports panel appears.

4 Scroll down.

The traffic sources appear.

Ⓐ *Organic* indicates clicks on unpaid search engine results.

Ⓑ *Direct/(none)* means someone typed the URL or used a bookmark.

Ⓒ *Referral* means someone clicked a link on an ordinary website or an ad link on a search engine.

5 Click **Referrals**.

The Referral Traffic panel opens.

D The number of referral visits and the percentage of all visits that the number represents appear here.

E The bounce rate for referral traffic and comparison with the site average appear here.

6 Scroll down.

F This panel lists domains from which people linked.

7 Click a domain.

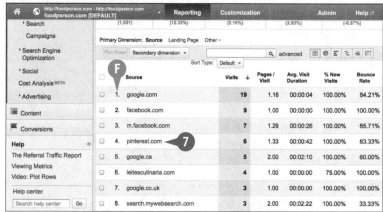

G This panel lists the *referral path,* or specific pages from the domain you clicked in Step 7 that linked to your site.

H You can click here to open the listed page in a new window.

Referral Path		Visits ↓	Pages / Visit	Avg. Visit Duration	% New Visits	Bounce Rate
G /pin/1234972147521754271/		2	1.00	00:00:00	100.00%	100.00%
2. /pin/1898549405108974271/		1	1.00	00:00:00	100.00%	100.00%
3. /pin/2327798744596561171/		1	1.00	00:00:00	100.00%	100.00%
4. /pin/3375589345401778991/		1	1.00	00:00:00	100.00%	100.00%
5. /pin/836685055492846021/	**H**	1	3.00	00:04:09	100.00%	0.00%

TIP

How can I tell where the referrers sent traffic?
On the page listing referral paths, click **Secondary Dimension**. A list drops down. Click **Traffic Sources**, and then click **Landing Page**. The list instantly disappears, and a new column, Landing Page, appears next to the referral path. That means when someone clicked the link on the page listed under Referral Path, he landed on the page at your site listed under Landing Page.

Find Important Keywords with Google

Y̲ou can find out what search terms people are using when they find your site through search engines. The Traffic Sources panels at Google Analytics show words and phrases that bring people to your site. When some terms show up frequently as a source of traffic to your site, it is a sign that you have done a good job using those terms in a search-engine friendly way. Otherwise, your content might not be ranked high enough for many people to discover you site through their search engines. To find those search terms, you first need to log in at www.google.com/analytics/ and click your site name.

Find Important Keywords with Google

1 Click **Traffic Sources**.

2 Click **Sources**.

3 Click **Search**.

4 Click **Overview**.

The Search Overview panel appears.

A The number and percentage of visits resulting from searches appear here.

B A graph of the number of visits from searches appears here.

5 Click **Keyword**.

C A list of search terms appears.

D *(not provided)* indicates a private search, as when a person is logged in at Google.com.

6 Click **Secondary dimension**.

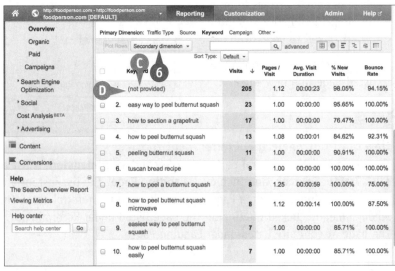

The Secondary dimension drop-down list appears.

⑦ Click **Traffic Sources**.

⑧ Click **Landing Page**.

The Secondary dimension drop-down list disappears.

Ⓔ The Landing Page column appears, showing where each search led, even when keywords are not provided.

Ⓕ Click ⊗ to eliminate the column.

How can I put this information to work?

These statistics can be especially useful if you decide to start placing online advertisements with search engines, such as Google AdWords, to bring traffic to your site. You can display the search terms overall, as on this example, or separate the organic and paid search data to see whether your ads are generating traffic.

What is the Advanced Segments item at the top of the page?

It lets you filter the results. Click **Advanced Segments** (Ⓐ), and a drop-down list appears. Click an item check box (☐ changes to ☑) (Ⓑ) to select, and then click **Apply** (Ⓒ). The page then lets you view, for example, the data only from visitors who stayed on the site after arriving via a search.

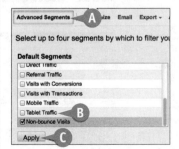

Find Useful Links with Google

One way you can find out whether your site is engaging readers is to look at whether they click on links that you provide on your site. The In-Page Analytics view that Google offers provides fascinating information that you can use as you work to keep visitors on your site longer. Specifically, In-Page Analytics displays an actual page from your site and identifies on which items readers clicked, and for each item what percentage of total clicks it contributed. You first need to log in at www.google.com/analytics/ and click your site name.

Find Useful Links with Google

1 Click **Content**.

2 Click **In-Page Analytics**.

A Statistics for pages that had user activity appear.

B The live home page display appears.

3 Scroll down.

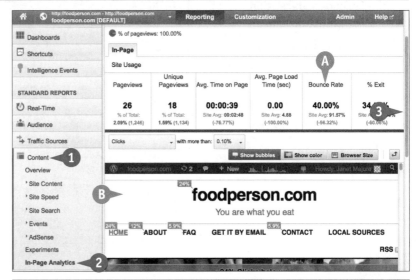

4 Position your mouse pointer over a bubble next to a link.

C A pop-up display gives details about activity on the associated link.

5 Scroll down.

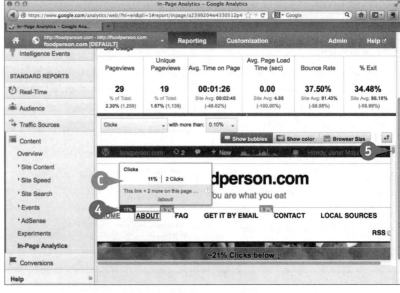

More clicked links appear.

6 Click a link.

After a moment, the link target appears within Google Analytics.

7 Repeat Steps 4 to 6 for as many pages as you want.

TIP

What is the Browser Size button about?

When you click **Browser Size** (**A**), a slider appears above the view of your page (**B**), and an orange screen or overlay (**C**) appears. The area that is not screened is visible by the percentage of page visitors shown on the slider, and the screened area cannot. You can scroll down to see what visitors see at the bottom of their screen when they first land on the page. You can move the slider to get an idea of what proportion of visitors can see what part of your page when they arrive.

Using Analytics Dashboards

You can get a big-picture view of your Google Analytics statistics by using the Dashboards feature. It allows you to select the data reports of greatest interest to you and see them all in one spot. You can add modules, select the data to show, and delete modules. You can have multiple dashboards, such as one for each website you track or one set for all traffic and one for e-commerce traffic. The default dashboard that Google creates for you is called My Dashboard. To start, you first need to log in at www.google.com/analytics/ and click your site name.

Using Analytics Dashboards

① Click **Dashboards**.

② Click **My Dashboard**.

My Dashboard appears.

Ⓐ Modules, or *widgets*, of various site measures appear.

③ Scroll down to see more widgets.

The other initial widgets appear.

④ Position your mouse pointer over a widget.

Ⓑ Tools appear, ✐ for editing and ✖ for deleting.

⑤ Click ✖ to delete a widget.

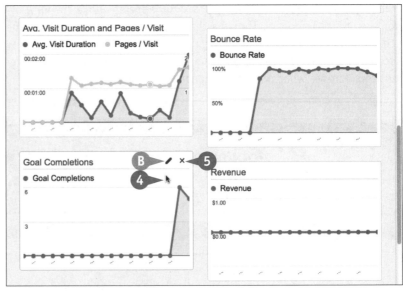

A confirmation dialog box appears.

6 Click **Yes, delete this widget**.

The widget disappears.

7 Click the edit tool on a widget (✏).

The Widget Settings dialog box appears.

ⓒ The display options appear.

Note: Widget Settings options vary according to the display option chosen.

8 Click the drop-down arrow to choose among dozens of content options.

9 Make other changes as desired.

10 Click **Save**.

ⓓ The edited widget appears.

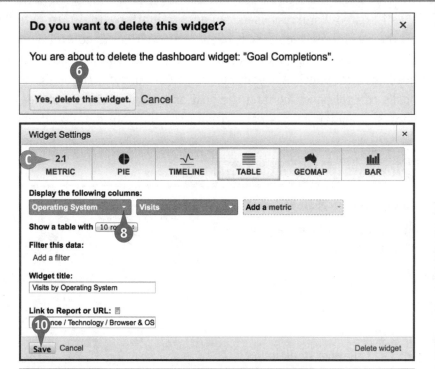

TIPS

How can I show more widgets at one time?
If you click **Customize Dashboard** at the top of the dashboard panel, a layout options box appears. Click a layout that provides more columns so that more widgets can appear across the top of the panel, and then click **Save**. The layout changes, and you can click in a widget's title area to drag it to a new column.

Customize Dashboard

How do I add a widget?
Click **+ Add Widget** at the top of the panel. The Add a Widget dialog box appears. You can choose the display, the content, or *metric,* and a filter for that content. Then add a title and a URL if you want the widget to link to other locations. The options are nearly endless.

View Statistics from Log Files

Self-hosted WordPress users can get straightforward, up-to-date data based on the log files that their web host keeps. Most likely, your web host's control panel offers that information analyzed by software such as AWStats or Webalizer. If so, you may need to activate the statistics on your host's control panel. Ask your host if you are unsure. If you do not see AWStats or Webalizer on your host's control panel, contact the host and ask if it offers another option. Some people like log files, because they let you see data without sharing your details with an outside party such as Google.

View Statistics from Log Files

Note: This example uses AWStats.

1 At your host's control panel, click **Awstats**.

The AWStats page opens to the current month's statistics.

A Links to other statistics on page appear here.

B You can click here to select dates.

C A summary of month's activity to date appears here.

2 Click **Origin**.

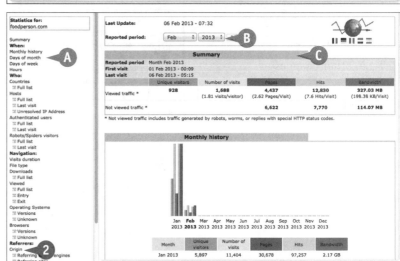

AWStats skips to sources of the month's traffic.

D Line for Direct address/ Bookmark/ Link in email shows the number or pages and the percentage of total entrances made to your site by visitors who typed a URL or arrived by clicking a bookmark or e-mail link.

E Line shows the number of pages and the percentage of total entrances to the site from search engines, which are itemized below.

F Line shows the number of pages and the percentage of total entrances to the site via links from other web pages. The list below shows linked-from pages.

3 Scroll down.

G Phrases used at search engines that led to site visits.

H Words used at search engines that led to site visits appear here.

I Links to a full list of search terms appear here.

4 Scroll up to view other data.

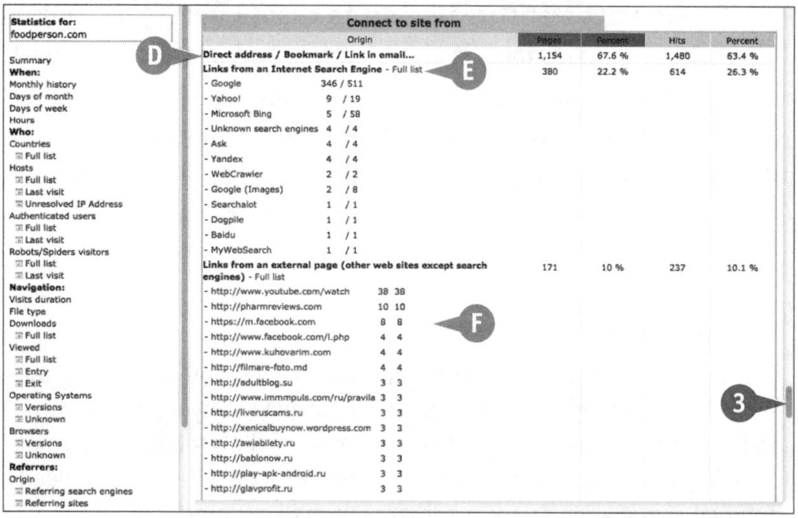

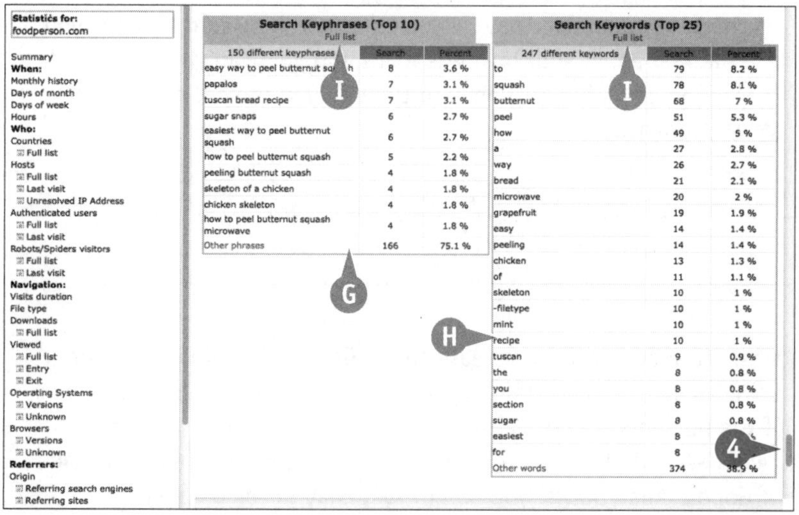

Statistics figure (top)

Statistics for: foodperson.com

Summary
When:
Monthly history
Days of month
Days of week
Hours
Who:
Countries
  Full list
Hosts
  Full list
  Last visit
  Unresolved IP Address
Authenticated users
  Full list
  Last visit
Robots/Spiders visitors
  Full list
  Last visit
Navigation:
Visits duration
File type
Downloads
  Full list
Viewed
  Full list
  Entry
  Exit
Operating Systems
  Versions
  Unknown
Browsers
  Versions
  Unknown
Referrers:
Origin
  Referring search engines
  Referring sites

Connect to site from

Origin	Pages	Percent	Hits	Percent
Direct address / Bookmark / Link in email...	1,154	67.6 %	1,480	63.4 %
Links from an Internet Search Engine - Full list	380	22.2 %	614	26.3 %
- Google	346 / 511			
- Yahoo!	9 / 19			
- Microsoft Bing	5 / 58			
- Unknown search engines	4 / 4			
- Ask	4 / 4			
- Yandex	4 / 4			
- WebCrawler	2 / 2			
- Google (Images)	2 / 8			
- Searchalot	1 / 1			
- Dogpile	1 / 1			
- Baidu	1 / 1			
- MyWebSearch	1 / 1			
Links from an external page (other web sites except search engines) - Full list	171	10 %	237	10.1 %
- http://www.youtube.com/watch	38 38			
- http://pharmreviews.com	10 10			
- https://m.facebook.com	8 8			
- http://www.facebook.com/l.php	4 4			
- http://www.kuhovarim.com	4 4			
- http://filmare-foto.md	4 4			
- http://adultblog.su	3 3			
- http://www.immmpuls.com/ru/pravila	3 3			
- http://liveruscams.ru	3 3			
- http://xenicalbuynow.wordpress.com	3 3			
- http://awiability.ru	3 3			
- http://bablonow.ru	3 3			
- http://play-apk-android.ru	3 3			
- http://glavprofit.ru	3 3			

Statistics figure (bottom)

Statistics for: foodperson.com

Summary
When:
Monthly history
Days of month
Days of week
Hours
Who:
Countries
  Full list
Hosts
  Full list
  Last visit
  Unresolved IP Address
Authenticated users
  Full list
  Last visit
Robots/Spiders visitors
  Full list
  Last visit
Navigation:
Visits duration
File type
Downloads
  Full list
Viewed
  Full list
  Entry
  Exit
Operating Systems
  Versions
  Unknown
Browsers
  Versions
  Unknown
Referrers:
Origin
  Referring search engines
  Referring sites

Search Keyphrases (Top 10)
Full list

150 different keyphrases	Search	Percent
easy way to peel butternut squash	8	3.6 %
papalos	7	3.1 %
tuscan bread recipe	7	3.1 %
sugar snaps	6	2.7 %
easiest way to peel butternut squash	6	2.7 %
how to peel butternut squash	5	2.2 %
peeling butternut squash	4	1.8 %
skeleton of a chicken	4	1.8 %
chicken skeleton	4	1.8 %
how to peel butternut squash microwave	4	1.8 %
Other phrases	166	75.1 %

Search Keywords (Top 25)
Full list

247 different keywords	Search	Percent
to	79	8.2 %
squash	78	8.1 %
butternut	68	7 %
peel	51	5.3 %
how	49	5 %
a	27	2.8 %
way	26	2.7 %
bread	21	2.1 %
microwave	20	2 %
grapefruit	19	1.9 %
easy	14	1.4 %
peeling	14	1.4 %
chicken	13	1.3 %
of	11	1.1 %
skeleton	10	1 %
-filetype	10	1 %
mint	10	1 %
recipe	10	1 %
tuscan	9	0.9 %
the	8	0.8 %
you	8	0.8 %
section	8	0.8 %
sugar	8	0.8 %
easiest	8	
for	8	
Other words	374	38.9 %

TIPS

How can I see which pages got the most traffic?
Click **Viewed** (**A**) under Navigation in the links list. The Pages-URL (Top 25) section appears. The subcategories (**B**) open new panels with more details. Full list shows all visited pages for the time period. Entry lists the pages where visitors arrived, and Exit shows from which pages visitors left. The Full list, Entry, and Exit panels also let you filter the results.

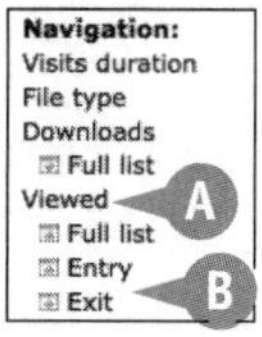

Navigation:
Visits duration
File type
Downloads
  Full list
Viewed — **A**
  Full list
  Entry — **B**
  Exit

Why do the statistics here differ from what I see on WordPress.com Site Stats or Google Analytics?
Each statistics tracker uses its own methods to sort, filter, and present the huge volume of data that comes in and out of a website. For example, AWStats shows referrers from probable spam sites while Google Analytics and Site Stats do not.

Choose Among Statistics Trackers

With numerous statistics trackers to choose from, you can find one that works for you. Three options are described in this chapter, and many others exist. Each has its strengths and weaknesses. Because statistics gathered over time generally are more useful than a short-term set of numbers, it pays to spend a little time thinking about what you want from your statistics. Knowing that can help you make the right choice. You can always change your mind, of course, and keep up your old tracker while the new one gathers more data.

Understanding Your Goals

Your need for a statistics tracker depends on what you are trying to achieve. You might simply be curious about how big your audience is and whether it is growing. At the other end of the spectrum, you may be using WordPress as the basis for an e-commerce site and you need detailed information to see whether your marketing efforts are succeeding. Your goals may lie somewhere in between. Perhaps you write a blog about your business focus and you want to know what share of your visitors responds to the link you provide that offers more information.

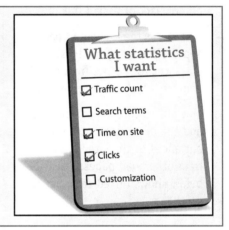

Determine Your Available Time

Most statistics trackers are easy to set up. The learning curve for using them and understanding the results, however, varies widely. If the numbers are critical to you and you have the time — or a helper — to follow and analyze results, you can take full advantage of Google Analytics. If you do not, you may need to go with something simpler.

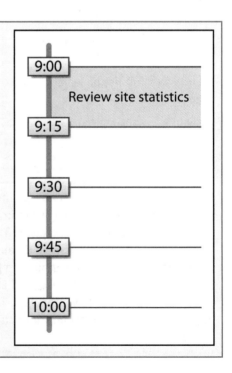

Know the Options

In addition to the trackers discussed in this chapter — WordPress.com Site Stats, Google Analytics, and AWStats — numerous other options are available, each with its own strengths and weaknesses. Here is a comparison of several options:

Clicky	http://clicky.com	Free up to 3,000 page views per month	Easier than Google Analytics but still provides significant, although fewer, statistical reports.
Google Analytics	www.google.com/analytics/	Free	Complex, with a wealth of options, including ability to track specific traffic goals and e-commerce. It can be especially useful if you place AdSense ads on your site, as described in Chapter 15. Navigation is difficult for the novice, and some people think Google knows enough about them without sharing their tracking information with the company. You also can add Google Webmaster Tools or use Universal Analytics for even more data.
Open Web Analytics	www.openwebanalytics.com	Free	You download this software to your computer, thus keeping your tracking details to yourself. Higher than average setup difficulty.
Statcounter	http://statcounter.com	Free up to 250,000 page views per month	Less detail, long-established. Has code for a counter widget to show on a WordPress.com blog and a WordPress.org plugin.
WordPress.com Site Stats	http://wordpress.com or http://jetpack.me	Free	Simple, straightforward, limited information.
Plugins	http://wordpress.org/extend/plugins/	Generally free	Various plugins offer some kind of statistics tracking. Each has its own WordPress.org page. Among the possibilities are WP-Statistics and Counterize. Search Meter tracks search traffic within your site. Other plugins, such as Google Analyticator and WP-Piwik integrate with the related statistics software.
Others	Numerous other statistics trackers exist. You can see a reasonably up-to-date list at http://en.wikipedia.org/wiki/List_of_web_analytics_software. Among them are KISSmetrics at www.kissmetrics.com, Mixpanel at https://mixpanel.com, Piwik at www.piwik.org, and W3Counter at www.w3counter.com.		

Understanding Your Statistics

You can do a lot to improve and understand your website traffic when you understand the statistics your tracker has gathered. The first step is in knowing what the terms mean and how you can use them. Some trackers use slightly different terms than others or apply them somewhat differently. Still, this primer should get you started, and then, you can begin interpreting your statistics. Note that interpreting those statistics is an art and a science and mostly beyond the scope of this book. Even so, you can get a general idea of how your site is doing.

Hits versus Visits

You want to know about visits, not hits. A *hit* is a call to your server for an individual item it stores. If someone lands on your home page, which shows your five latest posts,

Day	Number of visits	Pages	Hits	Bandwidth
01 Dec 2012	455	1,093	3,099	87.89 MB
02 Dec 2012	537	1,065	3,804	95.79 MB

each with one image, plus five widgets, the visit to that page accounts for at least 16 hits — one for the index file for your home page plus one for each post, image, and widget. A *visit*, on the other hand, is one session at your site by one visitor, as determined by IP address, the visitor's unique ID. If you have five visits to a page, those visits are probably more valuable than 16 hits.

Visits versus Visitors

A visit, again, is a session at your site by a *visitor*, also known as a *unique visitor*, as indicated by IP address. If someone visits your site, goes elsewhere, and then comes back, her return might count as a new visit, but not as a new visitor. At Google Analytics,

Visits: 992

Unique Visitors: 948

a visitor must spend 30 minutes away from your site before returning to count as a new visit. When you first start tracking statistics, nearly all visits will be unique visitors, because their IP addresses will be new to the tracker. If, over time, you have many visits and a big share of them are unique visitors, it means relatively few people are coming back. Hence, you need to work at getting visitors to return.

Entries and Exits

The *entry* or *entrance* numbers for individual pages represent the number of visitors who entered at that specific page during the time period being viewed. The term *landing page*

% Exit: 85.72%

also is used. Similarly, *exits* is the number of times visitors left your site from a particular page. If you run an ad campaign that directs an audience to a particular page, the entry number can give you an idea of your campaign's success. The exits figure may tell you that people leave your site from the home page — probably not good — or leave from a particular blog post or contact form — much better. Some programs list this information as percentages.

Bounce Rate

Bounce rate indicates the percentage of visitors who arrive at and leave from the same page without visiting other pages on your site. A high bounce rate generally is a sign that your site is doing a poor job of retaining visitors. You may have an overall site bounce rate — the overall percentage of visits that are one-page, in-and-out visits — and individual page bounce rates. The latter would be the percentage of visits to that page that result in bounces. Your highest bounce rate is likely to be on your home page if that is where your blog appears. Although blogs tend to have higher bounce rates than other sites, because many of your visitors arrive just to read your latest post, you want new visitors especially to click around your site and find reasons to return. When it comes to bounce rate, lower is better.

> **Bounce Rate**
>
> **91.79%**
> Site Avg:
> **91.79% (0.00%)**

Pages per Visit and Visit Duration

Both pages per visit and visit duration are measures of how engaged or involved your visitors are. If they like what they see when they arrive and if you make navigation easy, they are likely to visit multiple pages. If they spend 15 minutes on a single page, it's an indication that they like what they see and want to study it. More pages and more time add up to more increased odds that the visitors will interact by commenting or viewing other content as well as increasing the chances that the visitor may return.

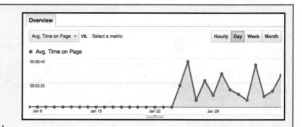

Which Statistics to Focus On

The statistics provided with WordPress.com Site Stats are probably the most important ones, at least when your blog is new. They let you know how many visits you are getting, where they are coming from, and which pages people are visiting. If you get more serious about understanding your traffic or try to make money from your site, you will need to pay closer attention to the other statistics available.

referrers   pages visited

hits   exit   visitors

entry   visits

bounce rate

CHAPTER 10

Maintaining Your WordPress Blog

When your WordPress blog is up, running, and getting readers, you want to make sure that it continues to work smoothly. Although WordPress.com users have fewer maintenance tasks than do self-hosted bloggers, everybody can benefit from a little blog upkeep.

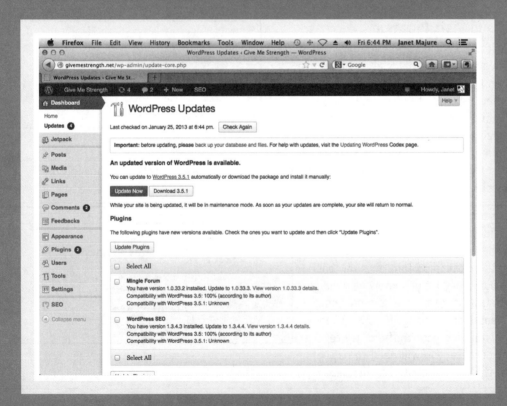

Understanding WordPress Backups

If you have a self-hosted blog, you are responsible for backing up your website. Doing regular backups assures that you do not lose data — or at least not much — should your database become corrupted or your host crash. You have many options for backing up your website. The critical thing is to do it regularly. WordPress.com users have some options for backing up the data, although not their database, on their sites.

What to Back Up

If your site is self-hosted, you need to back up the MySQL database that you created when you installed WordPress because the database stores all your blog posts and comments. You also need to back up the site, however. It contains your plugins, themes, uploads, scripts, and a few other files as well as the core WordPress files. WordPress.com backs up users' databases, but users can back up their content in various ways.

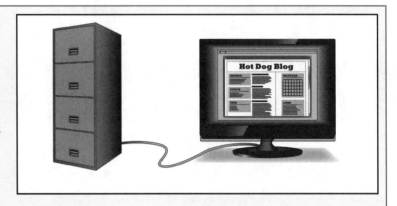

When to Back Up

You are wise to back up your files on a regular schedule so that you do not forget. Some people do it daily, others monthly. Frequency depends on how active your site is — or how much you are willing to lose. In addition, you should always back up before updating to a new version of WordPress.

Backup Methods

There are several backup methods for you to consider. You can use a plugin, such as WordPress Backup; a backup tool provided by your web host; a paid service such as BackupBuddy and the VaultPress service offered by the WordPress.com company Automattic, or a manual backup method. You may want to try more than one method to see what works best for you.

Web Host Tools

Web hosts that use the cPanel control panel have a tool set called Site Backup & Restore. Others provide phpMyAdmin, an interface you can use for backing up your site and database. Find more information by searching on *backups* at http://codex.wordpress.org.

How Long to Save Backups

Some people discard old backups when they create a new one. WordPress experts recommend keeping the latest three backups, just in case something has gone wrong along the way. Let your risk aversion be your guide.

Backup Instructions

Most web host tools are fairly self-explanatory, but contact your web host if you have questions. WordPress.org provides step-by-step instructions for backups using phpMyAdmin and MySQL tools. If you have trouble, also consult the WordPress.org forums.

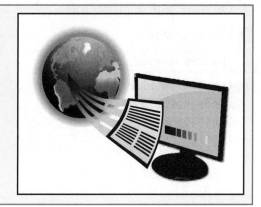

Back Up Using VaultPress

One of the simplest and arguably surest ways to back up your site is to subscribe to the VaultPress backup service. VaultPress is owned and operated by Automattic, the company that runs WordPress.com. Hence, it is intimately familiar with the WordPress.org software and has banks of servers that back up your site's changes more or less immediately. Manual backup options, such as through your web host, may leave you vulnerable to losing data since the last time you backed up. VaultPress requires a WordPress.com account.

Back Up Using VaultPress

① In your browser, go to http://vaultpress.com/jetpack/.

② Click **Buy Now**.

Note: You can choose a Basic or Premium subscription. This example uses the Basic subscription.

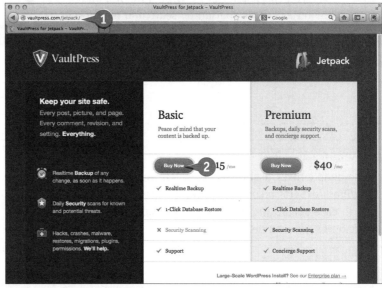

③ Click **Sign In with WordPress.com**.

A screen asks you to connect VaultPress with WordPress.com.

④ Click **Authorize**.

The Subscribe screen appears.

⑤ Complete the credit card information, and click **Subscribe at $15/mo.**

The VaultPress Plugin screen appears.

6 Click **Skip this step**.

7 Copy the registration key.

8 Click **Download the Plugin**.

A download dialog box appears. Save the vaultpress.zip file but do not extract.

TIPS

Why not provide the FTP information requested in Step 6?
You may provide the requested information during the setup if you like. You also can do it later or not at all, although providing it is a good idea. Giving VaultPress FTP access to your site allows faster operation and easier site restoration should the need arise. Chapter 3 provides information about FTP settings.

I have two sites at my web host. Will both of them be covered by my subscription?
No. You need to buy a separate subscription for each site. You can, however, view and manage them all from one location, your dashboard at VaultPress.com.

continued ▶

nce you complete the VaultPress setup, your work is done. After that, VaultPress automatically backs up any change you make to your site. Setting up, however, can seem a little confusing because once you authorize VaultPress to connect with WordPress.com, you still need to download and manually install and activate the VaultPress plugin. The plugin is not available through the WordPress.org plugin directory. Once the plugin is installed, you provide the registration key, and then VaultPress begins its backup of your data, your themes, and plugins.

Back Up Using VaultPress (continued)

9 At your site's administration panel, click **Add New** under Plugins in the left menu bar.

10 Install vaultpress.zip and activate the plugin.

Note: See "Install and Activate a Plugin" in Chapter 6 for detailed instructions.

WordPress confirms the activation, and a VaultPress banner appears.

11 Click **Register VaultPress**.

12 Click here and paste the registration key you copied in Step 7.

13 Click **Register**.

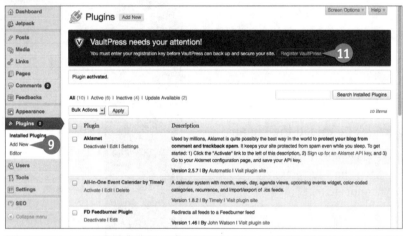

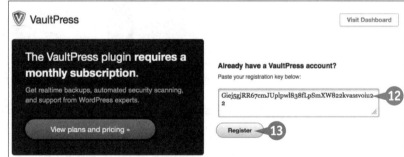

VaultPress immediately begins to do a full backup of your site.

Ⓐ This is a link to the screen where you may provide VaultPress FTP access to your site.

Ⓑ Backup progress is shown here.

Ⓒ New menu item, which lets you return to VaultPress panel, appears here.

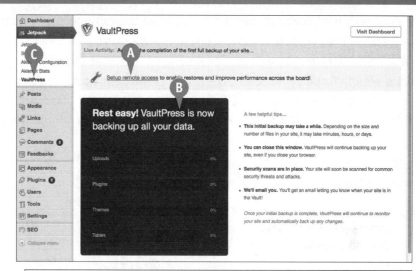

The VaultPress panel at your site displays results of the completed backup.

⑭ Click **Visit Dashboard**.

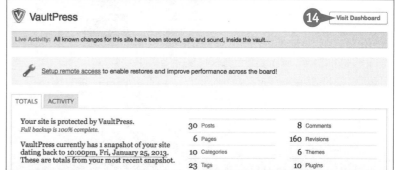

The VaultPress Dashboard appears in a new tab.

Ⓓ You can click here to link to tips for using VaultPress.

Ⓔ You can click here for links to information about your backups and site activity.

Why is it taking so long to do my backup, and will it always take so long?
The first backup takes longest because VaultPress is backing up everything you have on your site. Depending on how much data you have it could take hours. Once the initial backup is completed, backups occur automatically as you make changes.

How do I restore my site from a backup?
On your VaultPress dashboard, click **Backups**. The Backups panel appears. Click the **Restore** button next to the backup that you want to restore to your site. The restoration occurs automatically. For detailed instructions, go to https://vaultpress.com/help/site-restore.

Back Up Using Your Web Host

Your web host probably has a built-in, free backup manager of some kind. It may also have a paid version that costs less than services like VaultPress and BackupBuddy. One such backup option is called Site Backups & Restore. Because your web host already has your information, you need to do little setup. You may need to take responsibility for doing regular backups and storing them on your computer and perhaps to DVD. Contact your web host if you have questions about its backup options. This task uses Site Backups & Restore through cPanel, a widely used web host control panel.

Back Up Using Your Web Host

1 After logging on to your host control panel, click **Site Backup & Restore**.

A backup panel appears.

2 Click **Website Files**.

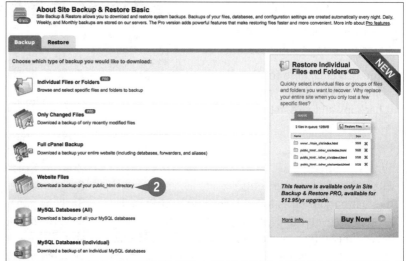

③ Click **Weekly System Backup** or another option if you prefer.

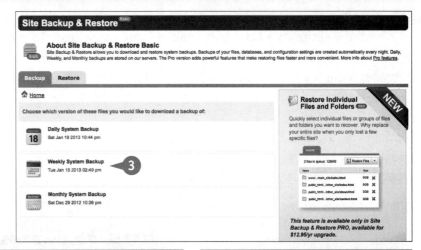

A dialog box appears.

④ Click **Start Archiving**.

When the archive is ready, the dialog box changes.

⑤ Click **Click Here to Download**.

A browser dialog box appears.

⑥ Make sure the **Save File** radio button is selected (◉).

⑦ Click **OK**.

The backup downloads to your default download location.

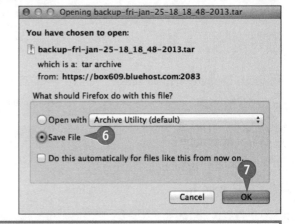

Should I back up my site files or my whole website?

You probably should backup your entire website periodically and your site files more frequently. Site files change more frequently and are easier to restore than an entire site archive should the need arise.

My web host says it backs up every day. Why do I need to back my site up myself?

Chances are your web host policies include one that says it does not guarantee it keeps backups of your files and that it recommends you create and keep your own backups.

Back Up Using Dropbox

Dropbox, a cloud storage service, when used with a plugin allows you to safely back up your self-hosted website to a third party and at little to no cost. To use this option, you need to sign up for a Dropbox account at www.dropbox.com. The free basic account provides at least 2 gigabytes of storage, more if you refer other people to the service. This example uses the WordPress Backup to Dropbox plugin. You need to install it to get started, as described in Chapter 6.

Back Up Using Dropbox

1 After installing and activating the plugin, click the new left menu item, **WPB2D**.

The WordPress to Dropbox panel appears.

2 Click **Authorize**.

The Dropbox sign-in screen appears.

3 Type the e-mail address you use at Dropbox.

4 Type your Dropbox password.

5 Click **Sign In**.

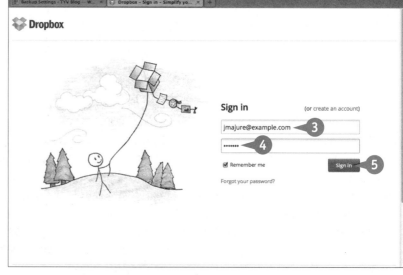

An authorization screen appears.

6 Click **Allow**.

Dropbox displays a Success! message.

7 Click the Backup Settings tab to return to the WordPress to Dropbox Backup settings.

8 Click **Continue**.

9 Select a day for backups.

10 Select a time for backups.

11 Select a backup frequency.

12 Click **Save Changes**.

WordPress saves the settings, and backups will occur at the set schedule.

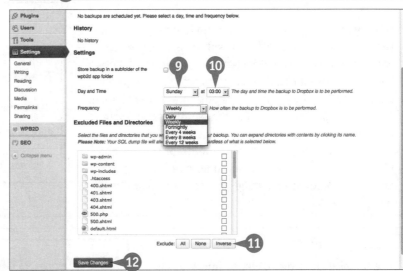

TIPS

Can I back up to another cloud service, such as Amazon S3 or Google Drive?

Yes. At least two good plugins are available. UpdraftPlus allows you to schedule automatic backups to those services as well as to Dropbox, an FTP site, and e-mail. BackWPup adds to that list backups to Microsoft Azure, Rackspace Cloud, and more.

How do I know if the backup is working?

You should go to your Dropbox account and check in the Applications/wpb2d folder to see if your backup is there. Even though the backup is automatic, you probably should check periodically, especially after installing WordPress or plugin updates.

Understanding WordPress Updates

One great and terrible thing about using the WordPress.org software is that developers are continually improving and adjusting the software. It is great, because it means WordPress regularly improves security, fixes bugs, and adds features. It is terrible, or at least frustrating, because that means you also must continually update your software. The updating process is simple for most users, but it does cause you to spend time on site maintenance that you might prefer to spend writing posts. Unfortunately, updating the WordPress software sometimes can create problems with plugins or themes. Hence, you need to pay attention to your updates.

Update Alerts

When a new WordPress software update is available, your current software lets you know, unless you are using a fairly old WordPress version. It strips a yellow alert banner across the top of every panel in your Dashboard (**A**) when a new version of WordPress is available. It also puts a number next to the recycling icon (⟳) in the administration bar that informs you of the total number of updates, including plugins and themes, available (**B**) on the items you have installed.

What Gets Updated

When you update WordPress, you update only the WordPress software itself. That software underlies all your site's functions and includes two themes, Twenty Eleven and Twenty Twelve. Chances are, however, you have customized your site by choosing a different theme and adding plugins. Updating the WordPress software does not update those parts of your site, and sometimes WordPress updates affect the operation of themes and plugins. As a result, theme and plugin developers who are staying current may issue updates, which you need to install separately.

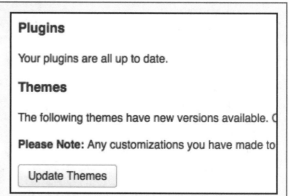

Need to Update

The temptation is great just to ignore updates. You may feel they are unnecessary, or their installation interrupts your workflow, or you do not want to have to learn about any new features or new ways to do the same things. You may worry whether an old plugin will work properly with the new software. Still, avoid the temptation to ignore updates. Failing to update increases your site's vulnerability to hackers and limits your ability to take advantage of new developments.

Update Two Ways

WordPress offers both automatic and manual means of updating its software. The automatic version can be started and completed in moments from your WordPress Dashboard. The manual version requires you to download the software to your computer, disable all your plugins, upload the software to your web host, and then reenable the plugins. While the process is simple enough, it is just a little more time-consuming than an automatic update.

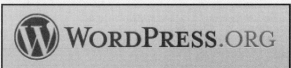

An updated version of WordPress is available.

You can update to WordPress 3.5.1 automatically or download the package and install it manually:

Automatic or Manual

You may want to do a manual update if you want to keep edits you made to the Twenty Eleven or Twenty Twelve theme or if the automatic update fails for some reason. In most instances, however, the automatic update works fine.

Update Requirements

Although usually not necessary, it is not a bad idea to check before updating to see that your web host meets the minimum requirements WordPress needs to run on the host. You can find them at http://wordpress.org/about/requirements/. At this writing, those requirements are for PHP version 5.2.4 or greater and MySQL version 5.0 or greater.

WORDPRESS.ORG

Requirements

After the Update

After you successfully update your WordPress software, WordPress presents a welcome screen in which it explains what is new in the new version. That information is general but lets you know what to expect. After you read that information, you can dismiss the welcome screen and continue with your content creation and management.

Welcome to WordPress 3.5

Thank you for updating to the latest version! WordPress 3.5 is more polished and enjoyable than ever before. We hope you like it.

WORDPRESS
Version 3.5

Update WordPress Automatically

If you have a self-hosted blog, you need to keep up with WordPress updates, a task that WordPress.com does for its users. Updating WordPress is a simple process, and it assures that you have the latest features and the latest security measures installed. Although updating can seem like a bother, especially because you really need to back up your site and database first, you are wise to stay current. Hackers are good at exploiting weak spots in old versions. Your Dashboard maintains a yellow alert whenever new versions of the WordPress software are available, so there is no excuse that you did not know it was time.

Update WordPress Automatically

1 After backing up your site, click **Please update now**.

The WordPress Updates panel opens.

2 Click **Update Now**.

WordPress presents a progress screen as it downloads and installs the update, and then it opens.

The Welcome to WordPress screen appears.

③ Click **What's New** and read the information to ease your transition to the new version.

④ Scroll to the bottom of the page.

⑤ Click one of the Return to Dashboard links to dismiss the welcome message.

TIP

My automatic update failed. Now what?

You are among the unlucky few. Worry not; you still should be able to update successfully. If an automatic update does not work, you can update manually. Here are some troubleshooting tips. Note that you must update manually if you are updating from a version earlier than WordPress 2.7.

- *Installation Failed* message: Simply try again; you may have had some Internet connection interruption.

- First message says *WordPress Updated Successfully*, but another message says *An automated WordPress update has failed to complete — please attempt the update again now*: Using your FTP program, open the directory or folder where WordPress is installed — that is, the folder that contains the WP-Admin folder. Look for and delete a file named .maintenance. Then try the automatic update again.

- *Fatal Error* message: Installation succeeds, but display is fouled up. Go to your plugins list and deactivate all plugins. Then try the automatic update again. When the update is complete, reactivate the plugins. If you still get the message, again deactivate all the plugins and then activate them one at a time, going to the site after each activation, until you identify one that may be causing the error.

- Repeated failure: Review the information at http://codex.wordpress.org/Updating_WordPress for ideas. Then, ask at the WordPress.org forums for help, or do a manual update, as described in the next section.

Update WordPress Manually

Maybe you are a hands-on kind of person, or maybe you have had trouble with the automatic update. In any case, you can orchestrate a WordPress update manually. Be sure to back up your site first, as described earlier in this chapter. The actual update process essentially consists of downloading and extracting the software to your computer, turning off all plugins, uploading the software to your web host using FTP, and then reactivating plugins. After you are done, it is a good idea to click around on your website to make sure everything functions properly.

Update WordPress Manually

1 After backing up your site, click **Updates** in the left menu bar.

The WordPress Updates panel opens.

2 Click **Download 3.5.1** (or whatever is the latest version).

Your browser opens a download window.

3 Click **Open with Archive Utility** (○ changes to ◉) if not already selected.

Note: Your computer may use a different program for extracting the Zip file.

4 Click **OK**.

Your browser downloads the file to your computer and extracts the Zip file.

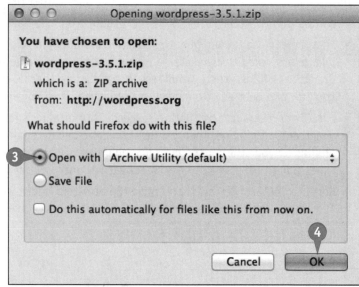

5 Click **Plugins**.

The Plugins panel opens.

6 Select all plugins (☐ changes to ☑).

7 Click the Bulk Actions drop-down menu and select **Deactivate**.

8 Click **Apply**.

The plugins are deactivated.

9 Using your FTP access, delete the folders called wp-admin and wp-includes from your site's root directory.

Note: Do NOT delete other files or folders.

10 Upload the new wp-admin and wp-includes from your extracted WordPress folder.

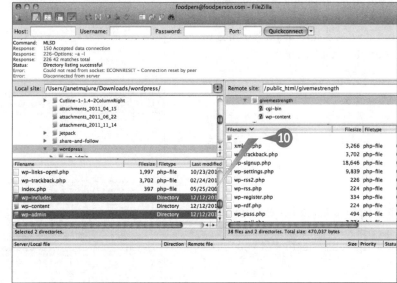

TIPS

Should I update my plugins and themes before or after I update WordPress?

Update WordPress first. The plugin and theme updates you have most likely are intended to work best with the new version of WordPress. After you update WordPress, you can update the plugins and themes as you turn them back on.

My web host used Simple Scripts to do my initial installation. Does that affect what method I use to update?

It should not. You can check with your host and Simple Scripts to see if it has an update ready. If it does, you can use Simple Scripts to update your software. If not, you can use either the automatic or manual update described in this and the previous sections.

continued ▶

Manual updating usually takes much longer than automatic updating, so allow time to upload the many files needed. Remember that upload speed is typically much slower than download speed. If you need more help with your manual installation, go to http://codex.wordpress.org/Upgrading_ WordPress_Extended. Once your update is complete, you need to review your website to see that things are functioning properly. If they are not, a plugin conflict may be responsible, so you may need to update plugins, also. The next section details how.

Update WordPress Manually (continued)

11 Upload the contents — not the folder itself — from the new wp-content folder to your existing wp-content folder.

Note: Overwrite any old files with the same names as the new files, but do not delete any other files in your old wp-content folder.

12 Upload the other remaining files from the download into the root directory of your site.

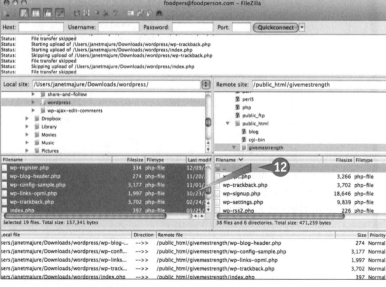

13 Go to your site's Dashboard at www.*yoursite*.com/ wp-login and click **Plugins**.

The Plugins panel opens.

14 Click the plugins you want to activate (☐ changes to ☑).

15 Click the Bulk Actions drop-down menu and select **Activate**.

16 Click **Apply**.

The plugins are activated.

Note: Some users prefer to activate plugins one at a time, checking the site after each, to detect any plugin conflicts with the new software.

17 Click the website name and visit the updated site.

Ⓐ If you have reactivated Jetpack, you need to click to reconnect your site to the WordPress.com servers.

18 Navigate around your site to see whether everything works correctly.

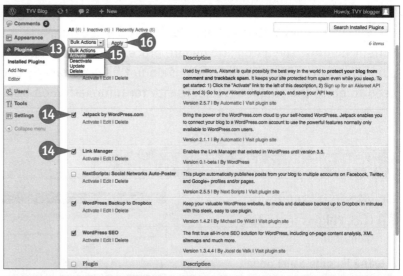

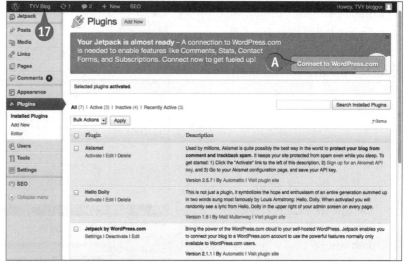

TIPS

When I tried to return to the Dashboard, I got a notice that said "Database Update Required." What should I do?

WordPress has detected that your database needs some updates to work with the updated WordPress installation. Go ahead and click **Update WordPress Database**.

Since my update, the layout looks weird. What do I do?

Make sure you have the latest versions of all your plugins and your theme. If you still have a problem, turn off all plugins. Then activate each plugin one at a time, checking your blog's performance after each activation. If you identify a problem plugin, leave it deactivated and contact the plugin developer to see whether an update is available. If it is not, you may need to seek a different plugin.

Install Plugin Updates Automatically

You can keep your website up to date and functioning safely by updating your plugins as well as your WordPress software. Your WordPress Dashboard alerts you to the existence of updates to your current plugins. The automatic update process works for most plugins. You can even update multiple plugins at once. Occasionally, plugins do not have automatic updates available. In those cases, you need to go to the plugin developer's site for information on how to update.

Install Plugin Updates Automatically

Update One Plugin

1 Click **Plugins** in the left menu bar.

The Plugins panel opens.

A A number indicates how many plugins have updates available.

2 Click **update automatically**.

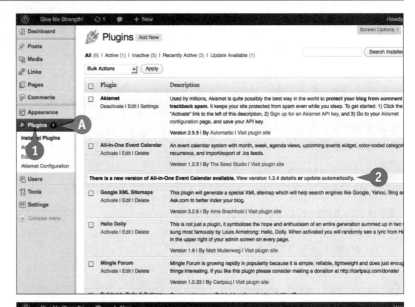

The Update Plugin panel opens and displays update progress.

3 When the update is complete, click **Return to Plugins page**, and update other plugins as needed.

Update Multiple Plugins

1. Click **Plugins** in the left menu bar.

   The Plugins panel opens.

2. Click **Update Available**.

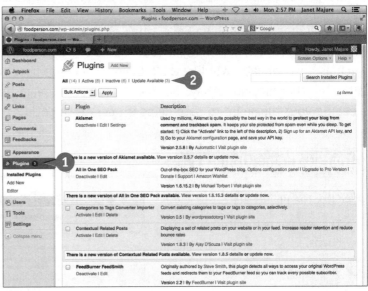

3. Click the **Plugin** check box (☐ changes to ☑).

   All available updates are selected (☐ changes to ☑).

4. Choose **Update** from the drop-down list.

5. Click **Apply**.

   All the updates are installed and activated.

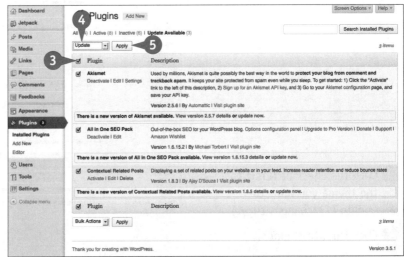

TIPS

I have a plugin that has not been updated for a couple of years. Do I need to do anything about that?

It depends on the plugin. It probably is a good idea to go to http://wordpress.org/extend/plugins and search for the plugin. Read the comments and problems that people have posted. If they worry you, chances are that a newer plugin has been developed that you can use to replace the old one.

How do I manually update a plugin?

You can simply replace it by deleting the old plugin and uploading the new version using the manual installation procedure mentioned in Chapter 6. However, in the likely event you want to keep settings, go to the plugin developer's page, accessible via your Plugins panel, and read the instructions there.

Install Theme Updates

In most cases, you can update your theme as easily as you can update your WordPress software and plugins. Although you may think of your theme as a visual presentation, it interacts with the WordPress software, especially if your theme engages some of the more complex and recent functions such as post formats. WordPress alerts you when you have themes installed that require updates, although that may not always be true if you use a theme that is not registered with WordPress.org. Keeping your theme up to date helps it operate smoothly.

Install Theme Updates

1 Click the update alert.

The WordPress Updates panel opens.

2 Scroll down to the Themes area.

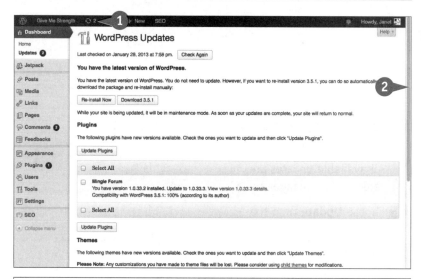

3 Click the check box next to the theme you want to update (☐ changes to ☑).

4 Click **Update Themes**.

The Update Themes panel appears, and the update begins.

Ⓐ WordPress confirms the successful update.

5 Click **Return to WordPress Updates**.

Ⓑ The update counter has decreased.

Ⓒ The Themes area of the Updates page indicates whether more theme updates are available.

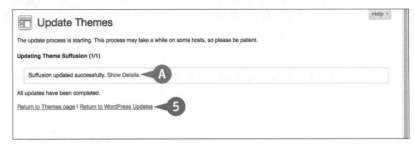

TIPS

Do I need to update all the themes I have installed?

You definitely need to update your active theme and the default themes that come with the WordPress software, Twenty Eleven and Twenty Twelve. You need to keep them up to date for testing purposes in case things go awry with your site. As for additional themes, updating is not essential as long as they are deactivated.

Will my settings get lost if I update?

As a general rule, no. The WordPress Updates panel warns that customization to theme files will be lost. That refers to changes in the code in the theme files, not to the theme's settings. If you decided to customize, try making a child theme. That option is discussed in Chapter 13.

Clean Out Outdated Drafts

Keeping your blog up to date also involves clearing out detritus that can distract you from your purpose, not to mention that it unnecessarily takes up space on your web host. Take a few minutes to get rid of it! This aspect of maintenance is probably easiest if you clear drafts every two weeks or every month. If you go too long, many drafts are likely to accumulate. When that happens, you may spend too much time trying to recall why you started a post or you may delete something you should have kept.

Clean Out Outdated Drafts

1 Click **Posts** in the left menu bar.

The Posts menu expands, and the Posts panel opens.

2 Click **Drafts**.

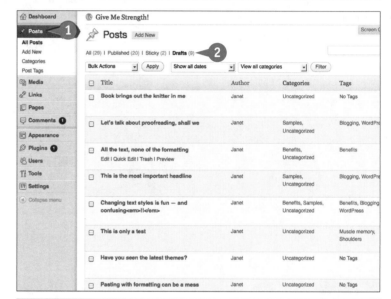

The Posts panel filters out all except draft posts.

3 Click the **Title** check box to select all drafts (☐ changes to ☑).

4 Choose **Move to Trash** from the drop-down menu.

5 Click **Apply**.

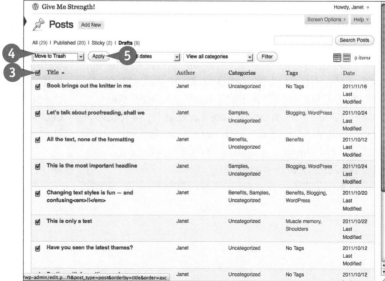

WordPress confirms the move to Trash and provides an Undo link.

6 Click the **Trash** link under the confirmation message.

The Posts panel filters out all but the posts in Trash.

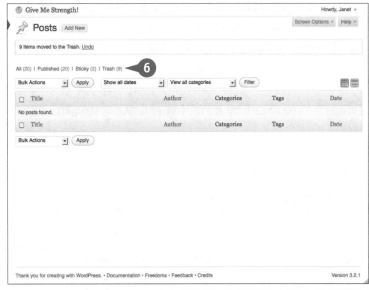

7 Click the drafts and other trash you want to remove (☐ changes to ☑).

8 Choose **Delete Permanently** from the drop-down menu.

9 Click **Apply**.

WordPress confirms that the posts you selected are permanently deleted.

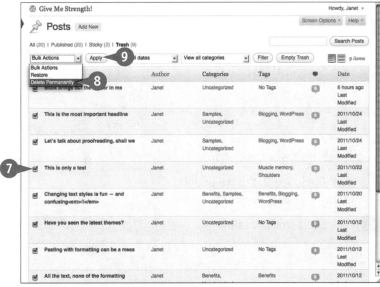

TIPS

Should I review the drafts before I delete them?

That would probably be a wise step, although if your blog is like most people's, chances are that drafts that have been sitting for more than six months are out of date — or you are not able to remember what your point was!

Do I have to delete all drafts?

Of course not. Feel free to review and delete drafts one at a time. If you position your mouse pointer over a particular draft, links appear under the post title. Click the **Trash** link to move it to the Trash. To delete it permanently, click **Trash** near the top of the Posts panel so as to view the trashed items. Position your mouse pointer over the post you want to eliminate, and then click **Delete Permanently** under the post.

Remove Post Revisions

You can keep your content database from getting bogged down by eliminating old post revisions. As explained in "Recall an Earlier Version of Your Blog Post" in Chapter 4, WordPress saves a revision whenever you save or update a post. It's a great feature, but over time those revisions can add up. A plugin can keep your database from accumulating too many of those revisions. The Optimize Database after Revisions option allows you to delete all or some revisions, and it does it on a schedule. Start by installing and activating the plugin the usual way.

Remove Post Revisions

① Click **Optimize DB Options** under Settings in the left menu bar.

② Type the number of revisions you want to retain for each post.

③ Choose a scheduling interval if desired.

④ Click **Save Options**.

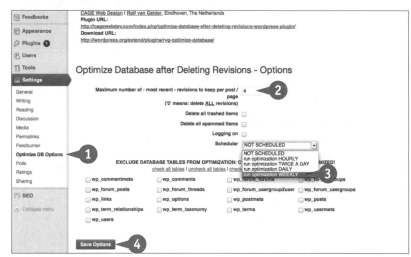

WordPress saves the options.

⑤ Click **Optimize Database** under Tools in the left menu bar.

⑥ Click **Start Optimization**.

Your site's first optimization runs.

Ⓐ Plugin activity appears here.

➐ Scroll to the bottom of the page.

Optimization results appear.

Ⓑ In this example, the database size is cut nearly in half.

Can I manually delete individual post revisions or turn them off?
Probably not. Although it is possible to edit your WordPress software to stop post revisions, there is no convenient way to delete revisions one by one.

How do I delete post revisions at WordPress.com?
You do not need to. WordPress.com maintains your database, so you do not need to worry about overloading your server. WordPress.com automatically stores up to 25 post revisions for each post or page you create.

Check Your Site for Outdated Links

You know you hate it when you click a link and get a *Page Not Found* message, so you can assume your readers will not like it if they find a broken link on your site. Fortunately, finding and fixing broken links is fairly simple. Try it occasionally! Even better, schedule it regularly. Depending on the size of your site, the process can be a little time-consuming, but it is worth the effort to keep your site up to date.

Check Your Site for Outdated Links

1 Go to http://validator.w3.org/checklink in your web browser.

2 Type your URL in the box.

3 Click **Check linked documents** (☐ changes to ☑), and type **4** in the box next to recursion depth.

The depth setting takes the link checker into directories beyond the home page directory.

4 Click **Check**.

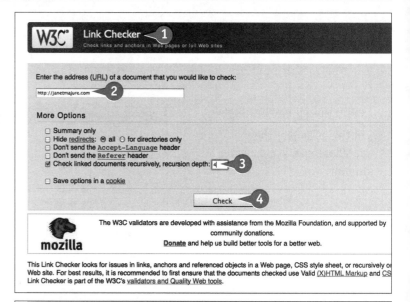

The link checker goes to work reviewing your site's links.

5 When the validator is done, click **the results**.

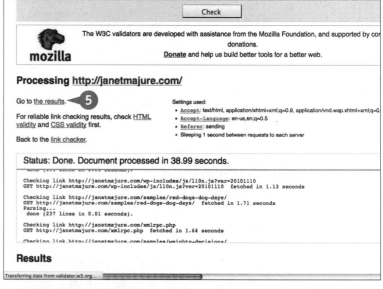

Lists of broken links and other issues appear.

⑥ Review the problem links. You can click them to see what happens.

Note: Some links may work but are flagged because they do not comply with the World Wide Web Consortium standards.

Ⓐ Details of issues and repair suggestions appear under each page's list of problem links.

⑦ Scroll down to see more results.

⑧ Above the list of broken links is the URL of the page link where the broken link or links appear. Click the link.

The page with the broken link appears in your browser.

⑨ When you find the broken link, correct it or delete it in the Edit Post or Edit Page panel.

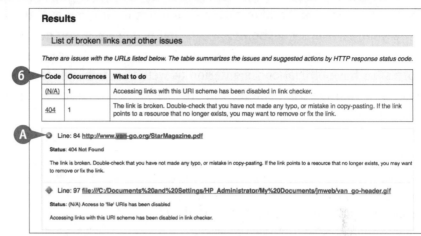

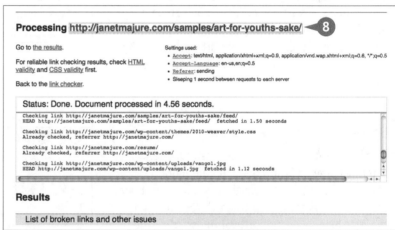

TIPS

Are there any other link trackers?
Yes, several. Perhaps you would prefer Xenu's Link Sleuth, a free program you can download for Windows, or the LinkChecker add-on for the Firefox browser. The Broken Link Checker plugin is another option for self-hosted blogs.

Why does the W3C Link Checker take so long?
The time it takes depends primarily on how much content your site has to check. If you check your links periodically, the Link Checker processing may be no faster, but you will have many fewer dead links to investigate.

Get to Know WordPress Support Options

The multiplicity of WordPress support options means you are almost certain to find the answer to your particular question. You can find it quicker if you go to the right places. Start at WordPress.org if you have a self-hosted website and at WordPress.com if your blog is hosted there. Both sites have official documentation as well as active user forums where someone else probably has asked your question before. You are likely to get a prompt response at either forum. Other support options also exist.

The WordPress.org Codex

A *Codex* is a bound manuscript, and that is the name that WordPress.org chose for its set of support articles, which you can find at http://codex.wordpress.org. Note that numerous contributors write Codex articles, and some are definitely better and more up to date than others. The Codex main page lists support documents by category, but note the links on the right side of the page as well.

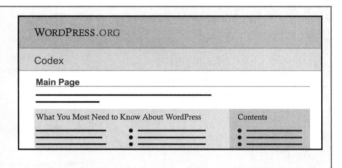

Official WordPress.com Support

Compared with those at WordPress.org, the support pages at WordPress.com are more consistent in style and timeliness, but even they are not always totally up to date. You can find them at http://en.support.wordpress.com. The main page lists topics that you may find helpful. Occasionally, WordPress.com Support articles may be helpful even to self-hosted bloggers.

Search for Answers

Both the WordPress.org Codex and the WordPress.com Support pages have search options, and both allow you to search the documentation as well as the forums. If you do not identify what you need by browsing the documentation, search the documentation and the forums. You are likely to find an answer.

Do Not Miss WordPress.TV

WordPress has numerous instructional and informational videos you may find useful. You can find them at http://wordpress.tv. Although many of the videos focus on WordPress.com, you also can find videos from WordCamps, conferences for WordPress enthusiasts of all descriptions.

Pose a Question

If you fail in your attempts to find an answer, you are welcome to post a question to the thousands of WordPress users who read the forums. You need to be logged in to post a question — or an answer. Make sure you follow posting etiquette if you want to get a good response.

Search the Support Forums

Enter a few words that describe the problem you're having.

[   ] (Search)

Posting Etiquette

Things that might be considered bad manners on the forums:

- Posting a question that has been answered many times before. Search first!

- Posting a *.com* question on the *.org* forum or vice versa. The most frequent misplaced questions seem to be people asking questions about plugins on the .com forums.

- Using a useless post title, such as "Help!"

WORDPRESS.COM

8 Things To Know Before Posting in WordPress.com

✔ FAQ   ✔ Linking   ✔ Remember...

✔ Search   ✔ Be polite   ✔ It's free!

✔ Be specific ✔ www.myblog.com

Good manners include posting a link to your site, being specific, and using standard grammar and spelling. And remember that in most cases volunteers and fellow users are trying to help, so be nice.

Find Support at WordPress.com

The support pages at WordPress.com provide just about any help you might need if WordPress.com hosts your site. The official documentation, accessible at http://en.support.wordpress.com, provides authoritative information on nearly all issues pertaining to WordPress.com. Unfortunately, that information sometimes is not up to date. The user forums at http://en.forums.wordpress.com tend to be more current, but sometimes yield confusing or conflicting advice from fellow users. You also can contact staff directly to seek help.

Find Support at WordPress.com

1 Go to http://en.support.wordpress.com in your web browser.

2 Scan for the general category that fits your question.

A More links appear at the bottom of the page.

3 Click the category that fits your topic.

Note: This example seeks help in creating a table in a post.

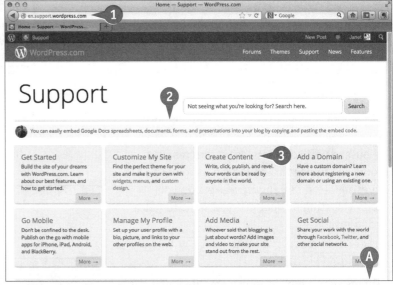

The support topic page opens.

4 Scan the page for the information you need.

B This section contains links to spots on the page you are viewing.

C This section contains links to related support articles.

If you find what you need, you are done.

5 If you do not see what you need, type a search term.

6 Click **Search**.

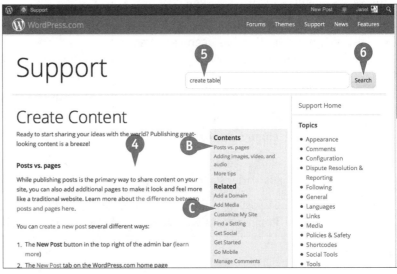

The search results for your term appear.

D Possible support articles appear at the top of the results page.

E Possible forum topics appear at the bottom of the page.

7 Click the link that seems most pertinent.

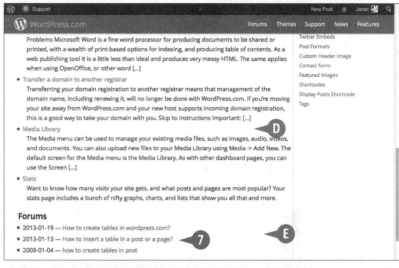

The article or forum topic opens.

8 Click the Back button (◀) to view more results, if desired.

Can I just go to the Support page and search as a first step?
Certainly. It is just a matter of how you like to work. Sometimes browsing works better than searching. It depends on how good your search term is. If you go straight to search, you may want to try different search terms until you find what you are seeking.

How can I get support by e-mail?
It is a multistep process. Go to http://en.support. wordpress.com/contact. There, you review common questions, then ask the question and review proposed answers, and then, after telling WordPress.com twice that you did not find the answer, a contact form appears. Complete it, and click **Contact Support**.

Find Support at WordPress.org

The forums and articles at WordPress.org cover much of the same material as at WordPress.com, and a whole lot more. That's because users of the WordPress.org software have many issues that WordPress.com users do not have to contend with, including installation, updates, plugins, and hundreds more themes. And because many of those add-ons are developed by people not directly involved with the WordPress team, the support is inconsistent. Still, most questions get answered either in the documentation, known as the Codex, or in the forums.

Find Support at WordPress.org

① In your browser, go to http://wordpress.org/support/.

Ⓐ This area contains links to documentation.

Ⓑ This area contains links to forums by category.

Ⓒ This word cloud displays support topics. Click one to see a list of discussions on that topic.

② Type a search term.

③ Click **Search**.

The search results appear.

④ Click an item.

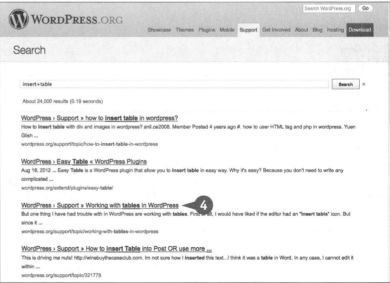

The item appears.

5 Read the full question and answers.

6 Click the browser Back button (◀) to look at more results.

7 Repeat Steps **3** to **6** as needed.

8 Click a related tag.

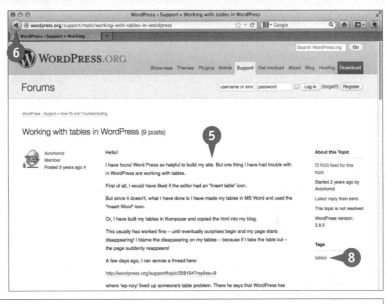

A list of forum topics appears, newest first, labeled with the tag you clicked.

Topic	Posts	Last Poster	Freshness
Adding Table on Plugin Activation / dbDelta	1	emailmike1994	15 hours
Moving from MS Expression to WordPress	1	BostonDan	1 day
Tables verses Divs	11	Andrew Nevins	5 days
Transparent table borders: how to w/ html vs css?	6	inaprettybox	5 days
[Plugin: SortTable Post] Displaying posts of just one category	13	infinetmkt	1 week
Home Page Extends When Not Supposed To	3	Andrew Nevins	1 week
[resolved] [Theme: Twenty Twelve] Why can't I add custom style classes to each cell or ?!?!	2	jamesinagiantpeach	1 week
How to JOIN tables with $wpdb	7	michael.mariart	1 week
Creating a custom page from tabular data	2	vtxyzzy	1 week
[resolved] How to insert a line break in tables	10	wackynation	2 weeks
[resolved] Photogallery TABLE with LARGE Text Options	3	calgarytech	2 weeks
[resolved] How to merge two database tables	1	alex.one	2 weeks
function convert_to_screen() no longer exists in template.php?	7	artichokelucy	1 month
WP-Reloaded Issues	6	TobiasBg	1 month
I would love for plugins to state if and how many tables they add.	19	12sp	1 month
Inputting multiple text entries to appear on site in a preformatted layout	6	vtxyzzy	1 month
[resolved] Aligning Multiple Images On A Page	2	athenacurrier	1 month

TIPS

How do I browse the documentation?
Position your mouse pointer over the Support menu item, and click **Docs**. The Codex opens. Choose among the topics listed to read the documentation. You also can browse the forums by clicking on one of the categories at http://wordpress.org/support/.

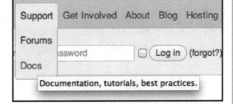

How do I submit my own forum question or answer?
First, log in at WordPress.org. There is a login area at the top of the Forums page. Click any forum or tag. An Add New button appears at the top of the page that you can click to add a new topic. At the bottom of existing topics, a Reply form appears. Older topics usually are closed to new replies.

Take Action When Your Blog Breaks

Blogs do break or crash, but they can be recovered. Most often, problems involve plugins or updates to your WordPress software — or even updates to your host's software. Because you cannot get into the code at WordPress.com, the host must resolve crashes there, but see the table in this section for some issues common to both WordPress types. Although crashes are frustrating and sometimes time-consuming, you may feel a bit less anxious if you have maintained a regular backup routine, as discussed in "Understanding WordPress Backups," earlier in this chapter.

Remain Calm and Take Notes

Take a deep breath and write down exactly what happened. Note any error message you saw or see, and when possible take screenshots. Try to recall what you did just before everything went wrong.

Turn Off Plugins

Even if you have not altered plugins lately, deactivate all plugins and see if your blog works. If it does, you may well have a plugin conflict. Turn one plugin on and view your blog. Repeat with the next plugin and so on until the crash recurs. Then deactivate that last plugin.

Install the Default Theme

Themes can cause strange behavior. The default theme, Twenty Eleven, is guaranteed to run on the latest version of WordPress. If you activate the default theme and the blog works okay, then you need to identify what is wrong with the theme you were running.

Reinstall the Plugin or Theme

Sometimes the code for the problem plugin or theme becomes corrupted. Using your FTP program — not the administrative panels — delete the plugin from the Plugins folder on your server, or the theme from the Themes folder. Then reinstall the plugin or theme, either manually or through the administrative panels.

Support Forums

If your problem is a plugin or theme you can contact the developer, or search on the plugin or theme forum if one exists. For other problems, search the forums at WordPress.org. If your question has not already been addressed, post a question and be sure to provide your URL and the error message or other behavior you are getting.

If All Else Fails

You may need to restore your site from a backup. Your web host should have a utility to help you do that, or you can find instructions at http://codex.wordpress.org/Restoring_Your_Database_From_Backup. You may need only to restore your database, or you may need to restore your site's files as well. These files include the WordPress software, plugins, and themes. If you have been using a backup plugin, backup service, or your host's backup option, the plugin, service, or host may help you restore your data and files.

Troubleshoot Common WordPress Problems

As with any computer program, WordPress poses problems for its users now and then.

Problem	Possible Explanation	What to Do
I forgot my password!	Brain freeze.	Go to your blog's logon page — http://*yourblog*.com/wp-admin (or http://*yourblog*.wordpress.com/wp-admin) — and click the lost password link. You still need to know your username and e-mail address. A password will be e-mailed to you.
Page does not display.	Server is down or your web connection is interrupted.	Check to make sure you can access other websites. If you can, your web connection is okay, so it may be a server at your web host, including WordPress.com. Wait 15 minutes and try again.
Page still does not display, although I have Internet connectivity.	Server is still down after waiting 15 minutes.	Contact your web host.
I made changes to my theme, but when I check it, nothing happens.	Your site is *cached* in your browser, which means a previous version is showing up.	Refresh your browser by pressing and holding Ctrl (⌘ on a Mac) and clicking the **Refresh** button on your browser.
I need to talk to a live person!	You are frustrated.	Try live chat. Read about it at http://codex.wordpress.org/WordPress_IRC_Live_Help. If your blog is hosted at WordPress.com, you can contact support at http://en.support.wordpress.com/contact. You may get a quicker response by going to www.justanswer.com or http://wpquestions.com, but you will need to pay a small fee.
No answers to my forum question.	You posted it in the wrong forum, you did not give it any tags, or your question was too vague.	Make sure you post WordPress.com questions at WordPress.com, and self-hosted blog questions at WordPress.org forums. You will note that WordPress forums are subdivided into categories such as Installation and Plugins. Use brief, descriptive tags, such as *comment plugin*, rather than *I cannot figure out why this is not working!*
Scheduled post did not appear.	You forgot to click **Schedule**.	After you save a draft to be published at a future date, you not only need to save the draft and okay the time for publication, but you also need to click **Schedule** to make it happen. When you do, the Status will read *Scheduled*.
Blog looks funny on different machine.	Different browser, different monitor.	The nature of web design is that the appearance of pages varies according to the monitor and the browser being used. You can get an idea of it at home by viewing your blog with different browsers or changing the display settings, such as resolution, for your monitor.

Make a Suggestion

H ave you noticed that your blog would work just about *perfectly* if only it would do that one thing that you want? If you are certain that the widget or plugin you need is not available, you can ask for it. WordPress.com and WordPress.org have different approaches to making suggestions, but both are fairly simple. In both cases, you need to log in before you can post suggestions.

Make a Suggestion

Send a Suggestion to WordPress.com Support

1. Log in to WordPress.com, and go to http://en.support.wordpress.com/contact in your web browser.

2. Skim the support topics listed, and click **I didn't find the right answer**.

3. Type your suggestion in the text box that appears.

Ⓐ Links to possibly similar information appear.

4. Click **I still didn't find the right answer** if the related information did not show your idea.

A contact form appears.

5. Provide the information requested, and click **Contact Support**.

Post an Idea in the Forums

1. Go to http://en.forums.wordpress.com/forum/ideas in your web browser.

2. Click **Add New**.

The New Topic box appears.

3. Type your suggestion in the New Topic box, add tags, such as *themes,* to describe your suggestion, and then click **Submit**.

Your idea appears in the Ideas forum.

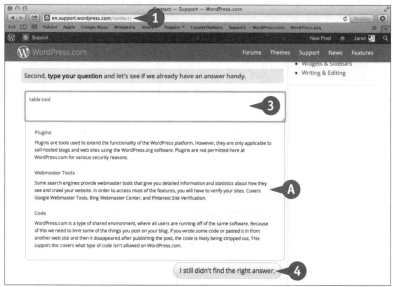

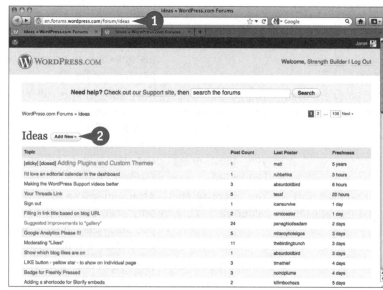

Make a Suggestion at WordPress.org

1 Go to http://wordpress.org/ extend/ideas in your web browser.

2 Scroll to the bottom of the Ideas page, and type a subject in the One line summary box.

3 Describe your idea in the Description box.

4 Type a keyword or two as tags.

5 Choose a category from the pop-up list.

6 Click **Submit Idea**.

Your idea is submitted for consideration.

Rate an Idea

1 After reading other people's ideas, click one you like or dislike, and then click a star to rate the idea.

Note: For ideas under consideration, you also can type a reply to add to the consideration.

B More ideas can be reviewed by their status.

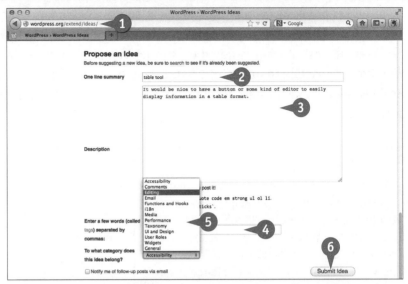

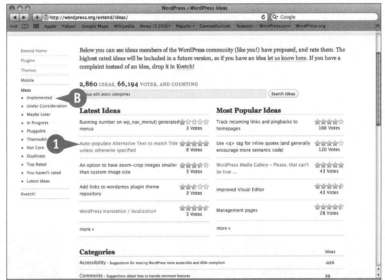

TIPS

Is there a way to propose something privately at WordPress.org?
Yes. Use the Kvetch page at http:// wordpress.org/extend/kvetch, which is largely for complaints. The page displays a random, anonymous complaint by a user and a simple box to state your complaint. Write it, and click **Kvetch it**.

How can I tell if my suggestion is being considered?
On the right sidebar of each idea's display is a status line indicating that the idea is being considered, has been addressed with a plugin, has been implemented, or has been assigned any of the other handful of status categories.

> **Status**
>
> Good idea! We're working on it

Read Blogs that Focus on WordPress

For better or worse, WordPress, like most successful computer programs, is always a work in progress. If you prefer, you can simply update your blog when WordPress tells you to, or you can keep abreast of what is going on so that you are not taken by surprise. Reading blogs about WordPress is useful regardless of whether you have a self-hosted or WordPress.com-hosted site. Besides learning about new developments, you also can find tips for operating your site more successfully.

Official Blogs

WordPress developers maintain blogs that apprise readers of new developments. At WordPress.com, keep the What's Hot module active and near the top of your Dashboard to see headlines of the latest official blog posts. If you are a self-hosted blogger, you can keep the WordPress Development blog active on your Dashboard. Or subscribe to either feed for your feed reader or to get posts by e-mail.

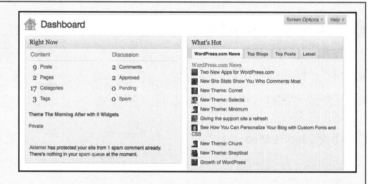

WordPress Help Blogs

Several bloggers write much useful information about WordPress. Check out http://planet. wordpress.org, which aggregates the blogs of several WordPress bloggers, which are listed on the site's sidebar. Another good, useful site is http://onecoolsitebloggingtips.com, which has tips for both the hosted and self-hosted versions. It is written by a regular contributor to the WordPress.com forums; and http://weblogtoolscollection.com, which posts information about new plugins and themes, among other subjects.

Helpful Sites about WordPress

Several other blogs and sites provide useful advice on a wide range of issues. These focus on WordPress, other aspects of blogging, or both. There is no need to read them all, but read at least one or two regularly to stay up to date.

Title	URL	Description
Copyblogger	http://copyblogger.com/blog	Content and marketing emphasis, with related tutorials.
DailyBlogTips	www.dailyblogtips.com	Blog tips with an emphasis on marketing.
Lorelle on WordPress	http://lorelle.wordpress.com	A longtime blogger on all things WordPress, for both hosted and self-hosted sites.
ManageWP Blog	https://managewp.com/blog	Good tips helpful to any WordPress site owner by a company that sells comprehensive WordPress management.
ProBlogger	www.problogger.net	Content emphasis rather than WordPress focus.
WP Realm	http://wprealm.com	Wide-ranging WordPress discussion, from news to the fairly technical.
WPBeginner	www.wpbeginner.com	Help especially for new users; offers Beginners Guide for WordPress.
Wplift	http://wplift.com	Ad-laden site but good tips, guides, and news.
wpMail.me	http://wpmail.me	Free, authoritative weekly e-mail newsletter about WordPress.
Yoast	http://yoast.com	Reviews, tips, and more by author of the Yoast WordPress SEO plugins. Knowledgeable and sometimes technical.

CHAPTER 11

Expanding Your Posting Options

You can take advantage of the most popular mobile devices, online tools, and other gear when you use WordPress for your blog. As a result, you can post from your phone, moderate comments from your tablet, compose offline, and even post by text message. In short, you can post in the way most convenient for you.

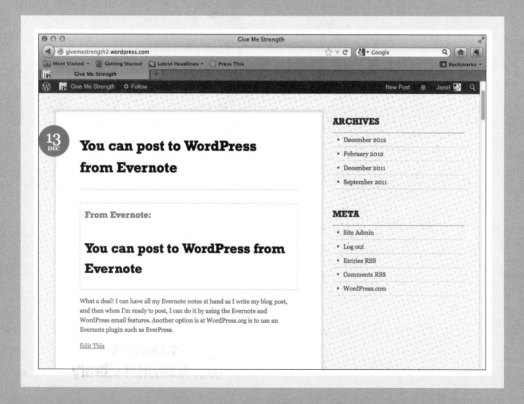

Set Up to Post with iOS App

When you set up your iOS device with the WordPress app, you can use your iPhone or iPad as a WordPress blogging device. The WordPress iOS app lets you write and edit on your device — even include images — and then post to your WordPress blog. First, though, you need to download and launch the free app from the App Store. The app is called simply WordPress, and the publisher listed is Automattic.

Set Up to Post with iOS App

1 Tap **Add Self-Hosted Blog**.

Note: See the Tip in this section for adding a WordPress.com blog.

2 Type your blog address.

3 Type your username.

4 Type your password.

5 Tap **Save**.

The app attempts to log you in to your site and opens an error message.

Note: If you do not see this message, the app logs you in to the Posts screen for your blog and you are ready to go.

6 Click **Enable Now**.

The WordPress sign-in screen appears with an empty password field.

7 Type your site's password.

8 Tap **Log In**.

The Writing settings page opens.

9 Scroll down to the Remote Publishing section.

10 Tap the check box next to XML-RPC (☐ changes to ☑).

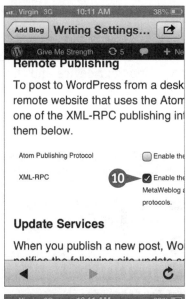

11 Scroll to the bottom of the page.

12 Tap **Save Changes**.

A WordPress confirms the change.

13 Tap **Add Blog**.

14 Repeat Steps 1 to 5.

The WordPress app opens to the Posts screen.

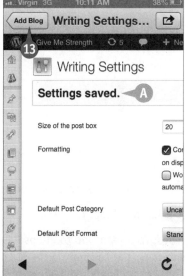

How do I add a WordPress.com blog?

Simply click **Add WordPress.com blog** on the initial screen. Then type your WordPress.com username and password. As soon as you tap **Done** on your iOS keyboard, the app begins to log you in. WordPress.com always has remote publishing enabled, so you do not have to enable it as you may need to do for a self-hosted blog. By the way, the app lets you keep up with multiple blogs.

Post from Your iPhone or iPad

Y ou can write on the fly using your iPhone or iPad once you have installed and set up the WordPress app, as described in the previous section, "Set Up to Post with iOS App." If your device has Siri, you can even dictate your blog post. Simply launch the WordPress app, tap to add a new post, and your device and the app give you everything you need to finish the job.

Post from Your iPhone or iPad

1 On the Posts screen, tap the **Add** button (➕).

2 Type a title.

3 Type a tag or two.

4 Tap **Categories**.

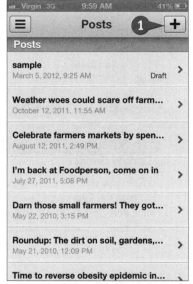

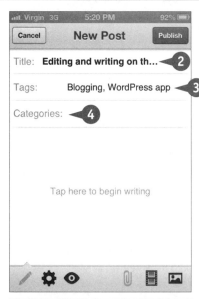

The Categories screen appears.

5 Tap a category or two.

Note: When you tap to choose a category, the category turns blue and a check mark appears next to it.

6 Tap **New Post**.

The New Post screen returns and displays your category selection.

7 Tap the writing area.

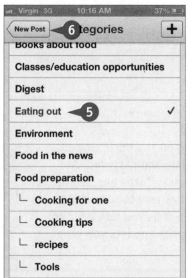

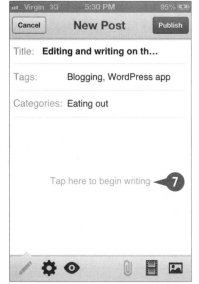

The keyboard appears.

8 Type your post.

9 Tap **Done** when you are finished.

The keyboard disappears, and the post with its title, tags, and categories appears.

10 Tap **Publish**.

A The Posts screen briefly displays an uploading message, and then adds your new post to the top of the list.

TIP

What do I do if I don't want to publish the item right away?
When you are ready to save your draft, tap the Cog (⚙) on the toolbar. When the Settings screen appears, tap **Status**, select **Draft**, tap **Done**, and tap **Update**. The item appears in the Posts list marked with Draft in red. To work on it later, just tap the item in the list, tap the posting area of the post screen, and make your changes. Then tap **Update**. If you want to publish it, tap ⚙, and change the status to Published the same way you set it to Draft.

Moderate Comments from Your iOS Device

With the WordPress app, you can use your iOS device to approve, reply, delete, or mark as spam comments on your blog. The app even lets you know you have comments pending. You start by launching the app and tapping the Comments option in the app's main menu. You can reach the main menu by tapping 🔲 from most any screen within the app. The comments list displays recent comments and identifies those that require moderation. Your blog immediately reflects the actions you take on your iPhone or iPad.

Moderate Comments from Your iOS Device

Approve a Comment

① Tap **Comments**.

Ⓐ The number shows how many comments need moderation.

The Comments list appears.

② Tap a comment that needs moderating.

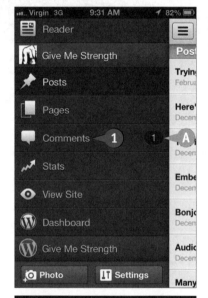

The comment opens.

③ Tap the checkmark (✔) to approve the comment.

The Comments list returns, with the approved comment at the top of the list.

Reply to a Comment

1. Repeat Steps 1 and 2 in the "Approve a Comment" subsection.

2. Tap the reply arrow (↩).

   The Comment Reply screen opens.

3. Type your reply.

4. Tap **Reply**.

After an upload message appears, the Comments list appears, with your reply at the top of the list.

Mark a Comment as Spam

1. Repeat Steps 1 and 2 in the "Approve a Comment" subsection.

2. Tap the flag (⚑).

   The comment disappears and the app returns to the Comments list. The spam comment no longer appears.

How do I delete a comment?

Tap the trash button (🗑). A confirmation screen appears. Tap **Delete**, and the comment moves to the comment trash. Remember, though, to use the spam flag instead (⚑) if the comment is spam. Doing so keeps the spam database up to date.

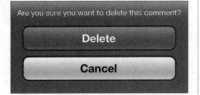

How do I recover a comment I accidentally marked as spam?

Go to the app's main menu and tap **Dashboard**. A dashboard like the familiar one online appears. In the Right Now pane, tap **Spam**. The Comments panel opens to a list of spam comments. Tap **Not Spam** under the comment you want to recover, and it returns to the regular Comments list.

Edit from Your iOS Device

You can add text formatting, change wording, or make any number of editing changes with your iPhone or iPad and the WordPress app. Simply open the post — or comment or page — and edit. When you save your changes, they appear online. Although the editing functions with the app are not as slick as those you might find in your favorite word processor, they are simple to use and more than enough to get the job done. You start by launching the app and opening the item you want to edit.

Edit from Your iOS Device

1 In the open post or page, select the text you want to change.

2 Tap the bold button (b).

Ⓐ The HTML tags for starting and stopping bold appear before and after the selected text.

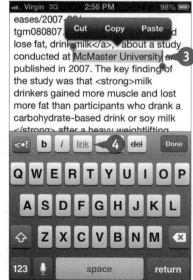

3 Select text to which you want to attach a hyperlink.

4 Tap the link button (link).

The Make a Link dialog box appears.

Ⓑ The selected text appears as the link text.

5 Type the link URL.

6 Tap **Insert**.

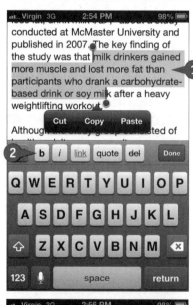

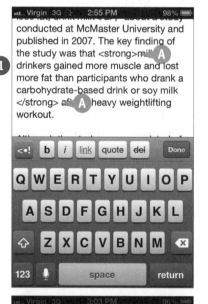

C The HTML for the hyperlink appears in the editing screen.

7 Tap **Done**.

The keyboard disappears.

8 Tap the preview button (👁).

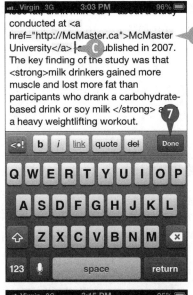

A preview of the post with the editing appears.

9 Tap **Update**.

The Posts list displays the post with an Uploading message. When the upload is complete, the post returns to its place in the Posts list.

TIP

What is that button, 📋, to the left of the 🅱 in the editing screen?

Whatever its name may be, tapping it reveals more style options. They are:

A Unordered list, typically a list with bullets.

B Ordered list, typically a numbered list.

C A list item. The code goes at the beginning and end of each item in your ordered or unordered list.

D Code, which defines text as computer code.

E More, which inserts a break in your post. For more information, see Chapter 4.

F A companion to 📋, 📋 switches the buttons back to those for bold, italic (𝑖), link, quote, and strikethrough (del) styling.

Post a Photo from Your iOS Device

With your iOS device and the WordPress app, you can take pictures and include them in your blog all with one device. The app lets you insert a photo from your phone into a blog post. If, however, you want to insert a photo that is in your blog's library on line, you can do that, too. Start the process by creating a new post, or, if you prefer, add a photo to an existing post. You can even take the photo while posting and add it straight to your post. It all depends on how you like to work.

Post a Photo from Your iOS Device

1 While writing or editing a post, tap the photo icon (🖼️).

The photo dialog box appears.

2 Tap **Add Photo from Library**.

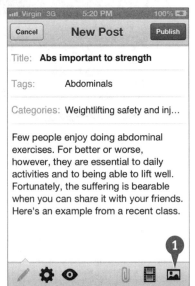

A photos permission dialog box appears.

3 Tap **OK**.

The Camera Roll appears.

4 Tap **Camera Roll**.

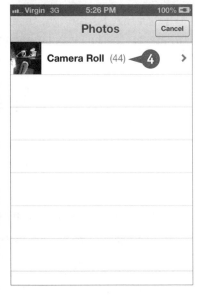

⑤ Tap the image you want to add to your post.

The Choose Image Size dialog box appears.

⑥ Tap a size. This example uses Original.

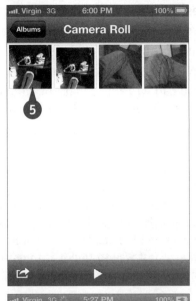

The Media screen shows the upload.

⑦ Tap **Publish**.

Ⓐ The new post appears at the top of the Posts list.

Note: Occasionally the app may temporarily show an upload twice in the list. The post most likely was uploaded only once, but you can look at your site to be sure.

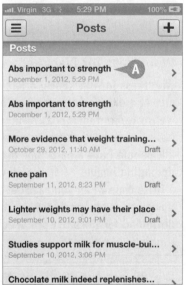

TIPS

Can I post a photo without starting a new post?
Yes, at least initially. Tap the **Photo** button (📷 Photo) on the app's main menu. Choose **Add Photo from Library** or **Take a Photo** in the dialog box that appears. A Quick Photo screen appears that includes the photo you chose or took and a space to add text. Then tap **Publish** on that same screen to finish.

How do I take a photo as I post?
Tap **Take a Photo** in the photo dialog box that appears when you use the 🖼 in a post screen or 📷 Photo from the app's main menu. Your iPhone or iPad instantly switches to camera mode. When you take the shot, a preview appears. You can choose **Retake**, which discards the image, or **Use**, which adds it to your post and Camera Roll.

Using Apps on Other Mobile Devices

Y ou can operate your WordPress blog not only from iOS devices but also from devices using Android, BlackBerry, Windows Phone, WebOS, and S60 or Maemo-powered Nokia phones. The apps work with both WordPress.org and WordPress.com blogs, and they work on the comparable tablet devices. If you have multiple devices with different operating systems, you simply set up each device with the appropriate app, and you can write or update or moderate comments from whichever one you have on hand. Like the computer-based WordPress software, the apps are free.

WordPress for Android

WordPress for Android opens with a graphical dashboard that takes you to the task you want to do, whether it is reviewing existing content or creating new content. A corner banner on the Comments button tells you how many comments are awaiting moderation. The app, which lets you easily write and format posts as well as images, works for both Android phones and tablets. You can download the app for free from the Google Play Store. The easiest way to find it is to go to http://android.wordpress.org and tap **Download from Google Play Store**.

WordPress for BlackBerry

WordPress for BlackBerry offers similar functionality as the apps for iOS and Android. You can get it at http://appworld.blackberry.com/webstore/content/5802. Although the reviews for the BlackBerry app have not been as good as those for iOS and Android — some, but not all, people have a hard time getting it up and running or have issues uploading images — it should work for you if you are willing to devote a little time when you first get the app. If you are not able to download it at App World, go to http://blackberry.wordpress.org/download for links to apps specific to the BlackBerry version you are running.

WordPress for Windows Phone

WordPress for Windows Phone has a nice clean interface and is available for longstanding Windows Phone operating systems as well as Windows Phone 8. It requires Windows Phone 7 or newer. You can get it at www.windowsphone.com/store and search for WordPress. Choose the app from Automattic. You also can go to http://wpwindowsphone.wordpress.com/download and tap **Download App**.

WordPress for Nokia

The app for Nokia and Ovi works with several phone models, but not with all. You can get a list of the models that work at http://nokia.wordpress.org. It also provides a link to the download. If you are not sure whether your phone is compatible, you can go to http://store.avi.com and click **Set device** to find the app that works with your device.

WordPress for WebOS

If you have an HP TouchPad, you can download the WebOS version of the mobile WordPress software. Because HP has abandoned TouchPad, the WebOS software has been released as *open source* software, meaning it is available without charge to anyone who wants to use it or change it. It is likely the software will be available in the future on additional devices, but for now it works only with HP TouchPad, and as of this writing did not appear to be updated. From your TouchPad, you can search the HP App Catalog for WordPress.

Other Mobile Options

WordPress developers continue to update and expand their mobile blogging options. You can keep up by checking in regularly at http://wordpress.org/extend/mobile. The apps listed on that page work with both the WordPress.com and WordPress.org versions of WordPress.

Post via E-Mail

If you like e-mail, you can use it to post to your WordPress site. First, you set up a secret e-mail account and enable e-mail posting at your site. If you self-host your blog and have Jetpack enabled, then WordPress.com generates a special e-mail address for you. Otherwise, you need to create such an account on your own. It is important to make that address as difficult to guess as you can, and WordPress helps you do so. In any case, you need to guard the address closely, because any message sent to that account automatically posts to your blog.

Post via E-Mail

At Self-Hosted Site with Jetpack Enabled

1 In the administrative interface, click **Users**.

Note: See the Tips in this section if you do not have Jetpack active on your site.

2 Click **Your Profile**.

The Profile page opens.

3 Scroll down until you see Post by Email.

4 Click **Enable Post By Email**.

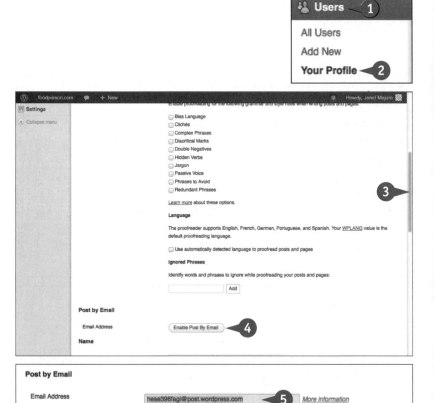

The screen changes and shows a computer-generated e-mail address.

5 Select and copy the e-mail address.

6 Start a new message in your e-mail software.

7 Paste the e-mail address in the To box.

8 Type a post name in the Subject box.

Note: The Subject line becomes the title or headline for the post.

9 Type your post.

10 Click **Send**.

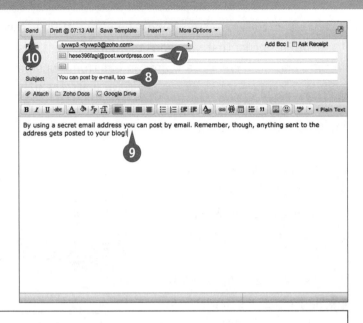

The e-mail post publishes to your blog.

You can post by e-mail, too

DEC
7
2012

By using a secret email address you can post by email. Remember, though, anything sent to the address gets posted to your blog!

TIPS

How do I set up posting by e-mail if I do not have Jetpack enabled?

First, create a secret e-mail account. Return to your WordPress administration interface. Click **Settings** in the left menu bar and choose **Writing**. Scroll down until you see the Post via email section. Type the account information for the secret e-mail account you created. You might prefer to go to the Writing Settings panel first, though, to copy one of the random strings of characters to use for your e-mail address. Click **Save Changes**, and you are ready to post by e-mail.

Can I use formatting when I write my e-mail message?

Yes. WordPress generally keeps basic formatting such as bold or underline if you are using Jetpack or WordPress.com. You can even attach images to the e-mail, and they are included in your post. You can read about more options at http://jetpack.me/support/post-by-email.

continued ▶

You get extra-easy setup to post by e-mail if your site is hosted at WordPress.com. When you tell WordPress.com that you want to enable e-mail posting, it automatically creates an e-mail address for you and even creates a vCard, an electronic business card that you can use to add the secret address to your e-mail address book. No matter which type of WordPress you use, you can disable e-mail posting at any time or change to a new e-mail address if you find that your secret address has been compromised. Nobody wants to see e-mail spam showing up as a blog post.

Post via E-Mail (continued)

At WordPress.com Blog

1 Under Dashboard, click **My Blogs**.

The My Blogs panel appears.

2 Beside the blog to which you want to send e-mail posts, click **Enable** in the Post by Email column.

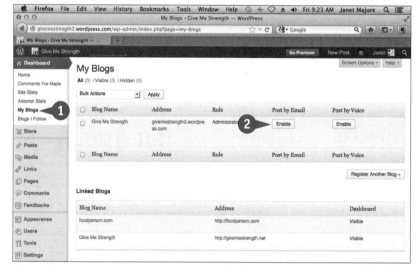

WordPress displays your e-mail address for posting.

3 Click the address.

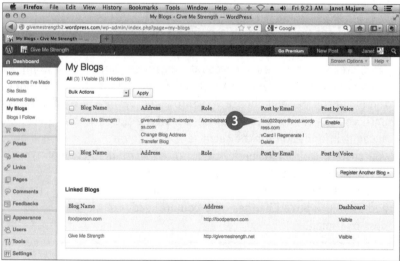

WordPress.com opens your default e-mail software and includes your secret address in the To field.

4 Type a title in the Subject box.

5 Type your post.

6 Click the send button ().

The e-mail post publishes to your blog.

How do I change the e-mail posting address if it is compromised?

At WordPress.com or Jetpack-enabled WordPress.org blogs, return to the location where you set up post by e-mail, and click **Regenerate** or **Regenerate Address**. A new address appears that you can to use to post by e-mail. For a self-hosted site without Jetpack, create a new e-mail address, add it to the Post by Email section of the Writing Settings, and click **Save Changes**.

How do I disable e-mail posting?

Again, return to the location where you set up e-mail posting. Then do the following, depending on your setup:

- At Jetpack-enabled WordPress.org blogs, click **Disable Post by Email**.

- At other WordPress.org blogs, delete the e-mail information under Post by Email and click **Save Changes**.

- At WordPress.com, click **Delete** under the e-mail address. The Enable button reappears.

Post with QuickPress

The QuickPress module on your Dashboard lets you write and publish posts or save drafts in a hurry. If you see something on the Dashboard that inspires you, such as a recent comment or news item, you can type your thoughts without so much as going to another page. You can publish your quick post straight from the Dashboard. If you prefer, you can save a draft. You can then preview the draft with a click from the Dashboard, or edit your draft in the posting panel.

Create a Post with QuickPress

1 Type a headline or title in the Title box.

2 Type your post in the Content box.

Note: You can add simple HTML tags such as \<b> for bold and \</b> for end bold.

A The media buttons are available.

B A Tags box lets you assign tags.

3 Click **Save Draft**.

WordPress saves your draft and clears the QuickPress entry boxes.

Note: You can publish immediately if you prefer by clicking **Publish**.

4 Click **Edit post** in the confirmation box.

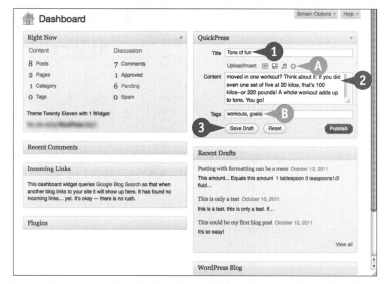

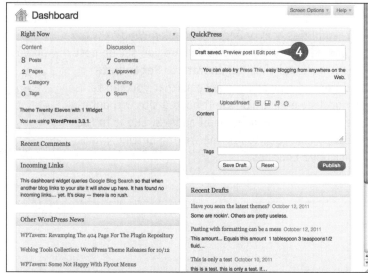

WordPress opens the post in the Edit Post panel.

5 Add to or change your post.

6 Click a category box (☐ changes to ☑).

7 Click **Publish**.

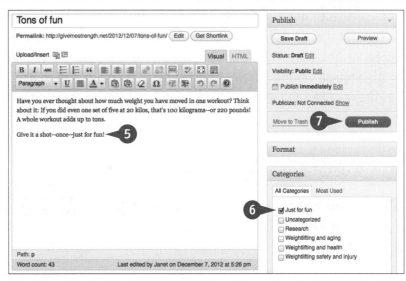

C WordPress confirms the publication.

8 Click **View post**.

Your QuickPress post appears on your blog.

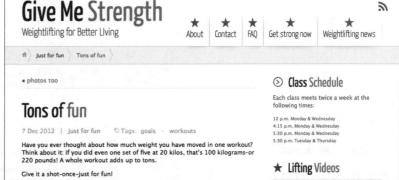

TIPS

Can I just click Publish from the QuickPress module?
Certainly. When you do, WordPress publishes the post to your blog and confirms its actions. Instead of providing a link to preview the post, the confirmation box provides a link to view the post. Click the link to see the post on your site.

Post published. View post | Edit post

What happens if I publish without editing to choose a category?
The post is assigned to your default category. In the example, the default category is Uncategorized. You can select or create a different default category on the Writing Settings panel.

Post via the WordPress.com Home Page

If you like things simple, you can post content via a stripped-down interface at WordPress.com. That interface lets you create a text post — with or without an image — or create a photo, video, quote, or link post. The interface makes sure the post is styled appropriately if you use post formats to distinguish among different post types. To get started, go to WordPress.com and log in. When you do, the member home page appears, with the Reader page active.

Post via the WordPress.com Home Page

1 Click **New Post** to open the posting panel.

2 Click **Text**.

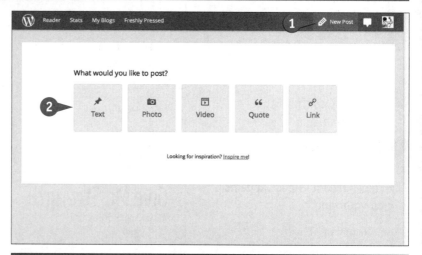

A posting box appears.

3 Type a title.

4 Type your post.

5 Type a tag or two.

6 Click **Publish Post**.

Note: The post is assigned to your default category as set in the Writing Settings.

WordPress.com publishes the post and gives a confirmation message.

7 Click **View Post**.

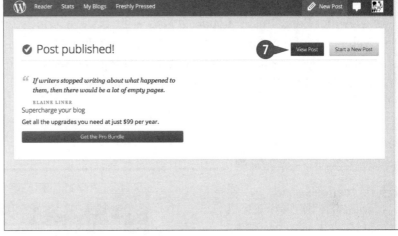

The new post opens on your blog.

Where do I find that interface for my self-hosted blog?
At this writing, the WordPress.org software does not offer this type of interface. If your self-hosted blog has Jetpack activated, you can go from the WordPress.com home page to a New Post panel on your WordPress.org site. To do so, position the mouse pointer over your name in the WordPress.com Admin Bar, then point to the WordPress.org site in the drop-down menu that appears, and click **New Post** in the flyout menu. An Add New Post panel appears.

How do I add a photo in the WordPress. com home page posting panel?
Click **Insert Photo** beside the post's title box. A File Upload dialog box appears. Browse your computer for the image file that you want to upload. Select it and click **Open**. WordPress uploads the image and adds it to your post.

Post with Press This

With just a click, Press This lets you capture text, images, and the web address from a site you are viewing. Press This is a *bookmarklet,* a bit of JavaScript stored as a browser bookmark. It grabs the web page information and places it immediately into a post-writing box. It does not get much simpler when you want to write about something you see on the web. First, however, you need to install the bookmarklet on your favorite browser. After that, the bookmarklet makes blogging about web information a snap.

Post with Press This

① On the Tools panel, accessible by clicking Tools in the left menu bar, click the **Press This** bookmarklet and drag it to the bookmarks or favorites menu bar of your browser.

Press This appears as a bookmark on your browser.

Note: You only need to install the bookmarklet the first time you use it.

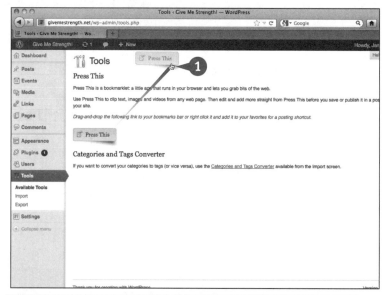

② Select the text you want to quote or comment on.

③ Click **Press This**.

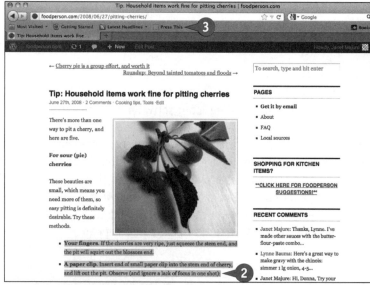

A Press This window opens.

ⓐ The web page's title appears in the Title box.

ⓑ Your selected text appears in the content box.

ⓒ A link to the page appears at the bottom.

④ Edit the title and content.

⑤ Click **Publish**.

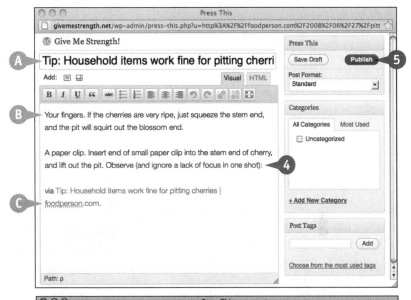

WordPress publishes your post and gives you a confirmation message.

Note: You can save a draft if you prefer by clicking **Save Draft**.

⑥ Click **Close Window** to return to the web page you were browsing.

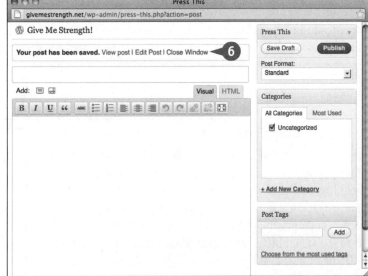

TIP

I cannot get the bookmarklet to work. What do I do?

You may be using an out-of-date version of your browser. Go to http://browsehappy.com to determine the latest supported version of Internet Explorer, Google Chrome, Firefox, Safari, and Opera and find links to the latest downloads of those browsers. You generally can determine the version you are running by launching the software, clicking **About Browser** under the Tools or Help or Browser menu — depending on your browser and computer operating system. Another possibility is that your bookmarks or favorites bar is hidden. Check your browser's Help to determine how to show it.

Consider Using a Blogging Client

When you use a blogging *client,* meaning a program that runs locally on your computer, you can write your blog post offline. In other words, you do not have to be connected to the Internet to write your posts or even to add media as you create your post. Many people like the interface with their blogging client more than they like the WordPress Write/Edit Post panels. Your preference may depend on your Internet connection or simply the way you prefer to work.

Advantages of Blogging Clients

Advantages vary by software, but a couple of advantages are fairly consistent among blog clients. One is that you can write posts without having to go online, and then you can post your creations, formatted and with images if you want, in fewer steps. Also, many clients allow you to use more keyboard shortcuts when typing and provide easy

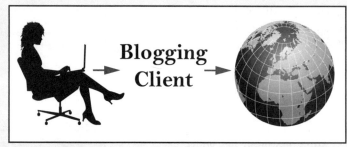

ways to do fancier formatting, including inserting tables. If you post the same content to multiple blogs, clients make easy work of it, and you have a local backup of your posts.

Available Blogging Clients

Windows Live Writer, which is for PCs only, is among the most popular clients, but several others are available, including clients for Mac and Linux. You can find lists at http://codex.wordpress.org/Weblog_Client or http://en.support.wordpress.com/xml-rpc for WordPress.com blogs. Microsoft Word for Windows, versions 2007 or newer, also has built-in blog client capability.

- 2 List of Client Software:
  - 2.1 Windows
  - 2.2 Mac OS X
  - 2.3 Linux
  - 2.4 Browser-Based

How Blog Clients Work

When you use a blog client, you write in the interface provided and you supply the logon information that you use for your blog. You then create your blog posts, and when you are ready to publish, the client publishes your post. Some clients can publish to multiple blogs.

Mobile Clients

In addition to the official WordPress apps described earlier in this chapter, other mobile clients are available for Android, BlackBerry, iPhone, Nokia, and more. Some work for both hosted and self-hosted WordPress blogs. Others do not, at least as of this writing. You can find lists by device at http://codex.wordpress.org/Weblog_Client#Mobile.

- 2.5 Mobile
  - 2.5.1 Android
  - 2.5.2 BlackBerry
  - 2.5.3 iPhone
  - 2.5.4 J2ME
  - 2.5.5 Nokia Phones
  - 2.5.6 PalmOS

Other Writing Interfaces

In addition to blogging clients that are on your computer, some third-party online blog-writing and browser extensions are available. They offer features such as seeking additional content for you from the web as you write or complex formatting options. They are listed at the same URLs as the clients and include WriteToMyBlog and ScribeFire. Remember, though, you do have to be online to work with these.

WriteToMyBlog

ScribeFire

Create a Post with Windows Live Writer

A popular blogging client, Windows Live Writer, is free, and you will recognize many functions if you are familiar with Microsoft Word. Windows Live Writer is an excellent blog client for PC users but is not available for Mac. You need to download the Windows Live Writer software at http://windows.microsoft.com/en-US/windows-live/essentials-other-programs and follow the usual installation process. You need only the Writer portion of the Windows Essentials package.

On a self-hosted blog, you need to enable XML-RPC, an Internet protocol that allows remote access to your website. WordPress.com has it enabled by default.

Create a Post with Windows Live Writer

Enable XML-RPC

1 While logged in to your blog, go to the Writing Settings page and click **XML-RPC** (☐ changes to ☑).

2 Click **Save Changes**.

Note: WordPress.com blogs always have this setting enabled.

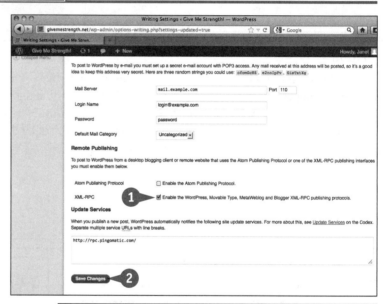

Configure Live Writer

1 Launch Windows Live Writer.

The configuration dialog box opens.

2 Click **Next**.

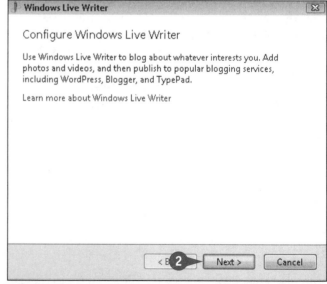

The blog service dialog box appears.

3 Click the **WordPress** radio button
(◎ changes to ◉.)

4 Click **Next**.

The blog account window opens.

5 Type your blog's web address.

6 Type your WordPress username.

7 Type your password.

8 Click **Next**.

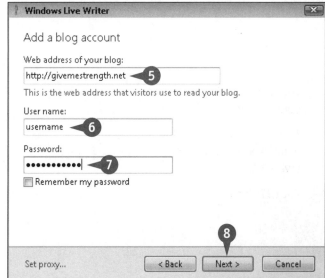

continued ▶   **405**

TIP

Can I just use Microsoft Word instead?
Yes, if you are using a PC, although Microsoft Word does not have as many built-in features as Windows Live Writer. For example, the Word version does not have the ability to upload and post photos from your hard drive the way Live Writer does, which negates one of the advantages of using a blog client. The Mac version of Microsoft Word does not have a blogging interface.

New blog post

After you install Windows Live Writer on your hard drive and set up connections to your blog or blogs, you can work offline to create posts complete with all the formatting you want and photos just the way you want them. Then you can upload that post and its associated media files in a single action. When you do, you can choose to publish the upload directly or to upload it as a draft to update later.

Create a Post with Windows Live Writer (continued)

Windows Live Writer sets up your account, downloads your existing categories and tags, and opens the Download Blog Theme dialog box.

⑨ Click **No**.

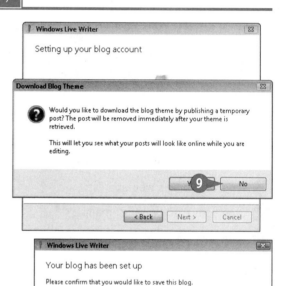

Windows Live Writer confirms your account.

⑩ Type a name for your blog for identification in Windows Live Writer.

⑪ Click **Finish**.

Windows Live Writer opens a writing and editing window.

⑫ Type a headline.

Note: The headline box outline disappears after you click outside the box.

⑬ Type your message.

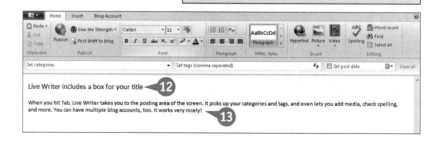

14 Click the menu icon.

15 Click **Publish**.

A sign-in screen appears.

16 Type your blog's username.

17 Type your blog's password.

18 Click **OK**.

Windows Live Writer uploads the post to your blog, publishes it, and opens the site for you to see.

Give Me Strength
Weightlifting for Better Living

★ About   ★ Contact   ★ FAQ

🏠 Blog

1 2 Next »

Live Writer includes a box for your title

DEC
8

When you hit Tab, Live Writer takes you to the posting area of the screen. It picks up your categories and tags, and even lets you add media, check spelling, and more.

TIP

Is it true that Microsoft is going to drop Windows Live Writer?
Much has been written on this question, but as of this writing Live Writer still works, and Microsoft has said it works with Windows 8. You never know how long any publisher will support its software. If you are worried, consider some of the alternatives mentioned in the previous section, "Consider Using a Blogging Client."

Move Your Blog from WordPress.com to WordPress.org

You can easily move your WordPress.com blog to a self-hosted WordPress.org site to get more flexibility in your blog's content. First, create a WordPress.org site, as described in Chapter 3. Then export your WordPress.com site using a built-in tool. You can keep the names of authors the same on the new site as on the old, or you can assign them to an existing author on the new site. Either way, in minutes your WordPress.com content is available on your self-hosted site.

Move Your Blog from WordPress.com to WordPress.org

1 On your WordPress.com site's dashboard, click **Tools**.

The Tools menu expands.

2 Click **Export**.

The Export panel appears.

3 Click **Export**.

The panel changes.

4 Click the **All Content** radio button (○ changes to ⦿).

5 Click **Download Export File**.

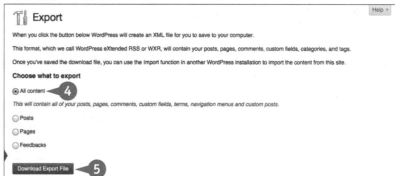

A dialog box appears.

6 Click the **Save File** radio button (○ changes to ⦿).

7 Click **OK**.

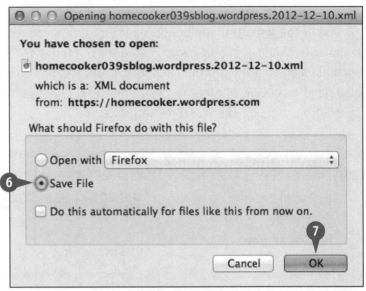

Your browser saves the export file to your computer.

8 Type *www.yoursite.com/* **wp-admin/import.php** in your browser's address bar, where *www.yoursite.com* is your WordPress.org site.

9 Click **WordPress**.

Why is my WordPress.com download taking so long?

If you have been keeping your site for a long time, you probably have a lot of posts, comments, and pictures, which make for a big database and a big download. It is nothing to worry about.

Will my WordPress.com site go away after I export it?

No. The site remains up and functioning. It is a good idea to post a notice telling readers that you have moved to a new address and to include a link to your new site. Even though you have uploaded your posts and so on to your new site, it still is good to have the old site for the benefit of any links in the web that go to your original posts.

continued ▶

The WordPress.org importer is a plugin that you install as you would most any plugin. After you install the importer, you import your WordPress.com database. In addition to the posts and comments, you can import pages, categories, and tags. You may also be able to import your media, such as images, although that import process has had some bumps. When you do your import, you also need to decide whether to create new users for the incoming authors or to assign authors' posts to existing users on the WordPress.org site.

Move Your Blog from WordPress.com to WordPress.org (continued)

The Install Importer dialog box appears.

10 Click **Install Now**.

A plugin installation screen appears.

11 Click **Activate Plugin & Run Importer**.

The Import WordPress screen appears.

12 Click **Browse**.

A file upload window appears.

13 Locate the downloaded WordPress.com export file and click **Open**.

The location appears in the box.

14 Click **Upload File and import**.

The screen changes to Assign Authors.

15 Click **Submit**.

WordPress completes and confirms the import.

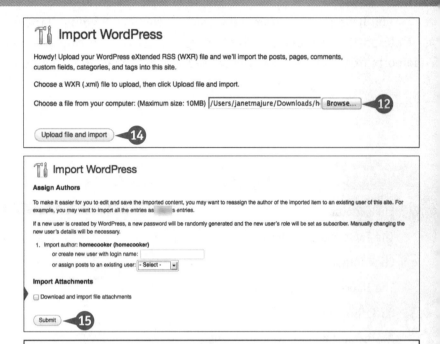

Import WordPress

Howdy! Upload your WordPress eXtended RSS (WXR) file and we'll import the posts, pages, comments, custom fields, categories, and tags into this site.

Choose a WXR (.xml) file to upload, then click Upload file and import.

Choose a file from your computer: (Maximum size: 10MB) /Users/janetmajure/Downloads/h [Browse...]

(Upload file and import)

Import WordPress

Assign Authors

To make it easier for you to edit and save the imported content, you may want to reassign the author of the imported item to an existing user of this site. For example, you may want to import all the entries as ____'s entries.

If a new user is created by WordPress, a new password will be randomly generated and the new user's role will be set as subscriber. Manually changing the new user's details will be necessary.

1. Import author: **homecooker (homecooker)**
   or create new user with login name: [   ]
   or assign posts to an existing user: [- Select - ▾]

Import Attachments

☐ Download and import file attachments

(Submit)

Import WordPress

All done. Have fun!

Remember to update the passwords and roles of imported users.

TIPS

What are the Assign Author options?
The importer includes a section for each author from the incoming site. The default setting imports the WordPress.com author's posts with the WordPress.com username. Alternatively, you can assign that author a new username at the WordPress.org site or you can assign the author's posts to an existing author at the WordPress.org site. After the import, go to the Users panel and confirm each person's privileges. See Chapter 14 for more information about user privileges.

What do I do to try to import my photos?
On the Import WordPress screen that includes Assign Authors, you can find a section called Import Attachments. Click the check box next to Download and import file attachments (☐ changes to ☑) before clicking **Submit**.

Import Posts from Another Blogging Platform

I f you have come to WordPress from a different blogging platform, you probably can import your old posts to WordPress. WordPress provides tools to help you make the transition. This example imports from Blogger, the widely used blogging platform from Google.

Import Posts from Another Blogging Platform

1 Click **Tools**.

The Tools menu expands.

2 Click **Import**.

The Import panel appears.

3 Click **Blogger**.

An Install Importer window opens.

4 Click **Install Now**, and then click **Activate Plugin & Run Importer** in the next screen.

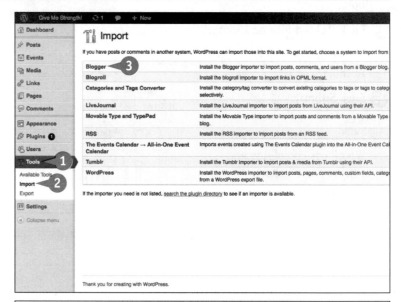

The Import Blogger panel opens.

5 Click **Authorize** to allow Google to send your Blogger data. The Google Accounts window opens.

6 Click **Grant access**.

A Blogger Blogs panel opens that displays all Blogger blogs associated with your Google account.

7 Click **Import** next to the blog you want to import.

Ⓐ The Posts and Comments columns indicate the progress of your import. If your previous blog was large, the import process may take a while. WordPress allows you to go to other pages and check back periodically.

8 When the import is finished, your Blogger posts and comments appear on your WordPress blog, and the Import button changes to Set Authors. Click **Set Authors**.

The Author Mapping panel opens.

9 Click the drop-down menu under WordPress login to associate the Blogger username with the WordPress user.

Note: You have only one choice if there is only one author on your WordPress blog.

10 Click **Save Changes**.

Your former Blogger entries now are published and listed with the author you selected.

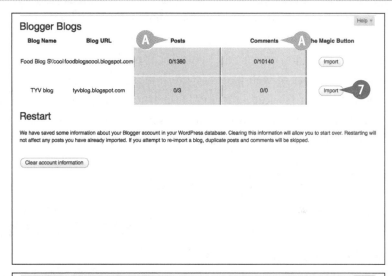

TIPS

I received a message saying the importer cannot authenticate my Blogger blog at Google. Is there anything to do?

You can go to www.google.com/support/blogger/bin/answer.py?hl=en&answer=97416. It explains how to export your blog, which creates a file you can save to your hard drive and then import to your WordPress blog.

My import was going okay and then stopped. What do I do?

Click **Clear account information**. It takes you back to the import panel. You can repeat the steps you took before, and WordPress resumes your import without duplicating posts.

Download and Install Evernote

With Evernote installed on your electronic devices, you can organize and keep track of the bits of information you need to produce great content for your blog. Evernote stores your *notes,* or individual items, online, and your local devices synchronize with the online account. You can write notes, clip bits of web pages, store images, and more — and then find the one you need wherever you are. The first step is to install Evernote on your various devices, such as your home computer, your laptop computer, and a smartphone. This book provides only an overview of this useful program, which is free for basic users.

Download and Install Evernote

1 In your web browser, go to http://evernote.com.

2 Click **Get Evernote, It's Free.**

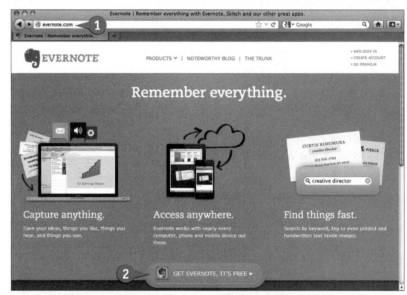

A download box appears.

Note: Your download and install process may differ, depending on your computer's operating system. This example uses Mac OSX.

3 Click **Save File.**

4 Use your system's normal method for installing the software.

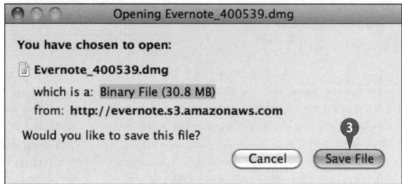

The Evernote license agreement appears for you to review.

5 Click **Agree**.

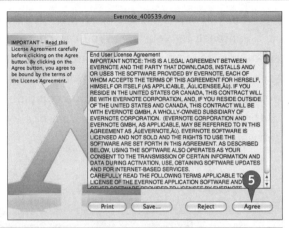

Evernote launches the New to Evernote dialog box.

6 Type your e-mail address.

7 Type a username.

8 Type a password.

9 Click **Register**.

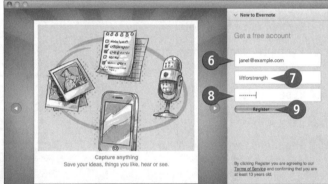

Evernote creates your account and launches the desktop application.

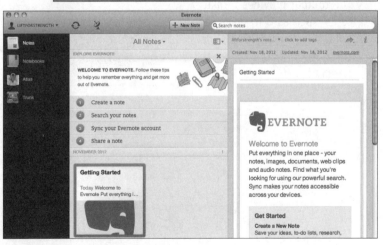

TIP

How do I download Evernote for my phone or my tablet?
From your device's web browser, go to http://evernote.com/evernote, and click the link to go to the download location at your device's app store, such as Google Play for Android or iTunes for iPhone. Or go straight to the app store and search for Evernote. Follow your device's usual app installation steps.

Create a Basic Evernote Note

When you create an Evernote *note,* you add to the collection of information, ideas, and images you need for your blog. You can create a note on your local computer or device, or you can create a note from Evernote online. You can add formatting — including different fonts, type styles such as italics and boldface, text of different color or size, and numbered or bulleted lists. The process is essentially the same on a computer, a mobile device, or online, although the appearance of the interface varies somewhat from one location to the next. Start by launching your Evernote software on your device.

Create a Basic Evernote Note

1 From the Evernote main screen, click **New Note**.

Evernote creates a new, blank note.

2 Type a title.

3 Type a note.

4 Highlight text you want to format.

A The toolbar provides format tools, such as **B** to make text bold. When you click a style, Evernote formats the selected text.

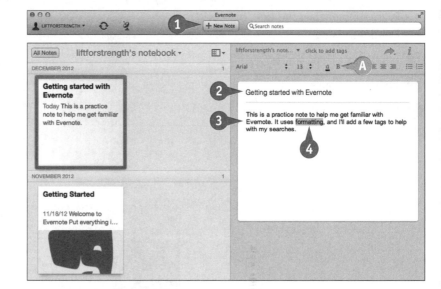

⑤ Click in the bar above the format tools.

Note: Before you click, the bar reads *click to add tags*.

⑥ Type a keyword.

Note: Choose words to help you organize or search for your note.

⑦ Press Enter (Return on a Mac).

⑧ Repeat Steps **6** and **7** to add more tags.

Periodically, Evernote uploads your note as you work. If you are not connected to the Internet, it uploads the next time your computer is online.

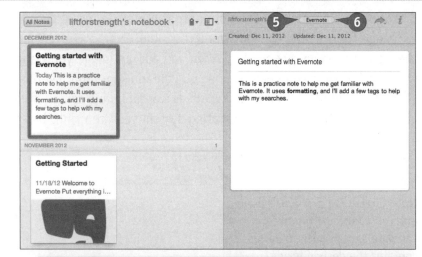

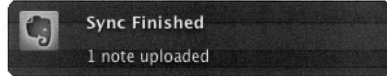

TIPS

How do I create a note online when I am on someone else's computer?

Go to http://evernote.com and click **Web Sign In**. A login screen opens. Type your username and password, and then click **Sign In**. Evernote opens to your online account page, and you can create a note from there. You also can e-mail a note to Evernote. Find the address by clicking your username at Evernote online and clicking **Settings**. The Account Summary appears and lists an e-mail address where you can send notes.

How do I delete a note?

From your computer, right-click the note you want to delete. Click **Delete Note** from the pop-up menu. The note disappears from your screen. To get it back, click **Notebooks** in the left menu bar, and then click **Trash**. Click the deleted note, and then click **Restore Note** to get it back. You also can restore notes online.

Create an Evernote Image Note

*S*toring an image on an Evernote note can provide visual cues for your blog or even store the image for use later on your WordPress blog. Evernote offers multiple ways to add images from the web or from your computer. When you add an image you want to a note, Evernote automatically stores it for when you need it, and you can add tags, too. Evernote even has built-in optical character reading capacity, so it indexes words in your image if you like. Interface details may vary according to the device and operating system you are using, but the basic actions are the same.

Create an Evernote Image Note

Note: Start with a new or existing note on your local Evernote software and an open folder that contains the desired image.

① In the image folder, click and hold on the image you want.

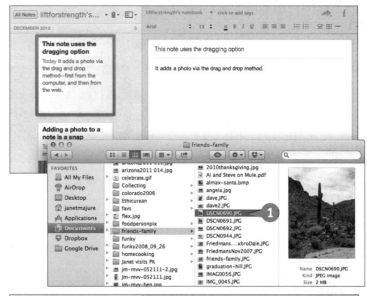

② Drag the image to the Evernote note.

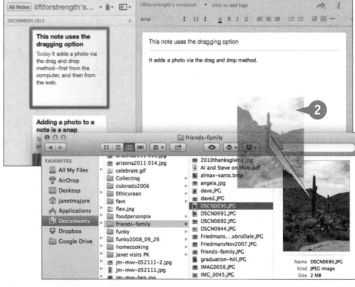

The image appears in the note.

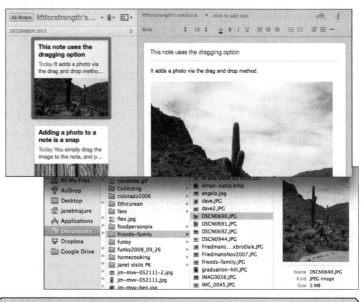

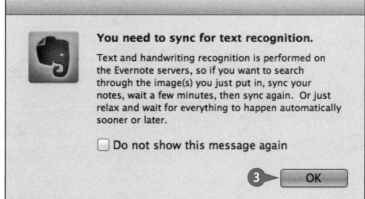

A dialog box appears.

3 Click **OK**.

Evernote saves and synchronizes, or *syncs*, your image note with the online Evernote servers.

You need to sync for text recognition.

Text and handwriting recognition is performed on the Evernote servers, so if you want to search through the image(s) you just put in, sync your notes, wait a few minutes, then sync again. Or just relax and wait for everything to happen automatically sooner or later.

☐ Do not show this message again

3 OK

TIPS

Is there any other way to add an image to a note?
Yes. There are several options. Among them, you can click the attachment icon (📎) in Evernote, and it opens a dialog box that lets you browse your computer for the desired image. You can copy and paste an image from your computer or the web. When at Evernote online, you can drag an image from a website onto a note in Evernote online.

What use is the text recognition feature?
Here is an example of how you might use this sophisticated feature: You are at an exhibit, and you want to record the details on an item's information placard. Using the Evernote app on your smartphone, take a photo of the card and when Evernote uploads it, it reads the text and enables you to search by words on the card.

Install the Evernote Web Clipper

You can install the Evernote Web Clipper on your computer's web browser to create an Evernote note with little more than a click. Web Clipper is a browser *extension,* or a tiny program, that works with your browser. Installation details vary according to the browser you use. If you installed Evernote for Windows as your computer-based Evernote program, you already have the extension for Internet Explorer. Otherwise, start by going to http://evernote.com/webclipper for links to the browser extensions for Firefox, Chrome, Safari, and other browsers. Click the link for the browser you are running. This example starts at the extension page at Firefox.

Install the Evernote Web Clipper

1 Click **+ Add to Firefox**.

A dialog box appears.

2 Click **Install Now**.

The dialog box disappears, and Firefox displays an alert.

③ Click **Restart Now**.

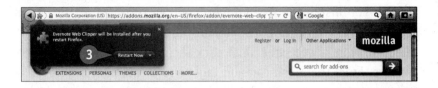

Firefox restarts.

Ⓐ The Evernote Web Clipper icon () appears.

What do I need to do to see the Web Clipper icon in Internet Explorer? I already installed the Evernote client on my computer.

The details depend on what version of Internet Explorer you are using. Check to see whether the Command Bar is visible. If it is, and you do not see the little Evernote elephant icon (🐘), look for a double arrow (>>) at the end of the command bar. Click it to see the rest of the commands. Check Internet Explorer Help (❓) if you do not know how to show the Command Bar in your version of Internet Explorer.

Using the Evernote Web Clipper

After you install the Web Clipper, you can turn just about any information on any web page into a note for future use in your blog posts. You can clip a whole page, an article, a URL, or a selection from a web page. Just click the Evernote Web Clipper icon and a Web Clipper dialog box appears. From there you can add tags, add a comment, and even search your existing Evernote notes. It is a great way to accumulate information for blog posts that link to web pages.

Using the Evernote Web Clipper

1 **On a web page**, select text or images you want to record.

2 Click the **Evernote** icon (▣).

The Evernote Web Clipper window appears, with your selection outlined.

A The web page's title appears automatically.

3 Type a tag or two.

4 Add a note to yourself if you want.

5 Click **Clip Selection**.

Note: Clicking the arrow reveals other clipping options.

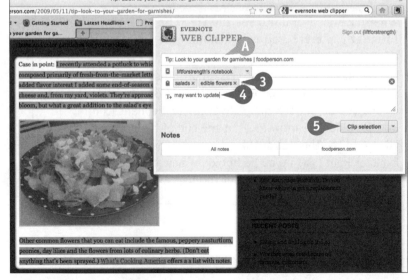

The Web Clipper window disappears.

Ⓑ A box advises you that clipping is underway.

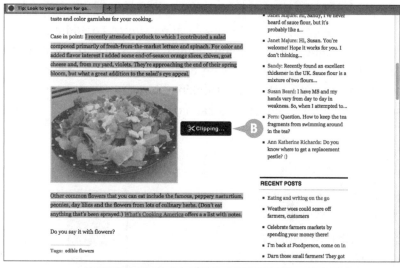

The clipping advisory disappears.

A Clip to Evernote box appears for a second or two in the corner of the screen, and then disappears.

Ⓒ You can click **View** or **Edit** to work with the clip at your Evernote online account.

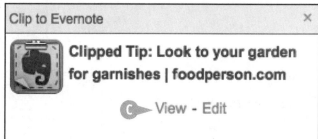

TIPS

How can I clip a selection and the URL at the same time?
When you clip a selection — or an entire web page for that matter — the Web Clipper automatically records the page's URL. Next time you look at that note, you can see the URL at the top of the note. Click the URL to go to the source of the note.

Do I have to be signed in to Evernote to use the Web Clipper?
If you click the Web Clipper icon and you are not signed in, the Web Clipper opens as a sign-in box. When you type your username and password and click **Sign In**, you see the clipping view of the Web Clipper and you are signed in with Evernote online.

Create an Evernote Notebook and Stack

If you create a set of *notebooks,* or collections of notes, you can keep your notes orderly. You even can create groups of notebooks, called *stacks,* to add a layer to your organizational hierarchy. If you have multiple blogs, you might have a stack for each blog and a notebook for each blog category. You may very well want a few notebooks for your other endeavors as well. You are well advised to spend a little time thinking about the way you want your notebooks organized before you accumulate a lot of notes. You can create them online or on your client Evernote software.

Create an Evernote Notebook and Stack

Note: This example creates a notebook at Evernote online.

1 Click the list button (▾) next to Personal Notebooks.

An option or options appear.

2 Click **New Notebook**.

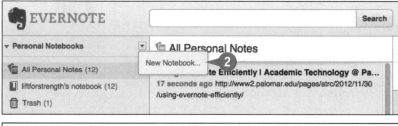

A dialog box appears.

3 Type a notebook name.

4 Click **Save**.

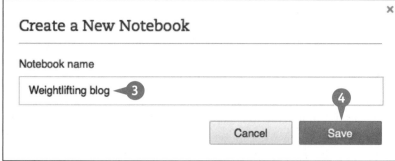

The dialog box disappears.

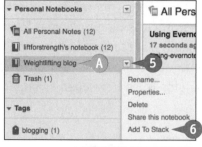

Ⓐ The new notebook appears in the Personal Notebooks list.

⑤ Click ▾ next to a notebook.

⑥ In the list that appears, click **Add To Stack**.

The list expands.

⑦ Click **New Stack**.

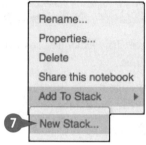

A dialog box appears.

⑧ Type a stack name.

⑨ Click **Save**.

The stack appears in the notebooks list with the associated notebook under it.

TIPS

How do I add notebooks to an existing stack?
Click ▾ next to the notebook name, and then click **Add To Stack**. Names of Existing Stacks appear under the New Stack option. Click the desired stack, and the notebook is added to the stack.

What are good categories and stacks for my blog?
The answer, of course, depends on your personal needs and preferences, but a starting point might be to have a stack for your blog and notebooks for post ideas, for potential blog roll sites, for reminders to yourself, and for draft posts.

Post from Evernote

If you keep your notes and links and more in Evernote, you can go a step further and post to your WordPress blog from your Evernote account. The easiest way is to set up your blog to post by e-mail, as described in "Post via E-Mail," earlier in this chapter. Then create your post in Evernote and send the post via e-mail to your WordPress site, where it immediately gets published. Watch for plugins to be developed to provide better integration between the two programs.

Post from Evernote

Note: This example uses Evernote online.

1. Type a title in a new Evernote note.

2. Compose your post.

3. Click **Done**.

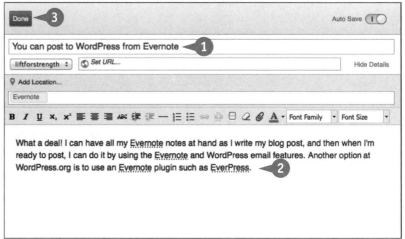

The screen changes, and a set of tools appears next to the note title.

4. Click the sharing icon (➦).

5. Click **Email**.

6 Type your secret WordPress e-mail posting address.

7 Click **Email**.

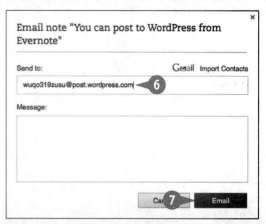

Email note "You can post to WordPress from Evernote"

Send to: Gmail Import Contacts

wuqo319zusu@post.wordpress.com ◄ **6**

Message:

Ca **7**   Email

Evernote sends the e-mail to your WordPress account, which immediately publishes the note as a new blog post.

8 Go to your blog address to see the results.

A The note title appears both as the post title and within the post.

You can post to WordPress from Evernote ◄ **A**

From Evernote:

You can post to WordPress from Evernote

What a deal! I can have all my Evernote notes at hand as I write my blog post, and then when I'm ready to post, I can do it by using the Evernote and WordPress email features. Another option is at WordPress.org is to use an Evernote plugin such as EverPress.

Edit This

TIPS

How do I get rid of the second appearance of the post title?

Go to your WordPress administration area to edit the post. In the Edit Post window, delete the second appearance of the headline and, if you like, the From Evernote: link. Although this adds a step to the posting, it still allows for simple posting from Evernote.

Why not just copy the post I wrote in Evernote and paste it into a new WordPress post?

You certainly can do that, and many people do. The advantage of posting straight from Evernote is that you can compose with all your notes handy and post it quickly. One cool thing is that when you e-mail the post, images are saved to your WordPress account. When you copy and paste, the blog post image remains based at Evernote.

CHAPTER 12

Expanding Your Content Options

You can liven up your website with all kinds of content without importing it into WordPress. Zemanta points you to usable content elsewhere on the web, and you can embed your content — and sometimes content created by others — from scores of sites. The possibilities are amazing.

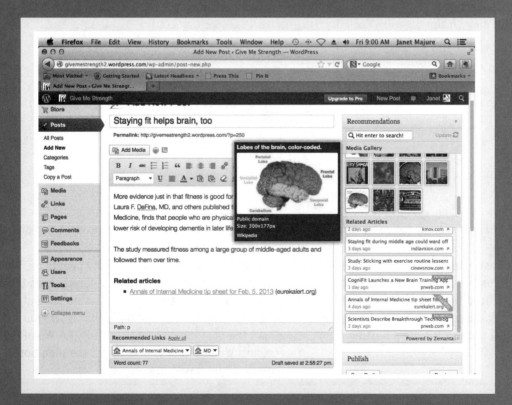

Understanding Shortcodes

Shortcodes give you, in effect, shortcuts for inserting code into your site. Knowing when and how to use them can make posting material faster and easier, and it often can give you more control over how your content looks. Both WordPress.com and WordPress.org have standard shortcodes available. The shortcodes are written especially for WordPress and therefore cannot be used in, say, e-mail messages to get the same results.

Shortcodes at WordPress.com

WordPress.com offers numerous shortcodes for everything from embedding audio and video players to inserting contact forms. It lists the available shortcodes at two locations — http://en.support.wordpress.com/category/shortcodes/ and http://en.support.wordpress.com/shortcodes, along with links to instructions and information about those shortcodes. Recent developments in embedding from several platforms have reduced the need for some of these shortcodes, but each service is slightly different.

Shortcodes at WordPress.org

WordPress.org offers just one standard shortcode, the gallery shortcode, but the WordPress.org software is designed so that you or developers can create your own custom shortcodes. As a result, you may find yourself using various plugin-related shortcodes. To use the gallery

shortcode, simply type **[gallery]** on a line by itself in the post writing and editing box, and WordPress automatically inserts a gallery in that location of all images attached to the post. You can customize the gallery to use images not attached to the post or to specify display options as described at http://codex.wordpress.org/Gallery_Shortcode. Of course, the WordPress Media Library, as described in Chapter 5, makes galleries easy.

Create Your Own Shortcode

WordPress.org users can create their own shortcodes, which can save time for actions you repeat. You can find instructions at http://codex.wordpress.org/Shortcode_API or you can use a plugin such as Shortcodes Ultimate. A little coding experience is a good idea, however.

Using a Shortcode

You can simplify many tasks with shortcodes such as those provided by default at WordPress.com. Many WordPress.org plugins have built-in shortcodes, too, which plugin developers usually explain how to use. Whatever your shortcode source, however, the use is fairly standard. You need to find the shortcode that you want, type it or paste it into a blog post or page, and then save the post or page. Some shortcodes may have variables that you can change. Follow the directions provided by WordPress.com or the developer to get the results you are seeking. This example uses the archives shortcode.

Using a Shortcode

1 In a post or page writing panel, type **[archives]** in the location where you want your archive list to appear.

2 Click **Save Draft**.

3 Click **Preview**.

A preview of the page or post with the archive inserted appears.

4 Click **X** to return to the page being edited.

Note: You can customize the archive using the options listed at http://en.support.wordpress.com/archives-shortcode/#options. The format is [archives optionname= optionchoice], and you can use more than one option. For example, you can type [archives type=monthly format= option] to create monthly archives in a drop-down format.

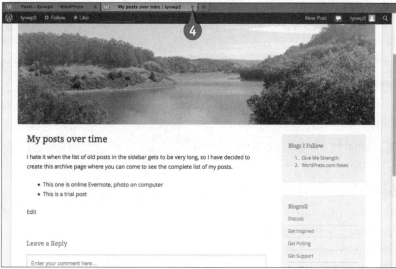

Identify Related Content with Zemanta

You can make your posts provide richer content when you use the Zemanta content-identification service. As you write, Zemanta identifies related articles and information elsewhere on the web to which you can link or simply read so that you can create better-informed posts. The Zemanta service is included in WordPress.com installations, although you have to activate it. At WordPress.org, you need to install a plugin to connect to Zemanta and get its recommendations.

Identify Related Content with Zemanta

Note: This example uses the service at WordPress.com.

1 In your administration panels, click **Users** and then click **Personal Settings**.

2 Scroll down to the Additional Post Content area.

3 Click the check box (☐ changes to ☑) to activate Zemanta.

4 Click **Save Changes**.

WordPress confirms the changes.

5 Click **Posts**.

6 Click **Add New**.

The New Post panel appears.

7 Start writing your post — typing enough to contain keywords or topics — and then press `Enter` (`Return` on Mac).

A Zemanta displays possibly related images and articles in the Recommendations module.

B Zemanta displays possibly related links.

8 Click an article to link to.

Note: For this illustration, the Recommendations module was dragged to appear at the top of the posting panel.

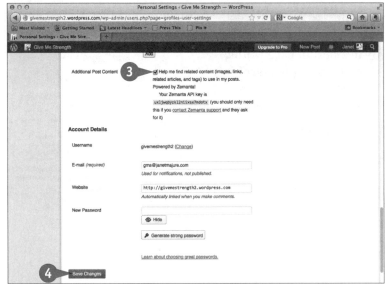

C The link appears in the Related articles section.

9 Click an image.

The image pops up, showing details about image size and license.

10 Click the image pop-up.

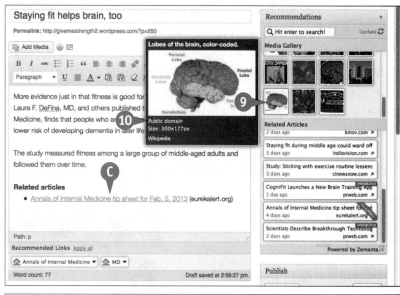

The image appears in the post.

D The Image Settings box appears, where you can change appearance and caption.

11 Click **Done**.

Zemanta embeds the image in your post.

12 Click **Save Draft**.

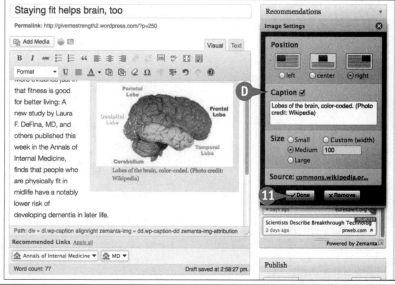

TIPS

How do I use the Recommended Links at the bottom of the post-writing panel?

Click a recommended link, and Zemanta automatically creates a link. The link uses the words that appear both in your text and in the Recommended Links button. It links to the location that you can see by positioning your mouse pointer over the link button. There, you also can click **Visit** next to the link target to see exactly where the link leads.

What plugin do I use to do this at WordPress.org?

Zemanta has three plugins with somewhat different functions plus one to identify related posts on your blog. Go to http://wordpress.org/plugins/ and search for Zemanta.

Insert a SoundCloud Audio Player

You can insert music from SoundCloud, a site where musicians and others post their work, on your WordPress site. Any music track or list with a Share button can be posted on your site. If your blog is at WordPress.com or if you have the Jetpack plugin activated at your self-hosted WordPress site, you can post from SoundCloud by copying and pasting a shortcode found there. Other WordPress.org users can use a plugin specifically for SoundCloud or use the HTML available at SoundCloud. Start by going to http://soundcloud.com and finding a track or list you want to share on your site.

Insert a SoundCloud Audio Player

At WordPress.com and Jetpack-Enabled Sites

1 Click **Share**.

A box appears that includes a shortcode labeled WordPress Code.

2 Click in the WordPress Code box and copy the shortcode there.

3 Paste the shortcode in a new or existing post or page at your site's administration panels.

4 Click **Save Draft**.

5 Click **Preview**.

WordPress opens a preview of the post in a new tab.

Ⓐ The SoundCloud player and playlist appear on your post or page.

⑥ Click **X** to return to the page being edited.

At WordPress.org Without Using Plugin or Jetpack

① Click **Share**.

A box appears that includes a box labeled Widget Code.

② Click in the Widget Code box and copy the code there.

③ In a new or existing post or page, click the **Text** tab.

④ Paste the code.

⑤ Click **Save Draft**.

⑥ Click **Preview**.

WordPress opens a preview of the post in a new tab showing the SoundCloud player.

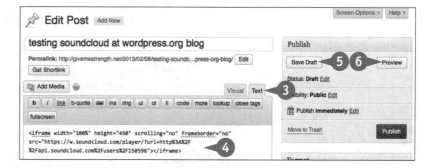

TIPS

How can I put a SoundCloud list in a widget?
At self-hosted sites, you can drag a text widget to a widget area and then paste the widget code there. Save the widget, and you are done. At WordPress.com and Jetpack-enabled self-hosted sites, you can use the WordPress shortcode.

Is there any advantage to using a plugin?
Yes, if you want to use SoundCloud tracks often. For example, the SoundCloud Is Gold plugin lets you see your SoundCloud tracks and favorites from within the WordPress Insert Media dialog box. Mostly, it is a matter of how you like to work.

Add Music with Spotify

You can add your favorite tunes from Spotify to your WordPress site by copying and pasting a link. This can be a simple option if you and your audience are signed up at Spotify. If your readers are not, they cannot listen to the Spotify player that you post. Spotify has much music to choose from, however, so if you are willing to accept that limitation you can start embedding your Spotify selections. Start by signing in to Spotify online or start the Spotify program on your computer.

Add Music with Spotify

At WordPress.com

1. At Spotify, right-click a song you want to embed.

   A pop-up list appears.

2. Click **Copy Spotify URI**.

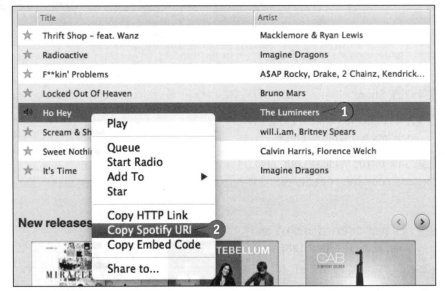

3. In a post or page, click the **Text** tab.

4. Paste the Spotify URI.

5. Click **Save Draft**.

6. Click **Preview**.

A preview of the post with the Spotify player appears in a new tab.

⑦ Click **X** to return to the page being edited.

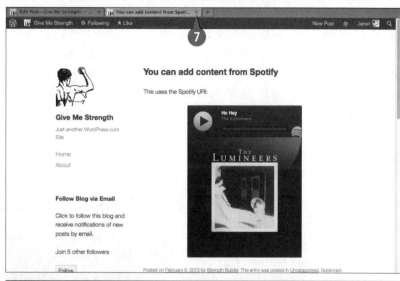

At WordPress.org

① At Spotify, right-click a song you want to embed.

A pop-up list appears.

② Click **Copy Embed Code**.

③ In a post or page, click the **Text** tab.

④ Paste the Spotify embed code.

⑤ Click **Save Draft**.

⑥ Click **Preview**.

A preview of the post with the Spotify player appears in a new tab.

TIPS

What happens if someone who is not a Spotify user clicks the player?

A dialog box appears. Someone who does not use Spotify must click **Not a user? Sign up** and complete the signup procedure to listen to the music.

If I use a plugin, will that allow people who are not Spotify members to listen?

No. At this writing, Spotify tracks are available only to registered users, no matter what means you use to try to access them. If you want all visitors to be able to hear the music without signing up, you need to try a different audio player.

Add Music with 8tracks

You can insert an 8tracks mix on your WordPress site with little effort, even without signing up at 8tracks.com, although you may want to. The site's content is composed entirely of playlists created by members, giving the playlists personality, compared with some sites that use computer techniques to choose music for you. Also, it does pay royalties to artists. To use 8tracks on your site you can use a shortcode at WordPress.com or, with a plugin, at WordPress.org sites. WordPress.org site owners also can paste the HTML embed coding in the Text tab of their posting panel.

Add Sound with 8tracks

1. Click the **share** button (⬀) on a playlist you want to embed at http://8tracks.com.

2. Click the **Embed** button (<>).

The Embed mix window appears.

3. Click the **WordPress shortcode** radio button (○ changes to ●).

4. Copy the code in the embed code box.

A. If you are using WordPress.org and do not have the plugin, you can click this link to get the 8tracks Shortcode Plugin.

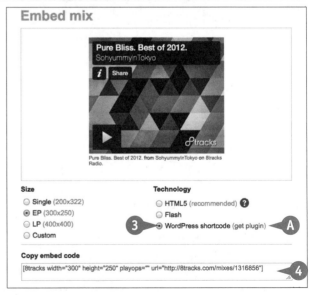

5 In a post or page editing box, paste the shortcode.

6 Click **Save Draft**.

7 Click **Preview**.

The post appears, with the 8tracks player in your post preview.

8 Click the **Play** button (▶) to start the playlist.

9 Click **X** to return to the page being edited.

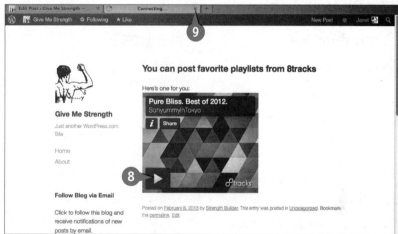

TIP

How can I post to my self-hosted site without the plugin?

Copy the HTML5 code that appears by default when you first click the **Embed** button (⟨⟩). On the Text tab of a post or page, paste the code in your page or post, and then save. You also can use that same code on a self-hosted site to post an 8tracks player in a widget.

Technology

◉ HTML5 (recommended) ❓

◯ Flash

◯ WordPress shortcode (get plugin)

Post by Voice at WordPress.com

You can create voice posts that are instantly published to your WordPress.com blog to add another dimension to it. First, you need to enable voice posting and get the telephone number and code necessary to post. Then dial up, enter the number, and start talking. As soon as you hang up, WordPress.com publishes your voice post to your blog. Hence, it is a good idea to write a script before you start talking, unless you are an amazing ad-libber. The default post title is "Audio Post," but you can edit that online or from your mobile app. Voice posting is not available to self-hosted bloggers.

Post by Voice at WordPress.com

① Click **Dashboard**.

② Click **My Blogs**.

The My Blogs panel appears.

③ In the Post by Voice column, click **Enable**.

A telephone number and code appear.

Note: Keep these secret, as any calls using the number and code are posted to your blog.

④ Copy the numbers.

⑤ Dial the telephone number.

⑥ If using a mobile phone, tap **Call** or press the **Send** button.

An automated response asks for your posting code.

⑦ Using your telephone number pad, enter the code.

The automated voice says, "Sweet."

⑧ Speak your message clearly into your phone.

⑨ Hang up when you are done.

The audio post instantly publishes to your blog.

⑩ Go to your WordPress.com blog.

⑪ Click the **Play** button (▶) to listen to your post.

Ⓐ The player changes appearance while playing.

Can I edit the audio recording if I make a mistake?

Yes, if you know how. Go to the Media Library, where you can find the MP3 file created in the posting process. Download the MP3 file to your computer, and then edit it as you normally would. When you are done, you must upload the edited file and insert it into your post.

What do I do if I mess up and I am away from my computer?

Not much, unless you have a smartphone — preferably with the WordPress app on it, as discussed in Chapter 11. In that case, you can go to the Posts panel and delete the mistaken voice post. Otherwise, all you can do is hope no one listens before you get to a computer.

Add Video with Blip.tv

You can post your Blip.tv videos at your WordPress blog by simply pasting the video's URL. You also can embed other people's videos. You should request permission to do so, unless the producer has made clear that its content can be reproduced. You could embed an episode from your series of videos on maintaining different types of garden tools in a post and then add text explaining more about the tools and their care. WordPress.com and Jetpack-enabled self-hosted blogs can use shortcodes as well as URLs. Start by choosing a video at http://blip.tv.

Add Video with Blip.tv

1 Position your mouse pointer over a video at Blip.tv, and click the **Share** button that appears.

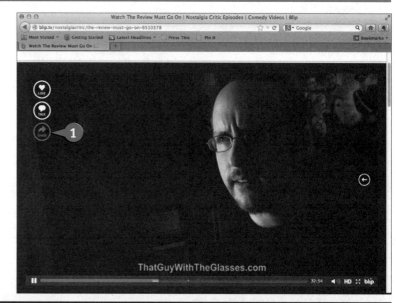

2 Click **Copy Link**.

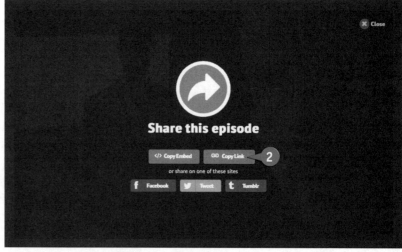

③ In a post or page in your WordPress administrative pages, paste the URL on its own line.

Note: Use the Visual editor on the posting page.

④ Click **Save Draft**.

⑤ Click **Preview**.

WordPress displays a preview of your post.

⑥ Click the **Play** button to play the video (⊙).

⑦ Click **X** to return to the page being edited.

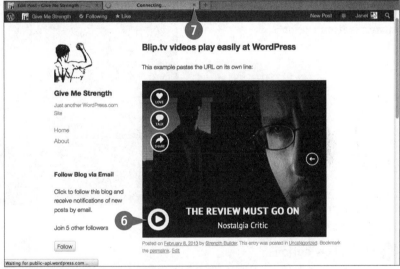

TIPS

If WordPress has shortcodes, why paste the URL?
The performance of Blip.tv embeds has been inconsistent. At this writing, the best way to embed on WordPress.com and WordPress.org sites — with or without Jetpack — is simply to paste the URL on its own line and not hyperlinked.

How would I use the shortcode?
Instead of copying the URL, click **Copy Embed** in the Blip.tv sharing window and then paste the code in a post or page's Visual editor at your WordPress.com or Jetpack-enabled self-hosted site. When you save the draft, WordPress converts the code to the shortcode. The results are the same as if you pasted the URL on its own line.

Add Video from Vimeo

Vimeo gives you another option for posting videos to enliven your blog. Although not as big a video-sharing site as YouTube, many people like Vimeo for its cleaner interface, significantly lower advertising profile, and lower incidence of spam-type comments. You can use a Vimeo video's URL to embed it in your post on WordPress.com, WordPress.org, and WordPress.org sites with Jetpack. If you want to customize the display, you can use the Vimeo embed code or a shortcode. Start by going to a video at http://vimeo.com that you want to share.

Add Video from Vimeo

1 Position your mouse pointer over the video, and click the **Share** button that appears.

Note: This example uses the customization option.

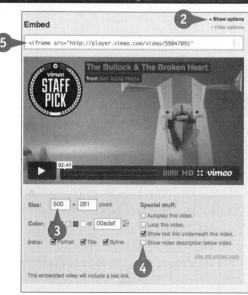

The Share This Video window appears.

2 Click **Show options**.

The Embed area expands.

3 Change the width to your preference. The height automatically adjusts to keep proper proportions.

4 Select a play option (☐ changes to ☑).

5 Click in the Embed box and copy the code there.

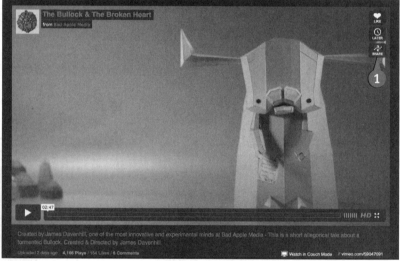

6 In a new or existing post or page panel, click the **Text** tab.

7 Paste the code.

8 Click **Save Draft**.

A At WordPress.com and Jetpack-enabled WordPress.org sites, the code changes to a shortcode.

9 Click **Preview**.

WordPress displays a preview of your post with your customizations.

10 Click the **Play** button (▶) to play the video.

11 Click **X** to return to the posting panel.

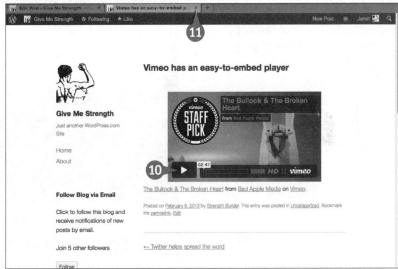

TIPS

How do I post a Vimeo video on my self-hosted blog without Jetpack?
You do it in the same way as described in this section. The only difference is that if you use the embed code instead of the URL, it does not change to a shortcode.

What am I supposed to do with the shortcode?
At this stage, probably nothing. If you want, you can change the width by changing the number after w= within the shortcode, and then saving. The shortcode does not keep some customizations you may have made at http://vimeo.com, but it does allow you to keep it on the same line as text if you want, unlike when you use the URL to embed.

Embed a SlideShare Slide Show

The SlideShare service can save your slide presentations, which you then can display on your WordPress site. At this writing, you can insert a SlideShare slide show by pasting the URL of the slide show you want to embed on its own line in the Visual editor of a post or page. That is true regardless of what type of WordPress installation you are running. For customizing, you need to use the WordPress.com shortcode at WordPress.com sites, but the embed code for WordPress.org sites. Start by finding the slide show you want to present at www.slideshare.net.

Embed a SlideShare Slide Show

1 Click **Embed**.

The Embed panel expands.

2 Click **Customize**.

A If you want the default presentation, you can copy the URL and paste it on its own line in a post or page-writing panel.

The Embed panel expands further.

3 Click the size you want.

Note: The selected size is white.

4 Click **Copy**, using the top Copy button for self-hosted bloggers and the bottom Copy button for WordPress.com bloggers.

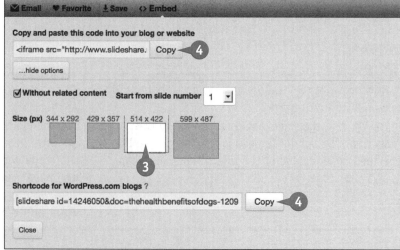

5 Click the **Text** tab.

6 Paste the code.

7 Click **Save Draft**.

8 Click **Preview**.

The preview opens in a new tab.

9 Click **Play** (▶) to show the next slide.

10 Click **X** to return to the page being edited.

My slide show is not working right. What do I do?

If you have trouble with your slide show operation, it probably is an issue to explore at the SlideShare support site at http://help.slideshare.com/home. You can check the forums at WordPress.com or WordPress.org for questions about embedding.

Can I adjust the size to fit my theme rather than the SlideShare default?

Yes. In the shortcode, change the value after w= (Ⓐ) to the desired width, in pixels, of the presentation. If you are using the embed code at a self-hosted site, change the value between the double-quotation marks after width= to the desired width, in pixels. The height adjusts proportionally.

[slideshare id=14246050&w=600&h=356&sc=no]

Ⓐ

Share Flickr Images

If you are among the thousands who post images to the Flickr website, you can share your images to your WordPress site without even leaving Flickr. First, set up your Flickr account to connect with your WordPress site. Then you simply click the WordPress share button at Flickr, and you can create your post. You also can use your Flickr photos in the WordPress.com Flickr widget at WordPress.com or via various plugins at WordPress.org. First, sign in at www.flickr.com, and find an image on your Flickr account that you want to include in a blog post.

Share Flickr Images

1 While signed in at Flickr, click your avatar.

A drop-down list appears.

2 Click **Your Account**.

3 Click **Sharing & Extending**.

4 Click **More sites**.

5 Click **WordPress**.

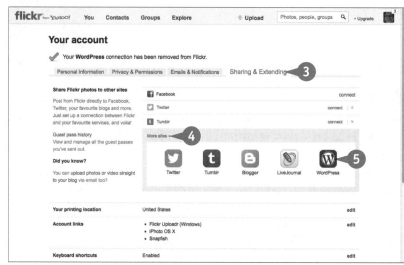

⑥ Type your blog URL in front of **/xmlrpc.php** already in the box.

⑦ Type your WordPress username.

⑧ Type your WordPress password.

⑨ Click **Next**.

Flickr returns to the accounts page.

⑩ Navigate to an image that you want to blog on your Flickr pages.

⑪ Click **Share**.

⑫ Click **WordPress**.

⑬ Type a post title.

⑭ Type the post text.

⑮ Click **Post**.

Flickr sends the post to your WordPress blog, which publishes it immediately, and Flickr shows a confirmation message.

TIPS

Can I publish to more than one WordPress blog from my Flickr account?

Yes. After you connect the first account, click the WordPress button on the account Sharing & Extending screen to connect another account.

How does the Flickr widget work?

First, on your Flickr photostream, scroll to the bottom of the page, right-click the RSS button (Ⓐ), and click **Copy Link Location**. Then, at WordPress.com, drag the Flickr widget to a widget module and paste the copied link in the Flickr RSS URL box. At self-hosted sites, you must use a plugin.

Using a Gallery Plugin

If you are not satisfied with the built-in WordPress galleries, you can find one more to your liking by using a gallery plugin at your self-hosted WordPress site. Numerous such plugins exist. Among the most popular is NextGEN Gallery, which is introduced here, although it has many more functions than this book covers. If you are at WordPress.com, you cannot use plugins, although some themes promoted as photoblog themes do a good job of displaying images. Among those are Ideation & Intent and the simple, straightforward Duotone. For NextGEN Gallery, install the plugin following the instructions in Chapter 6.

Using a Gallery Plugin

① Click **Overview** in the NextGEN Gallery plugin area on the Plugins panel after installing the plugin.

The NextGEN Gallery Overview panel appears.

② In the Plugin Check module, click **Check plugin**.

Ⓐ The plugin displays results of the check. If conflicts appear, follow the directions provided to resolve them.

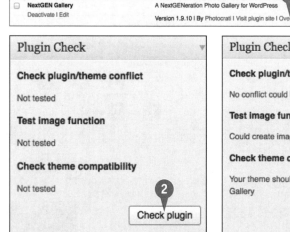

③ Click **Gallery**.

④ Click **Add Gallery/Images**.

The Add new gallery panel appears.

⑤ Type a name for your gallery.

⑥ Click **Add gallery**.

WordPress confirms creation of the gallery and shows the Upload Images panel.

⑦ Click **Select Files**.

A browser File Upload window appears.

⑧ Find your images, and then click **Open**.

Ⓑ The selected files appear here.

⑨ Pick the gallery from the Choose gallery drop-down list.

⑩ Click **Upload images**.

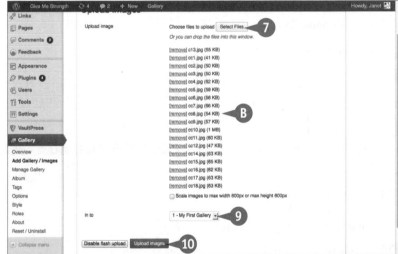

TIPS

What can I do if the upload does not work?
Click the **Disable flash upload** button. The default uploader uses Adobe Flash, which sometimes can be problematic. When you disable Flash, the Upload Images panel changes. Click **Browse** to upload your images via HTTP. The drawback is that you can upload only one image at a time.

Will images that I upload to NextGEN Gallery also appear in my WordPress Media Library?
No. NextGEN gallery has its own folder on your server where it uploads images. The default folder is wp-content/gallery, whereas the default media folder for your WordPress images is wp-content/uploads/*year/month*, where the dates of upload replace */year/month*. You can use the plugin and the Media Library separately, or NextGEN Gallery lets you import your Media Library folders.

continued ▶

When you use the NextGEN Gallery plugin, you not only have a flexible way to display your images, but you also have a way to manage your images. For example, you can use NextGEN gallery to resize and rotate images as a group. You can easily sort images in a gallery by filename or by date and time, among other options. You can group galleries, or sets of images, into Albums, or sets of galleries. You also can assign tags to your images, making it easier to find images by topic when your gallery gets big.

Using a Gallery Plugin (continued)

An upload progress screen appears, and then WordPress returns to the Upload Images panel when the upload is finished.

11 Click **Manage Gallery**.

The Galleries panel appears.

12 Click your gallery.

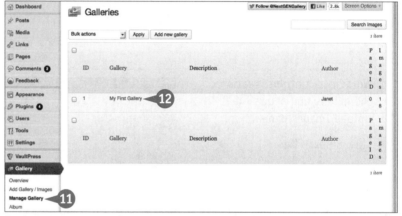

The Gallery: *Gallery Name* panel appears.

C This section toggles a module where you can rename the gallery and more.

13 Type a title, which also serves as alternate text for screen-readers.

14 Click the check boxes next to images you want to exclude (☐ changes to ☑).

D Click here to open a screen to sort gallery images.

15 Click **Save Changes**.

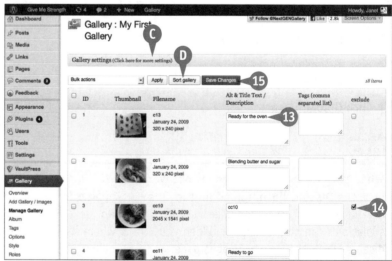

16 Click **Posts**.

17 Click **Add New**.

Note: You can click an existing post or draft if you prefer.

18 Click in the post where you want your gallery to appear.

19 Click the **NextGEN** button (🖼).

20 Click the Gallery box (▾) and choose a gallery from the list.

21 Click **Insert**.

E The gallery shortcode appears.

22 Click **Save Draft**.

23 Click **Preview**.

The preview opens in a new tab.

24 Click **X** to return to the post being edited.

TIP

Can I assign an image to more than one gallery?

Not exactly, but you can get the same results. In the Manage Gallery panel, click the check box next to each image you want in another gallery (☐ changes to ☑). Choose **Copy to...** from the Bulk Actions drop-down list, click **Apply**, and then choose a gallery in the dialog box that appears.

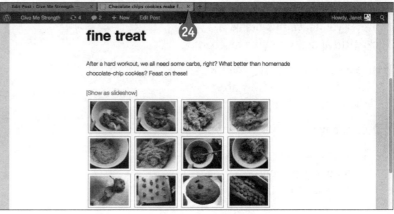

Display a Pinterest Feed

If your social media activities include Pinterest, you can share your Pinterest feed on your WordPress blog. At WordPress.com, you take advantage of an existing widget, and at WordPress.org, you use a plugin to accomplish your Pinterest feed. Having the Pinterest feed on your blog not only adds visual interest to your site, but it also can add traffic to your Pinterest page. The two forms of social media, in other words, have the potential to boost traffic at both. This example uses the Pinterest RSS Widget plugin for self-hosted bloggers.

Display a Pinterest Feed

At WordPress.com

1 Go to your Pinterest page and copy the URL.

2 In your WordPress.com Administration panel, click **Appearance**.

3 Click **Widgets**.

4 Drag the Flickr widget to a widget area.

5 Type a title.

Note: If you leave this blank, a Flickr title appears on your sidebar.

6 Paste your Pinterest page URL and then type **feed.rss** after the final / in the URL.

7 Click **Save**.

Images from your Pinterest feed appear on your WordPress.com site.

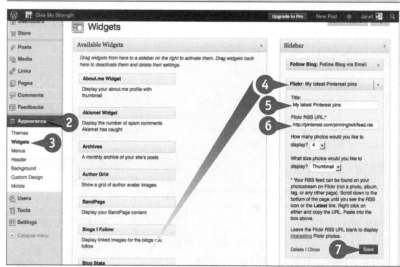

At Self-Hosted Blog Using Pinterest RSS Plugin

Note: This example assumes you have installed and activated the Pinterest RSS Widget plugin.

1 In your WordPress.org administration panel, click **Appearance** and then click **Widgets**.

2 Drag the Pinterest RSS Widget to a widget area.

3 Type a title for the widget.

4 Type your Pinterest username.

5 Type the maximum number of pins to display at one time.

6 Click **Save**.

Images from your Pinterest feed appear on your WordPress.org site.

7 Click the blog title.

Ⓐ Your site opens, revealing your Pinterest feed.

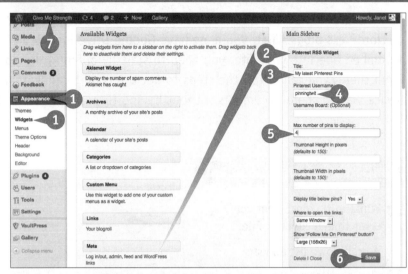

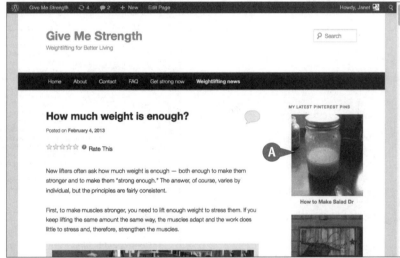

TIPS

How do I include a Follow Me on Pinterest button with my widget?

If you are using the Pinterest RSS Widget, that option is included in the widget box, and the button appears at the bottom of your Pinterest feed. If you are at WordPress.com, you need to go to http://pinterest.com/about/goodies. Click the **Follow** button you like, copy the HTML next to it, and then paste that HTML into a Text widget on your blog.

How can I change the way the images display in my sidebar?

There is no easy way to do so at WordPress.com. Self-hosted bloggers can change image size in the WordPress RSS Widget. If you want more display options and the ability to put pins on a page or post, try the Alpine PhotoTile for Pinterest plugin.

Embed a Google Document

If you use Google Drive to create and store documents, you can embed your documents into your WordPress blogs. First, you must have Google Drive installed and have documents stored there. To embed one into your site, you need to start by opening the document to embed at Google Drive. From there, you can follow the steps to get the code to allow you to do the embed. Doing so can be a nice way to share documents without having to post the full text as part of your blog.

Embed a Google Document

1 While in the document you want to embed, click **File**.

A drop-down list appears.

2 Click **Publish to the web**.

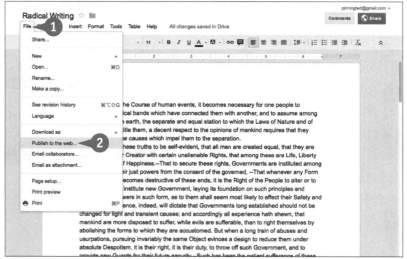

A dialog box appears.

3 Click **Start publishing**.

The box expands.

4 Copy the code in the Embed code box.

5 Click **Close**.

6 In a post at your blog, click the **Text** tab.

7 Paste the code where you want the document to appear.

8 Click **Save Draft**.

9 Click **Preview**.

Ⓐ The document appears in the post with a scroll bar.

10 Click **X** to return to the posting panel.

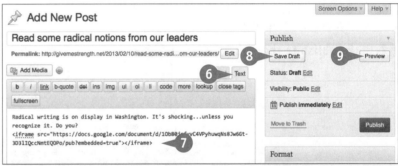

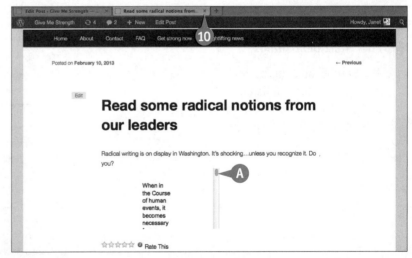

TIP

What do I do when I followed the steps, but my document does not seem to display?
Make sure your document is public. To do so, click **Share** in the upper-right corner of your documents screen. A window appears that shows who has access. If it does not say Public, click **Change** and click the radio button next to **Public on the Web** in the Sharing Settings box (○ changes to ●), and then click **Save**.

Embed a Google Spreadsheet

You can show good-looking tables in your WordPress blog by embedding a Google spreadsheet stored in your Google Drive online. After you sign up with Google Drive and create your public spreadsheet, you can embed the document by using code that Google gives to you. At WordPress.com, you can paste the embed code into a post, and WordPress converts it to a shortcode. At a self-hosted blog, you paste the code on the Text editor in a post. Wherever your WordPress blog, your spreadsheet then is accessible to all.

Embed a Google Spreadsheet

1 While in the document you want to embed, click **File**.

A drop-down list appears.

2 Click **Publish to the web**.

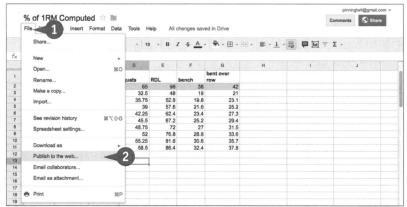

A dialog box appears.

3 Click **Start publishing**.

The Start publishing button changes to Stop publishing, and the lower portion of the window becomes active.

4 Click the Web page ⬍.

An option list appears.

5 Click **HTML to embed in a page.**

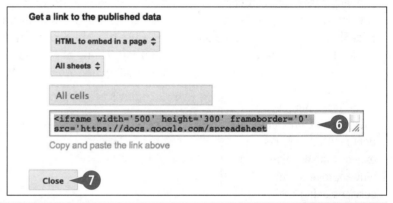

The embed code appears in the bottom box.

6 Copy the code.

7 Click **Close.**

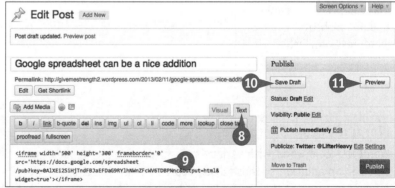

8 In a post at your blog, click **Text.**

9 Paste the embed code.

10 Click **Save Draft.**

Note: At WordPress.com, the code changes to a shortcode.

11 Click **Preview.**

A preview of your page appears in a new tab.

TIP

How can I adjust the size of the embed?
When you paste the code into the Text editor at your website, you can change the size by entering the parameters in the embed code. The embed code

```
<iframe width='500' height='300' frameborder='0'
src='https://docs.google.com/spreadsheet
/pub?key=0AlXEi2SiHjTndF8JaEFDaG9RYlhNWnZFcWV6TDBPNnc&output=html&
widget=true'></iframe>
```

includes these items, `width=` and `height=`. Change the numbers between the single quotation marks to the desired size, and save your changes. At WordPress.com the numbers are enclosed in double quotation marks after WordPress converts the embed code to shortcode.

Embed Other Content

Y ou can embed content from many services in addition to those mentioned in this chapter. However, each service seems to have its own idiosyncrasies as to how and whether it provides what you need for embedding content from the service on your site. The trick is to figure out what is possible from that service and on your WordPress site. Some of the services use the oEmbed protocol and have been approved by WordPress; they are easy to embed. Others require a little more effort. Choose what services are most important to you and decide whether you want to make them a part of your WordPress site.

The Easiest Way

In many cases, you can embed content from a service onto your site simply by pasting the URL of the content on its own line in a post or page, as described earlier in this chapter, such as Blip.tv, Flickr, SlideShare, and SoundCloud. Following is a list of more services that as of this writing permit such embedding at WordPress.org sites: Dailymotion, Funny or Die, Hulu, Instagram, Qik, Photobucket, Polldaddy, Revision3.com, Scribd, SmugMug, Twitter, Viddler, and WordPress.tv. Note that many of these URL-only

embeds also work at WordPress.com, even if they are not officially documented. You can expect that WordPress.org will approve more services using the oEmbed protocol. Find updates at http://codex. wordpress.org/Embeds.

WordPress.com Shortcodes

WordPress.com works with various sites to provide shortcodes for embedding content. For the following services, in addition to those discussed earlier in this chapter, WordPress.com accepts shortcodes they provide or converts their embed code to shortcodes. A complete list of WordPress.com shortcodes, which includes shortcodes for using content you have uploaded to WordPress.com, is available at http://en. support.wordpress.com/shortcodes/: Bandcamp; CNNMoney videos; Dailymotion; Gist; Google Calendar; Goggle Maps; Lytro; Memolane; Microsoft SkyDrive web apps for embedding Microsoft Excel, PowerPoint, and Word documents; Scribd; TED Talks; Wufoo for creating forms; and Instagram.

Plugins Can Help

If you have a particular service that you use a lot but are dissatisfied with the standard way that it or WordPress embeds the content, you may be able to find a plugin that helps. For example, you may want to try the Advanced YouTube Embed plugin if you use YouTube videos a lot. Some plugins, such as Easy FancyBox, let you customize the display of videos from multiple sources. The Google Doc Embedder takes advantage of the Google Docs Viewer to let your readers view a range of document types you embed. For example, they can view Adobe Illustrator files even if they do not have Adobe Illustrator.

Other Embeds at Self-Hosted Sites

At most sites where you can post content, you can find a way to share that content on your self-hosted site. Open the soundtrack, presentation, or video you want to embed, and you probably can find a share button. Click it, and you get code to copy and paste into the Text editor at your self-hosted site. In most cases, those embed codes involve scripts or iframes. WordPress.com does not allow use of those, except from sites with which it partners. A sampling of other sites where you can get code to embed on your self-hosted site are presentation sites such as Speaker Deck and Prezi, photo sites Shutterfly and Picasa, video site Metacafe, and audio site Chirbit.

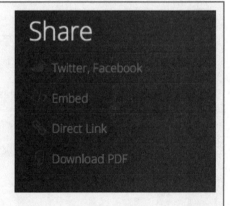

Embed Other Content

In addition to the content options in this chapter, as well as in Chapters 4, 5, and 7, you can enrich your content with other kinds of embeds. A world of content is available. For example, you can embed maps from Google or a weather map from www.wunderground.com/stickers on both WordPress.com and self-hosted sites. You also can embed a Google calendar. If you go to http://embed.ly/providers, you can see scores of sites with embeddable content. You can try the plugin, or simply visit some of the sites Embed.ly lists, such as SketchFab for 3-D models or a Timetoast timeline.

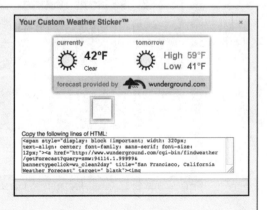

CHAPTER 13

Customizing Your Site's Look

You can further customize the way your site looks by digging a little deeper into your WordPress options. You can use featured images to highlight content, alter the post format, change the language displayed, and even change some theme templates if you have a self-hosted site.

Understanding Featured Images

Some themes allow you to highlight content by using featured images or to incorporate thumbnails of posts' images on the front page or with widgets. The featured images behave differently depending on your particular theme, and documentation for using them is not always the best. Still, you need to understand how they work if you want your theme to show images the way you expect it to do.

Featured Header Images

Some themes that have an image header allow you to display an image specific to your post. One of the default themes, Twenty Eleven, is such a theme. For it — and most — to work properly, the image has to be as big or bigger than the header image specifications.

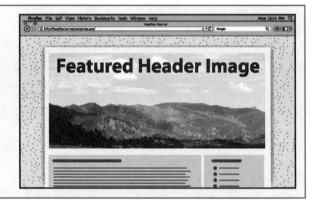

Featured Images as Thumbnails

Some themes use featured images as thumbnails or as a slide show; others combine multiple image sizes and display locations. Thumbnails can be especially useful when your front page shows only a few lines of your post, such as with magazine-style themes, and *sliders*, or slide shows, are a great option for image-heavy sites.

Expect a Learning Curve

Because the behavior of featured images is theme-dependent, understanding how featured images work is highly dependent on the quality of support from the theme developer. Be sure to read whatever documentation the theme developer provides for featured images. You can find a link to the theme developer by clicking **Appearance** in the left menu bar to reveal the Themes panel. At WordPress.com, you can get support from WordPress.com staff, except for premium themes. For them, contact the developer.

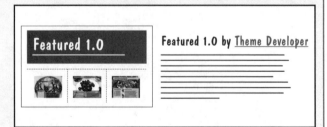

Featured Image Complexity

Adding to the potential confusion — and potential value — of featured images is that your theme may have multiple uses for featured images. For example, it may let you create a slide show that appears at the top of your blog page, or it may allow you to set featured images for categories, which can help readers navigate your website. Each of those featured image types may have preferred image sizes. If you choose a theme with multiple featured image options, plan to experiment a little to get the best results.

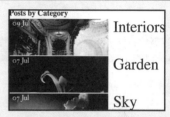

Some Featured Image Specifications

WordPress.com and WordPress.org share some themes. While the themes do not operate entirely the same across both platforms, their formats generally are the same. Hence, the list of theme-specific specifications that WordPress.com offers can be helpful for users of both types of WordPress. That list, which is not always entirely up to date, lists themes with featured images, where the featured images appear, and, in many cases, the preferred size or size limits for the images to be featured. You can find that list at http://en.support.wordpress.com/featured-images/#other-featured-images.

Gridspace

- Horizontal Featured Images: 384 x 285
- Vertical Featured Images: 248 x 330
- Square Featured Images: 384 x 384
- Logo: 180 pixels wide, flexible height

Find a Featured Image Theme

If you like the idea of using featured images, you can identify available themes by using the Feature Filter at your WordPress.com site. Find it by clicking the Appearance item in the left menu bar, and then click **Feature Filter** under your active theme. Click the **Featured Images** check box (☐ changes to ☑), and then click **Apply Filters**. At WordPress.org, click **Appearance** and then click the **Install Themes** tab, which opens the feature filter. Click the **Featured Images** check box (☐ changes to ☑), and then click **Find Themes**.

Features

- ☐ Blavatar
- ☐ Custom Header
- ☑ Featured Images
- ☐ Microformats
- ☐ Theme Options

Add a Featured Image

When you designate a featured image, you can call attention to the post associated with it. Doing so is a simple variation on uploading an image to your site's Media Library.

Add a Featured Image

1 While writing or editing a post or page, click **Set featured image** in the Featured Image module.

A If you do not see the Featured Image module, click **Screen Options** and then click **Featured Image** (☐ changes to ☑) to reveal the module.

The Set Featured Image window opens.

2 Click an image you want to feature.

The selected image appears in the Attachment Details panel.

3 Click **Set featured image**.

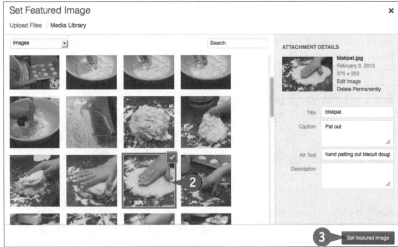

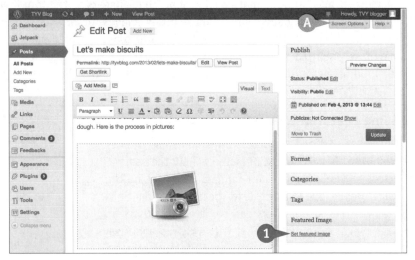

The posting page returns.

B The image appears in the Featured Image module.

4 Click **Update**, or **Save Draft** if appropriate.

5 Click **View Post**, or **Preview**.

Your post appears. In this case, the featured image displays at the top of the post.

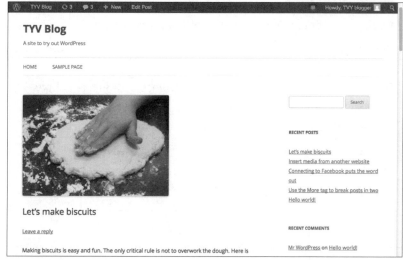

Why does my featured image not appear in the header as I expected?

Be sure to read the information that your theme provides. Some themes may require that your featured images fit specific dimensions. You can edit the image size in the Edit Media window. You can do so by clicking **Edit Image** in the Attachment Details pane of the Set Featured Image window.

How do I change the featured image if I decide I want a different one?

You can click the image in the Featured Image module to reopen the Set Featured Image window. Then click the image you prefer. Or, if you want to get rid of the featured image altogether, simply click **Remove featured image** in the Featured Image module on your post panel.

Understanding Post Formats

You can give your posts different looks by using different *post formats*. Not all themes support post formats, but if yours does you can take advantage of it from the New/Edit Post panel.

If you are code-savvy, you can add post format functionality to your WordPress.org theme. Get the scoop at http://codex.wordpress.org/Post_Formats.

Post Format Options

If your theme supports post formats, it lists available options in the Format module on the New/Edit Post panel. Different themes may have additional post formats. Particular themes style the formats differently, but WordPress intends them to be used as follows:

Standard	Basic post
Aside	Brief remarks, usually without a post title
Audio	A post of an audio file
Chat	A chat transcript
Gallery	Thumbnail on front page for post with image gallery
Image	Highlighted image
Link	For links
Quote	Highlighted quote
Status	Twitter-type personal updates
Video	A single video

Format

- ○ Standard
- ○ Aside
- ○ Link
- ○ Gallery
- ○ Status
- ◉ Quote
- ○ Image

Post Format Styling

The appearance of the different post formats varies widely by theme. At this writing, few theme designers have taken full advantage of post format potential, with about 10 percent of themes at WordPress.org listing the option. Indeed, you may not see much difference in published posts. If you are interested in this feature, be sure to look at a theme's demo of the formats you want before you commit to the theme.

LINK

Janet Majure

Posted on **October 10, 2011** | **Leave a reply**

ASIDE

They have a lot of nerve!

Posted on **October 10, 2011** | **Leave a reply**

Using Post Formats

Make your status updates stand out from your regular posts by using the Status post format. It is among several options that post-format-enabled themes may offer. Although the formats have intended purposes as noted in the preceding section, you can use them any way you want.

Using Post Formats

1 Click **Add New** under Posts in the left menu bar.

The Add New Post panel opens.

2 Write a title.

3 Write your post.

4 Click the post format you want (○ changes to ⦿).

Ⓐ If the Format module does not appear, click **Screen Options** and then click the **Format** check box (☐ changes to ☑).

5 Click **Save Draft**.

6 Click **Publish**.

WordPress publishes the post.

7 Click the blog name to go to the front page.

Ⓑ The post format may leave off the headline you typed.

8 Click the date to go to the post's individual post page, which includes the headline.

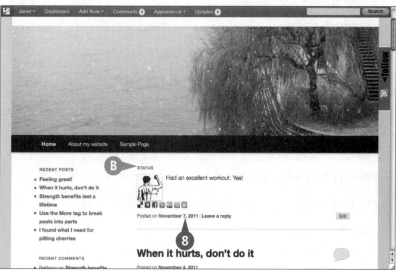

Understanding the Theme Editor

If you do not mind getting your fingers a little dirty digging in the code (not for WordPress.com blogs), you can personalize your theme even more by making adjustments to your theme in the theme editor, listed as Editor under Appearance in the left sidebar. You do not have to be a programmer to make it happen. If your adjustments are limited to changes in the *Cascading Style Sheets*, or CSS, you can do so at WordPress.com if you purchase the Custom Design upgrade, but you cannot edit any of the template files that operate the theme.

Theme Editor Components

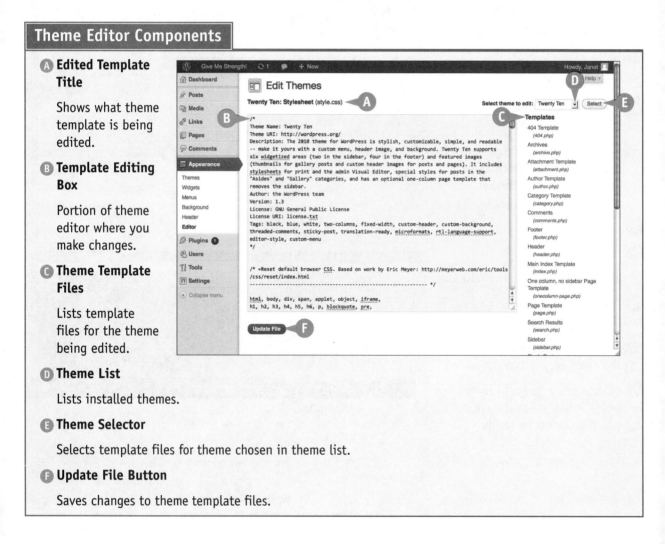

A **Edited Template Title**

Shows what theme template is being edited.

B **Template Editing Box**

Portion of theme editor where you make changes.

C **Theme Template Files**

Lists template files for the theme being edited.

D **Theme List**

Lists installed themes.

E **Theme Selector**

Selects template files for theme chosen in theme list.

F **Update File Button**

Saves changes to theme template files.

470

Theme Template Files

WordPress themes consist of several *PHP* templates, which are files written in the PHP scripting language, plus at least one Cascading Style Sheet, or CSS file. All themes have a file called index.php, and almost all have such files as header.php, sidebar.php, footer.php, comments.php, and more. For many templates, the Edit Themes panel lists a template title as well as the filename under it in parentheses. Self-hosted bloggers can make changes — carefully — to any template file. For a good overview of how the files work, go to http://yoast.com/wordpress-theme-anatomy.

Templates

404 Template
(404.php)

Archives
(archive.php)

Author Template
(author.php)

Category Template
(category.php)

Theme Editor Alternatives

If you are not comfortable using the theme editor, you may edit theme files in a text editor on your computer and upload them to your theme's folder. If you save an unedited version of the files, you can reload them if your changes mess anything up. Free source code editors such as Notepad++ or Komodo Edit make editing the files easier.

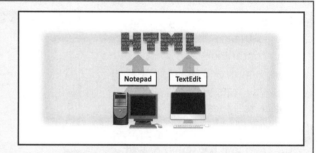

Common Changes

If you do not know PHP or HTML, keep changes simple. You may want to edit files to change text in templates or to insert code, such as from an affiliate advertiser, in a location such as a footer that does not have a widget to do it for you. CSS files also are commonly changed. You might consider creating a child theme, discussed later in this chapter, rather than changing your theme's files directly.

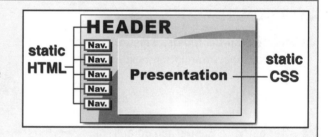

What to Change

It can be scary editing theme files. To be safe, *do not* change anything between a pair of angle brackets that start with <?php; *do not* change items beginning <div unless you know CSS; but *do* change text between common HTML tags such as <h3> and </h3>.

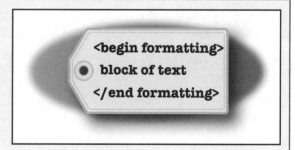

Add Copyright Information to the Footer

Adding a copyright statement to your blog's footer lets readers see at a glance what rights you retain, and you can use a plugin if you want for that purpose. Publishing the notice, though, is a good way to dip your toe into theme editing, because virtually all themes have a Footer template. The example in this section uses the Twenty Eleven theme. This example starts off taking a look at the footer in the public view before getting into the footer file in the Edit Theme panel. You might have other customizations that you want to do in the footer, and the approach is the same.

Add Copyright Information to the Footer

1 On your blog front page, scroll to the bottom to take note of how your footer looks and what it says, and decide where in that area you want your copyright notice to appear.

2 Position your mouse pointer over the text, and remember or write down what you see. In this case:

Ⓐ The text is a link.

Ⓑ You can read the *tooltip*, which is the additional information box.

3 After going to the Dashboard and clicking **Appearance** and then **Editor**, click **Footer (footer.php)** under Templates.

Footer.php opens in the edit theme file box.

Ⓒ This is the text that appears in the footer.

Ⓓ This is the link associated with the text.

Ⓔ This is the tooltip text.

Ⓕ This is the HTML <a> tag that starts the hyperlink.

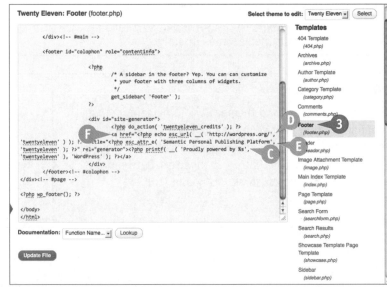

472

④ To insert plain text, click the mouse pointer just before `<a href=`, and type your copyright notice, such as **This site is licensed under the Creative Commons Attribution-Share Alike license, effective 2012 forward**.

⑤ Click **Update File**.

The changes are saved and published to your site.

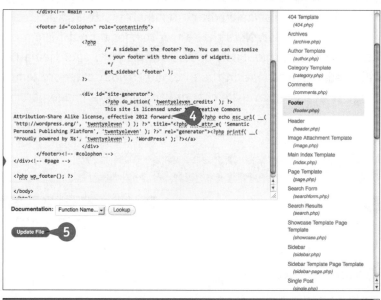

⑥ On your blog's front page, scroll to the bottom to review your changes.

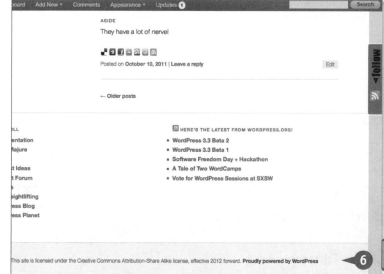

TIPS

Can I make a link in the copyright statement?

Certainly. Just use the HTML to do so. It is `<a href="http://www.place tolink.com">link name</a>`, where *www.placetolink.com* is the place to which you want to link and *link name* is the text you want to appear as a hyperlink.

Where can I find out more about copyrights? How about HTML?

You can get more information at www.copyright.gov. You also may be interested in the Creative Commons licenses, which you can read about at http://creativecommons.org. As to HTML, you can find many sources on the web, including www.w3.org, the HTML authority, or www. w3schools.com.

Add an Image to the Category Template

Another way to sample editing templates is to add an image to make the display of your category pages stand out. Note that a few themes do not have a category template. This example uses the Twenty Eleven theme. First, upload an image to your Media Library, as described in Chapter 5. You will need URL information there to add to your category template in the Edit Themes panel. Once the image is in place, save the changes to make the image part of your category template.

Add an Image to the Category Template

1 Click **Media** in the left menu bar.

The Media Library opens.

2 Click the image name.

Ⓐ You can also click **Edit** under the image name.

The Edit Media panel opens.

3 Select and copy the File URL for the image.

4 Click **Editor** under the Appearance menu to go to the Theme Editor.

5 Click **Category Template**.

The code for the Category template appears in the editing box.

6 After inserting your cursor immediately after `<header class="page-header">`, type `<a href="` and then paste the URL for the image you want, followed by `">`.

7 After the URL, type `"><img src="`, paste the URL again, and then type `"></a>`.

8 Click **Update File**.

9 Go to your site's front page, click a category, and see the image at the top of the category page.

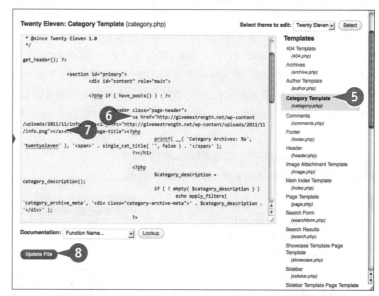

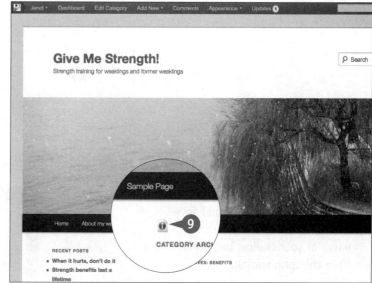

TIPS

I tried this, and I did not get the results I expected. What did I do wrong?

Unfortunately, it is impossible to say because themes handle category displays differently. To do serious editing, you need to understand PHP and HTML. Avoid putting text or HTML between PHP commands — that is, between `<?php` and `?>` — and at the very least you will not mess anything up.

Can I change or add HTML tags to text in the theme files?

Yes. It should work just fine as long as you use proper opening and closing tags. WordPress actually uses XHTML, a newer and more advanced markup language based on HTML. Read more at http://codex. wordpress.org/HTML_to_XHTML.

Create and Use a Page Template

By creating your own page templates, you can add pages to your theme that fit your needs. Perhaps you want a page that does not include a comments area, and your theme does not include such a template. You can have it by creating your own page template. You create the template on your own computer and then upload it to your WordPress host via FTP. The template then should appear on the template list when you create a page or post. This option is not available for users at WordPress.com. In this example, you create a template for a page without a footer.

Create and Use a Page Template

1 Using your FTP program, save a copy of the page.php file from your theme directory to your computer.

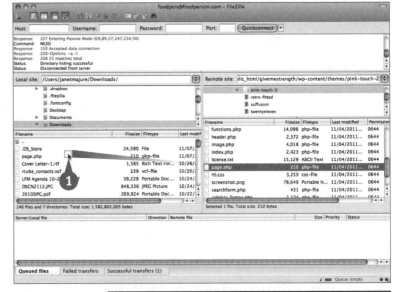

2 Open page.php with a text editor or a source code editor and save the file as no-footer.php, or a name of your choice, but it must have the .php ending.

3 Type `<?php /* Template Name: no-footer*/ ?>` at the top of the file.

4 Find and delete the line reading `<?php get_footer(); ?>`.

5 Save the file, and upload it to the directory where you found page.php.

6 In your WordPress Dashboard, expand the Pages menu and click **Add New**.

The Add New/Edit Page panel opens.

7 Click the drop-down menu next to Default Template to expand the templates menu.

8 Click **no-footer** to select the new template.

Note: The list of templates varies from theme to theme.

9 After typing a title in the title box and entering text or other content in the page box, click **Save Draft**.

10 When your page is ready, click **Publish**.

Your page is published and the Edit Page panel displays a View page link. Click the **View page** link to go to the page published with the new template.

Ⓐ The page has no footer.

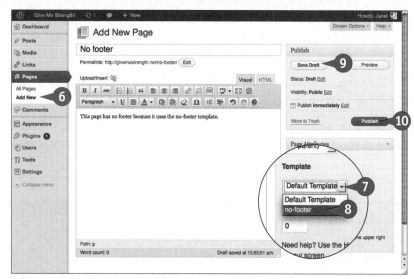

TIPS

Where do I find the page.php file?

You find it on your web host in your blog directory at wp-content/themes/*your_theme*/page.php, where *your_ theme* is the name of the theme for which you want to create a page template.

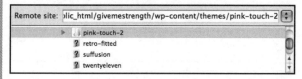

What else can I do with page templates?

Just about anything you want, but it is essential to know more about XHTML, Cascading Style Sheets (CSS), and PHP if you want to do anything at all complicated.

Introducing CSS

Cascading Style Sheets, or CSS, allow you to create standard styles for your blog's appearance. Your theme comes with a style sheet file, called style.css, which stores those standards. By using your style sheet, you can change all aspects of your blog's look without changing the way it works. Understand, however, that CSS can be fairly complicated. You may want to create a child theme, as discussed later in this chapter, to use your revised CSS.

You can use custom CSS on WordPress.com blogs only if you pay for the Custom Design upgrade. You can test the possibilities by clicking **Appearance** and then **Custom Design** under your theme name.

What CSS Affects

Your style sheet determines what font you use, the colors of headlines and links, whether images have borders around them, how text is aligned on the page, how lists are shown, and just about anything else visual on your page — even the page layout.

How CSS Works

Your WordPress theme is composed of a set of templates, and each template tells the web browser that displays your blog to get presentation information from your style sheet, which is exactly what happens.

Style Sheet Comments

You can open your style.css file in a text or source code editor. The file may have comments in it to help you understand its parts. Comments do not affect presentation. Comments appear between the characters / * and * /.

Style Sheet Rules

Each CSS rule consists of a *selector*, or the HTML element you are defining, and a *declaration*, which is the rule you are applying to that HTML element. In the CSS rule `body {background-color:beige}`, body is the selector and `{background-color:beige}` is the declaration.

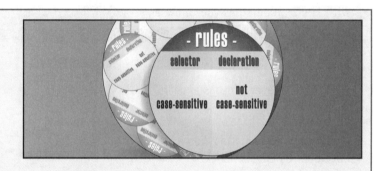

CSS Declarations

CSS declarations consist of a *property:value* pair, where *property* is the aspect of the element you want to define, and *value* is the definition. In the previous example, `background-color` is the property, and `beige` is the value.

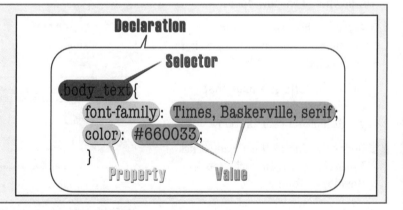

More CSS Information

If you want to learn CSS, which can get complicated, the authority is W3C, the World Wide Web Consortium. It has information on learning CSS at www.w3.org/Style/CSS/learning — in 40 languages! See also the excellent and free tutorials at www.yourhtmlsource.com and www.w3schools.com.

Try CSS with the Web Developer Extension

ortunately, you can test CSS changes without being a CSS whiz. When you use the Firefox extension called Web Developer, you can see how changes to your blog's CSS affect your blog's presentation. WordPress.org also recommends the extension called FireBug.

If you do not have the Firefox browser, you can download it from www.mozilla.org. The next section covers an extension for Google Chrome. If you prefer Internet Explorer, it has been catching up in the extensions department.

Try CSS with the Web Developer Extension

1 With Firefox running as your browser, go to http://addons.mozilla.org, and type **Web Developer** into the search box.

A list of developer add-ons appears.

2 Click **Web Developer**.

A new page opens listing Web Developer by Chrispederick.

3 Click **Add to Firefox**.

A download window opens.

4 Agree to the download and installation, and then restart Firefox as directed.

Firefox restarts at a page that profiles the developer and invites you to make a contribution.

5 Under the Firefox View menu, click **Toolbars**, and then click **Web Developer Toolbar**.

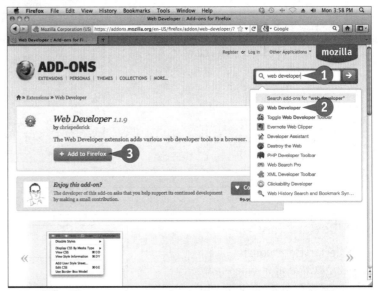

(A) The Web Developer Toolbar appears.

6 With your blog page open in Firefox, click **CSS** in the new toolbar, and then click **Edit CSS** in the menu that appears.

(B) Your style.css file opens in the Edit CSS pane of your browser.

(C) This example changes the h2 entry-title size to 6.0em.

(D) The type size changes instantly in the main part of your browser window.

Note: The browser displays what would happen if you changed the style sheet, but it does not actually change the style sheet.

TIPS

All I want to do is change the color of the headlines. How do I do that?

You need to specify the color in hexadecimal notation, such as #000000. Other options are to use a name specified in CSS3 or an RGB decimal codes, such as 0, 0, 0. Finding the right selector can be the trick. Fiddle around a bit with the Web Developer Toolbar and you will learn a lot about how CSS presents your site. You can find these and other color codes at http://en.wikipedia.org/wiki/Web_colors.

How do I find the selector?

The Web Developer Toolbar can help. Click the **Information** button on the toolbar and select **Display Element Information**. Now, click a headline whose color you want to change. A pop-up window displays information about the headline's styling. You also can use the Edit CSS search box to find all references to, say, h2 headings to find where the color may be defined.

Try CSS with the Chrome Web Developer Tool

If you like to work with the Google Chrome browser, you can get the Web Developer extension to help you view the CSS on your website and try your hand at making CSS changes without actually touching the style sheet. This extension is the product of the same developer who created the Web Developer Toolbar for Firefox. It seems to work better with Firefox than with Chrome, but it still can be a handy tool. Start by adding the extension to your Chrome browser, going to a web page you want to tinker with, and then give it a try.

Try CSS with the Chrome Web Developer Tool

1 In a new tab in your Chrome browser, click **Web Store** at the bottom of the page.

The Chrome Web Store opens.

2 Type **web developer** in the search box.

A list of matches appears.

3 Click **Extensions**.

The list shows extensions.

4 Click **Add to Chrome**.

A dialog box appears.

5 Click **Add**.

Chrome confirms the extension has been added.

6 Go to a page on your website.

7 Click the **Web Developer** icon (⚙).

A menu appears.

8 Click the **CSS** tab.

9 Click **Edit CSS**.

The Edit CSS panel appears at the bottom of the screen.

10 Select a CSS attribute you want to change.

This example changes a heading color.

11 Type a new color code.

Ⓐ The color change instantly appears in your web page.

Note: The change is temporary and is what you would see if you make the change in the actual style sheet.

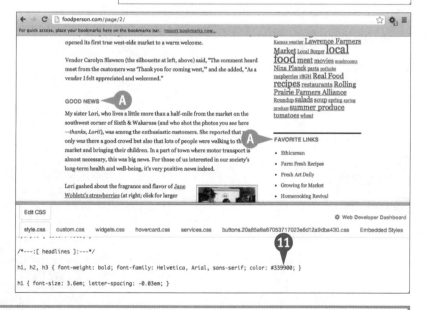

Where can I get help in using the Web Developer extension?

Alas, one drawback of the extension is that the support is not what it might be. Your best bet is to go to developer Chris Pederick's forums, at http://forums.chrispederick.com. You can click the Web Developer Issues category or search the forums for topics that may help you.

Create a Child Theme

You can protect your underlying theme files by creating a *child theme* when you change your CSS or other theme files at your self-hosted blog. A child theme consists of a folder with a CSS file and possibly other files. WordPress uses the contents of the *parent* theme on which the child is based, except for the items you include in the child theme folder. A child theme also means your customizations probably are preserved should the parent theme be updated. You need a text editor or programming editor such as TextPad, Notepad++ for Windows or TextWrangler for Mac, which are available for free.

Create a Child Theme

1 Using your FTP software, navigate to and open your site's themes folder.

Note: You can find it in the wp-content folder of your WordPress installation.

2 Right-click in the folder content area.

3 Click **Create directory** in the options pop-up.

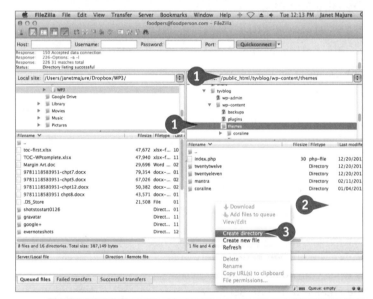

A Create directory box appears.

4 Type a new folder name in place of *New directory*.

5 Click **OK**.

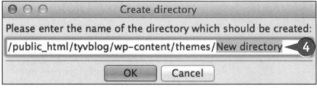

Ⓐ The new folder, or directory, appears in the wp-content/themes folder.

⑥ Double-click the folder for the intended parent theme, and write down the exact folder name, paying attention to capital and lowercase letters, for use in a moment.

The folder contents appear.

⑦ Click and drag style.css to your computer.

Note: The location on your computer is not important as long as you can find it.

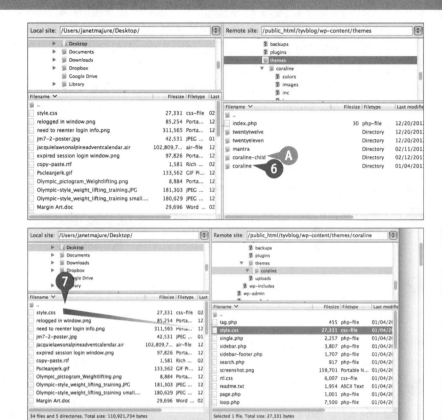

continued ▶

Does it matter what I name the child theme directory?

No. The important part is that you put it in the right location. You need to create the directory or folder in the wp-content/themes folder, *not* in the folder of the parent theme. You may find it helpful to name the directory using the parent name and some sort of child reference so that you have no trouble identifying it.

Do I have to use a text or code editor?

Yes. The style.css file cannot have anything extra in it. Word processors, which many people try to use, generate code that you do not see but that computers do. That extra code messes things up. The editors mentioned at the start of this section are free. Use one of them.

Create a Child Theme (continued)

The hardest part creating a child theme is editing the CSS and other files. Those topics are suitable for entire books of their own. The actual creation and activating of a child theme, however, is simple. After you create your child theme folder, you create a special child theme style.css file and upload it to your child theme folder. That is all WordPress requires. If you want to edit other templates in your theme, such as, say, the comment.php file, you can do so. When you save a file with the identical name in your child theme folder, it overrides that in the parent theme.

Create a Child Theme (continued)

8 Use your text editor to open the downloaded style.css file.

This example uses TextWrangler.

9 Press Ctrl+A (⌘+A on a Mac) to select all the contents of the file.

Note: You also may be able to do this from your editor's Edit menu.

10 Click **File**.

The File menu expands.

11 Click **New**, and then click **Text Document** (with selection) in the flyout menu.

A new document appears containing the original style. css contents.

12 Press Ctrl+S (⌘+S on a Mac) to save the new file.

A dialog box appears.

13 In the Save As box, type **style.css**.

14 Choose a new folder for the file. Create one if you do not already have one.

15 Click **Save**.

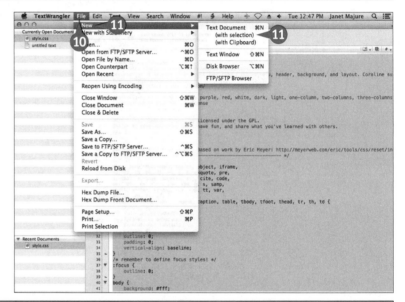

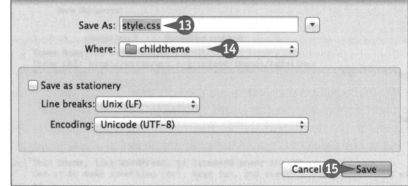

Edit the file header, which is the text between the opening /* and the first */ as follows:

16 Type a name for your child theme.

17 Delete the line labeled Theme URI.

18 Change the description to reflect your child's intent.

19 Delete the lines labeled Author, Author URI, Version, Tags, License, License URI, and any other text that appears before */.

20 Just before */, type `Template:` followed by the parent theme folder name on your host.

Ⓑ The edited header looks like this.

Note: This name is case-sensitive, so be sure to use the exact name as recorded in Step **6**.

21 Make and save whatever changes you want to the new style.css.

22 Using your FTP software, upload the new style.css to the child theme folder you created.

23 In your WordPress administration panels, click **Appearance**.

The Manage Themes panel opens.

24 Click **Activate** under your new child theme.

WordPress makes the child theme active.

25 Click the blog name to see your newly adjusted theme.

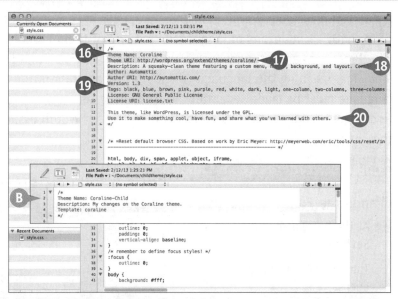

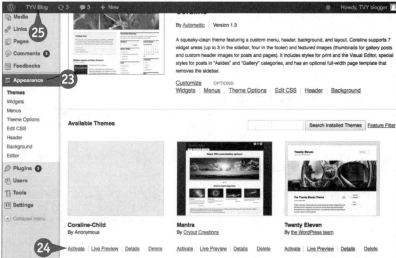

TIP

Do I have to use the style sheet from the parent theme?
No. Reusing the entire parent style sheet is simpler for beginners. However, you can call the parent style sheet in the header of your child style sheet. To do so, insert your cursor immediately after the */ that follows the template line, and type `@import url("../parentfolder/style.css");`. Then specify in your child style sheet only those items that you want to change. WordPress loads all other style matters from the parent theme's style.css.

Change WordPress.com Languages

You can make your WordPress.com site appear to readers or operate the administration panels — or both — in dozens of languages, and one of them probably works for you. Localized versions of WordPress.com are for languages from Afrikaans to Welsh and beyond. The settings for the *interface language,* meaning the language you see in the administration panels, and the publicly viewed language must be made separately. The separate settings, however, allow you to work and publish in different languages if you prefer. Log on to your WordPress.com site's admin panel to make the changes.

Change WordPress.com Languages

Change the Public Language

1 At the Dashboard, click **Settings**.

The General Settings panel opens.

2 Scroll to the Language area at the bottom of the page.

3 Click the **Language** drop-down menu.

The Language menu expands.

4 Click the language of your choice.

5 Click **Save Changes**.

The language for your blog's published pages changes.

6 Click the site name.

A The front page of your site appears, with WordPress-served text in the new language.

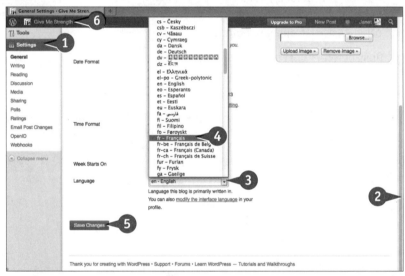

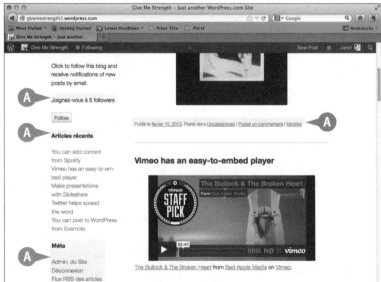

Change the Interface Language

1 At the Dashboard, click **Users**.

2 Click **Personal Settings**.

The Personal Settings panel appears.

3 Scroll to the Interface Language area.

4 Click the **Language** drop-down menu.

The Language menu expands.

5 Click the language of your choice.

6 Click **Save Changes** at the bottom of the page.

WordPress confirms the change in the new language, and the administrative interface now appears in the new language.

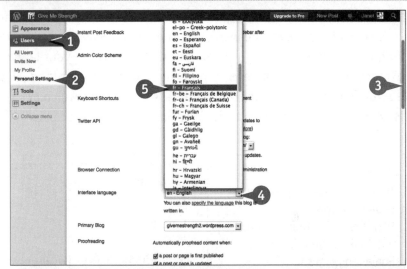

I changed the settings, but my posts are still in English. Why?
These settings change what WordPress does; it is up to you to write in the language of your choice. You can write in whatever language you want without changing the interface or public language, or *blog language,* WordPress uses on the published pages. If you change the blog language to French, German, Portuguese, or Spanish, the proofreader in your posts works in that language.

I changed the public language, but how can I type in a non-Roman script?
Go to www.google.com/inputtools/cloud/try. Choose a language from the drop-down menu. Type what you want to say using the equivalent Roman letters. Select the transliterated text, and paste it into a WordPress blog post or page. Save the post, and it saves the transliteration.

Change WordPress.org Languages

Translations of WordPress are not built in to the standard self-hosted WordPress installation, but scores of languages are available. The easiest way to change your WordPress.org installation's language is probably with a theme intended for use in your language or with a plugin such as qTranslate. The alternative is to find the .mo file in your language and follow a few directions. If you do not find your language, the WordPress community welcomes those who can help with translations. Maybe you can get involved with creating a new translation.

Find Your Language

In your browser, type **http://codex.wordpress.org/WordPress_in_Your_Language**, and look for your language. Some languages have complete, translated versions of the WordPress software, and you can find a link to translated support pages. Those languages include Basque, Catalan, Danish, Dutch, French, German, Indonesian, Korean, Portuguese, Sinhala, Sudanese, Swedish, Thai, Ukrainian, and Uighur. Other languages have add-on language files with a *.mo* extension that work with the English-language original software.

WORDPRESS.ORG

Codex

WordPress in Your Language

Languages: **English** • German • French • Chinese • (Add your language)

Add Language Files

After finding a link to an add-on language file at the previous URL, go to the .mo file and download it to your computer. If directions for installation are not available, go to http://codex.wordpress.org/Installing_WordPress_in_Your_Language for further instruction. If you do not find a translation but are willing to help create one, read the information at http://codex.wordpress.org/Translating_WordPress and get started!

WORDPRESS.ORG

Codex

Manually Installing Language Files

Languages: **English** • German • French • Chinese • (Add your language)

Get Support in Your Language

At http://codex.wordpress.org/Codex:Multilingual, you can find links to more-or-less complete translations of the WordPress documentation, or Codex, in numerous languages, though not in as many languages as the software.

Localization through Themes

A few themes are available that have built-in translations for some widely spoken languages. Go to the WordPress themes directory at http:/wordpress.org/extend/themes, and use *localize, localization,* or the language of your choice as the search term. One recent theme, RedLine, boasts more than a dozen language options and Catch Box has eight languages.

Localization through Plugins

Assorted plugins are available that can help you either install a language to your WordPress site or provide translations. Options include the popular qTranslate, which stores multiple languages. Others include xili-language to help you convert your site. If you would rather keep your English site but provide translations, a plugin such as Transposh provides translation in

many languages; the reader chooses. See http://codex.wordpress.org/Multilingual_WordPress for a discussion of the different approaches.

Using a Static Page as Your Home Page

You can give your site an entirely different feel by making your front page a static page, rather than the usual reverse-chronological presentation of blog posts. When people go to your domain, they see photos, text, or whatever else you want to display. Note, however, that this approach may not be a good idea if your theme has a complex home page, rather than the traditional newest-post-at-top format with a sidebar or two.

Using a Static Page as Your Home Page

① Click **Pages** in the left menu bar.

② Click **Add New**.

The Add/Edit Page panel opens.

③ Type **Home** in the title box.

④ Click **Save Draft**.

⑤ Click **Publish**.

The new page is published.

⑥ Click **Add New**.

A new Add/Edit Page panel opens.

⑦ Type **Blog** in the title box.

⑧ Click **Save Draft**.

⑨ Click **Publish**.

The new page is published.

⑩ Click **Settings**.

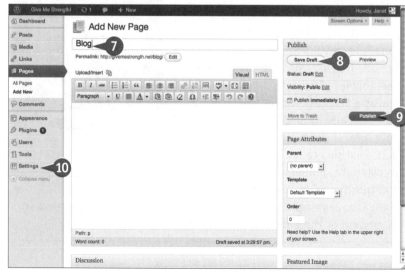

The Settings menu expands.

⑪ Click **Reading**.

The Reading Settings panel opens.

⑫ Click **A static page** (○ changes to ⊙).

⑬ Click the **Front Page** drop-down menu.

⑭ Click **Home**.

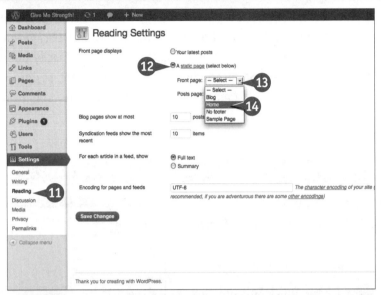

⑮ Click the **Posts Page** drop-down menu.

⑯ Click **Blog**.

⑰ Click **Save Changes**.

Visitors to your domain name now land on the page called Home and must click **Blog** to read blog posts.

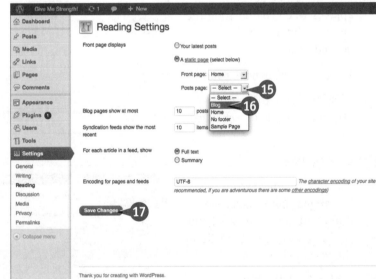

TIPS

Why is my home page blank except for the sidebar and comments box?
Presumably, when you decided you wanted a static home page, it is because you had something in mind you wanted your audience to see instead of your latest post or posts. You still must add the content you want — words, images, and so on. Do it as you would create content for any other static page.

Home

Leave a Reply

Do I have to name the blog page Blog?
No. You can name it whatever you want. If Blog does not fit the tone of your site, you can always call it News or Announcements or something else altogether.

Using Sticky Posts as a Static Page Alternative

You can make your blog's home page appear partly static and partly *dynamic*, or changing, thanks to sticky posts. Just mark one or more posts as *sticky*, and it or they stay at the top of your front page, with your latest blog post right after them. Sticky posts are a great way to welcome readers or announce policies. Some themes may have different styling for sticky posts. You may want to check your theme's styling to make sure you like it before committing to this approach. Making a post sticky could not be easier, however.

Using Sticky Posts as a Static Page Alternative

From the Posts List

1 In your Dashboard's left menu bar, click **Posts**.

The list of all posts appears.

2 Click the **Quick Edit** link that appears when you position the mouse pointer over the desired post.

The Quick Edit pane expands.

3 Click the **Make this post sticky** check box (☐ changes to ☑).

4 Click **Update**.

The post is published to the top of your home page, the Quick Edit pane collapses, and *Sticky* appears with the title in the Posts list.

From the Edit Post Panel

1 With the Edit Post panel open for the post you want to change, click **Edit** next to the Visibility setting.

The Visibility pane opens.

2 Click the **Stick this post to the front page** check box (☐ changes to ☑).

3 Click **OK**.

4 Click **Update**.

The post appears at the top of the blog front page, and *Sticky* appears with the post title in the Posts list.

Suppress the Date on Sticky Posts

1 Under Appearance, click **Editor**.

The Edit Themes panel opens to the style sheet, style.css.

Note: Your theme may have a different .css filename.

2 Find the code reading `.entry-meta...}`, and type `.sticky .entry-meta {visibility: hidden;}`.

3 Click **Update File**.

Your sticky posts do not show the original posting date.

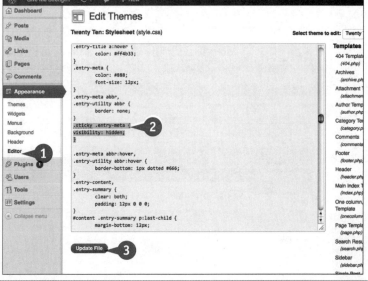

TIPS

Is there a limit to how many sticky posts I can have?
You can have multiple stickies, but if you wind up with a whole front page of static posts, consider using a page for the front and blog posts elsewhere, as described in the previous section, "Using a Static Page as Your Home Page."

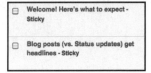

I tried to suppress the dates on the sticky posts as you suggested, but it did not work. What should I do?
It works with the Twenty Ten theme and others, but you may need to do things differently with your theme. Some CSS files may lack the `entry meta` line. Check with the theme developer or WordPress forums. You also could try a plugin, such as WP Date Remover.

CHAPTER 14

Managing Content and Multiple Users

Content management systems, or CMS, get much attention for the way they let multiple users work together or separately to create, edit, publish, and manage web content. WordPress lets you manage authors, members, content, and more.

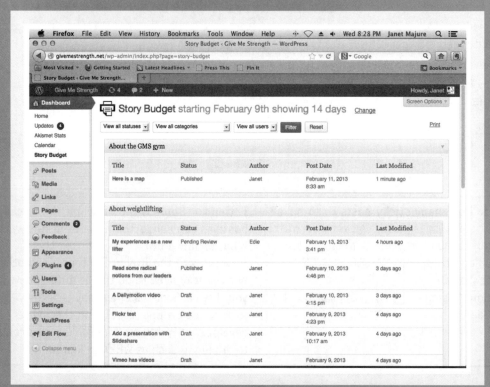

Understanding User Capabilities

As the site owner, you can decide who gets to write, edit, and publish content to your site. A critical aspect of using WordPress to manage content generated by multiple users is the permissions that you can assign to each user. Every WordPress site has a set of standard user roles that you can set up. These are Administrator, Editor, Author, Contributor, and Subscriber or Follower, depending on whether your site is self-hosted or at WordPress.com. Understanding and applying the roles appropriately make for easier-to-manage sites when you have more than one person involved.

User Roles and Capabilities

The standard set of roles that WordPress provides specify what *capabilities*, or tasks, a user can perform. When you create your site, you automatically get the Administrator role. When you add users, you can decide whether a user is an Administrator, Editor, Author, Contributor, or Subscriber/Follower. The Subscriber role is at WordPress.org; Follower is at WordPress.com. A sixth role, Super Admin, is for multisite installations, which this book does not cover.

Administrator Capabilities

As the Administrator, you can do anything WordPress or WordPress.com allows. Those capabilities include writing posts and changing themes and adding users. In most cases, the blog owner runs the site as the Administrator, but more than one person can have the Administrator role. If you add an Administrator, make sure it is someone you absolutely trust. Along with everything else, that other Administrator can change your role to, say, Subscriber.

Editor Capabilities

As implied by the role's title, the Editor role can write, edit, publish, and delete posts and pages by herself or by others. The Editor role also can moderate comments and manage categories, tags, and blogrolls. An Editor's capabilities deal mostly with content, as an Editor cannot change themes, plugins, users, and the like.

This week's blog post

Author and Contributor Capabilities

Authors can write, edit, publish, and delete posts that they wrote, but they cannot alter anyone else's posts. They also can upload images for their posts. Contributors can write and edit posts, but an Editor or Administrator must review and publish them. Authors and Contributors cannot create pages.

Subscriber/Follower Capabilities

If you have open registration available, Subscriber is the default role. Some blogs require registration to comment on blog posts, and when a reader registers, he or she gets the Subscriber role. A Subscriber can read blog posts, comment, and have a subscriber profile that defines his name, password, and so on. A WordPress.com registration fulfills that task for public WordPress.com blogs and creates Followers. Private blogs at WordPress.com have Viewers, not Followers.

Determining Roles

If you own a blog and want to have several contributors, a good practice is to give any new users the fewest capabilities that they need to complete their jobs. Limiting broader capabilities to only the very few who need them deters both miscues and malicious changes.

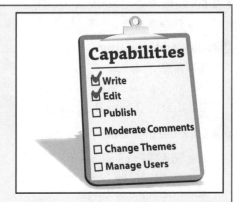

Add Authors and Contributors

You can turn your blog into a group blog by adding users as Editors, Authors, and Contributors. At the same time, you can control — or not — when and how content is published by setting permissions to fit your blog's needs. If you publish at WordPress.com, your fellow participants must have a WordPress.com logon. Added WordPress.org contributors need to have a valid e-mail address. To give other people access to your site, you add them in the Users panel in your blog's administrative pages.

Add Authors and Contributors

In Self-Hosted Blogs

1 In the administrative pages, click **Users**.

   The Users menu expands.

2 Click **Add New**.

   The Add New User panel opens.

3 Type a username in the Username box.

4 Type the person's e-mail in the E-mail box.

5 Give the user a password and confirm it.

6 Click **Send this password to the new user by email** (☐ changes to ☑).

7 Click the Role drop-down menu, and click a role.

8 Click **Add New User**.

   WordPress adds the user, sends the person an e-mail, and opens the Users list with the new user.

9 Click the username.

   The Edit User panel opens, where you or the new user can add or change settings.

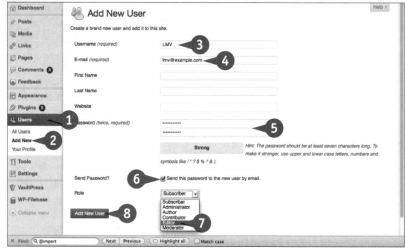

At WordPress.com

1 Click **Users** to expand the Users menu.

2 Click **Invite New**.

The Invite New Users to Your Blog panel opens.

3 Type up to 10 e-mail addresses or WordPress.com members' usernames, separated by commas.

4 Click the Role drop-down menu, and click the role you want for that user.

5 Customize the invitation.

6 Click **Send Invitation**.

WordPress.com sends an e-mail to the person and adds her name to Your Past Invitations list. The recipient must accept the invitation to be added and be or become a WordPress.com member for any role except Follower.

7 Scroll down to see the status of your invitations.

A You can resend invitations or delete invitations from the list.

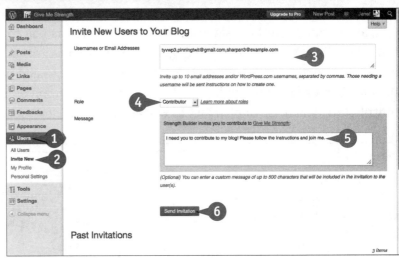

TIPS

How do new users add content?

New members of your site can access your administrative pages with their username and password in the same way you do, probably by going to *mysite*.com/wp-admin or *mysite*.wordpress.com/wp-admin, where *mysite* stands in for your site name. The available admin pages and tasks they can do depend on what their role allows. See the following section, "Work with Multiple Authors and Contributors."

How do I change a user's role?

Click **All Users** under the Users menu, click the user whose role you want to change (☐ changes to ☑), and then click the **Change role to** drop-down menu. Click the role you want, and then click **Change**.

Work with Multiple Authors and Contributors

You can enrich your blog's content when you start adding Authors and Contributors. You also can make running your blog significantly more complex as you try to maintain quality, consistency, and scheduling. You can simply add your partner as an Editor, as explained in the preceding task, if you want to make sure your partner can sign on to write and publish posts. If you want to make sure you can review material before it is published, maintain a posting schedule, or promote your contributors, you need to plan and to use plugins to achieve your goals.

Make a Plan

As with most activities involving publication, it is good to plan before acting. Before you start adding multiple people as users, make sure you understand what you want each person to do and what each user role allows. You can read the brief discussion in

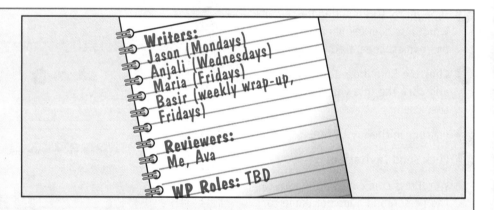

"Understanding User Capabilities," earlier in this chapter. To get the complete list of capabilities assigned to each user type, go to http://codex.wordpress.org/Roles_and_Capabilities. You can adjust users' capabilities, however, with a plugin.

Determine Workflow

Let us say you want to have six writers and have two people review and publish posts on subjects that you assign. You may trust the writers to submit whatever they choose. You need to decide whether each reviewer deals with three specific writers or

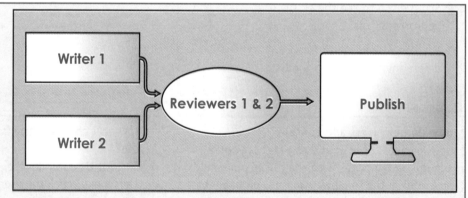

whether the reviewers take turns dealing with new posts. You may have some other workflow plan. You can always change your plan later if need be.

Start with Most-Restricted Role

When you start adding users, it is best to start them with the Contributor role. This approach is best from a human management rather than a software management perspective. That is, your participants will feel great

about getting promoted to a higher level of capabilities if they need them. Conversely, they might decide they do not want to contribute if you downgrade their role. The Contributor role has very limited capabilities, being able to write, edit, and delete their own unpublished posts but not upload files or publish posts. Capabilities can be altered with a plugin.

Give Your Contributors Credit

Depending on your theme, WordPress probably publishes the name of the writer on her posts. You can and should do more, however. Among the possibilities are providing users' profiles on the sites, publishing authors' profiles in a sidebar, and adding a brief author biography at the end of each post. Plugins at WordPress.org provided multiple ways to promote and credit your authors, and WordPress.com has two author widgets that take advantage of avatars.

Review Your Efforts

As anyone who has managed people knows, managing takes almost as much effort as doing a job yourself. After you see how your multi-author site is working, you can refine your setup, especially if you use some of the plugins discussed later in this

chapter. Among possible refinements are adjusting the capabilities of individual users, using a calendar to schedule posts, and more.

Manage Publishing Details with Edit Flow

The Edit Flow plugin automates and simplifies many tasks for you as the administrator of a site with multiple authors and contributors. It provides a handy way for you to give comments to writers before their work is published and for you to get e-mail notification when an author completes a post or makes revisions. Edit Flow lets you set up a calendar to plan your publishing schedule and create custom statuses for the different stages of your publishing process. Start by installing and activating the plugin from your self-hosted site's Install Plugins panel.

Manage Publishing Details with Edit Flow

1 Click **Edit Flow** in the left menu bar.

The Edit Flow panel appears, where it lists the Edit Flow modules.

2 Click **Configure** in the Notifications module.

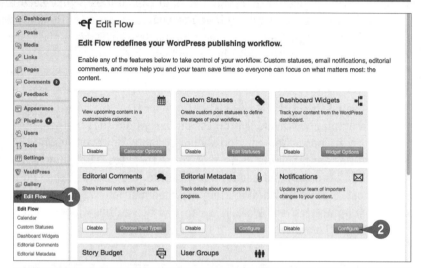

The Edit Flow: Notifications panel appears.

3 Click **Enabled** in the drop-down list.

4 Click **Save Changes**.

WordPress saves the change.

5 Click **Dashboard**.

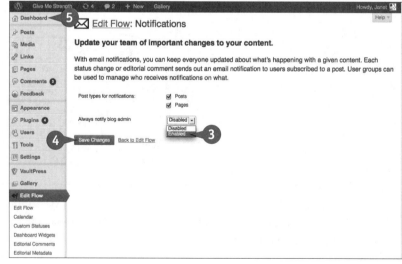

Your Dashboard opens.

⑥ Scroll down to view Edit Flow Dashboard modules.

Ⓐ Unpublished Content lists posts in your editorial queue.

Ⓑ Posts I'm Following lists posts that you are keeping track of.

⑦ Click **Pending Review**.

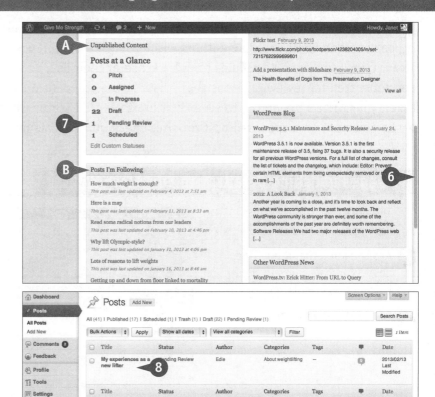

The Posts panel appears, with WordPress filtering out all except posts pending review.

⑧ Click a post that is pending review.

What statuses come with the plugin, and how do I change them?
Click **Custom Statuses** in the Edit Flow panel. The Custom Statuses panel opens, where it lists and defines the statuses that come with the plugin. As Administrator you always can see the custom status options in addition to the Published status after a post has been published. Contributors cannot change the status of a published post, even their own. The Custom Statuses panel lets you create new statuses, delete unwanted statuses, and set a default status.

Name	Description
Pitch - Default	Idea proposed; waiting for acceptance.
Assigned	Post idea assigned to writer.
In Progress	Writer is working on the post.
Draft	Post is a draft; not ready for review or publication.
Pending Review	Post needs to be reviewed by an editor.
Name	Description

continued ▶

Manage Publishing Details with Edit Flow (continued)

Edit Flow has enough functions that you probably will not use all of them at once. If you have been working with multiple authors without such a plugin, you probably will put it to work right away. Click the different modules to get a sense of their use, and then open a post that a contributor has submitted for review, a status that exists in the standard WordPress installation. You may have asked your writers previously to save their drafts as that status when they are finished. Now you can easily comment on a proposed post on-site. Check out the Calendar and Story Budget, too.

Manage Publishing Details with Edit Flow (continued)

The post opens in the Edit Post panel.

9 After reading the unpublished post, type comments in the Editorial Comments box.

10 Click **Submit Response**.

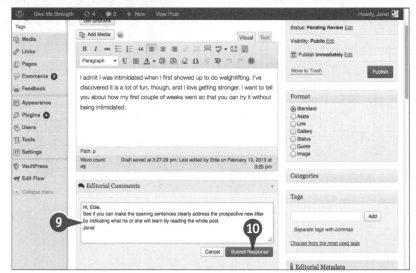

The comment is recorded, and a new Respond to this Post button appears.

11 Scroll up and click **Dashboard** in the left menu bar.

The Dashboard menu area expands.

12 Click **Calendar**.

C Published posts appear in gray on the publication date.

D Unpublished posts appear on the last date of activity.

E Options let you filter posts by status, category, or user — or a combination.

13 Click **Story Budget**.

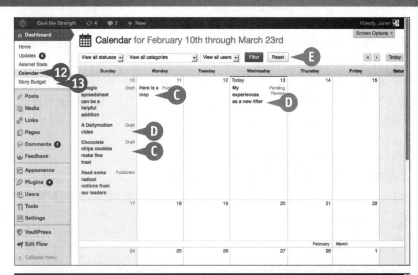

The Story Budget panel appears, listing posts by category during a specified date range. The default is from current date to 10 days ahead.

F This link lets you change the date range.

G Options let you filter posts by status, category, or user — or a combination.

14 Click **Edit Flow** to return to the Edit Flow panel.

TIPS

What does a Contributor see when he logs on to my site?

A Contributor sees much less than you do. The left menu bar, for example, excludes such major sections as Media, Pages, Appearance, and Plugins. He can see all comments and posts but can do nothing more with them than view them on the published site or in a preview. A Contributor can open his Profile panel, where he can change his password or choose a different display name.

How do I use the Editorial Metadata and User Groups?

Those modules offer more ways for you to keep track of posts and organize your contributors. This plugin, clearly, has many options and functions beyond those in this introduction. You can get more information at the plugin's home page at http://editflow.org, or by searching the forums at WordPress.org.

Manage Roles and Capabilities

Perhaps you want a contributor to upload images, unlike the Contributor default capabilities. Maybe you do *not* want editors to moderate comments, a capability that is standard for the Editor role. Two well-established plugins, User Role Editor and Role Scoper, allow you to alter the capabilities of existing roles or create new roles on your self-hosted site. At WordPress.com, you can use only the standard roles and capabilities. This example shows User Role Editor for changing role capabilities, which you can install and activate as you would any other plugin.

Manage Roles and Capabilities

Edit a Role

1 Click **Users**.

2 Click **User Role Editor**.

3 Click the **Show capabilities in human readable form** check box (☐ changes to ☑).

4 Click the **Show deprecated capabilities** check box (☑ changes to ☐).

Ⓐ The capabilities list changes to reveal readable capabilities and to hide those no longer supported in WordPress.

5 Click the Select Role drop-down ▾, and click **Editor**.

Note: This example edits the Editor role to remove page-related capabilities.

6 Click the check boxes next to all the page-related capabilities (☑ changes to ☐).

7 Scroll to bottom of module and click **Update**.

WordPress displays a confirmation dialog box.

8 Click **OK**.

WordPress updates the Editor role.

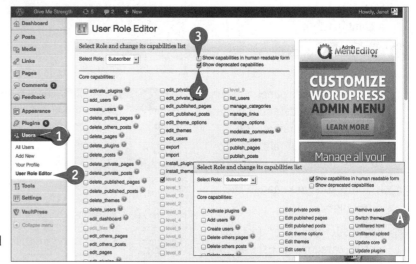

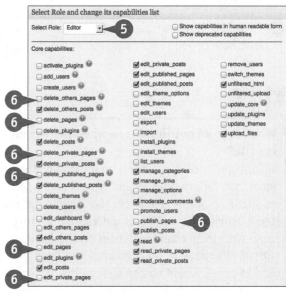

Create a New Role

1 In the User Role Editor panel, type a name in the Add New Role module.

2 Click the drop-down, and click **Subscriber**.

3 Click **Add**.

WordPress creates the new role using the Subscriber capabilities as the starting capabilities.

4 Click check boxes to add capabilities (☐ changes to ☑).

5 Click **Update**.

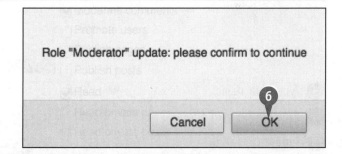

WordPress displays a confirmation dialog box.

6 Click **OK**.

WordPress updates the new role's capabilities.

Role "Moderator" update: please confirm to continue

Cancel   OK

TIP

Why does the Moderator role I created not seem to work? I gave it only the Moderate Comments capability.

Unfortunately, capabilities are not as clear cut as they seem. Some capabilities

☐ Delete posts

☐ Delete private [read about delete_posts user capability]

☐ Delete private posts   A   ☐ List users

☐ Install plugins

can be used only when the role has other capabilities. In this case, a role must have Edit Posts capability for the Moderate Comments capability to apply. The User Role Editor developer has written explanations for the capabilities marked with a question mark (A). Click one to open and read the explanation. Although it may be more detailed than the average user wants and is written in English by a nonnative speaker, he does a good job summing up at the end of his explanations.

Sign Up and Collaborate with Trello

The Trello online collaboration site lets you keep up with your blog-creating crew and help members work with each other. To get started, you need to sign up with Trello and add members to your *boards*, which serve as a basic organizing tool. You might create Trello boards for long-term blog planning, for assigning posts, and for marketing your website. You decide what you need for your site. Then you can make *lists* for each board, with each list item called a *card*. Those elements become more clear once you get started.

Sign Up and Collaborate with Trello

1. In your browser, go to https://trello.com.

2. Click **Sign Up**.

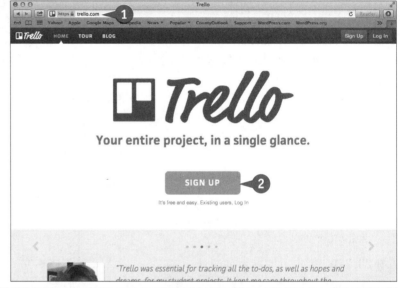

3. Type your name.

4. Type your e-mail address.

5. Type a password.

6. Click **Create New Account**.

Ⓐ Click **Google Account** if you want to sign up using your Google login.

Trello sends you a confirmation e-mail.

7 In your confirmation e-mail, click **Verify Address**.

Your browser displays your Trello page.

8 Click **New board**.

TIPS

What happens if I click Google Account in the sign-up process?
A Google Accounts screen appears. It asks you to allow Trello to get your e-mail address from your Google logon. If you currently are signed in at Google, and you click **Allow**, you are ready to use Trello. From then forward, you can log in using Google.

What is the Welcome Board that appeared when I signed up?
Click **Welcome Board**, and a sample board appears. It introduces you to Trello terms and concepts. Each column you see is called a *list*, and each item in each list is called a *card*. Click a card to view its options. Spend a little time on the Welcome Board to familiarize yourself with Trello.

Once you sign up at Trello, you can keep track of your own activity, but where Trello stands out is in group activities. When you create a board, you can invite others to join your board. When you do, the board appears on their Trello page. On a board, members can see what is going on with the project, add comments, create a checklist, attach files, and more. You can even have members vote on items, and you can decide actions members can take on your board. The possibilities are vast. This section just introduces you to Trello.

Sign Up and Collaborate with Trello (continued)

The Create Board dialog box appears.

9 Type a board name.

10 Click **Create**.

Your new board appears.

11 Click a list module, and type a new name.

12 Click **Save**.

13 Repeat Steps **11** and **12** for other lists if desired.

14 Click **Add Members**.

The Members option expands.

15 Start typing the name of a Trello member.

16 When the member's name appears, click the name.

Trello adds the member to the board.

17 Click **Add a card**.

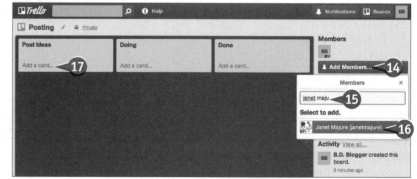

The module expands.

18 Type a card name.

19 Click **Add**.

Trello adds your card.

20 Repeat Steps **18** and **19** for more cards as desired.

21 Click a card.

Note: Step **21** is not shown.

The card opens.

22 Type a card description.

23 Click **Save**.

Trello saves the description.

B Click the **Assign** button to assign a card to a board member.

C Action buttons give options for refining your card.

D Use this area to record comments.

24 Click **X** to close the card.

The edited card appears in the list.

E Symbols indicate card activity.

F This is a symbol for a member assigned to an item.

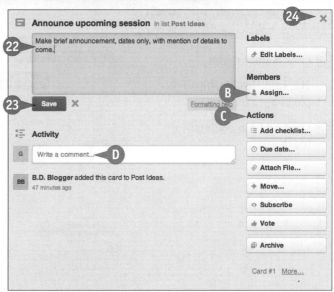

TIPS

Can I add someone who is not a Trello member?
Yes. Type the person's e-mail address in the Add Members box. Trello sends that person an e-mail message. The recipient then clicks a link in the message, and he must create a Trello membership to join your board. When he does, he is added to your board.

How do I move a card from one list to another?
You simply click and drag the task in question to the board where you want it to be. In this example, you probably would want to drag the updated card to the Doing list. As your work proceeds, you can move it again. You also can drag lists from one spot to another in your board. Trello gives you many options.

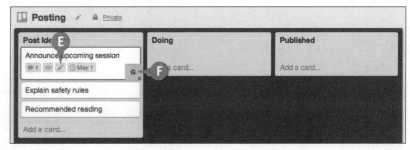

Add Registered Members

You can restrict your site content to registered members with the use of a plugin such as Paid Memberships Pro. It is a great way to deal with such issues as trying to make your organization's newsletter available only to organization members. This approach also allows you to put a public face forward to perhaps invite new members while restricting most content to registered members. If you want, you can charge for membership. Other plugins are available that do similar things. This example uses Paid Memberships Pro. Start by installing and activating the plugin the usual way.

Add Registered Members

1 Click **Memberships**.

The Paid Memberships Pro panel appears.

2 Click **Add a membership level**.

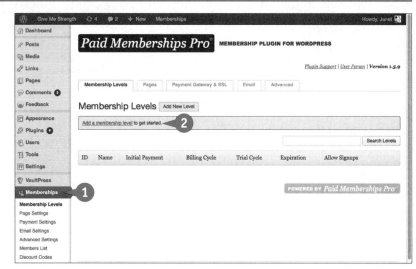

The panel changes.

3 Type a name for membership type.

4 Type a description.

5 Type a confirmation message for when someone registers.

6 Scroll down.

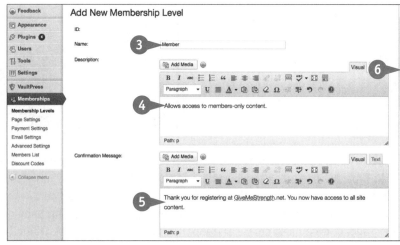

7 Type a registration fee amount, or type **0**.

8 Click category check boxes to make content available (☐ changes to ☑).

9 Click **Save Level**.

WordPress saves the membership level.

10 Click **Setup the membership pages**.

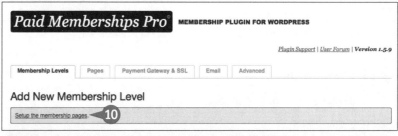

The Pages panel appears.

11 Click **click here to let us generate them for you**.

Paid Memberships Pro sets up the necessary pages.

12 Click **Email**.

TIPS

What does membership level mean?
The levels feature allows you to offer more than one type of membership. For example, you might have a free membership to allow access to some but not all content and a premium membership to allow access to all content.

How does the paid membership aspect work?
When you create a paid membership level, you specify the payment and frequency, if it is not a one-time fee. Most plugin users then connect their site to their business account with PayPal or with Authorize.net or both via the Payment Gateway & SSL tab at Paid Memberships Pro. When new users register, they provide the necessary information to pay via the payment options you select.

Paid Memberships Pro simplifies the plugin setup by creating the necessary pages for you and by having built-in messages, which you can edit, that individuals get when they register or need to log in. The plugin also prevents people from getting your protected content via RSS. Paid Memberships Pro lets you protect posts by category and by default makes pages public. Still, you can override the default to require member login on individual pages or on individual posts that are not in protected categories.

Add Registered Members (continued)

The Email Settings panel appears.

13 Type the e-mail address from which you want the plug-in to send messages to members.

14 Type the name you want to appear in the From line in e-mail messages.

15 Click **Save Settings**.

WordPress saves your changes.

16 Click **Advanced**.

The Advanced Settings panel appears.

17 Review standard e-mail messages and edit if desired.

18 Click the drop-down arrow ( ), and click **Yes-Show excerpts**.

19 Click **Save Settings**.

WordPress saves your settings.

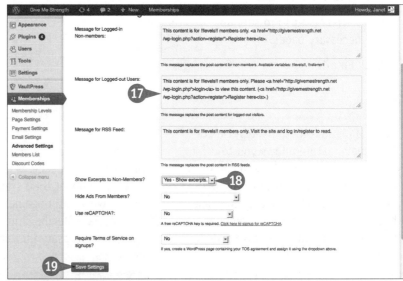

20 Position your mouse pointer over your name.

A drop-down list appears.

21 Click **Log Out**.

WordPress logs you out.

22 Click **Back to** *Your Site Name*.

WordPress opens your site's home page.

A A message tells viewers they must log in to view content.

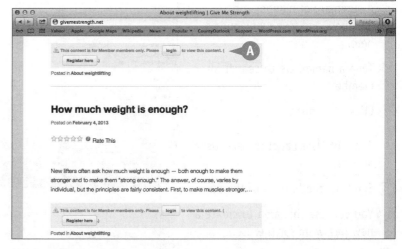

How do I protect a page from public viewing?

Open the page in the Edit Page panel. Locate the Require Membership module. Click the check box next to the member level or levels that you want to have access to the page (☐ changes to ☑), and then click **Update** in the page's Publish module.

Why do I get a restricted content notice when I click a Help link in the Paid Memberships Pro panel?

Because that is how the plugin developer makes money to maintain the plugin. You can sign up for the free membership, however, which makes some documentation, the forum, and a video available to you. By the way, it also makes a handy way to see how the plugin works from an audience perspective. You also can get some support by going to http://wordpress.org/tags/paid-memberships-pro.

Manage Registered Members

The Paid Memberships Pro plugin lets you keep track of your members' information from your WordPress administration panels. You can search the members, see how many members you have, and export their information to a CSV file. The plugin can be especially useful if you need to contact individual members or groups of members. You also can see when memberships expire if you want to remind members. This section assumes you have Paid Memberships Pro activated and you have members. For more on Paid Memberships Pro, see the previous section, "Add Registered Members."

Manage Registered Members

1. Click **Memberships**.

2. Click **Members List**.

   The Members Report panel opens.

   Ⓐ Click here to see the Filtering drop-down list.

   Ⓑ A summary of numbers of members and revenues appears here.

   Ⓒ Type a name here to search for a member.

3. Click a member.

   The Edit User panel for that user appears.

4. Scroll to the bottom of the panel.

   Ⓓ You can use this area to create a new password for the user.

5. If desired, click the **Expires** down arrow (▾) and click **Yes**.

   Dates appear next to Yes.

6. Set an expiration date if desired.

7. Click **Update User**.

   WordPress saves changes.

8. Click the browser **Back** button (◀).

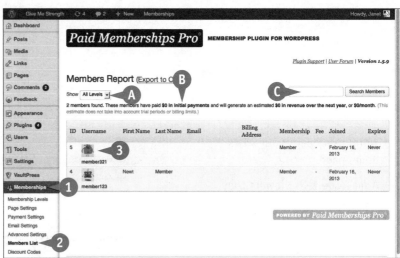

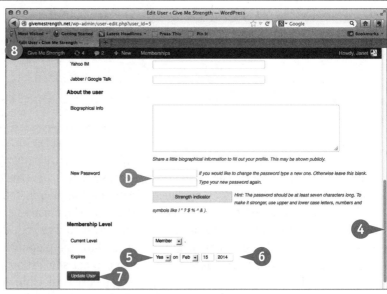

WordPress returns to the Members Report panel.

⑨ Click **Export to CSV**.

A download dialog box appears.

⑩ Click the **Save File** radio button (◯ changes to ◉).

⑪ Click **OK**.

The file downloads to your computer's default downloads location for you to use later.

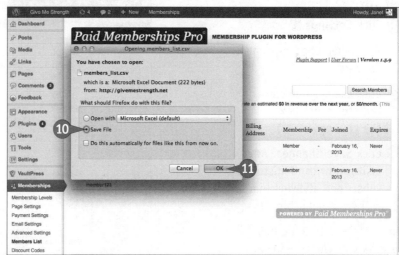

TIPS

What happens when a member logs on?
At this writing, a member's Profile page appears. This page allows the member to change his e-mail address, add biographical information, and change his password. The member then can click the site name in the menu bar to go to the site, or click the browser **Back** button (◀) to return to the page where he tried to read material. The login is retained, and he can see the restricted material.

Why does a member have access to the Dashboard?
If you sign on as a member — and you should so that you know what your members experience — and then click Dashboard, you will see that the member Dashboard shows none of your site's private information.

Create a Simple Member Community

You can avoid the formality of creating authors by letting people register and post with the P2 or PulsePress theme. At this writing, only P2 is available at WordPress.com. These themes let your subscribers post from the front page just as they might on many social network sites. Opening your blog to the world may invite unwanted contributions. At self-hosted blogs, a plugin such as Paid Memberships Pro can restrict content to registered users. Start by installing and activating P2.

Create a Simple Member Community

Set Up the Theme

1 Click **Settings**.

The General Settings panel appears.

2 Click the **Anyone can register** check box (☐ changes to ☑).

3 Click **Save Changes**. Any visitor now can register as a subscriber, allowing him to write and publish posts.

Note: Steps **1** to **3** are not necessary at WordPress.com.

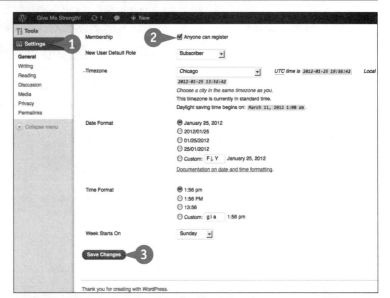

4 Click **Appearance**, and then click **Theme Options**.

5 In the P2 Options panel, click **Allow any registered member to post** (☐ changes to ☑).

6 Type a color code or choose a color by clicking **Pick a Color**.

7 Type a prompt that viewers will see to encourage posting.

8 Click **Update Options**.

WordPress saves the changes.

9 Click **Widgets**.

The Widgets panel opens.

10 Drag the Meta widget to a sidebar.

11 Give the widget a title to encourage members to sign up or sign in.

12 Click **Save**.

The widget is published to your sidebar.

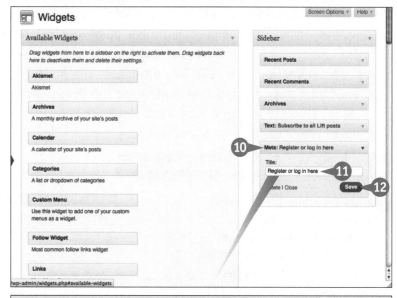

Use the Theme to Post

1 When you or a member is signed in, go to the site's front page, click, and type in the post entry box.

Note: P2 defaults to the Status Update post format, which includes no headline. If you want a headline, click the **Blog Post** button. Click the **Quote** and **Link** buttons for special boxes for quotes and links.

2 Add a tag if you like.

3 Click **Post it**.

The post is published immediately to your front page as you watch.

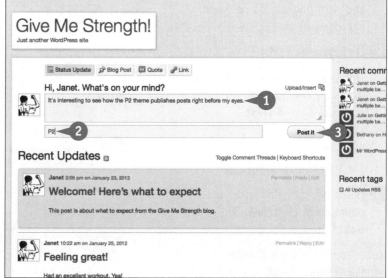

TIPS

Can each contributor have an author's page, and maybe a front-page login, too?
If you click an author's name, a page with all her posts appears. If you want more, WordPress.com has a widget that posts a grid of author avatars or a list of author posts. Also, plugins such as WP-Members for self-hosted blogs give the functions you want.

Can I get the social networking function with ordinary themes?
You can if your site is self-hosted, with the plugin WP Symposium. You install and activate it like any other plugin. Then you can create a mini social network, complete with an activity wall, friends, notifications, and more, and you can do it within your own theme in most cases.

Create a BuddyPress Social Network

Your own complete social network is possible with BuddyPress, which is owned by Automattic of WordPress fame. This complex plugin has plugins, which extend its functions. Be advised that BuddyPress is probably best for advanced — or patient — users, because of its complexity and limited documentation. This task only introduces the BuddyPress possibilities. You may want to go to http://buddypress.org and read content on the Documentation, Blog, and Support pages before you dive in. The first step in creating a BuddyPress network is to install and activate the plugin. BuddyPress is not available at WordPress.com.

Create a BuddyPress Social Network

1 After installing and activating the BuddyPress plugin and clicking **installation wizard** on the confirmation screen, review each item in the BuddyPress Setup panel's Components tab, and click any you do not want (☑ changes to ☐).

2 Click **Save & Next**.

The Pages tab opens, where you leave the default page settings, and click **Save & Next**.

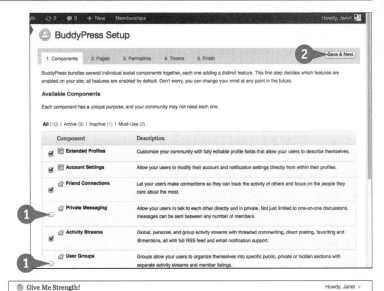

The Permalinks tab opens.

3 If you are satisfied with your permalinks, click **Save & Next**.

Note: You should not change permalink structure after your site is established.

The Theme tab opens with the BuddyPress Default theme selected.

Ⓐ If you prefer, you may select a BuddyPress-compatible theme that you already have installed. If you are not an advanced user, do not choose to install the BuddyPress Template Pack for your current theme.

④ Click **Save & Next**.

WordPress confirms your setup selections.

⑤ Click **Finish & Activate**.

WordPress activates the BuddyPress plugin and theme you selected.

TIPS

BuddyPress is not working the way I expected it to. How do I fix it?
The ins and outs of BuddyPress fill books and are beyond what can be covered here. Your best bet is to read documentation and to search or post at the BuddyPress support forums, at http://buddypress.org/support.

Should I try BuddyPress?
Go to http://testbp.org to get a taste of what running a site with BuddyPress might be like. In addition, try reviewing the information at the link in the preceding question to get a sense of what you are getting into.

Add a Forum to Your Blog

If a blog does not provide enough commentary to satisfy you, you can add a forum. Doing so allows visitors to start topics and respond to other people's topics, even if the visitors are not regular contributors. Among solutions at self-hosted blogs is Mingle Forum. Other popular plugins are Vanilla Forum and bbPress, which is created and maintained by the developers at Automattic Inc., the WordPress.com operator. Start by installing and activating the Mingle Forum plugin.

Add a Forum to Your Blog

1 Click **Add New** under the Pages menu in the left menu bar.

The Add New/Edit Page panel opens.

2 Type **Forum** in the title box, or type a different title if you prefer.

3 Type **[mingleforum]** in the Text editor view.

4 Deselect the **Allow comments** and **Allow trackbacks** check boxes (☑ changes to ☐) to *disallow* comments and trackbacks.

Note: If you do not see those options, make them visible by clicking the **Discussion** check box (☐ changes to ☑) under Screen Options at the top of the page panel.

5 Click **Save Draft**.

6 Click **Publish**.

7 Click **Settings** in left menu bar.

The General Settings panel opens.

8 Click **Anyone can register** (☐ changes to ☑).

9 Click **Save Changes**.

10 Click **Forum Structure** under the Mingle Forum menu in the left menu bar, which was added when you activated the plugin.

The Mingle Forum>>Categories and Forums panel opens.

11 Click **add new**.

The Add category module opens.

12 Type **Workout help**, or another name, under Name.

Note: You can add a description, but it is visible only to the site's administrator.

13 Click **Save category**.

The panel confirms that the category has been added.

14 Click **Add forum**.

The Add Forum panel opens.

15 Type a name.

16 Type a description, which readers can see.

17 Click **Save forum**.

The forum is set up and ready.

18 Click the site name and then the Forum page to see the results.

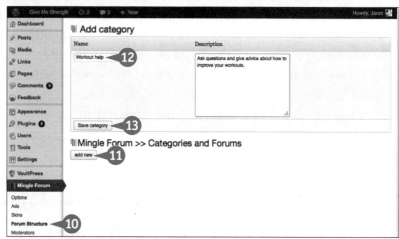

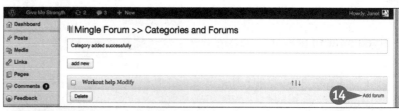

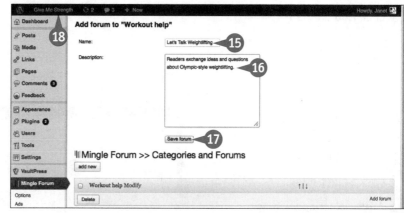

TIPS

How can I keep straight the Forum and Category terms on the setup?
They are confusing, and some might say the names are backward. You could think of *category* as one bulletin board and a *forum* as one topic pinned to the board. For most of us, the easiest way may be to set up a forum and category, look at the results, and change as needed.

Can I add a forum for my WordPress.com blog?
Not directly, but you can do so in indirect ways. First, do a Google search on *free forum hosting*, and set up a forum at the site of your choice. Then create a link to your forum in a Text widget on your WordPress.com site.

> **TALK IT OUT AT MY FORUM!**
>
> Get it by clicking GMS Forum.

Manage Documents

You can use your WordPress site as a portal to assorted documents that you want to store online and make accessible to others. Using the same technique as uploading images, you can upload word-processing documents, spreadsheets, and PDF documents for sharing. For this example, you make a page just for documents. This procedure works at either WordPress.com or WordPress.org. If your site is self-hosted, you may want to look at a plugin such as WP-Filebase Download Manager to provide more sophisticated document management functions.

Manage Documents

1. Create a new page by clicking **Pages** then **Add New**.

2. On your page, type the categories of the documents you want to upload.

3. Click where you want a link to your first document to be listed.

4. Click **Add Media** (⟨ Add Media ⟩).

The Insert Media window opens.

5. Click **Upload Files**.

6. Click **Select Files**.

7. A file selection window opens. When you locate the file you want to upload, click the filename.

8. Click **Open**.

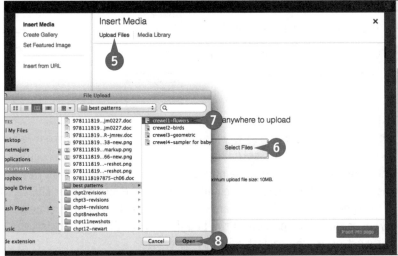

WordPress uploads the file and displays information about it in the Insert Media window.

9 Change the title, which by default is the filename, to what you want the link to the document to say.

10 Click **Insert into page**.

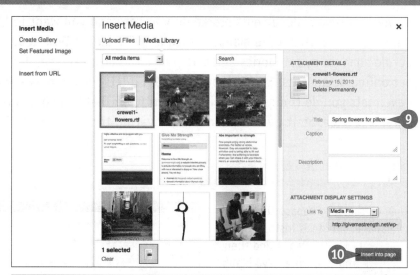

A A link to the file is inserted into the page where you positioned your cursor earlier.

11 Click **Save Draft**.

The page draft is saved.

12 Repeat Steps 3 to 11 for as many documents as you want to include.

13 Click **Publish**.

WordPress publishes your documents page to your site.

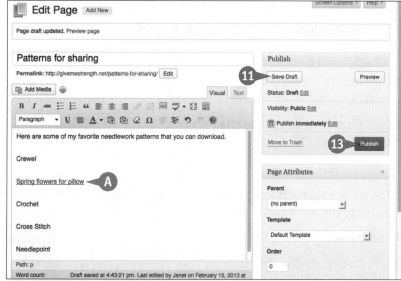

TIPS

Is there a way I can upload several documents at once?

Yes. After you click **Select Files** and the file selection window opens, you can click multiple files as long as they are in the same folder on your computer. Press and hold `Ctrl` (⌘ on a Mac) as you make your selections. After all the files are uploaded, click each item in the Insert Media window to see the attachment details and the button to insert the document.

I tried to upload a Rich Text Format, or RTF, file, but it would not let me. Why not?

WordPress.com has some restrictions on the file types you can upload, and it does not allow RTFs. Use one of the file types listed near the top of the Add Media window at WordPress.com.

📷 **Upload New Media**

Allowed file types: jpg, jpeg, png, gif, pdf, doc, ppt, odt, pptx, docx, pps, ppsx, xls, xlsx.

Manage Documents with a Plugin

If you have many documents stored on your site and you want to keep track of them and how they are used, you need a file manager such as WP-Filebase Download Manager. It lets you organize your documents by categories and sort them. You also can keep track of what is happening with your online documents. For example, the plugin lets you associate files with posts and attach them. It even lets you do things like limit bandwidth, so that someone does not try to download all your content at once. Start by installing and activating the WP-Filebase Download Manager plugin.

Manage Documents with a Plugin

1. Once the WP-Filebase Download Manager plugin is installed and activated, click **Pages** and then create and publish a new, blank page titled Documents.

2. Click **WP-Filebase**.

   The WP-Filebase panel appears.

   A Click here to open the help module.

3. Click **Click here to set the File Browser Post ID**.

   The WP-Filebase Settings panel opens to the File Browser tab.

4. Click **Select**.

   B A Posts tree window appears.

5. Click **Documents**, the page you created in Step 1.

6. Scroll to bottom of the screen and click **Save Changes**.

   WordPress saves changes and returns to the Settings panel at the Common tab.

7. Click **Categories**.

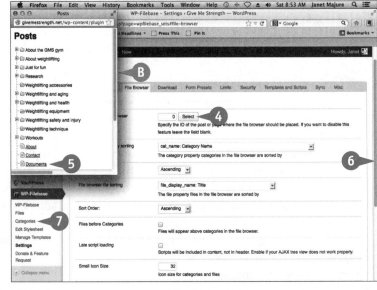

The Add Category panel appears.

⑧ Type a category name.

⑨ Type a category folder, using only lowercase letters, numerals, and hyphens.

⑩ Click **Add New Category**.

WordPress saves the WP-Filebase category.

⑪ Click **WP-Filebase**.

Note: Alternatively, you can click **Files**.

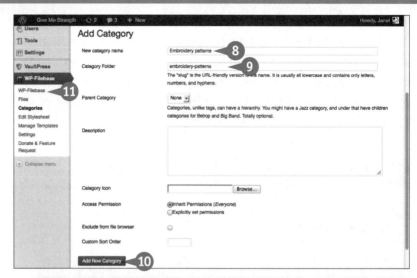

⑫ Click **Upload**.

A browser File Upload dialog box appears.

⑬ Browse to find files to upload, and click to select them.

⑭ Click **Open**.

WordPress uploads the files.

Ⓒ You can assign uploads to your category if desired.

⑮ Scroll down.

⑯ Click **Add File**.

WordPress stores the file.

TIPS

Can I upload files and assign categories later?
Yes. Click **Files** in the WP-Filebase menu area, and then click the file you want to add to a category. In fact, at this writing, if you upload multiple files at once and choose a category, only the last of the files uploaded gets assigned to the category.

Are the files saved to the Media Library?
No. WordPress saves the files to a folder specified in WP-Filebase. The default folder in your WordPress installation is wp-content/uploads/filebase. You can go to the WP-Filebase Settings panel if for some reason you want the files saved elsewhere.

continued ▶

Once you store your files with WP-Filebase, you can add them to your posts in various ways. WP-Filebase has templates that you can choose for how the file links appear in your posts. You also can protect files in numerous ways to make sure downloads are used in the manner and by the users that you want. The Settings panel provides most of the options. First, though, familiarize yourself with using WP-Filebase to insert documents into a post. The plugin has its own insert button in the posting toolbar to make it easy.

Manage Documents with a Plugin (continued)

17 In a new or existing post, click the **WP-Filebase** button ( ).

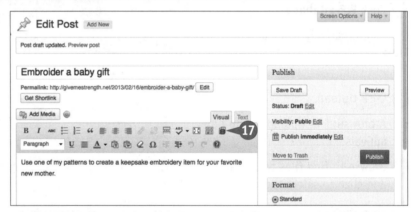

The WP-Filebase insert dialog box appears.

18 Click **Single file**.

D You can select a display option here (○ changes to ⦿).

19 Click the file you want to insert.

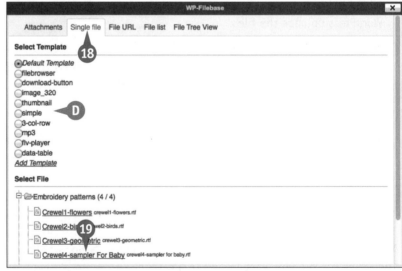

The screen immediately returns to the posting window.

E A shortcode appears in the file.

Note: If the cursor is not on a separate line when you start the insertion, the shortcode appears at the beginning of the post.

20 Click **Save Draft**.

21 Click **Preview**.

A preview of the post appears.

F In this example, the file is displayed in the default download display template.

22 Click **X** to close preview and return to the posting screen.

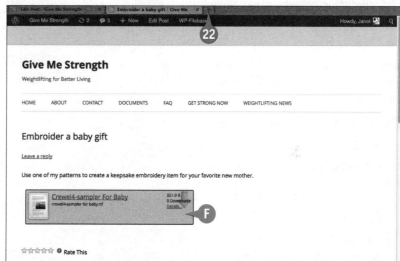

TIPS

How do I keep somebody from downloading everything all at once?
In the WP-Filebase Settings panel, click the **Limits** tab. There, you can limit downloads in several ways. These include limiting download transfer speed, or *bit rate;* setting a limit on the daily or monthly amount of data transfers allowed; and limiting the number of downloads by User type. Another option is to hide the downloads page by choosing **Private** in the Visibility area of the page's Publish panel.

What else can I do with this plugin?
The options are many. Review the various tabs on the Settings panel to get an idea of your options, from setting a default category or copyright license for uploads to using widgets that come with the plugin. Widgets allow you, for example, to list file categories or provide a file search box. You also can review the documentation at http://wpfilebase. com/documentation.

Add a Blog to an Existing Static Website

You can add a WordPress blog to your existing website with very little effort. That way, you get to keep the website you are known for while adding the dynamic content you can easily create with WordPress. You can add a self-hosted blog to your existing website via a subdirectory or subdomain, and both are described here. If your blog is hosted at WordPress.com, you must use a subdomain at your main site. It sounds complicated, but the task is fairly simple if you go step by step.

Add a Blog to an Existing Static Website

Use a Subdirectory for Self-Hosted Blogs

1. Create a subdirectory, or folder, called *blog* or some other name, in the root directory of your existing site.

Note: This example uses the cPanel file manager. You can use FileZilla for the same purpose.

2. Install WordPress into the blog directory.

Note: See Chapter 3 for installation information.

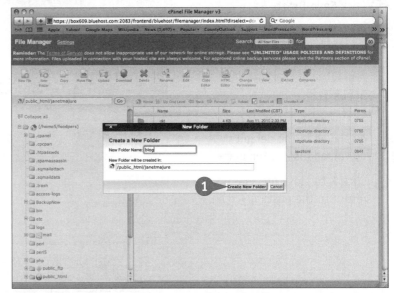

3. In your browser, type the subdirectory name in the address bar using the format **http://www.*yourdomain*.com/ *blogdirectory***, where *yourdomain*.com is the domain of your website and *blogdirectory* is the name of the new subdirectory.

Your blog page appears in your browser.

Note: Be sure to create a link to your blog from your site's home page so that your visitors can find it.

Use a Subdomain

1 Type **blog** as the subdomain in your web host's subdomains tool.

Note: This example uses the cPanel Subdomains tool.

A This field shows the directory where your blog content is stored.

2 Click **Create**.

A subdomain called blog.*yourdomain.com* is created, where *yourdomain.com* stands in for your site's domain. For a self-hosted blog, install WordPress into the subdomain's directory, and you are ready to blog.

Map a Subdomain to WordPress.com Blog

1 After you create a subdomain, create a new CNAME record at your domain registrar. It will look something like this: `blog.yourdomain.com. IN CNAME myblog. wordpress.com.` — where *myblog* is your WordPress.com username, and *yourdomain.com* is your site's domain.

2 Go to your WordPress.com Dashboard and click **Store**.

3 Click **Mapping** and follow the steps to add the subdomain and buy the mapping upgrade.

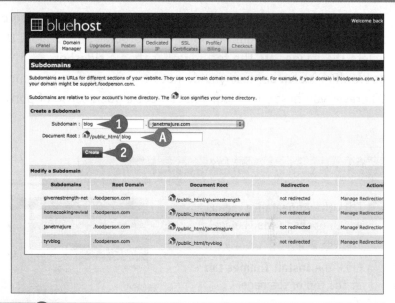

TIP

I added WordPress to a subdirectory at my site, but I cannot log on to the administration panels.

Your WordPress blog works just as if it were a stand-alone self-hosted blog, using http://www.*yourdomain.com*/blogdirectory/wp-admin to get to the administration pages. Again, *yourdomain.com* is the domain of your website, and *blogdirectory* is the name of the new subdirectory. Be sure to use the logon information you use for your WordPress administration pages, not your web host logon information.

Create a Portfolio of Your Photos or Art

The easiest and possibly best way to create a portfolio blog of your photos or art is through your choice of theme. Your portfolio or photoblog site is more than a blog with pictures. It is a blog where the images are the focus, rather than a sideshow for the words. Choice of theme is critical at WordPress.com because you do not have the option of using plugins to accomplish your goals. Wherever you host your blog, you can get a good sense of portfolio themes by using the theme filters.

Create a Portfolio of Your Photos or Art

① Click the **Appearance** menu, which opens to the Manage Themes panel.

② Click the **Install Themes** tab at the top of the page.

③ Click the **Photoblogging** check box (☐ changes to ☑).

Note: Another option is to search for themes using the search term *photoblogging* or *photography* or *portfolio*.

④ Scroll to the bottom of the page and click **Find Themes**.

Ⓐ A selection of themes appears that you can preview.

⑤ Click **Install Now** to install the theme of your choice.

The Install window opens, where you confirm that you want to install the theme. After the theme is installed, activate it.

Note: At WordPress.com, you merely activate your chosen theme.

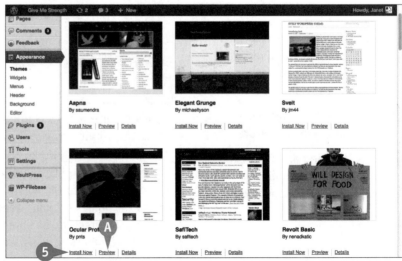

Considerations for Your Portfolio

When you choose a theme or a plugin to operate your photoblog, consider ease of use, whether it resizes photos for you, and whether it displays your photos to best advantage. After all, that is why you have a photoblog. On the other hand, you *can* put other themes to work for photos. The numerous portfolio-type themes, at both WordPress.org and WordPress.com, offer a selection of layouts and approaches to display. You should be able to find one that works for you.

Portfolio Theme Design Considerations

You can present photos — and other visual art — on a blog in more than one way, and you need to decide what works best for you: One great photo highlighted on the front page? A full-screen image on the front page? Perhaps you want to draw viewers in with a selection of photos on your front page. A theme generally makes all these options possible. If you only occasionally want to splash a big photo or gallery on your front page, you do not need a photoblogging theme; simply post a big photo or a gallery for an individual post as needed.

WordPress.com Themes to Consider

If you go to the Theme Showcase at http://theme.wordpress.com/ and click **Find a Theme**, you get more theme search options and information than via your Manage Themes panel. The showcase lets you enter search terms such as *photography* or *portfolio* or you can click **Subjects** under the filter heading. The possibilities include Art, Photoblogging, Photography, Portfolio, and Scrapbooking. Many are premium themes, but there are several free ones from which to choose. If you do not like any of those, however, you can take a different approach: Choose a plain theme such as Blogum, set the Reading settings to display just one post per page, and insert large images.

WordPress.org Themes to Consider

Your self-hosted blog offers numerous photoblogging themes. Search at http://wordpress.org/extend/themes/tag-filter. Among the free themes are Photographic, with a gallery-type front page; Pinboard, with numerous layout options; Portfolio Press, which includes post format options; Sliding Door, which has sliding images in the header; plus Origami, which also works for mobile devices. Popular premium themes include Photocrati, which has an e-commerce function as well as multiple formats.

CHAPTER 15

Making Money from Your Blog

You can make money from your blog, although making money probably is not the best reason for starting a blog or website. A blog is a great way to build your brand and to connect with customers. To make money directly, you have options that include placing ads on your site and setting up to sell products.

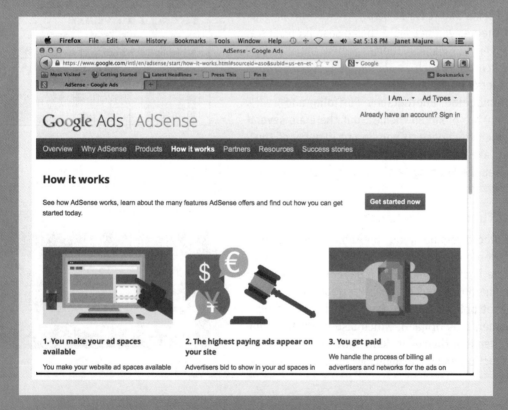

Introducing Blog Economics

You can make money from your blog directly, or you may boost your income more by building an audience and then garnering speaking engagements, consulting contracts, and writing or freelancing jobs in your field. It is wise, however, to have realistic expectations — and to avoid spending your as-yet-imaginary blog income right away. Entire books have been written about making money on your blog, and the possibilities continue to evolve. Before you decide you want to make money from, or *monetize,* your blog, it is good to know what is involved.

Expect a Slow Start

Unless you already have a big audience online somewhere else, you can expect that your audience will start small. If you blog consistently and create good content, your audience will continue to grow, but expect months to pass before you see any significant numbers of visitors. On the plus side, it probably is just as well the path to your door is lightly traveled while you work out the kinks in your presentation.

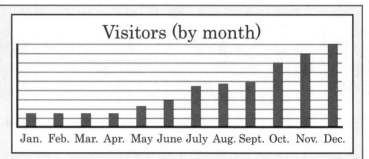

Visitors (by month)

Jan. Feb. Mar. Apr. May June July Aug. Sept. Oct. Nov. Dec.

It Is a Numbers Game

No matter what approach you want to take to make money by way of your blog, the more visitors you have, the better you will do. If you place ads or affiliate links as discussed in the next section, "Place Ads on Your Blog," you need many visitors before you can expect to collect much money as a result of the ads. Likewise, if you decide to charge for content, you need quite a few visitors before your restricted content pays off or before anyone starts downloading your e-book.

Ad Conversion		
Week	Visitors	Ad Clicks
1	100	0
2	110	0
3	112	2
4	115	0

The Competition Is Fierce

As you surely know by now, it does not take much to start a blog. All you need is access to a computer and the Internet, which means many, many other people are probably doing something like what you are doing. If you investigate the competition before starting your site, you know you are not alone. For your blog to succeed and for you to make money at it, you must be tenacious and work hard. Although some bloggers make handsome incomes, most make little money from their blogs.

food

Web   Images   Maps   Shopping

About 402,000,000 results (0.19 seconds)

Blog homepages for food

Content Is Key

The slow start makes sense when you realize that at the beginning you probably have very little content to attract search engines, and search engines bring the visitors apart from your existing network. Hence, you need to create a blog deep in useful information. Put up ads the first week if you want, but do not expect them to generate money until you have an audience, and that means content.

Right Now			
Content		**Discussion**	
469	Posts	1,204	Comments
5	Pages	1,150	Approved
24	Categories	0	Pending
211	Tags	54	Spam

Direct and Indirect Income

The leading sources of direct income for most blogs are revenue from Google AdSense ads and commissions from Amazon.com affiliate links. Less common sources are creating a *pay wall,* a barrier between readers and your content that requires a payment to get through, and selling products directly, which can be either intangible products, such as

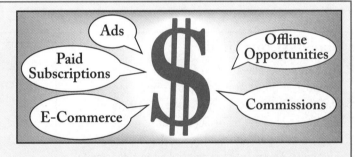

e-book downloads, or physical products, such as your handmade jewelry. Indirect income sources typically result after your blog has helped establish you as an expert in your field. With that reputation, you can get hired to conduct training, provide consulting services, or speak at conferences. Also, if you have an existing business, your blog can draw more customers to it.

Making Money Is Possible

A few bloggers have gotten attention for making a lot of money, and you also have the potential to do so. Making a lot of money, however, is not likely unless you are committed, consistent, and patient. Still, your blog can be a fine source of extra income, especially if you concentrate on a subject you love. Perhaps you keep your full-time job, but pay for your hobby and have fun at the same time by blogging about it.

Place Ads on Your Blog

One familiar way of making money on your blog is by placing ads there. These can be the Google AdSense ads you have seen on countless websites, but an assortment of other advertising media are also available. You are significantly more limited in your options if your blog is at WordPress.com. Its Terms of Service place major restrictions on ads. At WordPress.org, however, you can place as many ads as you want. Keep in mind, though, that too many ads are a turnoff to many people and could cost you an audience.

Advertising Possibilities

Advertising essentially is a means by which someone pays you for displaying an ad on your blog. You can contract directly with advertisers, sign up for an ad service or network, or use affiliate programs. Payments may be made for clicks on ads; for *impressions*, or the number of times the ad was viewed; or as sales commissions.

WordPress.com Limits

You can place any ads you want on your self-hosted blog. WordPress.com, however, significantly restricts advertising. Read the WordPress.com Terms of Service or contact support at WordPress.com if you have questions. Generally, Amazon Associate links are acceptable, but only if they are part of an original commentary about the item you are linking to.
Also, WordPress.com has its own WordAds option you can look into.

Advertising Networks or Services

The most popular ad system is Google's AdSense, which offers text and display ads. Other popular ad systems include Text Link Ads, Chitika, and Bidvertiser. The Adbrite system was scheduled to end service in 2013. Most often, these networks select ads to place on your site based on the content of your site.

Affiliate Programs

Numerous individual businesses offer affiliate programs, with Amazon being the best known. Many smaller businesses offer affiliate programs through affiliate networks, such as Commission Junction, LinkShare, or ShareASale. With affiliates, you choose the merchant or product to advertise, rather than the ad network choosing for you.

How They Work

Typically, ad networks provide a bit of code that you place on your site via a widget or by inserting it into your theme's files. The code keeps track of impressions, clicks, or both. Various plugins are available that you can use to manage ads, including ads that you sell directly to blog sponsors.

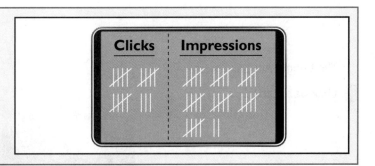

Ad Considerations

Some blogs make a lot of ad income, but most do not. Before you decide whether to include ads on your site, you may want to consider whether they are worth the effort to include and whether ads will detract from your blog content.

Add Google Ads to Your Site

Placing Google AdSense ads on your site lets you earn a few cents every time someone clicks an ad. Google lets you choose among a variety of ad types, including basic text ads and banners, and you can customize the ads to make them fit in with your blog design. You have an array of colors and sizes to choose among. WordPress.com does not allow use of Google AdSense. As a first step, you need to have or create a Google account and log on, and Google requires you to provide a postal address.

Add Google Ads to Your Site

1 Go to www.google.com and click **Advertising Programs**.

The Advertising Programs page opens.

2 Click **Get Started With AdSense**.

The Google Ads page opens.

3 Click **Get started**.

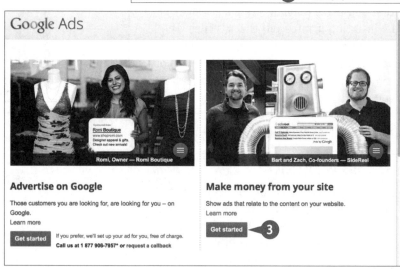

The Google Ads/AdSense page opens.

④ Click **Get Started now**.

The Step 1: Select your Google Account page appears.

⑤ Click **Yes, proceed to Google Account sign in**, and then sign in to your Google Account.

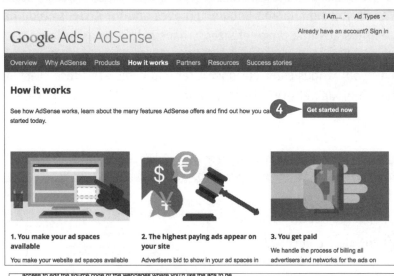

The Step 2: Tell us about your content page appears.

⑥ Type your site's URL.

⑦ Select a language from the drop-down menu.

⑧ Click to agree to Google's terms (☐ changes to ☑).

⑨ Click **Continue**.

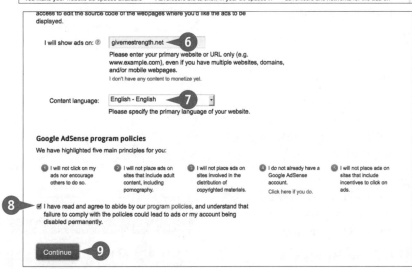

TIPS

Why do the program policies say I shouldn't tell people to click the ads?

Advertisers pay Google whenever someone clicks on their ads. Advertisers understandably want to pay only for clicks by people who are genuinely motivated to do so by the ad's content. Hence, you must agree not to encourage clicks or to click ads on your site.

What happens after I finish the application process?

You can spend some time reviewing the Google support for AdSense. Type **http://support.google. com/adsense/** in your browser. The main AdSense support page appears. Read support articles that catch your attention. As a new AdSense publisher, you might pay special attention to the "Work with your ads" and "Products" categories.

Once you sign up and Google approves you for AdSense, you have to create your ad or ads. Google offers ads in a range of sizes, from small buttons to large banners. You also can choose text-only ads or ads with media, which might be images or video. You also need to choose the ad style, which gives you various color options. After you complete those steps, Google gives you code, which you place in your website. After a few minutes, ads start to appear.

Add Google Ads to Your Site (continued)

The Step 3: Submit your AdSense application page appears.

⑩ Provide the information requested in the Contact Information section.

⑪ Scroll down to complete all the information, and click **Submit my application**.

Google shows an acknowledgment screen. It later notifies you by e-mail of your application status.

⑫ After your application is approved, which may take several days, sign in at google.com/adsense.

⑬ Click the **My ads** tab.

⑭ Click **New ad unit**.

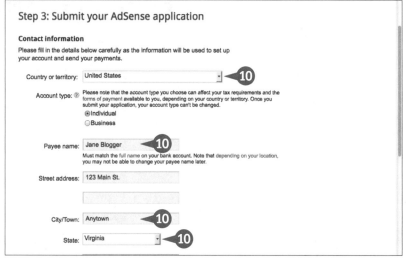

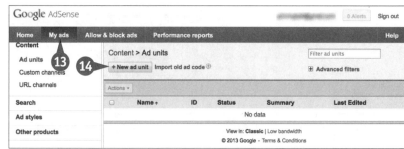

The Create new ad unit page opens.

15 Type a name for your ad display.

16 Select an ad size from the drop-down menu.

17 Choose whether to have text only, text and image/rich media, or image/rich media ads only.

Note: Not all ad types are available for all ad sizes.

18 Click the ad style you prefer.

19 When your ad selections are complete, scroll to the bottom of the page, and click **Save and get code**.

The Ad code box appears.

20 Click in the box to select the code, and then copy the code.

21 Click **Close**.

22 On your blog Widgets panel, create a text widget and paste the code into it. Ads start appearing in the widget space after a few minutes.

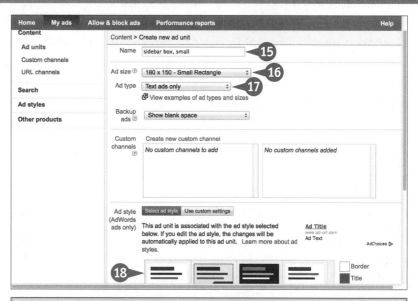

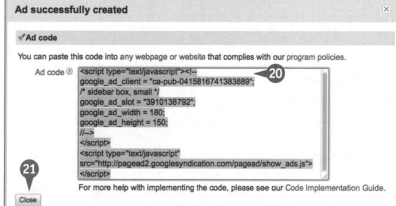

TIPS

I tried to put AdSense on my site at WordPress.com, where I bought my own domain, but the ads do not appear. Why?

As noted previously and on WordPress.com, you cannot put Google ads on your WordPress.com site, even if you paid for the domain upgrade. This question arises regularly but the answer is always *no* unless WordPress.com changes its policies, or unless you have a high-traffic VIP site, a *paid hosting* option WordPress.com offers to a select few. Try WordAds instead, as explained in the next section.

Is a widget the only way to implement AdSense?

No. You can incorporate it into your blog's theme templates by pasting the code in the location where you want the ads, such as in a footer or sidebar template. Another option is to paste the code into a sticky post.

Consider WordPress.com WordAds

If you want to run ads for money on your WordPress.com site, you can do it through the WordAds program operated by Automattic, the company behind WordPress.com. To do so, you must have your own domain — that is, your blog needs to be at *myblog.com* rather than at *myblog.wordpress.com*. Then you must apply and be accepted before the WordAds begin to appear on your site. Once ads begin running, WordAds pays monthly via PayPal. The service is fairly new, having been operating since early 2012, and continues to evolve. Get more details at http://wordads.co/faq/.

Who Qualifies

To qualify for WordAds on your WordPress.com site, you not only have to have your own domain, but you also have to have what the service terms *family friendly* and *brand-safe* content. When you apply, the service reviews your site and its content. Your site may be rejected if it has content unsuitable for a child — or your boss —

or if the content violates copyright laws or uses hate speech that might harm an advertiser's brand. Your site also needs to have enough traffic to interest an advertiser, but the amount is not defined. Note that WordAds is not available for self-hosted blogs.

What You Get

If your site is accepted, WordAds places ads served by its partners, which include Google AdSense and Federated Media, in two or three locations it chooses based on your theme. You have two choices of size and position of ads, although WordAds chooses the exact placement based on your theme. You cannot choose the

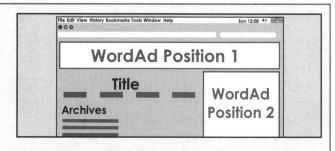

content of ads, many of which are videos. Once the ads begin to run, WordAds pays you monthly via PayPal after your earnings exceed $100. Payment generally depends on how many times an ad is viewed, but other factors come into play.

How to Apply

To apply for WordAds on your site, go to http://wordads.co/signup/. You have to sign in to your WordPress.com account before you can apply. When the Apply for WordAds page appears, follow the directions you see there. Note that you must be the owner of your site, not just an administrator. You may find that when you are signed in the signup page says, "We were unable to determine which public blogs you own." If that occurs, click the Contact link at the bottom of the page and submit a request for help to the WordAds staff.

What Happens After Submission

Response times vary, but numerous applicants have reported waiting weeks to hear from WordPress.com after submitting their WordAds application. Published staff reports say that they review each applicant's site and then activate WordAds in batches periodically. Thus, if you happen to apply just after a set of sites has had WordAds activated, you may have to wait weeks to know whether you get the ads.

Advantages of WordAds

The number one advantage of WordAds is that they are the only fully authorized advertising medium you can use as a blogger at WordPress.com. WordAds promotes its service to members as supremely simple to use. Indeed, once the service becomes active, you do not need to do much of anything except provide your PayPal information in hopes of payment. The operators also claim to go for top rates from advertisers and position the ads to complement your theme.

Complaints about WordAds

Many of the complaints about WordAds are the reverse side of the simplicity coin. That is, the simplicity of use also means you have no control to speak of. You cannot choose where the ads go, what size they are, what they look like, or what kind of business or product advertisements appear. Some WordAds site owners have complained that the video ads detract from their content or are not labeled adequately as ads. Moreover, at this writing you can find no support forum or support articles at http://wordads.co/, and the WordAds forum at WordPress.com has been closed, so all you can do for help is to submit a contact form at http://wordads.co/contact/ and wait.

Add Amazon Affiliate Ads to Your Site

I f you find yourself recommending products on your blog, you can make a little money by providing a link to a place where someone can purchase them — and earn a commission for you through an affiliate program. The commission is a percentage of sales and varies. Amazon.com Associates is the most popular such program, and you may be able to use it at WordPress.com. See "Place Ads on Your Blog," earlier in this chapter. Commission rates vary, primarily according to the product type sold. As a first step, go to https://affiliate-program.amazon.com and sign up.

Add Amazon Affiliate Ads to Your Site

① After signing in, click the **Links & Banners** tab to expand the drop-down menu.

② Click **Product Links**.

Ⓐ The Get Started Now button provides an introduction for new associates.

Ⓑ Search here to find a URL to add a text or image link on your site.

③ The Product Links page opens, where you search for the item you want to link to. When you find the item in the search results, click **Get Link**.

The Customize and Get HTML page opens.

④ Click the **Text Only** tab.

The page changes to display text link information.

⑤ Click **Highlight HTML**.

⑥ Press Ctrl + C (⌘ + C on a Mac) to copy the code.

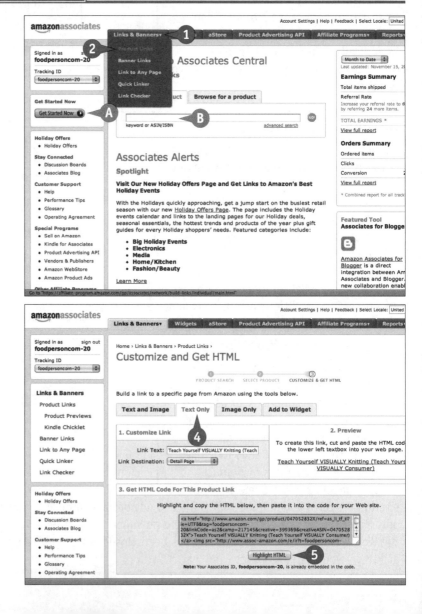

7 After logging in to your blog's administration pages and creating a new post where you want to add the text link, click the **Text** tab to go to the text post editor.

8 Paste the code in the place where you want the link to appear.

9 Click **Save Draft**.

The draft is saved with the text link to the product you recommend.

Note: The process is the same for adding a text link to an existing post. Simply open the post, click the **Text** tab, and paste the link.

10 Click **Preview** to see what your link looks like.

⦿ The coded Amazon link appears as a hyperlink.

11 Click **Edit** or click the **Edit Post** tab to resume writing your post.

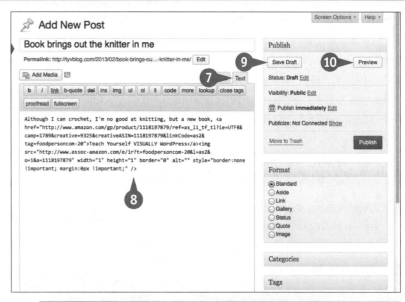

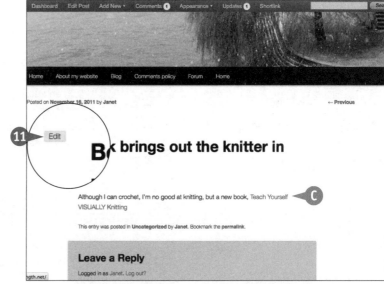

Can I use the other kinds of ads and links that Amazon offers?
Yes, if your site is self-hosted. You also can put Amazon and other affiliate ads in your sidebar. Many bloggers like the text links because they are unobtrusive, and WordPress.com frowns on image ads.

What are the Amazon widgets?
They are a form of dynamic ad, such as an Amazon search box or product slide show. Find out more about them and other Amazon Associates products and issues at the Help page at https://affiliate-program.amazon.com/gp/associates/help/main.html.

Add Amazon aStore to Your Site

You can add a store of sorts with the Amazon aStore option. It lets you choose a selection of products that you think your readers might be interested in and then present them on a separate page at your website — or at Amazon.com — so that your audience views the store contents as *your* virtual inventory. Amazon, however, handles all the billing, products, and shipping details. Then if someone buys a product after clicking a link in your aStore, you get a commission from Amazon. As a first step, go to https://affiliate-program.amazon.com and sign up.

Add Amazon A-Store to Your Site

1 After signing in at https:// affiliate-program.amazon.com/, click the **aStore** tab.

2 Click **Add an aStore**.

The Tracking ID page appears, listing the default ID assigned when you joined Amazon Associates.

Ⓐ Click this link to create a new tracking ID.

3 Click **Continue**.

The Create aStore Pages screen appears.

Note: This example creates a single-page aStore with hand-selected items.

④ Click the **Hide the category navigation** check box
(☐ changes to ☑).

⑤ Click the **Enable a link back to my site in the navigation** check box (☐ changes to ☑).

⑥ Click **Add Category Page**.

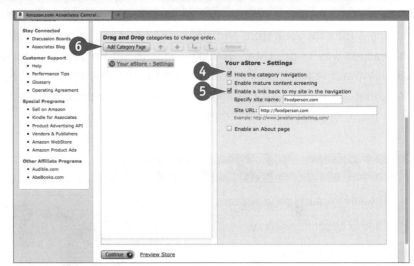

The right pane changes to Edit Category Page.

⑦ Type a category title.

⑧ Click **Add products**.

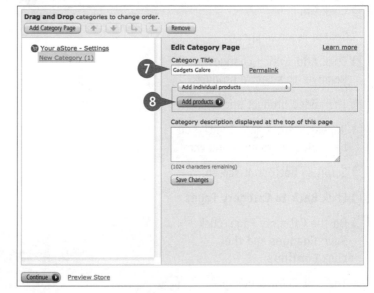

TIPS

Can I create an aStore for my WordPress.com site?
In general, no, but WordPress.com allows for a few exceptions. For example, an occasional WordPress.com website may have an aStore that lists products that the blogger has reviewed. That blog might periodically mention in a post, "See my aStore for all the books I have reviewed."

Can I do a store without categories?
You must have at least one category. Give it a name that works as a subtitle or tagline to your store's name. Add products to that category, and you have a one-page/one-category store. If you add other categories, they become separate pages in your store.

continued ▶

Add Amazon aStore to Your Site (continued)

Creating your Amazon aStore can be fun — and overwhelming. You have to choose products, titles, and a look for your store and then incorporate it into your website. Using a link in a widget is the easiest way to go. Later, you may want to set up your site such that your audience can visit your store without leaving your website. For now, though, concentrate on giving your store a look that coordinates with your site's look and on choosing products likely to be of interest to your audience, even if the product is not directly related to your blog topic.

Add Amazon aStore to Your Site (continued)

The Add Products page appears.

9 Choose a search category.

10 Type a search term.

11 Click **Go**.

Search results appear.

12 Click **Add**, which changes to Remove, to select a product.

Ⓑ The added product appears.

13 Repeat Steps **9** to **12** until you have all the products you want.

14 Scroll to bottom of screen.

15 Click **Back to Category Pages**.

16 On the Category Page, click **Save Changes** and then click **Continue**.

The Edit Color & Design screen appears.

17 Click and choose a color scheme from the drop-down list.

18 Customize the color scheme, if desired.

19 Scroll down to the bottom of the page.

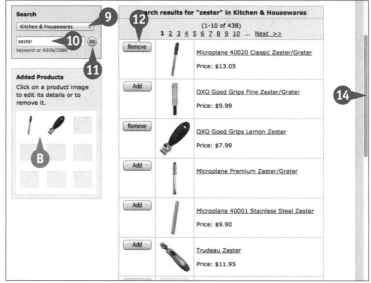

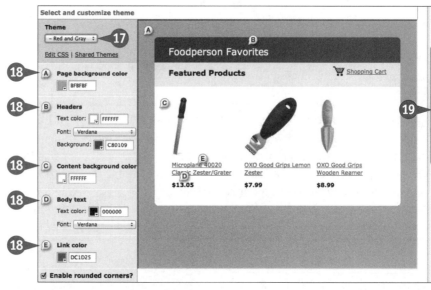

20 Type a name for your store.

21 Click **Continue**.

C ⦿ indicates the position of your store's sidebar.

22 Click the check box (□ changes to ☑) to select widgets you want.

D Position your mouse pointer over any item to see a popup of the widget's appearance.

23 Click **Finish & get link**.

The Get Link panel appears.

24 Click **Highlight HTML** and press Ctrl + C (⌘ + C on a Mac) to copy the code.

25 At your website's Widgets panel, click and drag a text widget to a sidebar area.

26 Type a title for the widget.

27 Create a link to your store using this format: `<a href="html-copied-from-amazon">`,*link text*`</a>`, where html-copied-from-Amazon is the HTML you copied in Step **24**, and *link text* is the text for your link.

28 Click **Save**.

The widget is published to your website, with a link to your aStore.

29 Click your blog name to see your site with the published widget.

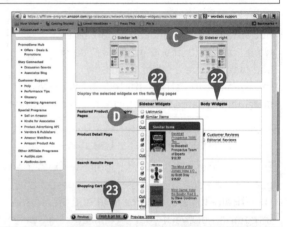

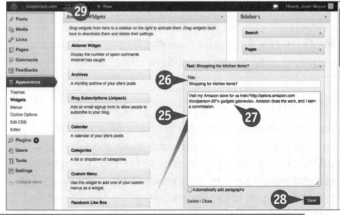

How do I make my aStore a part of my site?

Create a new blank page at your website and give it a title such as *My Shop*. Use a page template without any sidebars. Go to the Get Store Link panel at Amazon, and click the button next to **Embed my store using an inline frame** (○ changes to ⦿). Copy the resulting HTML. Return to the My Shop page, click the **Text** tab, and paste the HTML. Save and publish the page.

Get Set for E-Commerce

You can get going with online sales through a free or premium e-commerce plugin or a separate e-commerce provider that you incorporate into your site. As you consider options, keep in mind how many and what type of products you want to sell, how much time or money you can spend, and what solution you are most comfortable with. Adding e-commerce definitely increases the complexity of your website as suddenly you may need to consider shopping carts, credit-card acceptance, sales taxes, shipping rates, and order fulfillment. This book only introduces the subject.

E-Commerce Plugins

An e-commerce plugin may be the quickest way to get a shop on your website and may be the best solution for you if you have just a handful of products to sell. Plugins may not always have as much support as you want, especially if you opt for a free plugin, and may require a lot of hands-on

involvement in getting started. As WordPress shopping and commerce plugins have evolved, more of the developers charge fees, which are worth it if you get good support.

E-Commerce WordPress Themes

In many cases, you will be happier with your e-commerce plugin if you use a theme specifically designed for e-commerce. Themes created specifically for e-commerce hold out the prospect of having seamless integration between your e-commerce and website management functions. At this writing, nearly all e-commerce themes require payment for use, but the prices tend to be modest. The respected WooCommerce framework from WooThemes at www.woothemes.com/woocommerce/ is a good option with various themes.

E-Commerce Hosting

You also can choose to use a separate e-commerce host and integrate that store into your WordPress site via a subdomain. Or you can add your WordPress site to your e-commerce site — the only way to have e-commerce with a WordPress.com blog. The process is the same as adding a blog to a static site, as explained in "Add a Blog to an Existing Static Website" in Chapter 14. This might be the best approach if you have a large number of products. This option generally costs more but offers the most support. Well-regarded providers include Volusion, Shopify, and BigCommerce.

Before You Begin

If you have no retail sales experience, you may not have thought about the numerous hurdles you have to clear to be able to sell online. First, of course, you have to have something to sell. Then you need a way to sell it, meaning a shopping cart and a payment gateway.

Good Fits for E-Commerce

Not every business is well suited to e-commerce. However, e-commerce may be a natural extension of your existing retail business, especially if you have a product line that is not readily available elsewhere or that has a committed following. You also can sell intangible products such as e-books — a natural extension for many bloggers — or other digital products such as podcasts you have created or subscriptions to premium content.

Easy-for-You Payments

When people make purchases online, they expect to pay online. In most cases, the easiest way for you to provide a payment method is to sign up for a business account at www.paypal.com. The standard business account costs nothing to set up and allows your customers to pay with their PayPal account or with a credit card. In exchange, PayPal keeps a fee, 2.9 percent plus 30 cents per transaction at this writing. The drawback is that customers leave your website to pay. Others offering similar services include Stripe and Google Checkout.

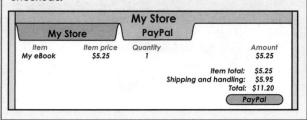

Easy-for-Customer Payments

The easiest way for customers is for you to use a payment gateway such as Authorize.net at www.authorize.net, and a credit card merchant account. These services typically have a setup fee, monthly fee, and transaction fees. The advantages are that customers pay right from your website, and you receive payment directly into your bank account.

Use an E-Commerce Plugin

An e-commerce plugin lets you manage your shop, your blog, and any other business pages you have at your self-hosted site all from your WordPress administration panels. You do not have to worry that a customer may become confused if he clicks your Store link and finds himself at a page that looks significantly different from your main site. Plugin options include WooCommerce, WP-eCommerce, and Shopp. You may want to try more than one before committing. This example uses WooCommerce, which requires a WooCommerce-compatible theme, such as Responsive, and sells digital products. To start, install and activate the plugin.

Use an E-Commerce Plugin

1 Click **Install WooCommerce Pages** in the banner that appears after activating the plugin, available at http://wordpress.org/extend/plugins/woocommerce/.

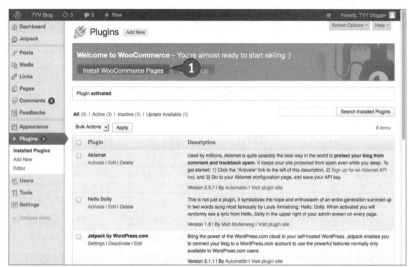

The plugin installs the pages and a WooCommerce menu section in the left menu bar and opens the WooCommerce Settings panel to the General tab.

2 Select your physical location from the Base Country/Region drop-down list.

3 Select the currency for payments.

4 Select All Countries or Specific Countries.

Note: The Specific Countries option creates another dropdown where you designate countries.

5 Scroll down, and review the Checkout and Accounts settings.

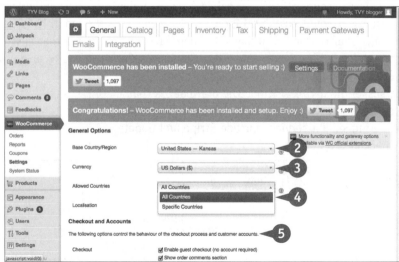

6 Click a color button, and type a color code or choose colors in the color-picker popup compatible with your site.

A Clicking ⓞ tells where each color appears.

7 Click **Save changes**.

8 Click your blog name to visit your site.

The home page appears, showing changes the plugin has made.

B The home page is static and has boilerplate text, and the blog stream has disappeared from view.

C A set of commerce pages appears in the menu bar.

9 Click ◀ to return to the administration panels.

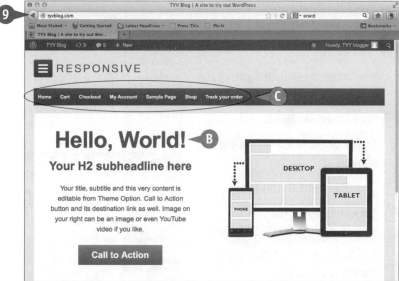

TIPS

How do I change the content on the new home page?
You may not need to if you use a different theme. This example uses the Responsive theme. To change the home page content for it, click **Appearance** in the left menu bar, and then click **Theme Options**. On the panel that appears, click **Home Page** and provide your content there. Click **Save Options** to finish.

What other theme options are available?
Search at http://wordpress.org/extend/ themes using the term *woocommerce* to find free WordPress themes that are set up to use WooCommerce. There are not many. Or you can go to www.woothemes.com to find a free or paid WooCommerce theme from WooThemes. It has about 30 available.

continued ▶

U sing the WooCommerce plugin is simpler than some plugins, and it offers many options. You can use it to sell tangible or intangible products. It can help you compute shipping and taxes, and provides featured items, sale items, and numerous business reports for you. It adds up to a lot of complexity and a lot of functionality. It takes time and effort, however, so do not expect to be ready overnight. Once you get your plugin set up, you still have to enter your products into your e-commerce system, for example.

Use E-Commerce Plugin (continued)

10 Click **Pages** and then click **Add New**.

11 Type a title for your blog page.

12 Click the **Template** drop-down list, and choose **Blog (full posts)** or **Blog Excerpt (summary)**.

13 Click **Save Draft**.

14 Click **Publish**.

Your page is published with your blog posts as its content.

15 Click **WooCommerce**.

The WooCommerce settings panel appears.

16 Click **Payment Gateways**.

17 Click the PayPal radio button to make PayPal the default payment gateway (○ changes to ◉).

18 Click **Save changes.**

19 Click **PayPal.**

20 Provide the PayPal information requested, and click **Save Changes**.

Note: You may want to click the other gateway links (Ⓓ) and click the **Enable/Disable** check box (☑ changes to ☐), and then click **Save Changes** to disable those gateways.

21 Click **Products**.

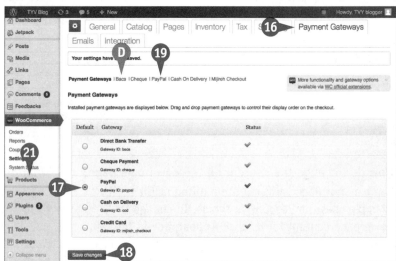

22 Click **Add Product**.

The Add New Product panel appears. As you work, the panel title changes to Edit Product.

23 Type a product name.

24 Type a complete product description.

25 Click the **Virtual** and **Downloadable** check boxes (☐ change to ☑).

Note: Step 25 does not apply for tangible products.

26 Click **Add Media** ( Add Media).

TIPS

Can I use my Authorize.net account as my gateway with WooCommerce?

Yes, although you must buy an extension, which at this writing costs $49 for a single-site license. It is set up to provide for secure payments without requiring you to have an SSL, or *secure socket layer,* certificate. On any tab of the Settings panel, you can click a link near the top of the panel labeled WC official extensions to find extensions, including for Authorize.net.

How do I handle shipping and taxes?

Those aspects require additional setup beyond what is described here. You can get an idea of what is involved by clicking the **Tax** and **Shipping** tabs in the WooCommerce Settings panels.

continued ▶

If you have never attempted to manage a retail establishment or a catalog operation, you probably never put much thought into how much information a retailer must keep track of, but starting an e-commerce site lets you realize quickly how much is involved. For each product, you need a description, a name, a price, and, if you are shipping it, you need to know how much each item weighs and what its dimensions are. You may also have inventory to track, orders to fulfill, and more. Fortunately, a good e-commerce site helps you handle those tasks and provides good records.

Use E-Commerce Plugin (continued)

The Insert Media window opens.

27 Click **Set Featured Image**.

28 Click **Upload Files**, and upload an image as you usually would.

29 When the image is uploaded type an image title.

30 Click the **Exclude image** check box (☐ changes to ☑).

Note: If you leave the Exclude image check box deselected the image also appears under the featured image.

31 Click **Set featured image**.

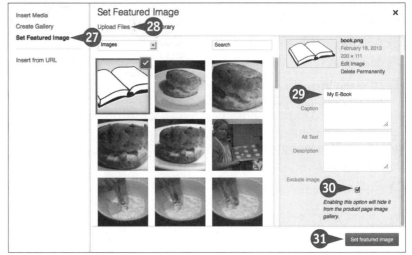

E The product window returns, with your product image in the Featured Image box.

32 Type a price.

33 Click **Upload a file**, and then browse for the product to be sold.

34 A media upload window appears, where you upload the file and then click **Insert into Post**.

35 Type a download limit if you have one.

36 Type a brief product description.

37 Scroll to the top of page, and click **Save Draft.**

38 Click **Publish**.

39 Click **View Product**.

The product page opens.

F The product title, featured image, price, and brief description appear.

G The detailed product description appears.

40 Click **+ New** and then click **Product**.

41 Repeat Steps **23** to **39** for other products.

TIPS

How can I add my products to WooCommerce if I already have them in a database?
You can import your product information from a CSV file with an importer. WooThemes, which manages WooCommerce, sells the Product CSV Import Suite for that purpose. You also can try a free plugin, WooCommerce CSV importer, available at http://wordpress.org/extend/plugins/woocommerce-csvimport.

Why do all my prices show up as free when I publish them?
You probably used a dollar sign ($) when you entered your price. The database requires numbers only, such as 2.99. If you include the dollar sign, the plugin evidently cannot read the numbers, and the item shows up as Free.

Index

Numbers

C

There's a Visual book for every learning level...

Simplified®

The place to start if you're new to computers. Full color.

- Computers
- Creating Web Pages
- Digital Photography
- Excel

- Internet
- Laptops
- Mac OS
- Office

- PCs
- Windows
- Word

Teach Yourself VISUALLY™

Get beginning to intermediate-level training in a variety of topics. Full color.

- Access
- Adobe Muse
- Computers
- Digital Photography
- Digital Video
- Dreamweaver
- Excel
- Flash
- HTML5
- iLife

- iPad
- iPhone
- iPod
- Macs
- Mac OS
- Office
- Outlook
- Photoshop
- Photoshop Elements
- Photoshop Lightroom

- PowerPoint
- Salesforce.com
- Search Engine Optimization
- Social Media
- Web Design
- Windows
- Wireless Networking
- Word
- WordPress

Top 100 Simplified® Tips & Tricks

Tips and techniques to take your skills beyond the basics. Full color.

- Digital Photography
- eBay
- Excel

- Google
- Office
- Photoshop

- Photoshop Elements
- PowerPoint
- Windows

...all designed for visual learners—just like you!

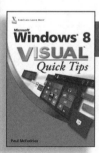